WHY
KETU
CAN HEAL

WHY
KETU
CAN HEAL

Understanding Ketu Spiritually

From the Best Selling Author of **"How to Overcome Rahu"**

ADDITTYA TAMHANKAR

White Falcon
Publishing

www.whitefalconpublishing.com

WHY KETU CAN HEAL?
Understanding Ketu Spiritually
Addittya Tamhankar

www.whitefalconpublishing.com

|| Shri Ganeshaya Namaha ||

I humbly prostrate before Sri Siddhivinayak Lord Ganesha.
At HIS behest, I offer this insightful book to all my readers.

|| JAI GURU ||

**I earnestly prostrate before the divine
spiritual master**

His Holiness Sri Jungli Maharaj

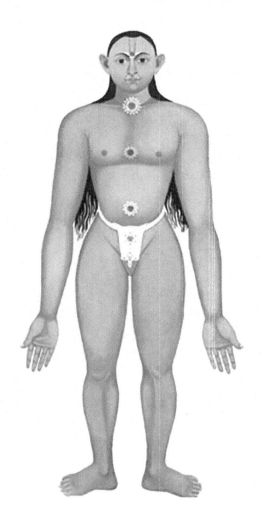

At the feet of My Beloved Master
His Holiness Mahavatar Babaji

I dedicate my book at the feet of the divine Master. This book is His blessings. His grace. When there was nobody to support me – You stood behind me. When people were trying to harm me – You stood behind me. When I was utterly foolish, stupid and ignorant – You stood behind me. When the whole world was making fun of me – You stood behind me. When I was bleeding profusely – You were healing me tirelessly. When I was about to give up – You motivated me to keep going. How can I express my gratitude towards You – You are my breath, You are my life. I pray to My Lord, My Master that may the readers experience the divine, May all, live with love & light.

Salute to the Great Himalayan Spiritual Master

I bow and prostrate before the great divine Himalayan spiritual master and healer – Dr. Ram Bhosale saheb. Millions and millions of births pass by – until a day comes, when you meet someone as great as divine and as compassionate as His Holiness Dr. Ram Bhosale saheb. Truly blessed to be in His omnipresence.

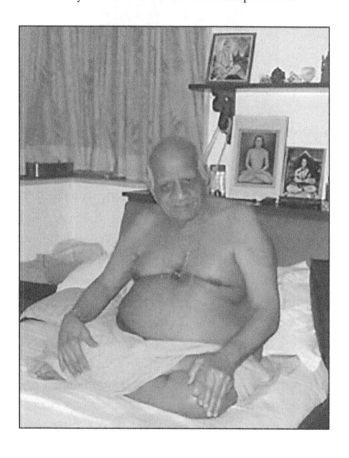

Tribute To My Dear Father

In the fond memory of my dear father,
Shri Arun Tamhankar – who left this world
when he was 47 yrs old.

A renowned journalist, a celebrity occult novelist, and a
learned astrologer - my father lived his whole life with
unwavering faith and compassion. With many television
serials, novels and leading magazines and newspapers of his
times; credited to his work, his commitment and passion
towards writing, and bringing spriritual awareness to
the masses is truly inspiring. His articles and his books
continue to motivate readers of all generations.
God bless His soul – today and always.

|| The Benevolent Bhagavan ||

Fondly remembering the benevolent Bhagavan - whose compassionate sharing and divine words enriched and motivated the 'journey' of my life in many ways that cannot be expressed in words.

With Love and Grateful heart, I humbly bow before **His Holiness Bhagavan Ramana Maharshi**.

|| Aum Sai ||

May the blessings of Sai Baba eradicate the ignorance within you and may His Grace instill the light of consciousness within you.

Ignorance is misery. Consciousness is bliss.

look within
be still.

**Your work is to discover your world within and
then with all your heart give yourself to it.**

๑ FOREWORD ๑
by
Stacy Lynn Imbasciani

I am a great admirer and friend of Addittya for some years now. We initially connected on LinkedIn and Quora. He is motivational, spiritually insightful and brings an awareness to all his readers. He has a strong belief in Meditation and the benefits it brings to everyone. He is highly accomplished with over 18 years of experience in Astrology. I admire Addittya's honesty and integrity that he brings to his writing.

Addittya's new book "Why Ketu can heal? - Understanding Ketu Spiritually" can bring you more clarity. Reading through this book will hopefully bring you to an understanding of the messages of Sri Ketu and what Ketu wants you to learn. When you learn the lessons of Ketu then you will find your bliss and happiness.

Ketu is the opposite of Rahu. Ketu is saying slow down, recharge and focus inward to transform your life. While Rahu focuses on the outside being too ambitious and this can lead to misery.

> Ambition is a poison but the label on the bottle says - it is pure nectar.
>
> **OSHO**

I am sure you will enjoy this book thoroughly as I did. You will also enjoy the "Gift of Consciousness", "How to overcome Rahu- A unique spiritual perspective on Rahu – The Ignorance", and "No Mind - The Journey Beyond". Addittya's books are a gift to all. I look forward to what Addittya has in store for us in the future!

- **Stacy Lynn Imbasciani**
  Reiki Grand Master L18
  New York, June 15, 2020

∾ ABOUT THE AUTHOR ∾

Based in Pune, Addittya Tamhankar is an internationally acclaimed author, celebrity spiritual astrologer, life coach, and visionary motivator. Addittya believes that with deep spiritual practice and meditation – **the solutions to all our miseries can be found**.

The solution to our problems is within us – all we need is to 'dive' within, turn inwards and explore our true self. From **18 years**, Addittya has been consulting and helping people from all walks of life to find the solution to their problems.

Addittya believes in selfless service. He believes and lives with the strong belief that: *"God is the creator and I am His humble servant."*

With his deep spiritual insights, Addittya has been addressing various problems and challenges that one encounters in life. Addittya believes in the *power of possibility* and works around to bring that positive change. His astrology consultation is purely spiritual in nature and is exercised solely for the benefit of the people.

By Profession –

- Addittya is a highly experienced, internationally travelled IT professional, documentation specialist with an MBA from the prestigious **Indian Institute of Management (IIM), Kozhikode**.
- Addittya also hold **Masters in English** and **Diploma in Multimedia Software Technology**.
- Practicing Astrologer and Numerologist (has consulted people
- across various geographies and from all walks of life)
- An innovative leader, executive coach & experienced counsellor
- with strong motivational mentoring and deep spiritual focus
- Internationally published & a proclaimed author

With a back to back success of his deeply insightful and international acclaimed books - "Gift of Consciousness", "Beauty of Acceptance – Tathata, "No Mind" and his Bestselling book on Rahu - **"How to Overcome Rahu"** – **Addittya Tamhankar** now comes with his spiritually inspiring and highly enlightening new book on KETU - **"Why Ketu Can Heal – Understanding Ketu Spiritually."**

Blessed with wisdom and enriched with insightful spiritual stories and beautiful quotes of spiritual dignitaries, and with an incredibly unique spiritual perspective of KETU in Astrology - **Addittya** once again inspires us all with his deep knowledge, wonderful writing and sharing. Committed to providing spiritual inspiration through his wonderful books, Addittya lives with a simple thought - that the more we are able to live in DETACHMENT – the more we can LOVE, the more we can SHARE, the more we can find HAPPINESS in our life. Detachment is the essence of KETU – KETU is detachment and spiritual progress is possible only through 'Detachment'. Addittya beautifully reveals the true essence of KETU and bring you closer to the state of realizing the immense significance of Ketu – Detachment. Through his own spiritual experiences – he has come to the realization that **'meditation can fructify only when you become more and more detached'**. Ketu is therefore closely related to Meditation – and to put it in Addittya's words – Ketu is Meditation.

Addittya lives his life with the realization that there is never **'the end'** to the journey called life, and that we exist in time, but we belong to eternity. To put it in his own words - **the 'End'** never happens, after every ending, there is a new beginning. After every dark night, a new morning begins. After every full stop a new sentence begins. The **ending is the beginning...**

Highlighted on multiple occasions as 'The most viewed writer in Jyotish' on Quora, and with a huge following on LinkedIn, and YouTube, Addittya Tamhankar continues to motivate and inspire people across geographies through his insightful sharing, wonderful writings, and wisdom. He can be reached by email. He is always open to help those who can 'understand' the language of the Heart.

E-mail: **Addittya.Tamhankar@gmail.com**
Visit Website: **www.astroinsights.co.in**

❧ PREFACE ❧

From Ashwini – the very first Nakshatra of the zodiac cycle begins the journey of Human Life. And Ketu is the Lord of Ashwini Nakshatra! From SHUNYA (KETU) begins the wonderful journey called – Life! And when the same KETU reaches the 12th house – comes the state of liberation – SHUNYA! 12th house is the house of final liberation, Moksha. It is indeed 'home' to KETU – in the 12th house KETU relaxes, here Ketu is back 'home'!

Going back 'home'! The whole essence of our spiritual 'journey' is going back home. To the source from where we have come. And the source is 'within'! And if we can understand this - if we can relate to this reality, then life can become the greatest gift that we can use for our self-growth, for our self-realization!

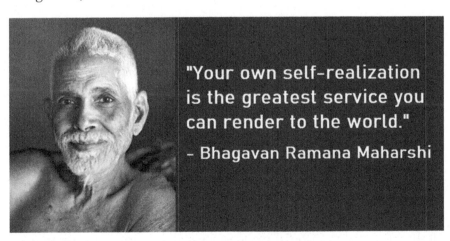

"Your own self-realization is the greatest service you can render to the world."
- Bhagavan Ramana Maharshi

Self-realization is not possible unless you start turning inwards. You come from zero - a nobody, and in the end - after death, you go back to zero - a nobody! In between - is the whole story of your life. The more you remain attached, the more you will suffer, the more you let go - the more you will rejoice. The more you are stuck on the circumference of your life - your status, your position, your ego - the more you remain miserable. The moment you start moving beyond the circumference, you find peace, and it is beautiful.

"You are nobody. You are born as a nobodiness with no name, no form. You will die as a nobody. Name and form are just on the surface; deep down you are just a vast space. And it is beautiful." - Osho

KETU is the only energy in our cosmic galaxy that can help us look within, and experience the vast space and the blissful silence within!

SHUNYA is from where the journey of life begins and SHUNYA is where the journey of life ends. The whole story of human life is from SHUNYA to SHUNYA. From NOTHINGNESS to NOTHINGNESS!

This NOTHINGNESS – this SHUNYA is KETU. We all are born from NOTHINGNESS, and we all finally immerse into NOTHINGNESS. KETU remains the very source of our life and KETU also remains the very source of our material dissolution – it is only when all that is material – your status, your ego, your attachments – all that is related to material world – when all is burned up – dissolved – that the REAL YOU will be born! In the Holy Bible, Jesus mentions that to experience GOD - to experience the ultimate TRUTH – one has to REBORN. KETU brings you to this state – the state of being REBORN! But to REBORN, one has to go through a certain pain – one has to die – but this death is not the death of his physical body – it is the death of 'I' (EGO) – it is the death of 'all learnings' – it is the death of all 'preconceived notions' – because it is only when you are EMPTY – that the divine can come to you – a 'cup' is useful – only when it is EMPTY!

This EMPTINESS is KETU. "Form is emptiness, emptiness is form" states the Heart Sutra, one of the best-known ancient Buddhist texts. God comes, love flows only when you become a 'NOBODY'! As long as you continue to live in the illusion that 'I AM SOMEBODY' – God cannot come to you, Love cannot flow unto you.

This thought or this idea that 'I AM SOMEBODY' – is the idea of RAHU.

And the moment you shift from 'I AM SOMEBODY' to 'I AM NOBODY' – you arrive in the abode of KETU, and it is here where you find peace, it is here where you find GOD, it is here where you find LOVE – unconditional love! Conditions are laid only when there is MIND in play – in the state of KETU – there is NO MIND – so where is the question of laying conditions? Everybody is welcome – there are no conditions, but only love, and deep understanding.

Understanding cannot be studied; nobody can teach it to you. Understanding can well up within you only when you start looking within - only when you start turning inwards. To raise the level of your understanding - you have to learn how to dive within yourself. And KETU makes it possible, KETU can direct you, motivate you to dive within. It is through the energy of KETU that you can be a light unto yourself. It is through KETU that you can become a true seeker!

Once it happened, a man asked Buddha, "Is there God?" Buddha answered, "NO - there is no God." Another man came and asked Buddha, "What do you think of God? Is there any God?"

Buddha answered, "YES - there is GOD." Late evening, an old man came and said, "There are people who believe in God and people who don't, I myself need to know if God exists, please help me."

Buddha did not speak – instead, he gave the answer through his actions. He sat beneath the tree, closed his eyes and went into deep meditation. The old man thought that this must be the answer - so he too sat down, closed his eyes and started meditating. After a while, the old man opened his eyes, touched the feet of Buddha and said, "Your compassion is great. You have given me the answer. I will always remain obliged to you." And then happily the man left.

Ananda asked Buddha, "To the first man you answered - God doesn't exist. To the second man, you answered, 'God exists.' And to the last man - you said nothing but just went into meditation. I don't understand your answers - please help me understand."

Buddha smiled and said, "The first and the second man just wanted an answer - they were not seekers. The last man was a seeker - he wanted to 'self-experience' God and not just 'know'. He was able to 'relate' - he was a seeker."

Buddha says - "Truth is not transferable. I cannot give you the Truth; nobody else can give it to you. But you can attain it on your own."

> **66**
>
> You have to seek. Buddha wants 'seekers', and the seeker is a totally different phenomenon. The believer is NOT a seeker. The believer wants to avoid everything, that's why he believes. The believer is always in search of a messiah, somebody who can chew for him. But if I eat, your hunger is not going to be satisfied. Nobody can save you except yourself. You have to be a seeker and NOT a believer.
>
> **OSHO**
>
> **99**

A KETU-ish man or a KETU-ish woman is a seeker and not just a believer. They are willing to 'jump' into the unknown – and it is only when you have the COURAGE to JUMP – that you can attain the unseen, the beyond! This COURAGE comes from KETU – because it is the MIND that hesitates to jump into the unknown – it is your MIND that goes on creating many illusions and doubts that stop you from 'jumping' – but a man who has NO MIND, a man who is NO MORE under the control of his MIND – a man who has become the MASTER of HIS Mind – such a man can JUMP – he has the COURAGE – he is a man of heart – he listens to his heart and JUMPS – simply jumps!

One of the most enlightening books that help us to realize the significance of 'Jumping' into the unknown – is the Holy Bible. In the Bible, it is mentioned that almost all of the 12 Apostles (disciples) of Jesus simply 'jumped' into the unknown – they had never known Jesus. Jesus meets them for the first time – and Jesus simply says two words "FOLLOW ME", and they all start following Jesus – no questions are asked, no doubts are raised – nothing – they simply drop everything – and start following this man who had something – Jesus Christ!

One of the most beautiful incidents is when Jesus meets Peter, the fisherman. Jesus is walking on the seashore, and on his way, he comes across Peter and looking at Peter – Jesus says, "Follow Me – I will make you the fisher of men."

Peter is an illiterate man, and he is meeting Jesus for the very first time in his life. He is not even aware of who Jesus is! But looking at Jesus, his glow, his aura, his peace, Peter is moved – he simply drops everything and starts following Jesus Christ – there is absolutely no show of intellectuality – no questions asked, no doubts raised – Peter simply starts following Jesus, and it is this Peter, the fisherman – who later is venerated as Saint Peter in the Christian community! You see – that is how KETU is – there is no head, no logic, no intellectuality. It is only when you are out of all these obstructions – that you can truly follow your heart – and the heart is intelligent, very intelligent. Peter was also a very intelligent man – he followed his heart, and one who follows his heart never fails, never.

Suddenness is related to KETU – Jesus meets Peter, and it is a sudden moment. In fact, Jesus meets all his other disciples (Apostles) in the similar way – in a sudden way! And they all must be KETU-ish – else they would not have been able to relate to Jesus and his omnipresence!

RAHU brings intellectualism. And intellectualism is nothing but noisy! The ancient scriptures mention that a demon was beheaded by Sri Vishnu. But because the demon had drunk the nectar of immortality – even though he was beheaded, he remained alive. And so the HEAD of this demon became RAHU, and the HEADLESS part became KETU.

Now let me clarify that this is a mythological representation – it is not factual, but it is very significant is passing the message – and the message is clear – very clear.

The message is simple – that as long as you remain in your HEAD – you remain RAHU-ish. And the moment you slip out of your HEAD – you evolve to the state of KETU – you become KETU-ish. And it is only when you become KETU-ish that you can understand the language of GOD. Silence is the language of GOD – says the Buddha!

Our journey begins from NOTHINGNESS (SILENCE), and it is only when you go back to 'SILENCE' – that you truly attain – you truly evolve.

Once a young man asked a divine master, "WHO ARE YOU?"

The master smiled and said, "WHO AM I? I am the 'Silence' that exists between your two words - don't ask the same question again."

Silence is the language of God - the whole journey is towards SILENCE - a time should come in your life - in your 'journey' when you are no more in search of silence - you become the 'silence' - a blissful silence!

Once you become a blissful 'silence' – you are completely healed, and it is only when you are healed that you can heal others!

This state of 'silence' comes by practicing meditation. KETU is meditation. Meditation happens only when there is NO MIND, NO HEAD. And KETU is that beautiful state – a form in which there is NO MIND, NO HEAD.

So, it is necessary for you all to start moving from the extrovert state (RAHU) towards the introvert state (KETU). The whole story of human life is between these two ends – RAHU and KETU. As long as you remain at the RAHU end – you may gain a fat bank balance, you may attain fame – but what is the use of such money and fame?

> Fame is foolish, it is pointless, meaningless. Even if the whole world knows you, how does it make you richer? How does it make your life more blissful? How does it help you to be more understanding, to be more aware? To be more alert, to be more alive?
>
> **OSHO**

By being wealthy and famous – you may have a very cosy lifestyle – but that's all! By no way does money or fame makes you a wise person!

You become wise only when you are able to LET GO!

Knowledge is learning something every day, wisdom is letting go of something every day.

As long as you remain in the tight clutch of RAHU – you will never LET GO. You will continue to CLING. And Buddha says – "You only lose what you CLING to!"

There is one beautiful verse of Jesus. Jesus says, "One who goes on saving, will lose. And one who is willing to lose, will gain." Quite a topsy-turvy mathematics, and yet so true, so true!

Many people come to seek solution, but they are unwilling to LET GO. They want REVENGE, they want to HOLD ON, they are not willing to LET GO and unless you are not willing to LET GO – there is absolutely no solution to your problem. You may visit many temples and churches and mosques and shrines – and yet you will remain in misery – because ATTACHMENT is the very root of your misery, your suffering.

> The ROOT of MISERY and SUFFERINGS is ATTACHMENTS.
>
> **BUDDHA**

You cannot forgive. Then some 'intellectuals' come up with a nice quote – they say "FORGIVE – but never FORGET" – Now this is typical RAHU-ish. This is just an 'appearance' of forgiving – RAHU is good at making 'fake' appearances that look real.

Now when you say - you will forgive but you will NOT forget – it simply means that you are still unwilling to LET GO in its TOTALITY! It is a HALF WAY that you have chosen and HALF WAYS are not of much help – HIGHWAYS are!

And the HIGHWAY is to LET GO in its TOTALITY – so much so that there is absolutely no grudge, no thoughts of resentment in your being – only then can you truly experience the peace, and the bliss that you seek.

RAHU is behind BIG things. KETU is more interested in small things!

One day, a man came and said to the master, "I want to be happy, but to be happy, I need to do something great - something greater than life."

The master smiled and said, "There is NOTHING greater than LIFE. LIFE itself is far greater than anything in this world. And you need NOT have to do great things to become happy - to find happiness. Happiness is found in small things, and if you cannot find it in small things then you will never find it anywhere else."

Only a man who realizes the significance of small things, small incidents, small moments - can find happiness - can truly experience happiness.

> **❝**
> The EGO always says these are small things, seek the big, seek the huge, seek the great, seek God, seek Buddhahood. I say to you - there are no great things, only small things. Love well, love deeply. Enjoy small things. There is no other point, and there is nowhere to go. Drop hopes and drop desires and just BE. Suddenly you will find you have always been a Buddha. Buddhahood is our intrinsic nature.
>
> **OSHO**
> **❞**

As long as you remain focused on the OUTSIDE – you will be driven by jealousy, by comparisons, by greed, by lust, by ignorance. This IGNORANCE is RAHU. Rahu wants you to TURN ON – whereas the real answer to all your problems and miseries is found when you TURN IN.

The message of Ketu is to Turn in. But you are more concerned about turning on. And that's Rahu. Ketu helps you to turn in - Rahu provokes you to turn on. Rahu makes you extrovert - you are too much focused on the - other. You become excited by the - other. The other - is the world. Rahu compels you to focus on the outside world. Ketu encourages you to focus within by turning inward. The real 'journey' begins when you are no more turned on - but you start to turn in.

"KETU is the driving energy that enables you to overcome the mind and realize the SELF."

People come, and people go. Someone today is a friend - tomorrow becomes a stranger. Situations change, people change, the MIND is always changing - the nature of the mind is to change! What remains STILL - is the SELF. One who is meditating - is coming closer to the SELF, overcoming the MIND - and then he or she is no more dependent on who turns what. Whoever comes - is welcome, whoever goes - is also accepted with gratitude. Such a person remains STILL - the external changes won't affect him or her anymore - because he is no more focused on the outside - he is turning inward - focusing on the SELF.

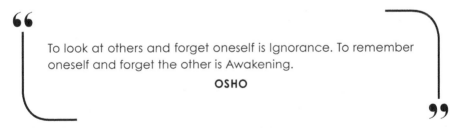

To look at others and forget oneself is Ignorance. To remember oneself and forget the other is Awakening.

OSHO

Once you are awakened - once awareness comes to your being, then you are no more dependent on the - other.

"There is NO other," says Bhagavan Ramana Maharshi.

Oneness (Advait) comes only when you reach the ultimate state of consciousness - when there is NO other! It is the stage of Enlightenment - the stage of Buddhahood.

Ketu enables you to reach the stage of Enlightenment, and it is only when you are enlightened that you can truly heal. At the very root of the healing energy - remains the benevolent Ketu.

Without Ketu - you cannot heal. With Ketu, you can heal. And it is beautiful.

The very source of your healing is found in your ability to LET GO!

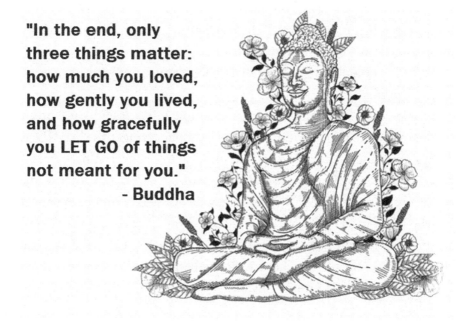

"In the end, only three things matter: how much you loved, how gently you lived, and how gracefully you LET GO of things not meant for you."
- Buddha

The nature of KETU is to LET GO. What is necessary is that you 'connect' with your KETU – so that the 'right channel' starts playing on the 'screen' of your life. The 'channel' of meditation!

Once you realize the significance of this 'channel' – once you get 'connected' to the channel of meditation – then all that you seek; can be attained, and can be experienced. It takes time; it is not that you start meditating and everything will change in one day – meditation is a process that needs time, intensity, devotion, persistence and efforts.

Always remember - no one succeeds without effort. Those who succeed owe their success to perseverance.

The greatest blessing that rarely comes our way – is the blessing that slowly and steadily makes us realize the immense significance of turning inwards! Many births have gone by, and if we continue to focus outward – then this cycle of birth and rebirth and the many hardships that the physical body has to go through – will never end! It will end only when a time comes in our life – when we stop focusing outside and start focusing WITHIN.

Someday, I will die. Someday, everyone has to die. But this death, this end of our life has to be a blissful end. We come crying in this world, but we should be able to leave this world - laughing, smiling, and in a joyful state! This state is possible only if you can expand your consciousness. And to do so, this world is the place to be.

Always remember – you are not here by accident. There is a purpose for your birth, and it is only when you start turning inwards – when your KETU energy is activated that you would realize the purpose of your life. But for that, you have to first start meditating.

That is the message, that is the only message of KETU – Turn inwards and Meditate.

And that is the sole purpose of this book – to push you into your inner space – to uplift you from your miseries and to provide you with a 'key' that can direct you towards the REAL GROWTH – the Growth Within.

I prostrate before my beloved master, without HIM, I am lifeless, with HIM, life flows through my veins. With HIS blessings and love, I now offer you all with this insightful book that can help you open the many 'closed' doors of your life – doors that were never locked but only closed.

Always remember – 'doors' are not locked, they are only 'closed' – the moment 'Awareness' comes – you can push open the closed 'door' and experience the many wonderful moments of life. The 'push' enabler is AWARENESS. And Ketu is the bridge that helps you to move from Ignorance to Awareness. The more you read this insightful book, the more you would come to realize the significant role that KETU plays in our life and in our spiritual journey.

It is necessary to remember that the real 'journey' is the journey within. Look within, turn inwards and let the 'journey' begin…

Meditate.

Love & Light

- **Addittya Tamhankar**
  July 21st, 2020

Email – addittya.tamhankar@gmail.com
Website – www.astroinsights.co.in

CONTENTS

Question 1

Why Ketu can heal?

The MIND cannot heal. The SELF can.

To realize the SELF - one has to move from MIND to NO MIND state.

KETU becomes the BRIDGE that helps you to move from the MIND to the NO MIND state. And you can HEAL yourself only when you reach the state of NO MIND. When there is NO MIND - the TRUTH descends like a glowing light - and when you are touched with the grace of the divine light - you become a true healer!

It all begins when you attain the state of NO MIND.

KETU is NO MIND.

When the mind disappears, thoughts disappear. It is not that you become mindless; on the contrary you become mindful.

OSHO

The moment there is NO MIND - the moment you are out of the prison of MIND - you can heal, you can forgive, you can transform into the most beautiful person that the world has ever known! BUDDHA was such a beautiful person. He was one of those enlightened men who walked on this planet with NO MIND and healed millions and millions of people through his divine messages - through his divine touch - his grace and his blessings. So much so that even today across the world - in plush malls and in modern hi-tech buildings, you will find his beautiful statues! Hundreds of years have passed and yet Buddha continues to attract millions and millions across the globe. What is the secret?

The secret is the beauty of KETU - which represents **DETACHMENT**. The secret is the quality of Ketu - which represents **WITNESSING**. The secret is the nature of Ketu - which represents **ACCEPTANCE**. The secret is the essence of Ketu which represents the ability to **LET GO**.

> Meditation is a surrender, it is not a demand. It is not forcing existence your way, it is relaxing into the way existence wants you to be. It is a Let-Go.
>
> **OSHO**

Meditation is to LET GO. So the very foundation of meditation is in the essence of LETTING GO. That makes KETU extremely significant when it comes to meditating. It is ONLY WHEN YOU ARE ABLE TO LET GO that you can HEAL yourself and when you are able to heal yourself - you can heal others! KETU remains the master key that enables you to HEAL yourself and HEAL others!

Unless you learn to HEAL yourself - how can you learn to heal others?

But people miss to understand the fact that HEALING has to happen first within your being - and there is absolutely nobody who can heal you than your own SELF.

"The only disease you have is your inability to see you have the power to heal yourself." – Ralph Smart KETU ENABLES you to realize the fact that you have all the ABILITY to have the power to heal yourself!

Ketu can move you towards Detachment.

When you are detached - you can enter into the state of WITNESSING.

> You know only two ways; either to be angry, be violent, destructive or to repress it. You don't know the third way, and the third way is the way of the buddhas; neither indulge nor repress – Just WATCH, Just be a WITNESS.
>
> **OSHO**

When you are able to WITNESS all that is happening in your life - you can Let Go.

When you are able to LET GO - you are no more holding anything to your chest - you feel lighter. When you Let Go, you create space for better things to enter in your life.

When you feel lighter - you can slowly learn to **ACCEPT** all that life provides you with a sense of **Gratitude.**

> No amount of self-improvement can make up for any lack of self-acceptance.
>
> **ROBERT HOLDEN**

There is NO SELF IMPROVEMENT unless and until you are WILLING to live in total self-acceptance.

And the moment you learn **to live your life with total self-acceptance** - something beautiful starts flowering within you - and it is called - Meditation! And then you are no more the same - everything around you is the same but you are NO more the same and that is the beginning of a wonderful journey- spiritual journey!

Your spiritual journey begins only when you are able to live your life in the state of:

- Detachment
- Witnessing
- Let GO
- Turn Inward

And KETU brings all of the above beautiful stages to your life - and that makes KETU a great enabler that enables you to heal yourself and heal others as well!

KETU is peace - because when there is NO MIND - where is the question of noise? The MIND is noisy - the SELF is quiet. The whole purpose of Meditation is to 'enable' you to QUIETEN THE MONKEY MIND. This Enabler is your KETU - without KETU, the idea of healing is next to impossible!

In the Indian context - the most striking representation of KETU is SHRI GANESHA!

The ancient sages have mentioned in the scriptures that KETU has NO HEAD - meaning NO MIND. Lord Ganesha also has NO HEAD - meaning NO MIND! And, therefore whenever you visit Lord Ganesha temple, you feel peace within. When there is NO MIND - peace showers upon you. The Elephant face is NOT his head - it is just a symbolic representation of deep wisdom. Because elephants are considered the wisest beings.

If you really want to HEAL yourself - you all must worship Lord Ganesha. Worshiping Lord Ganesha is like worshiping the positive energy of Sri KETU. Indirectly, you are praying to KETU - and if your prayers are heartfelt prayers - coming from the depth of your heart then KETU certainly can help you to overcome obstacles – and, therefore, Lord Ganesha is addressed as VIGHNA HARTA (meaning Destroyer of All Obstacles).

And what can be the biggest obstacle than the obstacle of being IGNORANT! Therefore, when you worship Lord Ganesha - the first change that you would experience is the destruction of your IGNORANCE. And how this happens? By making you SELF AWARE. Because IGNORANCE can only be wiped out when the LIGHT OF AWARENESS - CONSCIOUSNESS instils within you! Lord Ganesha (KETU) enables this - by helping you become more and more aware of yourself. Lord Ganesha encourages you to look within - turn inwards and meditate. So the greatest LORD of all - is LORD GANESHA - especially when it comes to the Art of Healing - and there is absolutely no doubt about this.

What blocks you from turning inward is your MIND. This MIND is ruled by Moon. Moon has two nodes - North Node and South Node.

North Node is called Rahu in Vedic Astrology. This RAHU is totally desirous by nature - in fact, we all are born out of desires! RAHU is what triggers our physical birth!

South Node is called Ketu in Vedic Astrology. And KETU is totally disinterested, detached and has absolutely NO DESIRES. KETU is what triggers our spiritual birth - it is through KETU that we are **REBORN!**

Jesus says to Nicodemus - **"To experience God - to experience the divine - You have to be Reborn. You have to be born again."**

"In reply Jesus declared, *"I tell you the truth, no one can see the kingdom of God unless he is **born again.**"*

- John 3.3 (Bible Verse)

Nicodemus was a great scholar of Jerusalem. And he was very old than Jesus. He wanted to meet this young man. He had been hearing a lot about Jesus - His miracles, His divine message, His love, His Grace - and so within his heart he had a wish to meet Jesus, but the question was - HOW?

Because Jesus was a carpenter's son, and Nicodemus was a great scholar, the whole town of Jerusalem had high regards for him, they respected him. How would they feel, what would they say IF he goes to meet Jesus who was not even half of his age?

So fear was there - Status, Name, Reputation - you see - and so Nicodemus was not sure how and when to meet Jesus. After a lot of thinking, he found a way. He decided to meet Jesus on a dark night when the whole town is asleep. He sneaked out of his house on a dark night and went to meet Jesus. Jesus was sitting beneath a tree - and Nicodemus rushed to Jesus - touched his feet and said "Jesus......"

Jesus looked at Nicodemus and said, "What is it that you want from me?"

And Nicodemus said, "I want you to help me realize GOD - experience the divine - experience the beyond."

And that is when Jesus said, "For that, you have to be reborn."

Nicodemus did not understand, he said, "What do you mean? Should I go back to my mother's womb? Please explain..."

Jesus said, "To be reborn - first you have to die. But this death is not of your physical body - this death is of all your preconceived notions, learning, ideas, intellectualism, EGO - until all of this is dropped - death cannot happen and unless death happens - you cannot be REBORN!"

Nicodemus was listening. Jesus said, "Look at you - even to meet me, you have chosen a dark night - you cannot come to meet me in daytime - because what will people say? A great scholar going to seek guidance from a carpenter's son! And if you cannot face people - then how will you face GOD!"

Nicodemus's eyes became wet. He realized how foolish he had been his whole life - he realized the futility of all the EGO, the Status, the Intellectualism, the Respect that he had been carrying all his life. At that moment - everything that he had been running after seemed to be of absolutely no value - before this beautiful gracious man called Jesus! He bowed before Jesus, he could not control himself, he started crying - it was a very intense moment - and it was also the turning moment of Nicodemus' life - he was 82. Jesus raised him up and Nicodemus said, "Master, help me to be REBORN..."

Unless the death of your intellectualism and EGO takes place - how can you be reborn?

KETU signifies death. Ketu signifies absence. Ketu signifies dropping all that makes NO sense to your REAL GROWTH. And it is through KETU that death of your EGO, your intellectualism (MIND) happens - and then you are REBORN.

KETU, therefore, is your master through which you are reborn!

But why certain people 'suffer' because of KETU? Because they are the followers of RAHU. They are so much fired up by their DESIRES that they cannot DROP, they cannot DETACH, they cannot LET GO - their whole DNA is of RAHU. Then they tend to suffer - though this suffering is of their MIND. Beyond Mind, there is NO Suffering!

"Pain is physical; suffering is mental. Beyond the mind there is no suffering. Pain is essential for the survival of the body, but none compels you to suffer. Suffering is due entirely to clinging; it is a sign of our unwillingness to move on, to flow ith life."
 - Sri Nisargdatta Maharaj

KETU is against pleasure seeking. A yogi is against a bhogi. And so when you are a BHOGI - the period (DASHA) of YOGI (KETU) will not go well with you - because KETU is trying to help you with the language of the SELF - the language of Meditation - Ketu is here to help you understand the forgotten language. Buddha is here to help you REMEMBER the forgotten language.

REMEMBER. Just REMEMBER. It is the most beautiful word - 'REMEMBER' and it has great significance. The last word of Gautama Buddha was 'Sammasti'. It means 'Remember'. Remember what is your inner space. Just remember. Sammasti.

"There is nothing to achieve, and there is nothing to become. You are already that which you have been seeking in all your lives in different ways, on different paths. But you have never looked inward. Look in. And whenever you have time, you know the path. Just go again and again to the inner space so that your fear of disappearing is dropped, you start enjoying being nobody, and you start REMEMBERING the forgotten language." - Osho KETU is simply asking you to remember - just remember your inner space. Sammasti.

But those men and women who are just NOT willing to slow down and turn inward feel lost during Ketu period or certain Ketu transits. They assume that it is because of KETU - though the real reason is TOO MUCH indulgence in material pleasures.

9

But if such men and women consciously try to understand the message of KETU - then the same KETU period can become a turning point of their life - it can become a point when you start turning inward.

> To achieve that state of lasting happiness and absolute peace, we must first know how to calm the mind, and to concentrate and go beyond the mind. By turning the mind's concentration inward, upon the self, we can deepen that experience of perfect concentration. This is the state of Meditation.
>
> **SIVANANDA**

A spiritually-inclined person will make the most out of KETU DASHA (period) or KETU transits.

While a pleasure-seeking, ignorant, —materially-driven person will find KETU periods difficult because the beautiful, deeply, spiritually-motivating KETU goes against his pleasure-seeking, material nature. They simply cannot understand KETU, they don't listen to what KETU is saying - what this phase of life is saying and hence they get frustrated.

> Don't be angry at life. It is not life that is frustrating you, it is you who are not listening to life.
>
> **OSHO**

When you turn a deaf ear to the KETU phase of your life - then frustration comes over. The period of KETU or the transits of KETU are simply to AWAKEN you. KETU may bring certain pain - but that pain is NOT to hurt you - but to AWAKEN you. People become AWAKE only when the thorn goes deep and wounds them! Ignorant men and women are shallow beings - they see only the thorn and the pain that it causes - they miss to realize the higher purpose of the pain - and because they miss to understand and realize the higher purpose behind the failures, the pain - they continue to miss life - they think that they live - but in reality they don't live - they simply continue to EXIST.

Living happens when you start tuning inwards - when you start spending quality time with yourself by meditating. Until you remain an extrovert - you continue to exist - the moment you become introvert - turn inwards - meditate - you start living!

And KETU is the only medium - the only energy that can help you turn inwards and meditate - KETU is Shri Ganesha. The ancient scriptures mention that wealth comes, wisdom comes through Lord Ganesha. It is only when you turn inward - that you can become wise. And it is only when you become wise that wealth will naturally start flowing towards you. The key is turning inwards - and that's the very nature of KETU - that's the very nature of Shri Ganesha.

Ketu (Shri Ganesha) is the master key through which the many treasures within you can be unlocked. Ketu can heal - the larger question is, "Are you willing to let him heal?"

Jai Shri Ganesha. Jai Guru.

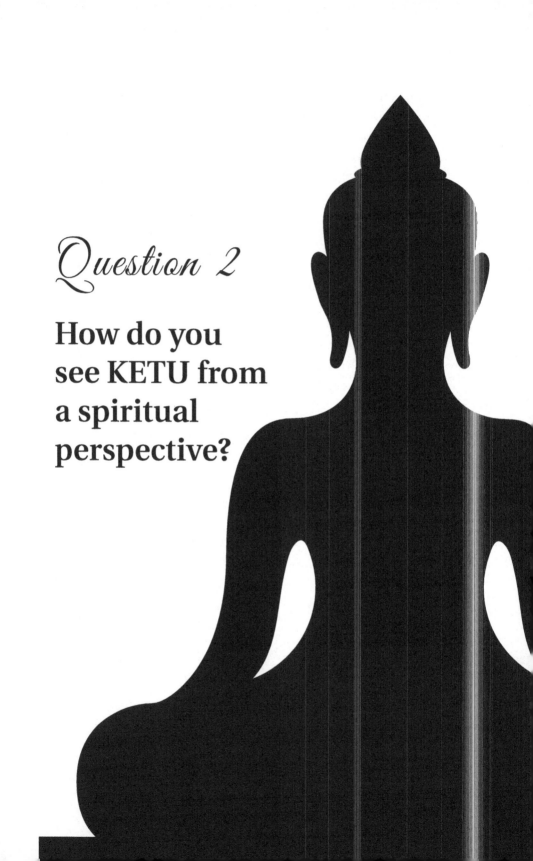

Question 2

How do you see KETU from a spiritual perspective?

K etu is NO MIND. Rahu is ALL MIND. Insanity is KETU. Sanity is RAHU.

And **yet** it is **'insanity'** that attains enlightenment much easier than your so-called 'sanity'!

A very sane person cannot 'JUMP' - and unless you 'JUMP' - there is no possible way to experience the divine, the beyond, the unseen!

To 'Jump' - one got to have a certain madness within - one got to follow his heart and not the mind!

That is how Arjuna is - that is how Sariputra is - that is how Peter, the fisherman is - they simply surrender - they 'jump' - they have the courage to jump (to surrender) - because they have 'Truth' within - they are truthful - they are following the heart and NOT the mind. They are KETU-ish and not Rahu-ish!

Peter, the fisherman is meeting Jesus for the very first time and Jesus says,

"Look into my eyes, I will make you the Fisher of Men - follow me."

A beautiful painting of Jesus meeting Peter, the fisherman - what a beautiful incident - the Master meeting the disciple for the first time! Peter is taken aback - he is looking at the stranger whom the people called Jesus - Isa!

And Peter, the fisherman could 'feel' that this is something - this is something else - the voice of this man, the eyes of this man - His glow, His bliss, His peace, His aura - and Peter cannot control himself - he simply bows before Jesus, kisses Jesus's feet and drops everything - everything is dropped and Peter, the fisherman starts following Jesus!

No questions are asked, no doubts are raised, nothing - just the WORD OF THE LORD - the WORD OF JESUS - and Peter starts following the most beautiful man the world has ever known - JESUS CHRIST!

You see - that is how life changes, that is how an illiterate man transforms into the greatest saint - SAINT PETER!

Peter, the fisherman can become SAINT PETER - KETU can become the enlightened being.

Only the HEART can FEEL! Only the HEART has Courage. Only the HEART can follow the TRUTH! Only someone as insane as Peter can throw away everything - drop everything and follow the master! The whole world would have called Peter - mad - his family, his wife, his children - they all would have called him insane, mad - crazy - but in the end, it is this Peter, the illiterate fisherman who becomes **Saint Peter** - the greatest Saint that the world has ever known! It is this Peter who becomes one of the 12 Apostles of Jesus.

How many people in Jerusalem would have laughed at Peter? They would have called him - a mad man who follows a carpenter's son! An insane man who has lost his head. But the reality was something else - it was NOT Peter - who was insane - he 'appeared' to be insane to those who could not hear the divine 'music' that Peter could hear in the omnipresence of Jesus Christ!

> And those who were seen dancing were thought to be insane by those who could not hear the music.
> **FRIEDRICH NIETZSCHE**

A certain madness is necessary to experience beyond! There are two types of madness - one that evolves through ignorance - where you fall below the mind. And the other that evolves through consciousness - where you rise above the mind - beyond the mind!

Meditation and Madness come at a common point - a common similarity but only at one point - both happen outside the mind. In every other sense - they are different.

The whole world stays away from a mad man. The whole world calls KETU - the mad man - the no-head man - but I tell you - there is nobody in this universe who is as wise as KETU - who has the capacity, the capability to 'attain self-realization' as KETU!

It is NOT the sane man who can attain - it is only the insane man - who can attain - who can go beyond - because he has NO MIND - he has the COURAGE - he has the FAITH - you only have to show him the 'right door' - the 'right way' - and a mad man can become the most enlightened man that the world would have ever known!

There was **one man** - who really did a miraculous job – and HE was the only man, after centuries! HE transformed many mad men into enlightened beings. He went all over India seeking and searching for mad people. In all the madhouses, anywhere that he heard there was a madman, he would go. He travelled all over India his whole life, searching for mad people. And HE turned many mad people into enlightened people.

HIS disciples asked him, "Why are you wasting your time with mad people when sane people are available to work upon, and they want your time?"

And HE would say, "You don't understand. **To bring a sane person out of his sanity is very difficult.** But **to bring out a madman is very easy** because *in a way he is already out but from the back door.* He has tasted something of the outside; we have only to show him the right door and say, 'Please don't go out from the wrong door, go from the right door. Being out is perfectly right, but choose the right door'."

HIS name was **Meher Baba**! A beautiful man, an enlightened man - an Avatar, a holy man who never uttered a single word and remained silent his whole life and yet moved millions of hearts in India, in the US and at all the places wherever he went - he transformed the whole meaning of life - changed the whole perspective towards life! Meher Baba - the benevolent, compassionate master whose remains are restored in the town of Meherabad near Ahmednagar, Maharashtra!

A **mad man** is ahead of you - he is ahead of you because **he has NO MIND.**

A **spiritual yogi** is ahead of you - he is ahead of you because **he too has NO MIND.**

The **only difference** between a mad man and a great yogi is of the CONSCIOUSNESS! The mad man is out of his mind - but because of utter ignorance. The yogi is out of his mind - but **with total consciousness!**

"I am everything that you take me to be, and I am also beyond everything. If your conscience says that "Baba" is the Avatar, say it even if you are stoned for it. But if you feel he is not, then say that you feel "Baba" is not the Avatar. Of myself I say again and again, I am the Ancient One — the Highest of the High."
- Meher Baba

Only a man who has attained - who has realized HIS self - can be so sure of himself - that he is willing to be **stoned** and he is also willing to take you under HIS wings! Beautiful. Only Jesus was willing to get nailed - only Meher Baba is willing to get stoned - the true Masters are fearless - they have nothing to fear - the MIND fears - the divine masters have gone beyond the mind - out of the Mind - CONSCIOUSLY!

And that is why the compassionate divine master **Meher Baba** says - that in a way a mad man is already 'out' - but through the wrong door - just a shake, just a **touch of conscious guidance** and it is easy to help him move out through the right door - through the door of consciousness and NOT ignorance!

But a sane man - a so-called intellectual man is completely trapped in his mind - it is difficult to get him out - he is so much stuck in his monkey mind!

One has to go *beyond the mind* to experience the spiritual bliss of desirelessness.

MEHER BABA

How beautiful is this, and how true, how deep is the grace and compassion of **Meher Baba**! I salute the compassionate benevolent divine master - a man who spent his whole life in helping the mad people find the 'right door' - the door of consciousness!

Your MIND is your problem. And it has been a problem not in this birth but for millions and millions of births that you have been through. You have become the MIND - when in reality you are NOT the mind. But to self-realize this truth - you first have to dive within - look within and this is possible only with one energy - and the name of that energy is Sri KETU!

"Do not listen to the voice of the mind. Listen to the voice of the heart. The mind wavers, the heart does not. The mind is the home of doubts, reasoning and theories. The heart when purified becomes the dwelling of the Beloved. Rid your heart of low desires, malice, selfishness and God will manifest in you as your true self." - Meher Baba

So, first you have to understand KETU - else you will go on reading hundreds of books on astrology and all you would become is a lovely 'Parrot'!

And I am here to help you all - **to help all those meditative souls** to come **out of this monkey mind** and instead of 'parroting' the books of astrology (because many of those books are also written by 'parrots') - I would love to see you all **turning inwards and realizing the true essence of astrology**, of life, of the breath that you inhale and exhale every moment. That's meditation - to BE HERE NOW - in this NOW moment - in this present moment - to be conscious - to BE - just BE yourself - don't BECOME!

RAHU is in the rush to BECOME. And KETU is happy to BE. Understand the difference. Savour the difference.

A RAHU-ish man cannot stop, cannot pause, cannot sit back. Such a man is always running behind power, pleasures, ambitions - that is how Alexander the Great was running - one kingdom after the other - and yet the whole world was never conquered - Diogenes, the divine master had said to him, **"Come, join me, relax with me."** But Alexander said, **"I will come back, master - but only when I conquer the whole world!"**

And Alexander was never able to come back. He died. Neither the whole world was conquered nor the world within was conquered - in reality - Alexander is the loser, a great loser. And that is how **you too would be** - if you are not willing to pause, to introspect, to look within.

Desires (RAHU) never end. After one desire is fulfilled - the other is standing in a queue and like a FOOL - you continue running behind your desires until you drop down dead in the graveyard! And still your 'running' never stops - you again take birth to satisfy your new desires and that is how for millions and millions of years, you all have taken many births and rebirths - and still the cycle continues. Life repeats itself mindlessly until you become mindful - until you become meditative - until you start turning inwards.

This is not the only life - that you had SEX or are looking forward to having SEX - for millions and millions of past lives - you have had sex - and still, look at you - you are still doing the same thing - nothing has changed - the PATTERN remains the same - only the outward 'design' changes!

The difference between you and the meditative man is that - the saint, the yogi too had sex in the past lives - but this life - they have become conscious - a moment in their life came - when they realized - what a monkey they had been - and from that moment they dropped the idea of sex - sex transformed into super consciousness and life was never the same - everything was the same - but they were not the same - then there was a dance, a music and life became a garden of bliss! The life of a true SAINT is blissful. HE will never stop you from having SEX - HE would simply like you to 'observe' your actions consciously - HE would wait - HE would wait for hundred more years - until you - yourself realize the futility of SEX - and the day you would self-realize - there is no need to put that saffron dress on your body - celibacy has to come from WITHIN and not through the fancy show-off by wearing the dress of a monk or saffron clothes!

But who wants to listen? RAHU is hovering over the MIND. And the majority have become the MIND - and so the daily chores of life continue - miseries continue - you say "I am living" - but in reality - you are not living, just existing!

It is difficult, very difficult to transform a sane man - a sane man is too noisy - he is too into his mind, caught by his mind - and the mind has many desires, the mind is ambitious - the mind is very clever - very cunning - the mind makes you believe that AMBITION is PURE NECTAR - when in reality, AMBITION is PURE POISON.

The hurdle between YOU and your happiness, your joy, your peace - is AMBITION. Ambition is of the MIND and not of the HEART. The Heart is fearless, but the Mind is fearful.

> **66**
>
> An ambition is out of fear. All ambition is out of an inferiority complex. Because you are afraid to be yourself.
>
> **OSHO**
>
> **99**

RAHU is the NORTH NODE of the Moon. The Westerners call RAHU as the NORTH NODE. It is the Head of the Moon. But when the MOON is with KETU - there is absolutely no HEAD - how will the MOON operate? How will the Mind operate? There is absolutely NO MIND. So MOON KETU conjunction is one of the most beautiful conjunctions and I have seen many great yogis with KETU MOON conjunctions.

KETU MOON - **a Yogi.**

RAHU MOON - **a Bhogi.**

Two ends. And between these two ends is the story of human life!

KETU is on the side of Jupiter. Jupiter loves KETU. Meher Baba, the Guru - loves Madmen. They are living with NO MIND - you just have to show them the right door - and they are out - liberated!

KETU - is that mad man - who IF bestowed with the grace of the divine master (GURU) - can transform into the most enlightened man - the world has ever known!

An enlightened man is a man who has NO MIND - who has gone beyond the MIND - who has reached to the depth of his heart - now his heart is speaking - his heart is singing, his heart is sharing - the MIND no more exists - it has merged - it has become quiet! Such a man is truly enlightened - that is how the Buddha is - Jesus is - Krishna is, that is how the divine masters are - living with NO MIND - but with total consciousness!

A wise man will look open-minded to you; in fact, he is without mind, not open-minded and closed-minded; a wise man is a no-mind.

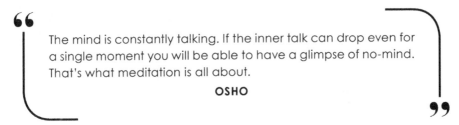

The mind is constantly talking. If the inner talk can drop even for a single moment you will be able to have a glimpse of no-mind. That's what meditation is all about.

OSHO

A mad man has no-mind. KETU has no mind. All you need is the **grace of the divine master** and the same KETU **swings to the greatest height of meditation** - of spirituality that one can ever imagine!

And that is how - KETU is the favourite of Sri Guru (Jupiter)! Jupiter loves Ketu. I love Ketu. Without KETU there is no way out - KETU is NO MIND - the only thing missing is - the guidance - the 'torch' - the moment the 'torch' switches on - KETU quickly moves from the 'wrong door' (IGNORANCE) to the 'right door' (CONSCIOUSNESS)! That is how Meher Baba with his deep compassion and grace - transformed many mad men into enlightened beings and that is why Baba says that it is far easier to transform a mad man into an enlightened being - because in a way he is 'out' (out of mind) - but through the 'wrong door' (ignorance) - you just have to show him the right door - just a touch of grace - and a mad man can transform and reach greater heights than your so-called **sane people!**

A Guru is not someone who holds a torch for you. He is the torch.

SADHGURU

Sane people are a real pain. A sane man is intellectual and intellectuality is of the MIND! The MIND is intellectual - the HEART is intelligent.

The master will tell a sane man to do a certain thing and he will ask you 100 questions. But when the master tells a man who follows his heart - to 'jump' - he will 'jump' and a time comes when the same man who 'appears' MAD to you - **reaches the greatest heights** of the same valley **in which he had jumped!** That is how Peter - reached the highest altitude - he became Saint Peter! That is the power of faith - an illiterate fisherman can become the greatest saint the world has ever known!

> They say: think twice before you jump. I say: jump first and then think as much as you want.
>
> **OSHO**

Krishna says, "Shoot, - Arjuna - just Shoot the arrow from your bow." And Arjuna is such a beautiful man - such a great disciple - such a faithful man - I think ARJUNA is one of the greatest disciples - the world could have ever known - shooting the arrow on those **who once had been so close to his heart** - Imagine what would have happened to you? Your hands would have started shaking - but ARJUNA is ARJUNA - he loves Krishna - he loves HIS master - and it is this love - this unwavering FAITH that gives strength to Him - and Arjuna without 'thinking' (NO MIND - KETU) shoots the arrow! The MAHABHARAT was won by the PANDAVAS but the true credit goes to ARJUNA and HIS immense love for his master - Sri Krishna - how to express such a love - how to! Language is really poor - words cannot suffice!

When I say 'Jump' - I mean the courage to SURRENDER in TOTALITY!

Once it happened, a so-called sane person came - intellectual, Harvard educated - and he said to Osho, "You say you are Bhagwan - then show me - your true Avatar."

Osho smiled and said, "But for that - first you have to become ARJUNA!"

Arjuna 'Jumps' - Peter the Fisherman 'Jumps' - Sariputra 'Jumps' - only those who have dared to JUMP have reached the higher altitudes - don't give me those big talks - first, look within - turn inwards and ask yourself - are you ready to JUMP? Are you READY?

Only a refined, well-aspected KETU can 'Jump' - that is how KETU is beautiful – Yes, I LOVE KETU - and I am against all those who have defamed KETU.

KETU is not meditating. KETU is meditation. It is a LET GO. I am KETU. I am meditation and so should all those who are following the path of TRUTH be. It is only KETU - meaning your willingness to meditate to turn inwards – that **can help you get ready.**

> When the disciple is ready, the master appears. And when the disciple is truly ready the master disappears.
>
> **LAO TZU**

What a beautiful quote by the most divine master - LAO TZU! I love LAO TZU - I simply love this great master.

When the student is truly ready - the teacher disappears! How meaningful, how deep, how true and how touching. Simply beautiful! When you are truly ready to spread the message of love - then the master moves on - the master disappears! Beautiful.

People come with all sorts of questions - and 90% of them are FAKE - it is a pain to entertain such men and women - but this is KALIYUG - what to say! So then, I listen. People have all sorts of fancy ideas about spirituality - they want to KNOW - **but who really wants to listen to the TRUTH** - because TRUTH is hard - very hard! To experience true spirituality - you should be ready - ready to JUMP - to surrender in totality - ask yourself - look around and you will find 90% are not willing to jump - to surrender - they say they are - but deep within is the fear - and the fear will never go away until the MIND goes away!

Until there is NO MIND - until you start moving away from RAHU - towards KETU - you cannot experience enlightenment! And to experience the beyond, one should be ready to go through the fire of suffering - so are you ready? The majority are NOT. They want to have a cosy life, fat salary, fat business first - and when everything is there - then they start getting fancy ideas of spirituality - then they want to sit in an air-conditioned room - and meditate! Now nobody knows whether meditation happens in true sense - except that some relaxation happens - but relaxation has to be of the MIND and not the body - the meditation classes that you spend millions on - they cannot help you - meditation is not something to be learned - it is within you - it comes naturally to human beings - just the way - the art of catching a mouse - comes to a cat by birth! But the business of meditation has begun - the world is vast - people are many - and so such so-called meditation school 'traps' continue to work - because who wants to know the truth - **the fake are celebrated** - **the truth is ignored** - it has always been ignored and yet it is only the truth that has prevailed!

"All truths passes through three stages – First, it is ridiculed. Second, it is violently opposed. Third, it is accepted as being self-evident." – Arthur Scopenhauer

A certain madness is necessary - only then can you JUMP - that is why the great MEHER BABA says again and again that - yes, it is far easier to transform a mad man into an enlightened being - simply because, he CAN jump - he has the courage! KETU has courage. You see - that is why KETU is fearless, courageous - brave - because he is totally mad - totally out of mind and that is good - the only thing needed is the touch of the master and this KETU goes a long way - becomes the greatest spiritual master the world has ever known! That is how I love KETU - that is how I worship KETU - that is how you too would worship KETU only if you understand KETU!

Everything is possible - only if you are willing to JUMP! Jump first, think later.

You will jump only if you are out of your MIND! Peter 'jumped' because the MIND stopped working - the MIND became quiet the moment JESUS came before him, and the moment there is no mind - the heart wells up and you can jump only when the heart wells up - and the mind has become quiet!

Ignorant people and astrologers have simply ridiculed KETU - they will never understand KETU - because to understand KETU - first, you have to understand your mind - the monkey mind - overcome it - only then can you understand the depth of KETU - else you will go on reading hundreds of books on KETU and still never realize the beauty of KETU!

Meher Baba realized the beauty of KETU (MADNESS) - he had no knowledge of astrology - to understand astrology - you don't have to parrot the books of astrology - you simply have to dive within - and understand your 'self' first! And to a man - to a great master like Meher

Baba who has self-realized - needs no knowledge of astrology - he is astrology - he is the moon and he is the sun - what more is required?

And Meher Baba did a phenomenal work - HE transformed many KETUs - madmen into enlightened beings!

"It is a strange world. Here, really great things are never rewarded. Nobody has bothered about Meher Baba. Mother Teresa will get a Nobel prize because she looks after poor orphan children, and nobody thought of giving a Nobel prize to Meher Baba who really did a miraculous job – and he was the only man, after centuries."
- Osho

Contact with Guru - Jupiter - transform the erstwhile mad man or mad Ketu!

And that is why KETU in the zodiac sign of Pisces and Sagittarius - the sign of Guru (Jupiter) is exalted - in other words – it has all the possibilities to become enlightened! In Pisces - Ketu is tremendously happy, delighted, in fact, Ketu is truly exalted in Pisces - the 12th zodiac - the beyond!

You see how beautiful astrology can be - only if it is coming through your 'self' - through your awareness - your consciousness!

The key to growth is the introduction of higher dimensions of consciousness into our awareness.

LAO TZU

There is NO middle ground for KETU. Understand this - this is of great significance. KETU is either totally mad - or - totally enlightened. There is absolutely no middle ground - either KETU will take your life OR he will sacrifice HIS life for you! Either he is a mad murderer or he is a great saint.

And that is how KETU is extreme. Because the sign of SCORPIO is of extremism - KETU finds home in SCORPIO! Look how beautiful the essence of astrology can be - only if it is coming through the 'self' and not from the books!

Ketu is home in Scorpio. Donald Trump has KETU in Scorpio along with MOON! The world thinks that HE is a MAD person - but in reality, HE is a genius.

The same comfortable KETU in Scorpio becomes exalted in Sagittarius and also in Pisces - both are its favourite places - they belong to Jupiter - the Master - and Ketu finds peace in the abode of the Master!

Scorpio KETU - is all on his own - meaning KETU shows all its colour with full force. Disruptiveness is the core nature of Scorpio KETU and that is what Donald Trump is doing - look at his decisions - they are all disruptive in nature - bold and courageous! No other President 'dared' to STOP the funding of billions of dollars to Pakistan - but Donald Trump did it. He stopped the funding to Pakistan. He also criticized Pakistan openly - which no other US President had done in the history of American Politics! That's Ketu in Scorpio and in Trump's case - KETU is with his Moon - but Moon is in Scorpio, so you see some negative shades also to his overall personality.

KETU in Sagittarius is a changed man - here in the abode of the master - of Jupiter - Ketu is elevated and so he becomes more understanding, more insightful - more tolerant and also brings some great qualities of a warrior - or righteousness!

KETU in Pisces - is the most beautiful placement. Great saints are born with KETU in Pisces - here KETU is beyond the point of elevation - in fact, here KETU has gone beyond the MIND - here KETU has truly helped the native to 'attain' enlightenment! KETU in Pisces and KETU in 12th house are the best placement for spiritual progress.

Look at this - this is beautiful. In reality - we all are born with NO MIND - that is how the very FIRST NAKSHATRA (STAR) of our zodiac galaxy is - ASHWINI - the star of KETU!

> **66**
> You were born as 'No-Mind'. Let this sink into your heart as deeply as possible because through that, a door opens. If you were born as a 'No-Mind' – then the mind is just a social product. It is not natural, it is cultivated.
> **OSHO**
> **99**

The journey is from No-Mind to No-Mind - in between these two ends is your struggle with life - a life that has evolved through your own KARMA!

Just the way a calf finds its mother among thousand cows - similarly your 'KARMA' comes searching for you - no matter where you are - at which place you are - your KARMA will catch you soon! And that is why all the holy scriptures of all religions emphasise on one thing - CLEANSE YOUR KARMA!

Being grateful for all that you have, being able to forgive, able to love, able to remain conscious about your intentions, and able to have a positive attitude is a sign of leading a progressive life.

SHANI is your KARMA.

KETU is the method - the way to cleanse your KARMA!

So Ketu coming over SHANI - from a spiritual perspective - is a wonderful development - wherein now - you will start focusing on cleansing your Karma - you will become more conscious, you will start transforming inside out!

For a materialistic RAHU-ish man - this transit can be problematic - because he has no interest in cleansing his karma - so then KETU becomes a pain for him - and he goes through many mental troubles!

So you see - KETU is a boon for spiritual people - and the same KETU is a beating for material people!

The real problem is, therefore, not KETU but RAHU! RAHU is a staunch enemy of SATURN. These are two contrast energies, understand this - this is of significance.

Saturn likes all that is within the system - and Rahu likes all that is outside the system! That is how RAHU pushes a person to commit adultery - to commit corruption - to commit murders - to commit theft - all that goes against the SOCIETY NORMS!

So, rather than worrying about KETU - you all should focus on overcoming the RAHU - the DESIRES within you! But how to overcome desires during this 1.5 years phase? And you will find your answer in the beautiful quote of NEEM KAROLI BABA - the divine master to whom the Apple CEO - Steve Jobs had come to meet. Many western followers came to seek Baba's blessings - and Baba would say to them - "Go and meditate like Christ - He lost himself in Love."

How to overcome RAHU - Desires? And Baba answers so beautifully:

> **66**
> If you want to see God, kill desires. Desires are in the mind. When you have a desire for something, don't act on it and it will go away. If you desire to drink this cup of tea, don't and the desire for it will go away.
> **NEEM KAROLI BABA**
> **99**

Always remember, the planets are innocent, the stars are innocent - they have no intention to harm anyone - they are just 'energies' that exist - what matters is HOW YOU RECEIVE those energies – and, therefore, it all begins with YOU!

If you are raising the level of your consciousness - then the planetary energies will be received at the higher altitudes - and the higher altitudes are always positive.

So, my appeal to all my readers is that - focus within you - you can change your life - only if you can transform yourself from within.

Raise the level of your 'antenna' — only then can you receive high quality 'signals'. Focus within and start meditating.

Once Buddha was in a deep discussion with the emperor. Suddenly, a very old monk came - he must be 90 years old, he bowed before the master and said, "I am very sorry to disturb you - but I have to leave and I must reach the other monastery before it gets dark. I have come to touch your feet and seek your blessings."

Buddha looked into the eyes of the old monk and asked, **"How old are you?"**

And the old monk said, "I am four **years old."**

Buddha smiled and said, "You can leave, my blessings are with you."

The emperor was shocked - when the old monk left, he asked Buddha, "How come the old monk **who looks beyond 90 years** – says that he is **four years old?"**

And Buddha said, "Real age **is the point from where you start turning inwards** - and you have been asking me all sorts of stupid questions - so I thought why not to give you the real thing. That is why I asked the old man - his age - so that you stop asking all stupid questions and start asking some sensible question."

Your money, your status, your cars, your bungalows, your sexuality - everything is going to turn into ashes someday - then what comes with YOU? Only the growth that you have attained WITHIN - only that comes with you! And that is why a great Sufi saint says - The real beggars are those who have been chasing the FALSE GOLD (material pleasures) all their life. Because after your body is burnt on the pyre - what comes with you is not the FAKE GOLD that you have been holding so tightly to your chest but only that which you have realized WITHIN - by turning inwards - by becoming detached - be being more and more meditative.

Spiritual growth is the REAL GROWTH.

> **66**
>
> Spiritual growth requires the development of inner knowing and inner authority. It requires the heart, not the intellect.
>
> **GARY ZUKAV**
>
> **99**

Sant Kabir would visit a village and he would look around - observe the ignorant people and then he would say, *"Sadhu - this is a town of dead people."*

Dead people meaning people who are ignorant - who have no consciousness - all that prevails within them is EGO, GREED, LUST and ANGER. They live their whole life focusing on the 'Makeup' – yes, they look beautiful but like those perfect PLASTIC ROSE FLOWERS - they look good - but that is all - they have no fragrance to their existence - they remain a PLASTIC DOLL - a plastic rose - all their life!

Once, I had a ride in a private aeroplane - in the US. It happened so that when I was working in the US office in San Jose - one evening, one of my office mates asked, "Addittya, will you come with me? I want to show you my private aeroplane."

I could not say 'no' — she had been a close colleague.

I got into her car and she drove me to a huge aeroplane parking ground. It took almost 2 hours to reach. Then we got inside the parking premise - it was huge - so huge that it had almost 500 private aeroplanes parked. She said, "The planes you see are private aeroplanes and the owners pay their monthly parking rents."

She showed me the way towards her aeroplane. It was a beautiful, small private aeroplane for just two. We got inside - she got that small beast - started. And within a few minutes - we were up in the sky - and

I could see the whole of San Francisco Bay Area. I said, "You are flying so nicely - it is so great to see you flying the aeroplane!"

And she looked into my eyes and said, "Today, I got my flying licence and you are the first to go!"

Now that was a good shot on me - I was wondering if this lady is going to get me down safely! But we did. Then I asked her - what she did with this aeroplane. And she said, "I use it sometimes to go for lunch with my husband."

So you see - life can be rosy - it can be so much rosy that you may get distracted from the real thing - the real you - your 'self'!

You have to focus within - you have to stay away from distractions and that is possible only when you remain rooted deeply within!

> **"**
>
> When there are thoughts, it is distraction; when there are NO thoughts, it is meditation.
>
> **SRI RAMANA MAHARSHI**
>
> **"**

Like Arjuna - remain focused on the 'eye of the fish' - meaning on your 'self'. Meditate - the transit of KETU over SHANI is a beautiful transit for coming closer to your 'self' - so meditate.

Even though you may be RAHU-ish - if you are turning towards your 'self' - if you are moving inwards - then you too have the rare opportunity to experience much relief during the coming 18 months of RAHU KETU transit - but only if you are seriously taking the efforts to turn inwards.

> **"**
>
> I want the world to realize that turning inward is the greatest joy. In comparison, any other pleasure is a regressive step.
>
> **SADHGURU**
>
> **"**

You are missing many opportunities that God has been showering upon you because you are so much focused on the outward! When there is so much for you to experience and explore within!

Come, come towards your 'self' - spend some quality time in meditation - focus on the name of the Lord - no matter whose name you take - as long as you remain focused on the name of the Lord. The way is within and not without.

Remember this. Sammasti. That was the last word of the Buddha.

The last word of Buddha is so touching, no, it is not a sermon, no, it is not any kind of instruction - HE simply says one word - one last word – 'Sammasti' - REMEMBER. That's all. Just one word and the whole universe is revealed through this one last word - REMEMBER – 'Sammasti'!

Remember what your inner space is. Just remember. There is nothing to achieve, and there is nothing to become. You are already that which you have been seeking in all your lives in different ways, on different paths. But you have NEVER looked inward. Look in. And whenever you have time, you know the path. Just go again and again to the inner space so that your fear of disappearing is dropped, you start enjoying being nobody, and you start remembering the forgotten language.

One word - a very significant word of the Buddha - 'Sammasti' - Remember. And then the most beautiful man who once walked on this planet - left us all - he left his physical form though he remains in millions of hearts - my heart - your heart - every heart that loves the Buddha! I love the Buddha. – No, I am not a Buddhist and yet I love HIM - because to understand the Buddha - you don't have to become a Buddhist - you just have to be here now - in this present moment and **let** HIS insightful words - His message reach you - merge within you.

Just listen - just remember your peace within - Sammasti!

The flower may die, but the fragrance will go on and on spreading to the very end of existence. A person who has attained to love may die—his love continues. *Buddha* is dead, his love continues. That is how I love HIM, that is how you love HIM - we have never seen him in physical form and yet we love him - the most beautiful, wise and enlightened man who once walked on this planet.

The message of the Buddha is in one line - "Look within - Meditate. Discover your 'self'"- it all sounds KETU-ish - because Buddha is KETU - KETU is wisdom and Buddha is not a name, it is not a title, it simply is a stage of enlightenment - KETU is that enlightenment - the moment KETU comes in contact with Jupiter - you are no more the same - everything around you is the same - but you are no more the same - a great transformation is happening within you and you are set on the greatest journey of your life - *the journey* **within!**

The only journey is the journey within.
RAINER MARIA RILKE

KETU is the energy that can move you within. Your struggle with RAHU will only come to an end when your journey with KETU begins!

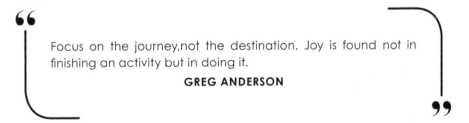

Focus on the journey, not the destination. Joy is found not in finishing an activity but in doing it.
GREG ANDERSON

Rahu is 'attachment'. Buddha says the root of suffering is attachment!

Ketu is detachment. Detachment is the key to your peace, your joy, your bliss.

Your mind must become a river of detachment. Your Heart must become a Sea of Love - says the divine master Sri Chinmoy.

> If we fearfully cling to what we have, we will never be able to discover who we truly are.
> **SRI CHINMOY**

You only lose what you cling to - says the Buddha!

Rahu makes you cling (attach) to all that you come across - you have to move beyond Rahu - you have to move beyond attachments - you have to move **beyond the Mind**. And that's meditation!

> Remember – meditation is not something that is done by the mind, it is the absence of the mind. When the mind stops, meditation happens. It is not something out of the mind, it is something beyond the mind.
> **OSHO**

The journey of your life begins from attachments - but it only starts *flowering* when you start moving from RAHU towards KETU - from outward towards inwards - from IGNORANCE towards CONSCIOUSNESS - and then there is a song to it - music - and life is no more the same - then life is transforming into a garden of bliss.

Find your bliss. Look within. Turn inwards.

Move from Rahu (desire) - towards Ketu (desireless) stage. It may take a million births but every long journey begins with a small step. Take the step towards the beyond - move away from the MIND and move more and more close to your Heart!

The very center of your heart is where life begins
RUMI

Your heart is the most beautiful place on earth. Focus on your heart - listen to the voice **within** you - **Meditate.**

Jai Shri Ganesha. Jai Guru.

Question 3

What role does KETU play in human life and how it contributes to spiritual life?

KETU is ZERO. KETU is SHUNYA (शुन्य) - Ketu is a Nobody. And yet Ketu can get you to Everybody.

"When you become SHUNYA, when you become absolutely NOTHING, a NOTHINGNESS, a NOBODY- then you have attained."

— Buddha

And it is only when you ATTAIN - when you SELF-REALIZE - when you are Enlightened that you can HEAL! And so I have been saying again and again - that at the ROOT of HEALING POWER - is the most benevolent KETU - one who has NO HEAD - and only one who has NO HEAD can JUMP - and only one who can JUMP - can ATTAIN - can experience the BEYOND.

> **66**
>
> They say: Think twice before you jump. I say: Jump first and then think as much as you want!
>
> **OSHO**
>
> **99**

Such men are very few. One in a million. People want to know many things - they talk a lot - so much of 'knowledge' they exhibit - and yet when it comes to taking the 'JUMP' - they start shaking - they start raising many doubts - and so ARJUNA is one in a million. ANANDA is one in a million. PETER is one in a million. They JUMPED - they simply jumped WITHOUT thinking - when you THINK - the MIND is at PLAY - the HEAD is at play - and the MIND won't let you JUMP - ARJUNA, ANANDA, PETER - these were great souls who had overcome the monkey mind - and so when KRISHNA says to ARJUNA - "SHOOT - SHOOT at that old man - BHISHMA- follow your DHARMA."

ARJUNA simply shoots - he simply shoots his ARROW at that old man who loved him the most - whom he also loves the most - BHISHMA! But when the MASTER says, "SHOOT" - ARJUNA simply SHOOTS - that is the stage of NO MIND - that is the most beautiful stage of KETU!

When Jesus meets Peter, the fisherman for the VERY FIRST TIME and says, "Peter - follow me - I will make you the fisher of men."

Peter, the fisherman simply drops everything and starts following JESUS. He is not even aware of who JESUS is! He is an illiterate man - and yet he could SEE that this man is something else - that the words of this young man are so deep - his eyes, there is so much GRACE - that

Peter simply could not even THINK - he simply 'JUMPS' into the unknown - and that is KETU - that is COURAGE - it is only through the State of NO MIND - KETU - you can become COURAGEOUS – Peter, indeed, was the most COURAGEOUS man and the same PETER, the fisherman goes on to become one of the 12 Apostles of Jesus and later is revered as Saint Peter in the Christian Faith!

Ananda - what an innocent man he was. Yes - he had some ignorance - but he simply was so much devoted to BUDDHA that he followed HIM for 40 years - like a shadow - he remained with BUDDHA - Ananda becomes the Shadow of Buddha - Ananda was also a PRINCE - he belonged to a ROYAL family - he was the elder cousin brother of Buddha - and yet he JUMPED - he left everything behind and came in search of his younger brother - whom the world had been addressing as the BUDDHA! And Ananda loved Buddha - but his love had become possessive. And the moment your LOVE becomes POSSESSIVE - KETU takes a backseat - and when KETU (DETACHMENT) takes a backseat - your spiritual progress - your enlightenment is blocked!

And that is what happened with ANANDA. He spent 40 years with BUDDHA and yet he could NOT attain.

And now when BUDDHA was dying - when BUDDHA was about to leave his human body - Anand started crying - he could not control himself - he broke out with such a cry that Buddha noticed it and said, "Ananda, why you cry?"

Ananda said, "I am not crying because you are leaving - I am crying because once you are gone - there will be nobody of your calibre for centuries to come and I am still not enlightened. Those who came after me - have been enlightened with your Grace - but I... haven't yet been enlightened...why?"

Buddha said, "Ananda - when you met me for the first time, you laid three conditions - those conditions became a hurdle between you and your attainment."

Ananda remembered those three conditions - those three conditions were to help him stay with Buddha and he stayed for 40 years - but no luck, enlightenment never happened to him. Ananda asked, "Now what?" Buddha said, "Now I have to die first - only then you will be enlightened - with my death - all your conditions that I had accepted will cease - you will then attain."

And it is said that after Buddha died, Ananda attained enlightenment. Conditions block you - when you love - let there be NO Conditions.

> **"**
>
> The word – Progress – is the basic disease of the modern age. What is the need? All that can be enjoyed is available, all that you need to be happy is Here & Now! But you create CONDITIONS and you say that unless these CONDITIONS are fulfilled you cannot be happy – as if by being happy you are going to oblige the whole universe.
>
> **OSHO**
>
> **"**

KETU has NO CONDITIONS. Because KETU operates WITHOUT HEAD - WITHOUT MIND.

So, a REAL DISCIPLE - a REAL FOLLOWER when follows the MASTER - he would never remember the BLOWS of the Master - because there is NO HEAD - all that there is - is the HEART and the HEART can only FEEL - the HEART cannot HOLD on to anything - in true sense - the HEART is DETACHED by nature - what makes you ATTACHED is your MIND – and, therefore, the MIND is always against KETU - because it knows - that the energy of KETU can eliminate all the illusions that the MIND goes on creating.

It happened once, Hassan and a few Sufi Mystics were walking through the forest and they all met Rabiya - the Great Sufi Saint. Expressing their love for the master - Hassan said, "None is sincere in his claims to the Love of God unless he patiently endures the blows of His Lord." Rabiya smiled and said, "This smells egoism." Sakik said, "None is sincere in his claim unless he gives thanks for the blows of the Lord." Rabiya again smiled and said, "This must be still bettered. Still some ego is there." Malik said, "None is sincere in his claim unless he delights in the blows of his Lord." Rabiya again smiled and said, "Good but still needs to be improved. A very subtle ego is still hiding like a shadow." Then they all said, "Rabiya - you yourself say - you guide us." And Rabiya, one of the greatest Sufi Saints – said, "None is sincere in his claim UNLESS he FORGETS the blows in beholding his lord." How beautiful is this. They loved the master - but they could not FORGOT the blows - here Rabiya is saying - when love is total - the blows cannot be remembered. So where is the question of being delighted to receive the Master's blows or thankful or tolerating the blows - the Blows simply do not exist - a devoted disciple forgets the blows in beholding his compassionate Master!

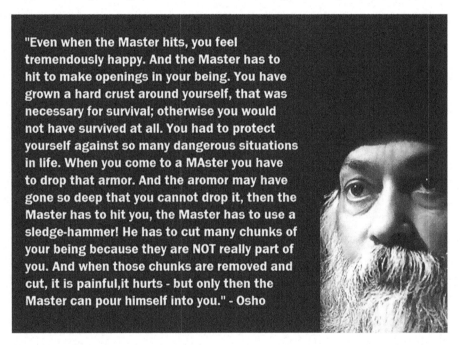

"Even when the Master hits, you feel tremendously happy. And the Master has to hit to make openings in your being. You have grown a hard crust around yourself, that was necessary for survival; otherwise you would not have survived at all. You had to protect yourself against so many dangerous situations in life. When you come to a MAster you have to drop that armor. And the aromor may have gone so deep that you cannot drop it, then the Master has to hit you, the Master has to use a sledge-hammer! He has to cut many chunks of your being because they are NOT really part of you. And when those chunks are removed and cut, it is painful,it hurts - but only then the Master can pour himself into you." - Osho

The Master can pour himself into you - only WHEN you have NO MIND. Only when you have overcome the MIND - only when your MIND is merged into your HEART and there is NO MIND - but tremendous intelligence!

KETU, therefore, brings Intelligence - but this intelligence is very deep, very unique and very rebellious by nature! TRUTH has always been rebellious. JESUS was rebellious - he goes to the PAGAN TEMPLES and asks the people to stop DOING BUSINESS on the name of these PAGAN GOD IDOLS. Mohammed was rebellious - He too went against the BUSINESS OF RELIGION and the Corruption that was happening on the name of GOD and IDOLS - BUDDHA too was rebellious - he too went against the Corruption that was happening on the name of religion. INTELLIGENCE is always rebellious by nature - the SOCIETY cannot FACE the intelligent - the SOCIETY always is afraid of an intelligent Man or an intelligent Woman. The SOCIETY is always afraid of KETU - because KETU brings Intelligence and Intelligence can unmask the FAKE and bring forth the TRUTHS!

> **"**
> Intelligence is dangerous. Intelligence means you will start thinking on your own; you will start looking around on your own; you will start not believe in the scriptures; you will believe only in your own experience.
>
> **OSHO**
> **"**

Intelligence is of the heart consciousness (also addressed as God consciousness in the West or Krishna Consciousness in the East). NEVER confuse Intelligence with Intellectualism.

Intellectualism is of the HEAD - Mercury.

Intelligence is of the Consciousness - SUN. And the way towards CONSCIOUSNESS is paved by KETU! Therefore, it is the SIGN of LEO - where KETU presides like an EMPEROR - by taking the lordship of the NAKSHATRA - MAGHA!

How beautiful is all this and how beautiful it can be - there is no limit - there never was! So, LEO, the sign of SUN (Consciousness), has its FIRST NAKSHATRA as MAGHA ruled by Sri KETU! That is why SUN feels HOME in the NAKSHATRA of MAGHA - SUN is extremely comfortable in the ROYAL ABODE of KETU (MAGHA Nakshatra)!

Hence, MAGHA is called the ROYAL ABODE - ROYALITY is closely associated with KETU - but the ROYALITY - the KING - the RAJ YOG that KETU brings is something beyond this material world - you become the KING of KINGS - but you roam NAKED - and yet you become the KING of KINGS - you become a Diogenes - he had NOTHING and yet he had THAT - which Emperors and Kings never had - he was one of the greatest YOGIS of the WEST - a great SAINT - now tell me - when you say 'I am the KING' - there should be absolute FREEDOM - no worries - no tensions - no obstructions - no obsessions - no possessions - such a FREEDOM - neither ALEXANDER the GREAT had and nor any EMPERORS who have been through this human world! SUCH A FREEDOM only JESUS had, MOHAMMED had, MAHAVIRA had, KRISHNA had, BUDDHA had - only a YOGI can experience TOTAL FREEDOM and only that man or woman who can experience TOTAL FREEDOM is the REAL KING - KETU enables you to reach the state of TOTAL FREEDOM - therefore, the NAKSHATRA OF MAGHA is addressed as the ROYAL ABODE - the REAL KING's SEAT - because it is here where you become a great YOGI - or you get the CAPACITY to become a great YOGI.

Yogi PARAMHANSA YOGANANADA had LEO Ascendant with MAGHA Nakshatra rising (KETU). And what a great Yogi he was - what a beautiful Autobiography he wrote - that it moved the hearts of millions across the globe - my salute to His Holiness Paramhansa Yogananda.

SUN feels home in the NAKSHATRA of KETU - MAGHA.
CONSCIOUSNESS feels home in the ABODE of KETU.

The Sign of LEO, therefore, is NOT in its entirety BENEFICIAL for the SUN. The SUN feels home - the SUN has all the abilities to expand your consciousness - ONLY as long as it is placed in the MAGHA Nakshatra of the SUN SIGN.

The moment SUN moves to PURVA PHALGUNI - it starts becoming uncomfortable - therefore, I meet many who wonder that why SUN in-spite of being in LEO sign - does NOT favor in its totality. PURVA PHALGUNI is VENUS Nakshatra and SUN energy is in contrast to VENUS. SUN wants to UPLIFT you - and VENUS wants you to remain ATTACHED to material PLEASURES - how can this MARRIAGE work?

So, SUN in LEO works beautifully - helping you to grow spiritually - as long as it is in the NAKSHATRA of MAGHA. Interestingly, many ROYAL FIGURES are also born on MAGHA - LEO ASCENDANT - when KETU connects with material planets - ROYALITY comes - when KETU connects with spiritual planets - SPIRITUALITY of HIGHEST NATURE comes - in both cases - you remain in the ABODE OF KETU - MAGHA - the ROYAL ABODE - that's why the ancient seers have HIGH REGARD for MAGHA - the nakshatra of KETU.

KETU is SHUNYA. ZERO. The WEST mentions the state of SHUNYA as EMPTINESS. NOTHING. NOBODY.

It is good to be a Nobody. Because LOVE happens only when you are in true sense a NOBODY! If you remain "I am somebody" (EGO) - Love is not possible. God is not possible. So, it is necessary to self-realize the significance of being a nobody - the significance of NOTHINGNESS, the significance of EMPTINESS. And only that man and woman can understand this significance - who is meditating, who is coming closer and closer to the Self - the consciousness.

Such a man, such a woman can relate to KETU - can listen to what it is saying, can follow its directions.

The label on the DOOR says - To open the door - PULL. But you are Pushing and Pushing and Pushing - how will the door open? WHEN

46

the JOB is lost - you continue to hit the same spot again and again - WHEN LIFE wants you to explore other opportunities. All your life, you have been PUSHING the DOOR - because you know only one way - you have never tried to explore the other way - the way to PULL open the DOOR.

And this is deep and this is something every individual should meditate upon - and this happens only when you have the support of Ketu. Only then you can turn inward - only then you can EXPLORE the many possibilities of OPENING the DOOR.

GOD has been knocking on your DOOR - many times - but what stops you from opening the door is your belief - you believe that there is only one way to open the door - it is your belief that comes in between your EXPERIENCE - and the IRONY of this human world is that people go by BELIEFS and NOT by Experiences!

Whenever KETU is in a specific planet's nakshatra - Ketu brings NOTHINGNESS to the matters of that planet. Through this NOTHINGNESS - Ketu wants you to PULL the Door and walk out - experience the ultimate FREEDOM from those matters that are ruled by that planet. DETACHED.

One day, Mohan came and said, "Addittya, how come I never had a chance to meet my mother? When I was 4, she left me - and then I just know that somewhere she is ALIVE - but neither she contacted me and nor I. So how do you see this happening? Please help me with your insights on this strange happening of my life - the absence - total absence of my MOTHER in my life.

I said, "Mohan - nowadays you have started to think a lot - that is not good. Thoughts become hurdles to your progress in meditation. So beware."

Mohan said, "But this has been troubling me for many days and months and so your answer will help me to understand and move on."

Sometimes you have to answer - Mohan was a close follower - with a strong focus on meditation. Not answering him would have blocked his progress in meditation, so I said, "Mohan, look at your birth chart - open it."

Mohan opened his birth chart and I said, "Look where your MOON is."

Mohan said, "Moon is in the SIXTH house. But I have many friends who have MOON in the sixth and still they have their mothers - there is no absence of Mother in their lives."

I smiled and said, "Look further...KETU is in which Nakshatra?"

Mohan said, "ROHINI."

I asked, "Who is the lord of ROHINI Nakshatra?"

Mohan said, "MOON."

I said, "Moon rules the matters related to MOTHER. KETU in MOON's Nakshatra - is bringing SHUNYATA (EMPTINESS) in the matters of MOTHER. Further, your MOON is also in conjunction with KETU - so again the EMPTINESS related to MOTHER becomes severe. So in the dictionary of your life - the word MOTHER is absent and will remain absent. Now LET GO - do not get stuck in the matters of MOTHER because KETU wants to liberate you - it is the way of KETU telling you - that MOVE ON - just the way when the doctor pricks the 'baby' inside the womb of a pregnant woman - COMES OUT - LIBERATED - FREED – similarly, KETU in this life wants you to MOVE ON - and NOT get attached to the matter related to MOTHER. Now get on with your life and focus on your MEDITATION."

> **❝** Kabir will suggest meditation, Buddha has suggested meditation, I suggest meditation. Meditation is a different approach: it has nothing to do with God, it has something to do with you, with your mind. It has to create a silence within you, a deep utter silence. In that utter silence you will start feeling the presence of God.
>
> **OSHO** **❞**

KETU is MEDITATION. And MEDITATION is a LET GO. Understand this - and I specifically appeal to all my close followers and readers - this is very deep.

KETU is Meditation. And Meditation is a LET GO - you will come to the state of SHUNYA - EMPTINESS only when you are able to LET GO - and KETU - the energy of KETU is precisely helping you to LET GO - Mohan was able to LET GO of his attachment with his MOTHER - but not everybody is like MOHAN - they come with questions - but they are NOT willing to or able to FACE the TRUTH - listen to what KETU has to say - to what LIFE has to say!

Understand the FACT - that the ABSENCE that KETU brings - the SHUNYATA (EMPTINESS) that KETU brings is simply to AWAKEN you and help you to MOVE ON - it is a clear signal - that you better remain DETACHED from the matters that are connected with KETU - BECAUSE KETU - the MASTER knows that unless you become DETACHED from these matters - you will NOT evolve - you will NOT mature - you will NOT GROW in the true sense!

When KETU is in a positive nakshatra - it simply empowers KETU - and that is a progressive sign for the native. Ketu LOVES Jupiter - he understands that the Master can channelize him in the most effective way. In fact, KETU is made for JUPITER - the Master. Ketu is just the way HANUMAN is - always devoted to the Master. Always!

So, when KETU is in VISHAKA NAKSHATRA which is ruled by JUPITER - KETU feels home. Feels comfortable. Had it been any other planet Nakshatra - Ketu would have simply moved its bulldozer on those planets and the matters they bring along. But in Vishaka Nakshatra - KETU gets a certain depth - if Jupiter is well placed then this placement can help in spiritual progress of the native.

Always realize the fact that YOU (and when I say YOU - it is meant for not just the questioner but to all my followers and readers) - can connect with the MASTER - only when there is NO HEAD (KETU)!

You have to ask yourself – What are you? A student or a disciple?

The relation of a Student with the Teacher is of the HEAD.

The relation of a DISCIPLE with the MASTER is of the HEART!

The Disciple can melt into the Master - only when there is NO MIND. Only when he or she has reached the state of NO MIND.

66

Meditation is the state of no-mind; no society within you, no conditioning within you – just you, with your pure consciousness.

OSHO

99

In the state of NO MIND - TRUTH descends like a light unto you. Then the Master appears - then the communication between you and the Master happens - and it all happens in SILENCE - deep Silence.

Real communication happens in silence, deep silence. MIND makes a lot of noise. That is one reason that I stay away from the crowd. A few selective people only I choose - because they are taking efforts to move beyond mind - through meditation.

A talkative person is a headache. This 'talk' has led to so many miseries. Mohan asked, "How?"

I said, "How does a relationship begin?"

And Mohan said, "Talk - through talking."

"That is right - first the man and the woman start 'talking' - then they talk more and more - over the phone - in person - and then this talking slowly starts transforming into the first step towards a bonding - a relationship!"

So 'Talking' is the first step - and this talking is all of the MIND and the MIND is monkey. The MIND goes on and on and on - and you start feeling that this woman is something - or - this man is something - the MIND is cunning - it knows how to attract through talking - you never know what lies beneath the talking - what is the REAL AGENDA!

And so, a common man falls in love through the medium of TALKING - COMMUNICATING. But a YOGI will never fall in love - because a YOGI has least interest in TALKING. Moreover, he also can easily understand what is the hidden agenda behind your talking - your communicating.

KETU dislikes Talking. Rahu likes Talking. A man ruled by RAHU talks a lot - let me tell you all that TALKING or COMMUNICATING can bring fortunes to your material life - and there is absolutely NO DOUBT about this. BUT the more you get inclined towards talking and talking - the more you go on losing your SELF - the more you move away from your SELF. So in the eyes of the world - you become RICH - but within, you become poorer and poorer.

"By talking and talking - externally you may be gaining something, but WITHIN you are certainly losing contact with *Yourself*. You are getting closer to people while you are becoming further removed from yourself. And the more adept you become at this game, the harder it will be for you to go into silence." - Osho

With folded hands – I, therefore, insist everybody who wants to contact me - that do NOT spend your time and my time in TALKING - just email me and if I can respond, I will - because the whole purpose of my sharing with you all - is to help you all MOVE towards your SELF - to MOVE you all towards SILENCE.

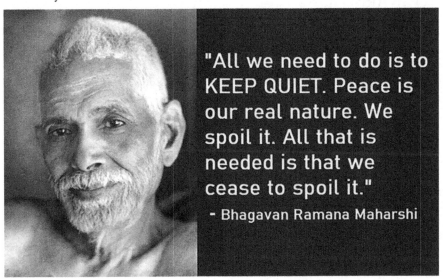

"All we need to do is to KEEP QUIET. Peace is our real nature. We spoil it. All that is needed is that we cease to spoil it."
- Bhagavan Ramana Maharshi

KETU rejoices in SILENCE. The YOGI rejoices in SILENCE. The whole journey of this human life is to move towards SILENCE - and that SILENCE has to be a BLISSFUL Silence - a meditative silence.

Those who cannot understand the TRUTH - will ask you, "Tell me the TRUTH?"

But how can you tell the TRUTH - when the one who is asking is still at the base level - is still an ignorant fellow! Jesus also remained silent - when he was asked at the very last moment when he was put on the CROSS - the Roman Prefect had asked, "What is the TRUTH?"

And Jesus remained silent. He just looked into the Prefect's eyes - and pure SILENCE. It was Buddhist Silence - because TRUTH can be shared - can be given only if there is a certain depth of UNDERSTANDING!

KETU can help you all - to bring a certain depth of understanding because KETU can TURN you INWARDS and only that man and that woman can have a certain depth - who is turning inwards - who is meditating - who is coming closer to the SELF - the Consciousness!

People are running and running and seeking a MASTER - a real MASTER - my question to them is - Are you ready to become a true disciple?

People want to see KRISHNA - the question is - ARE YOU READY TO BE ARJUNA?

Only when you have become a true disciple that you can SEE the Master - Feel his love - Feel his Grace.

The word DISCIPLE is very beautiful - it means one who is 'Ready to learn'. Discipline means creating a Space for learning. Disciple means one who is Ready to Learn. But when can you learn? Only when you drop all your EGO, your PREJUDICES, your NOTIONS and IDEAS only when YOU BECOME TOTALLY EMPTY - SHUNYA - that you can become a true disciple!

This state of being SHUNYA - EMPTY is what KETU brings - only IF you are able to resonate with its energy - can you develop - grow - in the true sense.

The 'cup' is useful ONLY because it is EMPTY! Form is EMPTINESS, EMPTINESS is FORM, states one of the most revered Buddhist Texts.

As long as you are PACKED with all the KNOWLEDGE that you have collected all along your life - how can the REAL - the TRUTH penetrate into your being - you are already packed - Houseful.

Unless there is EMPTINESS - you cannot grow inside out - you may go on repeating the words of Buddha but you will not become a Buddha - to become a Buddha - you have to first become EMPTY - a NOBODY - rejoice in NOTHINGNESS.

KETU, when related to Jupiter, is always beneficial for spiritual growth - the question is whether you are ready.

And so come, come you all - and realize the fact that this is the only moment - the PAST is NO more - and the FUTURE is not yet - this moment - NOW is the only moment and time is running - you have to decide which way you have to move on with your journey - RAHU or KETU?

What you choose is what you become. You are always free to choose but you are never free from the consequences of the Choice that you make!

So choose wisely - when you look around and you see people who have got exactly what they have wished for - you may get carried away by thinking that they are the ones who are LUCKY - but let me tell you all they are NOT the lucky ones - the lucky ones are those who DO what they are meant to do - who come with a mission - a purpose and work towards making that mission a success, a celebration.

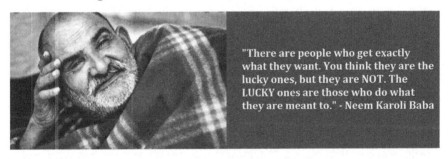

"There are people who get exactly what they want. You think they are the lucky ones, but they are NOT. The LUCKY ones are those who do what they are meant to." - Neem Karoli Baba

An Army officer fights to save his country - he may lose his life - but he has done what he was meant to do. Such men and women who work for others - whose sole purpose is to DO what they are meant to - are the LUCKY ones and not those who get exactly what they want.

But not everybody can understand this - the majority have become slaves of their MIND and the MIND ensures that you never get to the bottom of the TRUTH.

KETU helps you to overcome this Monkey Mind. Through KETU you can detach yourself -and the moment DETACHMENT starts coming over you - you can start experiencing the happiness - the love - the peace you have been seeking all your life.

The key is DETACHMENT. The way is through WITNESSING.

Witnessing is the way. Remain a witness while you do a certain action. Do it without getting attached - if you are feeding someone - feed but by being detached. If you are helping someone - healing someone - do it - but remain a witness - just the way a MILITARY DOCTOR on a battleground does.

What does he do? He simply heals the wounded soldiers - one by one. He is NOT attached - he is simply devoted to his ART OF HEALING - he heals one soldier and moves on to the next - and then next and next and next - that's all! There is absolutely no attachment - whatever he does - he does out of care, out of love - but that love is NOT attached - it moves on to the NEXT - and that's KETU - KETU heals and HE can HEAL because there is absolutely NO ATTACHMENT to what he does. There is absolutely NO AGENDA to what he does - there are absolutely NO expectations to what he does - he simply does what he is meant to do - and such a man is a lucky man - such a man is truly a blessed man, says the divine saint Neem Karoli Baba.

KETU is Emptiness. Shunya. Only when you become a Shunya can you WITNESS. Only when you start LETTING GO - can you Meditate. And only when you meditate that you can come to your own realizations - you can heal yourself - and only when you can heal yourself that you can HEAL others! The whole spiritual journey begins from KETU - for the way towards the TRUTH - is within and KETU is the only energy in this whole universe that can encourage you - empower you to look within and begin on the most wonderful journey of your life - the Journey Within.

66

You have no need to travel anywhere. Journey within yourself, enter a mine of rubies and bath in the splendour of your own light.

RUMI

99

54

The only journey is the JOURNEY WITHIN - and my fellows, this is exactly what KETU's message is - those who can relate to this divine message - can EVOLVE during KETU's Dasha, transits and those who cannot - will simply continue to live a miserable life.

Every Kundli is either inclined towards KETU (LET GO) or RAHU (ATTACHED/CLINGING/HOLDING). So, first comes RAHU KETU and then begins the whole story of planets - that is how critical these two ENDS are - one is HITLER (RAHU) and the other is BUDDHA (KETU) and they are two polarities that can never meet - you cannot say, "I am a philosopher and I am spiritual." - You are either a PHILOSOPHER (RAHU) or you are pure SPIRITUAL (KETU)!

Philosopher is like a blind man. He simply goes on and on and on - applies a hell of LOGIC - he may try to figure out how KRISHNA looks - but he has never experienced the divinity of Krishna. He may repeat the words of BUDDHA but he has NEVER EXPERIENCED the divinity, the essence of BUDDHA. You see - a philosopher is all logic WITH ABSOLUTE NO REAL EXPERIENCE.

But a Spiritual person and what a beauty he is. He is so simple, so straight and he speaks so less - he is not lost in his PAST and he is NOT worried or thinking about his FUTURE - because he is absolutely aware that PAST is NO MORE and FUTURE is NOT YET - he is perfectly aware that LIFE is flowing NOW - in this PRESENT moment - and so he lives moment to moment - he has absolutely NO interest in applying any logic or calculations - he is simply happy to - BE HERE NOW - Meditation happens only when you are able to BE HERE NOW - when your MIND is in your control and is concentrating on this NOW MOMENT. Such a man EXPERIENCES the TRUTH - and so whatever he shares is through HIS OWN EXPERIENCES - he is NOT imagining - he has actually experienced and so a SPIRITUALIST is NOT a philosopher. And a PHILOSOPHER is NOT a spiritualist.

TRUTH is hard - it may hurt - it may lead to ignoring this answer but as long as it is read and thought through - it can benefit a few.

You all have to decide your way - if you all ask me then I would say - live your life as an ordinary man or woman. Just be ordinary but let there be so much of Godliness - divinity - worship - selfless service to your being - to your life that you become special - a truly special CHILD OF GOD!

> ❝ Be ordinary, but bring a quality of awareness to your ordinary life. Bring God to your ordinary life; introduce God into your ordinary life. Sleep, eat, love, pray, meditate, but don't think that you are making or doing something special – and then you will be special.
>
> **OSHO** ❞

RAHU has dragged you all into the many lustful temptations, greed, low desires, ambitions - you all have gone through this - many must be going through this - and many may be in the waiting list to go through all of this - this RAHU showers plenty of money - just to make you 'blind' (ignorant) - then you start doing many mistakes - many foolish decisions - and then when you are tightly caught in RAHU's grip - which is your own past karmic creation - you start feeling utterly miserable - all the doors appear to be closed and there seem to be NO WAY OUT!

But KETU is on the other end - you miss to notice the Master - you miss to realize that while you were totally DRUNK in the abundance of money, power and fame - on the exact other end - a very old man was observing - waiting to see when you will WAKE UP - and the day you WAKE UP - you start moving towards HIS ABODE - then you are truly changing - then you are truly transforming - then there is a song to your life - then the bud starts transforming into a beautiful flower!

That old man - KETU always waits - to see when you WAKE UP. At times, he makes someone as common as me - as his medium to WAKE UP some of you - the process continues - like me - the old man has many such mediums - out of a million - one may WAKE UP and even that is a great development. There are souls who seek liberation and there are souls who are more interested to SERVE HIM by being HIS Servant - God's Servant.

I am one of HIS servants. Some of you also may be His servants. Always remember - A faithful servant never retires. You can retire from your career but you can NEVER retire from the service of GOD!

> " If you feel proud, let it be in the thought that you are the servant of God, the son of God. Great men have the nature of a child. They are always a child before Him; so they are free from pride. All their strength is of God and not their own. It belongs to Him and comes from Him.
>
> **PARAMHANSA RAMKRISHNA** "

Always remember - there is absolutely no reason to FEAR anybody or anything as long as you are walking on the PATH OF TRUTH. The beauty is NOT in advancing spiritually - the real beauty is to LOSE YOURSELF IN HIS LOVE - in HIS DEVOTION - in HIS SERVICE.

> " The Goal of Krishna Consciousness is not to be spiritually advanced; it is to be servant of Krishna."
>
> "

The best way to find peace, to find bliss, and to experience abundance of Joy - is by losing yourself in the service of others! KETU exactly wants this - you have to let go all of your 'ME-ness' - the 'I' should fade away.

The Holy Bible emphasizes on the fact that unless 'I' (the EGO) becomes less - the way out is impossible. The way out is possible only when 'I' becomes lesser and HE (GOD) becomes Greater.

> " HE must increase, but I must decrease.
>
> **JOHN 3:30** "

Krishna says to Arjuna – "You surrender to ME and I will take care of you."

Arjuna surrenders. Only a man who is turning inwards can surrender - only a man who is detached can surrender - only a man who is selfless can surrender - only a man who has overcome the monkey mind can surrender - only a man who has become love can surrender - Arjuna surrenders - the question that you all should ask yourself is that - WHY CANNOT YOU SURRENDER?

KETU is all about Letting Go - Ketu is all about SURRENDERING - KETU is all about living your LIFE in TOTAL SURRENDER.

SURRENDER is the most miraculous word. All religions and scriptures written under this sky simply encourage you to live your life in TOTAL SURRENDER.

> **"**
>
> Meditation is a surrender, it is not a demand. It is not forcing existence your way; it is relaxing into the way existence wants you to be. Meditation is a Let-Go.
>
> **OSHO**
>
> **"**

After surrendering yourself to existence - to God - there is nothing left to be done. You find your peace, you find your joy and then life starts transforming into a garden of bliss...this is how it happens...this is the way of its happening.

And so come you all - let us meditate - many lives have gone-by - one more human life has come our way - and so it is for you all to decide what to do with this precious human life - spend it by focusing on the outside OR value it by turning inward and evolving to the higher realms of consciousness.

Finally, it all comes down to CONSCIOUSNESS.

KETU is beautiful - KETU is immensely precious - because KETU can make you turn inward and it is only when you start turning inwards that you can come closer to your consciousness!

Bhagavan Ramana Maharshi - the divine Yogi says, "When we turn the mind inwards - God manifests as inner consciousness."

To all my followers, readers and fellow travellers - I appeal - everyday morning and evening - spend some quality time with yourself - turn inwards and meditate - meditate and meditate. Just REMEMBER your inner space and go back again and again - your peace is WITHIN you, your happiness is WITHIN you - all you need is to turn the mind's concentration inward - and meditate.

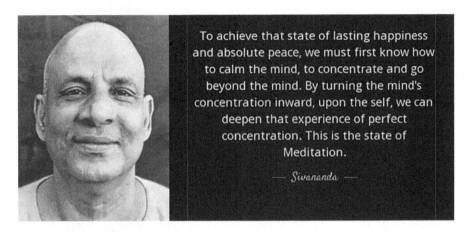

To achieve that state of lasting happiness and absolute peace, we must first know how to calm the mind, to concentrate and go beyond the mind. By turning the mind's concentration inward, upon the self, we can deepen that experience of perfect concentration. This is the state of Meditation.

— *Sivananda* —

A time should come in your life when you don't have to meditate anymore - you become meditation! **And that is the maturity state of Ketu - that is the real beginning - the ending is always the beginning!**

The 'journey' never ends, it never can.

Jai Shri Ganesha. Jai Guru.

Question 4

Can Ketu give huge fame and wealth?

For Ketu - Fame is Foolish. For Jesus - Fame is useless. For Buddha - Fame is a nuisance. But who is willing to listen to the truth? Prophet Muhammed never was interested in Fame.

The divine masters rejoice in their Aloneness. Ketu represents Aloneness. Aloneness is NOT behind FAME. It is a different story if FAME follows aloneness - but ALONENESS never is behind FAME. KETU is never behind Fame.

Only a man who can rejoice in ALONENESS can understand LOVE.

The First Lesson of Love is to Learn How to be Alone.
OSHO

Only a man who finds his BLISS in ALONENESS can understand LIFE.

Ketu understands Life. A Yogi understands Life - through Yogic practice - one can understand life.

The divine master - the real Yogi does Love - but their love is detached and because it is detached - it has a certain fragrance, a certain depth.

KETU represents **Detachment.**

Attachment is the strongest block to realization.
NEEM KAROLI BABA

The divine masters find their bliss when there is absolutely no greed, no quest for money - Ketu represents absolute disinterest in **Money or Sex or Fame.**

KETU IS SIMPLY HAPPY TO BE - LIKE A HEALER - a REFINED KETU (YOGI) continues with his Journey from one place to the other - from one village to the other - He moves but he moves in his own bliss, his own peace.

The place/territory that BUDDHA moved along came to be known as BIHAR. It is an outcome of two words - BUDDHA & VIHAR - VIHAR means 'going around' and so the territory or province in which Buddha moved around came to be known as BIHAR. All that *Buddha* talks about is India, and by India he meant only *Bihar*, because he had never gone anywhere else during his lifetime. BIHAR means TOUR - during his lifetime, BUDDHA toured only in that area - that's why the name became BIHAR. In short - BIHAR means BUDDHA's tour area.

But the greatest irony is that the people of BIHAR never accepted BUDDHA wholeheartedly - they condemned him, the Brahmins or the Pandas ridiculed his teachings - and so BUDDHA spent his whole life in the land of BIHAR - travelling to many villages and towns of BIHAR - for 40 years he walked around - shared such a wealth of wisdom - so much of love - so much affection - how beautiful this man must be - but that is how this human world is - when the MASTER is on the physical plane - the world never realizes HIS worth - and then when his body dies - when he leaves this human world - people start realizing - start building statues and temples and shrines!

It is the greatest irony of this human world that the state that condemned Buddha was later named after HIM - in HIS remembrance!

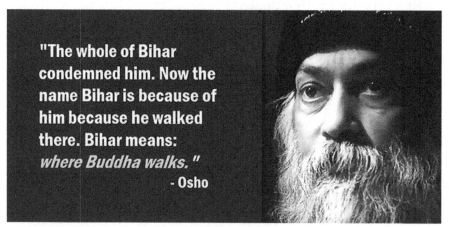

"The whole of Bihar condemned him. Now the name Bihar is because of him because he walked there. Bihar means: *where Buddha walks.*"
                                                    - Osho

Where BUDDHA walks! Where KETU walks! And what a beautiful man - BUDDHA was.

The only beautiful man who once walked on this planet - and his name was - Gautama Buddha.

Mohan asked, "What was so significant about Gautama Buddha that makes HIM so special - so lovable - so divine - so precious than the entire divinity put together?

Looking into Mohan's eyes - I said, "Buddha was the only one - a man after many centuries who came to help us all realize that what we seek on the outside - is WITHIN. Buddha showed us the way - he was the only one who helped us to realize that RELIGION begins only when you start TURNING INWARD."

KETU exactly is what BUDDHA has been saying all his life - and that is - TO TURN INWARD!

And all my close followers and readers are now well aware of the fact that KETU is the WAY - that only KETU can help you to TURN INWARD - MEDITATION is possible only when you have the blessings of SHRI KETU.

And so FAME has nothing to do with KETU - because KETU is NOT interested in wasting time by focusing on the outside - KETU is deeply interested in FOCUSING WITHIN. KETU is the wise energy that helps you realize that FAME IS FOOLISH - FAME cannot help you GROW INSIDE OUT. KETU is that divine energy that lets you realize that FAME, POWER, MONEY, SEX, PLEASURES are NOT the answer that can help you attain the lasting happiness that you seek.

"I hope everybody could get rich and famous and have everything they ever dreamed of, so they will know that it is not the answer." – Jim Carrey

The questioner is looking for FAME. I hope he gets what he wishes for. In fact, I hope that all of you get what you wish for. Just so that at the end of your life - **IF YOU BECOME AWARE** - IF by any chance you start turning inward - you start meditating - then you would realize - that it's Not the Answer.

But people don't listen. And they will not because they are destined to go through a certain suite of experiences - until they WAKE UP - until they SELF REALIZE.

There was a young man. He must be like Mohan. Always eager to seek the master. Always in search of a master. And so, one fine day - he set out in search of the real master - a true master. Just outside his village - he found an old man sitting beneath a tree. And he went to the old man and said, "I am looking for a real master - can you tell me in which direction should I move on? Right or Left?"

The old man was engrossed in his bliss, engrossed in his meditation - his eyes looked different - there was a certain grace, and there was so much love in his whole being - looking at the young man, he smiled and said, "Beta - you go towards the right direction...and take care of yourself."

The young man thanked the old man and set out on his journey - journey to search the master - the real master. And he spent 20 years searching for the master - but all he found was FAKE masters - FAKE Babas - FAKE Saints - and so finally, with frustration he decided to go back to his village.

On his way back - he again came across the same tree - the same old man - and the old man was in his own bliss, seated beneath the same tree - and suddenly the man's heart moved...his eyes started flowing with tears - he could NOW realize that - THIS OLD MAN - is his Master - the man rushed, he was running - he was crying - his whole being was shaken - he ran and ran and he came and he fell upon the old man's feet and he said, "MASTER...master...master..."

And the old man raised him up and said, "Raghu - how long you made me wait! I have been waiting for 20 years for you..."

Raghu - was that young man's name. Raghu said, "You know my name...you know everything then why you NEVER told me when I met you for the very first time and asked you for the direction to seek the master?"

The old man - the divine master smiled and said, "One has to REALIZE by HIS own awareness - it is okay that it took 20 years for you to selfrealize that I am your Master - I have been waiting for you - 20 years you were looking for the master - and here I was waiting for my Raghu - and see now you have arrived."

Raghu kissed the hands of the Master and said, "But all those 20 years were wasted…"

The Master said, "You are wrong. Those 20 years have not been wasted - those 20 years enabled you to realize what is FAKE - to realize how shallow this human world is - those 20 years brought you to a stage where you COULD differentiate between what is REAL and what is NOT - so how can you say that those 20 years were wasted?"

For everything, there is a certain PROCESS which each one of you has to go through. You may think that the PROCESS was useless - but GOD knows what HE is doing with your life - it is through HIS PROCESS that you evolve - you mature - you self-realize - this is how it happens - this is the way of its happening!

It took 20 years for Raghu to realize - who his master is! It may take 50 years for some of you and it may take just 5 minutes for some of you - it all depends on your SELF-AWARENESS - the greater the awareness - the greater is the SELF-REALIZATION OF the TRUTH.

And KETU brings this SELF-REALIZATION.

RAHU makes you go round and round and round - until you start coming back to the source - the master - until you realize that what you had been seeking - was always within you - and not anywhere else!

RAHU will give you FAME - and this FAME will then take away the peace, the joy, the bliss from you.

KETU will pull you away from FAME - and then once you are in your own secluded place - you can meditate - you can focus within - there are no disturbances - there is no greed that can distract you - there are no temptations that can stop you from meditating and rejoicing in your bliss.

FAME needs extrovert nature - the very basic example of extrovert nature is that of a Journalist. Only when you are loaded with RAHU that you can become a GOOD JOURNALIST. Reporting - NEWS - MEDIA - this all is a perfect place that drives FAME - and it all comes under the influence of RAHU.

This AGE is of RAHU and so MEDIA is very powerful. JOURNALISTS are more empowered than Policemen! They can cause much more harm to you than anybody - that is how the MEDIA is powerful - the POLITICS (SATURN) of today is DRIVEN by the empowered MEDIA (RAHU).

KETU is a simple man. He is BUDDHA, He is Jesus, He is Muhammad - He is Mahavira - He is all that what MEDITATION is - He is all that what spirituality is - and HE is least interested in the affairs of RAHU - of FAME - of WEALTH - of SEX - of Pleasures.

And yet, HE is always found to be happy - in his bliss - in his eternal joy, in his eternal peace.

> **"**
> If you do not find peace within, you will not find anywhere else. The Goal of Life is the attainment of Peace and not the achievement of power, name, fame and wealth.
> **SIVANANDA SWAMI**
> **"**

Ketu gives you Peace. KETU gives you Detachment. KETU ENABLES YOU TO HEAL YOURSELF.

So, KETU has absolutely nothing to do when it comes to bringing Fame and Wealth to you. But KETU has a lot to do when it comes to Healing yourself - because it is only when you can heal yourself that you can heal others! Ketu has a lot to do when it comes to bringing peace to your heart. Joy to your heart. So YES - KETU has absolutely no role when it comes to giving you Fame and Wealth - BUT KETU can give you those wonderful experiences and journeys that FAME AND WEALTH CANNOT GIVE YOU!

KETU is MEDITATION. And Meditation gives you NOTHING - and yet you are blessed with EVERYTHING!

> **"**
> Buddha was asked, "What have you gained from Meditation?" Buddha replied "Nothing. However, let me tell you what I have lost: Anger. Anxiety. Depression. Insecurity. Fear of Old Age and Death.
> **OSHO**
> **"**

Unless you become EMPTY - how can you be filled with the DIVINE?

KETU enables the coming of this EMPTINESS!

The inner emptiness is the path towards God.

Emptiness is everything. The Ending is the beginning.

Form is Emptiness. Emptiness is Form, states the Heart Sutra - one of the best known ancient Buddhist texts. The essence of all things is Emptiness - Nothingness - and KETU represents the state of Emptiness - the state of Nothingness.

> KNOCK – And HE'll open the door. VANISH, And He'll make you shine like the Sun. FALL, And He'll raise you to the heavens. Become NOTHING, And He'll turn you into EVERYTHING.
>
> **JALALUDDIN RUMI**

To meditate is to become NOTHING. It is only when you become a NOBODY that GOD can come to you - LOVE can come to you. If you remain - 'I am SOMEBODY' - then Love cannot be experienced in its true sense and God cannot be experienced in its true form.

It is only when you DROP your EGO - you DROP the idea and the illusions that 'I AM SOMEBODY' (Rahu energies) - that you can truly realize the energy of KETU - the energy of the divine source.

Evolved souls can benefit themselves through KETU. But souls who are still caught in many temptations - suffer at the hands of KETU. Because KETU wants you to SLOW DOWN, to SIT, to Meditate, to LET GO, to FORGIVE, to DETACH - but a common soul cannot understand the **language of KETU.** Buddha spends his whole life in helping people to REMEMBER this forgotten language - the language of meditation - the language of Ketu.

HIS last word before his DEATH was SAMMASTI - which means 'REMEMBER'. Just REMEMBER your inner space - your inner peace.

> " There is NOTHING to achieve, and there is nothing to become.
> You are already that which you have been seeking in all your
> lives in different ways, on different paths. But you have never
> looked inward. Look in. And whenever you have time, you know
> the path. Just go again and again to the inner space so that
> your fear of disappearing is dropped, you start enjoying being
> NOBODY, and you start REMEMBERING the forgotten language.
>
> **OSHO**
> "

But this Truth - not everyone can realize. This language - not everyone can understand. Some of my close followers can but the majority cannot. So, this answer may be collapsed but as long as it remains it can benefit a few.

There are men and women - who want to be spiritual but who also want to become millionaires. And this is how you all mess up with your life. You either be on this side or you either be on that side. You either be on the side of RAHU - OR - you either be on the side of KETU. When you try to find a middle-ground - you end up with absolute disaster!

You either be CONTENT with what you have or you remain a GREEDY man.

And it is perfectly fine to be GREEDY - every man goes through this process - those who remain 'asleep' die in ignorance - those who 'awaken' - become wise!

So, it is OKAY if you are GREEDY - a few more hundred lives will come your way - a few million more sufferings - more miseries - more painful experiences.

It is only when you are HIT HARD that you WAKE UP. It is only when you DO TOO MUCH - that you realize your foolishness - so being greedy is a process - which every man and every woman goes through - what MAKES THE DIFFERENCE though is - that NOT every man and every woman WAKE UP - they continue to live in utter ignorance - leading them to more RAHU and RAHU and RAHU - until a day comes when you realize that it is TIME to turn inwards - and that's KETU!

Turning inwards - meditating is KETU.

Whenever someone comes to me - with a desire to become a millionare, to rise to the TOP - to have more and more power - I wish him luck. Let him Go - Let him be Ambitious - because a DAY WILL COME when such a person will realize that AMBITION is NOT PURE NECTAR but PURE POISON.

But this REALIZATION has to come from within yourself.

It is said that Alexander the Great was too ambitious by nature. Diogenes, the divine saint had said to him, "Enough. Now come and relax with me. Just RELAX. You have conquered ENOUGH. ENOUGH IS ENOUGH. Now come back Alexander - come back."

But Alexander was fired up with AMBITION - just like many of you. He said, "Master, I will come - but only WHEN I HAVE CONQUERED the WHOLE WORLD."

Diogenes had looked at him and said, "Nobody comes back - because this AMBITION NEVER ENDS."

But Alexander won't listen. Who wants to listen? Everybody comes with a face to listen - but when the TRUTH comes - they are not willing to FACE - they go back.

Alexander also had to go back to war. HIS AMBITION won't let him REST in PEACE - until a day came when he died and his body was kept to REST in PEACE.

Neither the whole world was conquered, nor the world within was realized. And if anybody would ask me - then I would say again and again and again that Alexander died as a poor man - an utterly poor man.

AMBITION is a 'BOTTLE' of POSION but whose Label says, "It is PURE NECTAR".

This AMBITION won't let you all rest in peace - you want to run and run and run behind FAME, POWER, MONEY and when Diogenes asks you to come back - you all give the same reason that Alexander had given - he had said, "I will come back - when I am done with my AMBITION - with my desires."

But he never was able to 'comeback' - and that is what happens with every man and woman who is fired up with Ambition. This Ambition is

RAHU. And RAHU ensures that you never settle - you continue to run and run and run - until you drop down – are taken to the Graveyard and a nice label is placed on your Grave - that says "Rest in Peace."

And this is the greatest JOKE of human life - when you are ALIVE - you are not in Peace - nobody tells you to take rest - but when you are gone - when you are dead - People place a very nicely decorated label on your grave - 'Rest in Peace.'!

The TRUTH is - the FACT is that AMBITION never ends - DESIRES never end - after one ambition is achieved - another stands before you - after one desire is fulfilled - a new desire is born - and you are always standing in queue - the queue just never ends!

And the queue will end - only when the DESIRES will be dropped - when AMBITION will be curbed - only then peace is possible, only then joy is possible and this is what KETU is saying - but a RAHU man or woman cannot understand - they continue to 'debate' - and debates don't bring forth the TRUTH. Meditations do.

So come, come you all and let us meditate. Those who are wishing for FAME - let them have it. Those who are wishing for Money - let them have it. Those who are wishing for SEXUAL PLEASURES - let them have it. Those who are wishing for POWER - let them have it - AND those who are wishing for NOTHING SPECIFIC but HIS LOVE and GRACE - only those come with me and sit down and meditate.

The world of RAHU operates at one End.

The world of KETU operates at the other End.

Life begins with RAHU - Birth comes because of RAHU (desires) and Death comes because of KETU - but THIS DEATH is NOT PHYSICAL DEATH - this DEATH is of all your illusions that RAHU creates - it is only when the MASK OF RAHU is dropped that you are REBORN - but to be REBORN - DEATH is necessary - this DEATH is the bridge towards the DIVINE TRUTH - the DIVINE BLISS – and, therefore, Jesus says to Nicodemus that to experience TRUTH - GOD - LOVE - you have to be REBORN. Let this be very clear that ENLIGHTENMENT happens through DEATH - this DEATH is enabled by KETU and if you ask me - then I will say again and again - that such a DEATH is beautiful.

"Enlightenment is a destructive process. It has nothing to do with becoming better or being happier. Enlightenment is the crumbling away of untruth. It's seeing through the façade of pretence. It's the complete eradication of everything we imagined to be true." - Adyashanti

Physical DEATH cannot bring transformation as much as the DEATH of all your illusions that RAHU creates - DEATH of your EGO that your MIND feeds on.

So, such a DEATH comes only to the CHOSEN ONES. Remember - it is GOD who chooses MEN - it is the MASTER who chooses the Disciple.

God chooses first, then you start feeling hunger for Him. Men cannot choose God – it is God who chooses Man.

OSHO

Jesus chooses Peter, the fisherman. How beautiful was Peter - an utterly illiterate man - and yet when he meets Jesus for the first time - the very first time and Jesus says, "Follow Me - I will make you the fisher of Men." - Peter simply drops everything - everything is dropped - no intellectual questions, no logic - no head - just the heart - just the conscious decision and Peter simply decides to Follow Jesus - and whole life changes - everything around him remains the same - but Peter, the fisherman is no more the same - he goes on to become one of the most revered Saints of Christian Faith. Peter, the fisherman transforms into Saint Peter - that is the beauty of FAITH, of PATIENCE, of DEVOTION, of LOVE!

But who wants to listen? Millions and millions of souls are born every moment and every moment millions of them leave the human body - this cycle of birth and rebirth continues - and it simply goes on and on and on - until someday - you develop the qualities of PETER - of

ARJUNA - of ANANDA - of SARIPUTTA - then some change is possible - then the repeating PATTERN of your lives after lives CAN change - the question is - Are you WILLING TO?

But people are interested in FAME. WEALTH. SEX. MONEY. POWER. Let it be so.

KETU will never interfere. Understand this - this is significant. KETU will never interfere in your affairs - the MASTER will never interfere - the old man never interfered - he never told RAGHU - the TRUTH. HE let Raghu go his way to seek the MASTER - when in reality he himself was his Master! HE never told him the Truth - he let him self-realize the truth and just for that - he waited 20 years beneath the same tree! How beautiful is the heart of the master - how can I express - I am speechless - I am truly speechless.

The GURU - the master always lets you have your way - that is the way of the True Master - the Real Master.

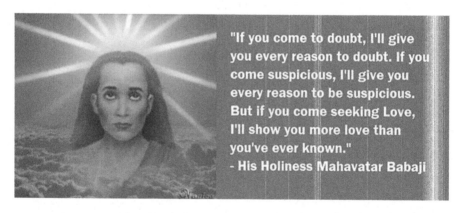

"If you come to doubt, I'll give you every reason to doubt. If you come suspicious, I'll give you every reason to be suspicious. But if you come seeking Love, I'll show you more love than you've ever known."
- His Holiness Mahavatar Babaji

Fame is short-lived. Wealth is short-lived. But what can be experienced for eternity is the BLISS, the JOY, the PEACE - WITHIN and yes - KETU bestows upon you all of this - that is ETERNAL in nature and NOT Short-lived.

Rahu gives all that is short-lived.

Ketu gives all that lasts for eternity.

Understand the difference. Savor the difference.

Life is short. Active years of life are even shorter. It is for you all to decide which way you want to go. The Way of Rahu is open. The Way of Ketu is also open. What you choose is what you become. You are always free to make a CHOICE - but you are NEVER free from the consequences of the choice that you make!

My father was a famous man in the late 80s - but his fame was short-lived - he died when he was 47. He must have had planned many things - but he wasn't aware of what is to happen the next moment. Fame is NOT the answer - people think that FAME is the answer to all miseries - but let me tell you all - it is the other way round - FAME brings many miseries than otherwise - it is a HARD TRUTH - very few could resonate with, but I thought why not share the real thing!

So, REAL is what we all have to be. The society is FAKE - filled with a majority of hypocrites - and the more the REAL you will be - the more you will be condemned, banned, ridiculed. Always remember - Jesus was crucified by this same society - Muhammed was forced to leave Mecca by this same society - Buddha was ridiculed and offended by this same society - Sai Baba was ridiculed and offended by this same society - Sant Dyaneshwar was outcasted by this same society - that's the way of this human world - if Saints could not get away with it - what to say about you or me.

Many times it happens - people come, then they say, "I understand everything that you are saying - BUT..."

You see - this BUT never goes away - and I can understand these BUTs - the desire is there - the ambition is always there - and that is perfectly fine. After all, this human birth is because of certain desires, certain ambitions - I always tell, "Do whatever your heart wishes to as long as you don't cause harm to anybody."

Follow your Hurt - attain all the Fame and whatever you all have wished for birth after birth - until a day comes, until a moment comes - when there will be NO Buts - when you will simply be able to say, "I understand."

That will be the moment of your transformation - that will be the day when you all will be REBORN - that will be the day when the flowering will happen - when the blossoming of your inner being will begin - God will wait for that day - the master will wait for that day - the old man waited for 20 long years - the master can always wait - there is absolutely No rush - you all can have your RIDE - until you self-realize - what is TRULY beneficial for your GROWTH - until you all self-realize - WHAT is REAL GROWTH.

The whole story of human life is between the two ends of RAHU and KETU - the journey of birth begins from RAHU (Focusing outside) - and should move towards KETU (Focusing Within) - that is the true sign of progress - that is the true mark of REAL GROWTH.

Jesus says - Nobody is Late - even if you arrive in the 'evening' - you will be provided with the same wages (blessings). Even if you are too much caught into the desires (Rahu) AND you have realized lately your foolishness - and you have started turning inwards - overcoming the desires - the temptations - then you are also not late - you are welcome - you will be provided with the same Grace - the same Blessings. In the KINGDOM OF GOD - there is absolutely no discrimination between who is Early and who is Late - as long as you come - as long as you start moving towards the Direction of Ketu - turning inwards - meditating and taking **efforts** to realize your SELF.

"No one succeeds without effort....those who succeed owe their success to perseverance." – Bhagavan Ramana Maharshi

KETU encourages you to keep going WITHIN - to meditate - to LOOK WITHIN.

If God comes and ASKS, "What do you want - RAHU or KETU? FAME or BLISS? LOGIC or LOVE? HEAD or HEART? Ignorance or Consciousness?"

Then *what will be your Answer?*

Your answer will define your FUTURE. And GOD has been asking you all - the same question - birth after birth...

What you are experiencing in this life is based on the ANSWER that you have chosen. If you want to raise the quality of your life - then the ANSWER needs to be REVISED - ask yourself and I say it to you all - ask yourself - Are you ready to revise the ANSWER?

The current course of your life can be REVISED only when you are **ready** to REVISE the ANSWER that you have been giving all your births after births.

The Master appears when the Student is READY, says Lao Tzu - the divine master.

Your READINESS is important for you to realize the true essence of life. My sharing, my answer is simply to help you all - Find the right Answer.

Meditate.
Jai Shri Ganesha. Jai Guru.

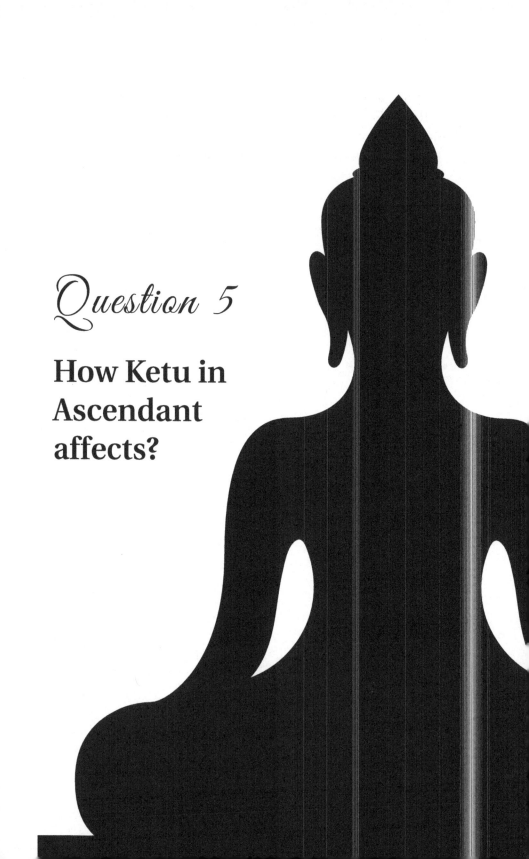

Question 5

How Ketu in Ascendant affects?

Ketu 1 = "I Quit". A Ketu 1 man would easily give up. In fact, he is much quicker to give up. He can drop everything - without giving any thought! So, such a man has the potential to become a sadhu - a monk - and **if other aspects are supportive, if Jupiter (Guru) aspects** - then he can also become an enlightened man!

Ketu 1 is not so good for material life simply because the material world expects you to run and run and go on clinging to everything that you come across - giving up in the material world is as good as suicide! Who will give up his wife, job, children and set out on a journey that has no return ticket?

Sitting in an air conditioned room and thinking about sadhus, spiritualism, miracles is something that the majority can do with much pleasure - but giving up everything - a beautiful wife, sweet children, big house, big car and stepping out to explore the unknown, the beyond - is not everybody's cup of tea!

KETU 1 can do it. But ONLY and ONLY when the other aspects are also supportive of his or her spiritual growth! Else KETU 1 leads the native through many tragedies of life - he simply gets so much trapped in the dangerous 'games' of this material world (Maya) - that life becomes a problem - which has no solution.

Ketu - when gets the positive support of Jupiter - then you see 'dust' transforming into 'gold' - 24 carats gold!

In the West - there was such a man - a great divine mystic. And his name was Diogenes. It is said that the stories of his miracles reached Alexander the Great. And Alexander wanted to meet Diogenes - a naked man - who roamed across villages and towns - Alexander the Great, the Emperor was seeking a meeting with a naked mystic - Diogenes!

It is said that one day, Diogenes was walking - and he observed a dog drinking water from the river. He looked at the begging wooden bowl that he had kept for himself - that was his only possession, that was his only property - his only asset!

Diogenes was a great spiritual master - and so a thought came to him - "If the dog doesn't need a bowl to drink water - then why am I carrying this wooden bowl with me?"

And that very moment - Diogenes threw the wooden bowl - now everything was dropped - there was nothing to care for - and smiling to himself, Diogenes continued to walk through the narrow lanes of Greece.

A KETUISH man can drop everything - can **detach** much faster than a Rahuish man! Always remember this.

RAHU's nature is to CLING.

KETU's nature is to DETACH.

> "
> Your heart must become a sea of love. Your mind must become a river of detachment.
>
> **SRI CHINMOY**
> "

A man who is clinging - cannot give up. And if you cannot give up - you cannot experience the beyond. Buddha says - you only lose what you cling to! RAHUISH men will go on and on and on - they may give long lectures on spiritualism - but when it comes to dropping everything - giving up everything - when it comes to renunciation - they will find many reasons.

Only a KETUISH man has the ability to 'Jump'. A certain madness is required to experience beyond. KETU has that 'madness' - and that is why Meher Baba always emphasized that it is far easier to help a mad man to attain enlightenment than a sane person! Because a sane person is in his 'head' - and so he goes on asking many questions, he is trapped in his intellectualism - it may take many births for him to understand the essence of Truth - the eternal.

Meher Baba says, "To bring a sane person out of his sanity is very difficult. But to bring out a madman is very easy because in a way, he is already out but from the back door. He has tasted something of the outside; we have only to show him the right door and say, 'Please don't go out from the wrong door, go from the right door. Being out is perfectly right, but choose the right door'."

And Meher Baba turned many mad people into enlightened people. In deep love, I salute His Holiness - **Avatar Meher Baba.**

> **"**
> I have come not to teach but to awaken.....I am the Ancient One. I belong to no religion. Every religion belongs to Me. My own personal religion is of – My being the Ancient Infinite One and the religion I share with you all is of Love of God. This love can be practiced by anyone, high,low, rich, poor, and every one of every caste and creed can love God.
>
> **AVATAR MEHER BABA**
> **"**

KETU is loved by Shri Guru (Jupiter). The dilemma is that many 'Rahuish' men are always trying to wear the mask of KETU and making a good business of 'spiritualism'! The real KETU men - the real Diamonds are far away from the glamor, the fame, the 'connections'. Because they are perfectly aware of how fake this world is - out of one million only a few would be true diamonds, the rest all just 'glitter' - there is no real 'substance'.

RAHU is so clever that He may fake spirituality - in the morning he may do all the 'drama' of how spiritual he is - and when it is dark - when it is night - his true colors come out - then he will engage himself in sex, liquor, pleasures and much more! I call such men 'Spiritual Hawks' - meaning they simply 'use' fake spiritualism to loot many innocent men and women. These are RAHUISH Babas and Sadhus - Spiritual Hawks. The nature of the hawk is to find its prey! These spiritual hawks are always in search of a nice 'PREY'.

KETU can help you to overcome the MIND. In fact, KETU and MOON (MIND) are totally contrast in nature. KETU is willing to give up, to LET GO. But the MIND is not and never willing to LET GO. The nature of the MIND is to cling, and it is this 'clinging' nature that brings many miseries to your life. You become a slave of your MIND and then begins the journey of many miseries…the mind is a beautiful servant, but a dangerous master!

Ketu 1 — has the ability to 'JUMP'. And only that man and that woman can truly experience spiritual bliss who has the ability to 'JUMP' into the unknown. It requires tremendous courage. And courage comes only when you are following the TRUTH!

> "
> To accept the challenge of the unknown is courage. The fears are there but if you go on accepting the challenge again and again, slowly, slowly those fears disappear.
> **OSHO**
> "

A man who is less of logic and more of love - can JUMP! Peter, the fisherman 'jumps' - Arjuna 'jumps' - Sariputta 'jumps' - the greatest disciples have had the courage to jump - this jumping is possible only when your birth chart is inclined towards KETU - and KETU 1 from that perspective - indeed becomes a 'blessing in disguise'!

Imagine - just imagine - a stranger comes to you, and you don't even know his name and the stranger says — **"Look into my eyes, follow me and I will make you the Fisher of men."**

You would say, "Who are you?" And then you may ask him a **hundred more questions.** *Raise millions of doubts. You see that is how the common man is* — a slave of the Mind. And the Mind is logical, the heart is illogical and yet it is the heart that knows the truth.

Peter the fisherman— What a beautiful soul he must be. Innocent, totally illiterate and so much faithful. Faith has no questions. Faith can see something precious that your MIND (logic) cannot. And Peter could see, he could see that this man is something — His voice, His lingering fragrance, the depth of His eyes — there was so much love, so much compassion in those beautiful eyes — he could sense the divinity — he falls at this man's feet and says, **"I am ready to follow you."**

Everything was dropped in one second and **Peter the fisherman starts following this man whom he has met for the very first time in his life**. And soon Peter learns that the man he is now following is no other than — **Jesus Christ!**

I have absolutely no doubt that Peter the fisherman is a KETUISH man — because it is only Ketu who has no logic, and only a man who has no logic - can dare to jump into the unknown — and Peter 'jumps'. Later, it is this same Peter the fisherman who goes on to become one of the 12 Apostles of Jesus Christ! The Christians have venerated Peter as one of the greatest saints. **Peter the fisherman** becomes **Saint Peter.** That is the beauty of faith, that is the beauty of Sri Ketu. That is the beauty of the heart! A man who follows his heart - always finds something precious that a man of logic cannot. The MIND is mechanical. The HEART is spiritual! The MIND is intellectual, the HEART is intelligent.

The Bible mentions that **Jesus** holds the feet of *Peter* in HIS holy hands - and pours water - the Master is washing the feet of His Disciple - Peter!

Jesus came to Peter, and Peter said, **"Lord, are you going to wash my feet?"**

And Jesus replied, **"You do not realize now what I am doing, but later you will understand."**

"No," said Peter, **"you shall never wash my feet."**

Jesus answered, **"Unless I wash you, you have no part with me."**

"Then, Lord," Peter replied, **"not just my feet but my hands and my head as well!"**

How beautiful is this - how to express this love - the master coming towards the disciple, the disciple coming towards the master - it is pure oneness - where there is no student and there is no master - but pure ONENESS!

> **"**
> Look within, there is no difference between yourself, Self and Guru. You are always Free. There is no teacher, there is no student, there is no teaching.
>
> **H.W.L POONJA (PAPAJI)**
> **"**

Just a touch of Sri Guru and **Sri Ketu liberates** you. Ketu leads you to the ultimate freedom from the unending cycle of birth and rebirth — Moksha. That is why 12th house - the house of liberation is home of Ketu! Ketu can do great things when it is placed in the 12th!

People have some crazy ideas about Moksha. As if you attain Moksha only when you die. That is not true. And the truth is that Moksha is attained — right **when you are alive in this human form.** Enlightenment - the stage of self-realization is Moksha - liberation! That is how Buddha attained, that is how Jesus attained, that is how the Mahavira, Muhammad, the divine masters attained liberation **while being in human form. Human birth is, therefore, very critical to your spiritual progress.** And so don't wait to die — liberation happens only when you are perfectly alive!

It happened once, Sariputta - the closest disciple of Buddha, came and asked Buddha, "How can I be liberated?"

Buddha said, "Do not come to me, go elsewhere - because I cannot liberate you, I can only liberate you from this 'you'. Always remember 'I' is never liberated. One is liberated from the 'I'. So if you are looking for your liberation, go somewhere else. But yes, if you want liberation from yourself, you have come to the right place. I will make you free from yourself. So do not ask how you will be liberated. You will not survive in your liberation. You should ask how to be free from this 'I' - how to be liberated from this 'I'."

Moksha or Liberation is possible only when you are liberated from this 'I'!

And you will be able to do so - you will be able to liberate yourself from this 'I' (Ego) - only when you surrender yourself to your Guru, your Lord - in totality.

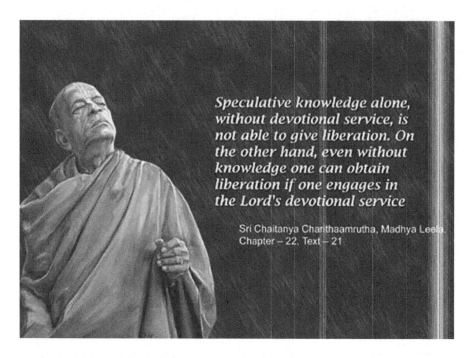

Speculative knowledge alone, without devotional service, is not able to give liberation. On the other hand, even without knowledge one can obtain liberation if one engages in the Lord's devotional service

Sri Chaitanya Charithaamrutha, Madhya Leela, Chapter – 22, Text – 21

KETU 1 is a good setup for at least moving away a bit from the 'I' - becoming less egoistic. It is a positive placement from a spiritual perspective. Such a man **can trim down his Ego - if and only if** - proper guidance is provided and proper support from Jupiter is in his birth chart.

Ketu 1 — is least bothered about being too careful or cautious — and so they become **an easy target. Soft Target.**

Target. In the technology world — the shady men and women try to HACK or HIJACK your private emails or bank accounts.

In the supernatural world — the **black magicians** try to HACK or HIJACK your **mind** and in turn, control your life. Understand the truth - the majority of the population is ruled by the MIND. They become the MIND. So when a black magician captures your MIND - you instantly become a puppet in his hands! Once your MIND is hijacked— then you dance — on the tunes that the black magician plays. **It is a dangerous world** and **it is more dangerous when you have no head (Ketu 1) and** *no proper guidance.*

Such a Ketu can either make you a mad man, a NO sense man or a great enlightened man but only when Jupiter takes control of this KETU through its fifth or seventh aspect. It depends a lot on the sign placement of Jupiter and **whether Jupiter is Yogakarak.** For Leo, Cancer ascendant, Aries, Sagittarius ascendant — the touch of the Guru (Jupiter) works miraculously. For the rest — on a mediocre level.

You may either find someone as beautiful as faithful as Peter the fisherman who later becomes Saint Peter OR you may come across an utterly foolish man who goes on repeating the same mistakes again and again and then starts blaming others for his own faults!

Now when such a Ketu has no aspect from the Guru (Jupiter) — life becomes HELL. Simply because now there is absolutely no consciousness — such a man then becomes an easy victim of Black Magic.

Somebody may wonder— how is Black Magic performed?

There are many ways of doing black magic. Around the world, right from India to the US, the Middle East to the Far East - the ways differ - though the goal remains the same - to TARGET someone - and cause much suffering.

One has to understand that you cannot hold all hands that are so passionately busy in casting or doing black magic on you — **but you can always hold your MIND — meaning — control your MIND!**

Samshani black magic **is done in the graveyard** — where millions of dead bodies are burned on the pyre — while you see the 'smoke' everywhere — this smoke is Rahu. Rahu is smoky. Ghosts or souls of dead men — also appear smoky. Rahu represents these ghosts or let's say, ignorant desirous souls.

Now let's say — your enemy wants to cast a black magic spell on you **so that you start suffering.** Your enemy goes to the black magician.

The black magician first asks for money. Once he receives money then he asks, *"What is the name of your target's mother and father?"*

There are millions of men with the name of — let's say 'Bhavesh'. But the real target Bhavesh can be tracked down by his mother's and father's name.

The ghost or the evil soul that is sent by the black magician - will need these details to track down to the actual **targeted Bhavesh.**

Next — to ensure that the attack hits the target accurately— the black magician asks for Bhavesh's used clothes or any of his used belongings. A pair of his used clothes is enough for the magician to cast the BLACK MAGIC spell on Bhavesh.

Every material that you use — has **your vibrations absorbed in it. And when it comes to casting a spell on you - what can be the best material** *than the clothes you wear on a daily basis?*

That is why - never share your used clothes with anyone. Whenever you want to get rid of your old clothes - just leave them without letting anybody know that you are the owner of those clothes OR - just donate them to unknown strangers - who don't have any information about you.

Once your old clothes are handed over to a black magician then the evil spirits are provided with your used clothes — they catch the scent of your vibrations absorbed in those clothes and then they track you down by following your body physical SCENT! And once they reach you- near your aura - the evil spirits try to create disturbance in your Aura - which in turn impacts your HEALTH, your MIND, your PEACE, your HAPPINESS.

Vashikaran - meaning 'taking you in control' or causing harm to your marriage, damaging your career prospects - and all such terrible and horrible actions are executed through the means of black magic - you never know - who is doing it all - behind the curtains - behind your back!

And this is how millions and millions of innocent men and women are targeted by the use of evil spirits (black magic) — every day — around this world. **And Ketu 1 becomes an easy target - for the black magicians or for those men and women in your life - who want to HARM you - from behind the curtains - using black magic.**

Interestingly — the person **who pays the black magician** *for targeting you* is always **someone very close to you! Always.** Someone who is either from your friend circle or someone who is a member of your extended family.

Never trust the person who is very close to you, chances are that HE or SHE may betray you.

That is how Judas betrayed Jesus. **Judas was very close to Jesus.** Judas was hoping - perhaps unknowingly, that he would be Jesus's successor. It was not intentional towards being the successor. But he was so close to Jesus that it was assumed that it will be Judas who will succeed Jesus. Jesus showered his love and blessings on him, but the day Jesus says: **"NOBODY IS GOING TO BE MY SUCCESSOR. I HAVE NOT COME HERE TO CREATE A DYNASTY. MY KINGDOM IS OF THE OTHER WORLD - THE KINGDOM OF GOD."** - the distance of just one foot became a distance of thousands of miles. That same night, **Judas betrayed Jesus.** He sold Jesus to the enemies for only thirty pieces of silver coins. Of course, it was done in a very emotional, hasty way - again unconsciously.

This is how you all behave **when you become angry** - in a very emotional, hasty way - unconsciously. This is how your **anger** - your **ignorance** leads you to much suffering and pain.

> You will NOT be punished FOR your anger, you will be punished BY your anger.
>
> **BUDDHA**

When Judas sold Jesus for thirty pieces of silver, he was not aware of what exactly he was doing and what it was going to lead to. On the day Jesus was crucified, Judas was in the crowd with tears in his eyes and he threw away those thirty pieces of silver. He didn't think that this was going to be the consequence of an act done in ANGER, RAGE, FRUSTRATION - he was not thinking that it would mean crucifixion. Twenty-four hours after Jesus' crucifixion, he hanged himself from a tree and committed suicide.

Anger comes when you become ignorant - selfish - and there is absolutely no consciousness to your existence - that is when you commit a horrendous act.

SIN happens only when you are **not conscious of *what you are doing*** - that is the only time when SIN happens. In the absence of consciousness - SIN happens. The negative energies (magicians, witch) try to invoke negativity within you - try to pull you away from the consciousness - and if you become a victim to their 'GAMES' - then sooner or later you commit a SIN - that later you regret heavily.

Judas committed suicide - it is a sign of **deep** regret.

A saint was asked – "What is Anger?"

The saint smiled and gave a beautiful answer. He said "It is punishment we give to ourselves, for somebody else's mistake.

Christians don't talk much of Judas, but it has always happened with all divine masters. It is a strange thing - **that those who were very close** have *gone far away:* those who were far away - had never thought, dreamed of being very close - **came close!**

Buddha was betrayed by his cousin brothers; Mahavira was betrayed by his son-in-law. In both cases, the situation was the same as Judas, because they were so close, they naturally hoped - without being conscious - that they were going to be successors.

It has always happened, it is always happening. Visit any ashram, any monastery, any Muth - and you will find the one who is very close to the master - is unconsciously thinking of being the successor! But tell me - tell me - who can be the successor to Jesus - to Gautama Buddha - to Mahavira? Nobody. If God wanted - then HE would have created hundreds of Jesus, hundreds of Gautama Buddha, hundreds of Mahavira - but God created only One Jesus, One Gautama Buddha, One Mahavira - and the same God has also created One YOU! But ignorance leads you to BECOME - when in reality, you should BE YOURSELF!

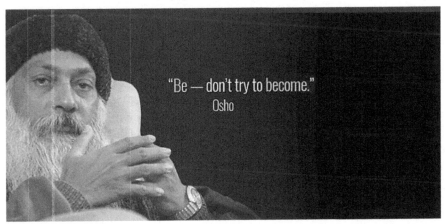

"Be — don't try to become."
Osho

Once it happened, a very old monk was on his death bed. Any moment he would die. Many of his followers had gathered around his bed. And they all were weeping - the old monk also started crying - the followers were surprised - one of them asked: **"Master - why are you crying?"**

And the old monk said, "I am crying not because - death may catch hold of me at any time - I do not fear death but I am crying because I am wondering **what will I answer when I will confront God** and God will ask me -

'Tao- I had sent you to live your life by **being yourself - by being Tao** - but then **why did you spend your whole life in** *becoming* **like somebody else?'** And when God will ask me this question - **then what answer would I have!** My whole life - I had been trying to BECOME like Jesus, like Buddha, like Mahavira - and God would say, 'If that was possible - then I would have created hundreds of Gautama Buddhas, Jesus Christ, Mahavira, Guru Nana, Kabir - but I made only ONE Gautama Buddha, ONE Jesus Christ, One Mahavira, One Muhammed, One Guru Nanak, One Kabir and I also made just ONE TAO - that is YOU! And still, look what you have done - you have spent - or rather wasted your whole life in BECOMING like somebody else - when I would have loved to see you living By BEING YOURSELF!' And that is my pain - that is my dilemma - that what am I going to answer God - once I am dead. That is why my eyes are filled with tears - you can say - these are the tears of awareness - consciousness - at this last moment of my life - I have become conscious - how beautiful it would have been - **had I become conscious of my actions - a little early** - *life certainly would have changed for better. But now there is no time - death may come anytime.*"

Your (when I say you or your - it is meant for all my readers and not just the questioner) - Your life would also change for better - the day you stop trying to BECOME and just BE - by being yourself - by being rooted within yourself.

> **"**
> Once you are rooted in your own centre, nothing from outside can move you.
>
> **OSHO**
> **"**

KETU 1 - trouble from marriage partner. Wife/husband is not of good nature, generally is hot-tempered - and leads to many problems to the native in one way or the other.

KETU 7 - cheating from marriage partner. Marriage partner of the native generally indulges in extramarital affairs. Here the partner wants more SEX, more THRILL, more PLEASURES - which a KETU 7 woman or man cannot provide. Then the partner starts 'looking out' - and then the 'other woman' becomes the reason for marriage breakup or in modern language 'divorce'!

KETU 7 native is submissive by nature, usually listens and trusts blindly. But the husband takes undue advantage and cheats the native.

So in any way - RAHU KETU AXIS on 1st and 7th or 7th and 1st makes **no** good to marriage or marital bliss. The only difference is that RAHU 7 - gives immense sexual pleasures - while KETU 7 hardly offers any sexual pleasures - just a couple of honeymoons and they are done!

So here - when KETU is in the ascendant - the native may suffer in his or her marriage - but that does not mean that he or she is deprived of SEXUAL PLEASURES. SEX is enjoyed much in life - though marriage life continues to go through many challenges which are more of illusionary than realistic.

Our ancient seers were so insightful - they were perfectly aware that unless and until - SEXUAL LIFE - is experienced to the fullest and sexual desires are fulfilled - **there is no way ahead for the soul to progress spiritually - to evolve - to mature in true sense.** That is why the ancient seers celebrated the sexual union called marriage! Marriage is a sexual union - validated and accepted by society - it brings a certain sense of completeness to the human existence whose roots are in the many desires - which have to be fulfilled before the spiritual journey begins!

But as time passed by - ignorance took over - SEX became a Stigma - in fact in India - even if you spell the word 'SEX' - immediately you are condemned and ridiculed as if SEX is some kind of sin. We forgot the fact that we all are born out of love - out of sex.

> 66
> Sex is not to be condemned, not to be repressed but immensely respected, because we are born out of it. It is our very life force. And to condemn the life force is to condemn everything.
> **OSHO**
> 99

The true source of a harmonious sexual union - is **LOVE.**

"LOVE is the real thing. And when sex happens without any sexuality in it, it is divine."
- Osho

Compassion can cure more sins than condemnation. But society is prone to condemn first - the society never gives you a SECOND CHANCE - once you are 'labelled' - you are labelled for life!

But the divine masters will NEVER JUDGE YOU.

To the woman who is labelled as a **'bitch'** - to a woman who has committed adultery - **Jesus** says, *"Who am I to judge? The matter is between you and God. If you think you are doing something wrong - do not do it again."*

The heart of the divine masters is filled with love - pure love - there is no judging - because if you go on judging - *then when will you be able to love?*

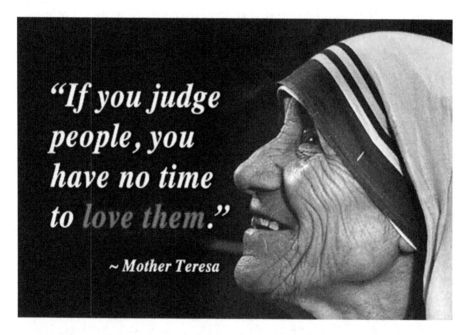

Love brings life. Without love - we are as good as a temple without the diety. With love - comes the deity - the temple is no more a deserted place - it becomes the most crowded place - the most revered place!

KETU 1 makes you a dry person. On top of that - KETU in Taurus ascendant - is like you are totally dried out of love - you become less sensitive - more reactive - and all of this leads you to many problems in a relationship or marriage. KETU 1 simply states that you are too much focused on the outward, when in reality, you should focus within. You are too much obsessed with your sexual partner or wife. You are too much obsessed with what the society thinks about you - all of this is not of any help.

And because you remain too much entangled into other's life - misery, tragedies, and sufferings become a part and parcel of your life. The only way out is to learn to focus on your self-growth - the partner (good or bad) - is the manifestation of your past life karma - so instead of blaming the partner - learn to ACCEPT the partner - the way he or she is.

The solution to KETU 1 placement - is in one sentence- **"Learn to live in suchness - in total acceptance."**

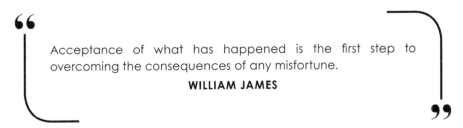

Acceptance of what has happened is the first step to overcoming the consequences of any misfortune.

WILLIAM JAMES

A man who ACCEPTS all that life provides with a sense of GRATITUDE - becomes the Buddha!

And so to all my readers and followers and fellow travellers - I encourage you all to learn to ACCEPT - it is only through ACCEPTANCE that you can truly move on with your life. And it is only when you are able to move on with your life - that you can truly progress!

But the question is - HOW TO ACCEPT?

Only through a LET GO!

You are not able to ACCEPT - because you are holding the matter so tightly to your chest - this nature of clinging (RAHU) brings many miseries to your life.

Buddha says - LET GO - just LET GO and the moment you do so - you feel relaxed - a great relief comes to your body, your mind, your soul.

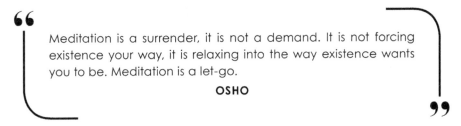

Meditation is a surrender, it is not a demand. It is not forcing existence your way, it is relaxing into the way existence wants you to be. Meditation is a let-go.

OSHO

Meditation is a LET GO. When you meditate - you cannot hold any grudges against anybody - only then your meditation can fructify. A meditative person ignores those who cause him trouble or who cheat him. He never lets the outside world disturb his inner peace. You will never find a true meditative person seeking revenge - he will simply let GOD handle his life. He lives in total surrender - He lives in LET GO - He lives in total ACCEPTANCE. He is a man of awareness. He lives moment to moment - without regretting his PAST and without worrying about his Future. He is a meditative man. Ask yourself - can you also live like him? Can you live in total acceptance? Can you live by surrendering yourself to God - in totality?

If you answer is Yes - then you have no reason to worry. The sky is clear and you are ready to fly!

This 'sky' is your consciousness. When you live in total SURRENDER to your Lord - when you live with unwavering FAITH - when you live by following the TRUTH - the sky (consciousness) is always clear and then who can stop you? The whole universe welcomes you - the whole eternity accepts you with love. Lao Tzu - the divine master says - to a mind that is STILL - the whole universe is available.

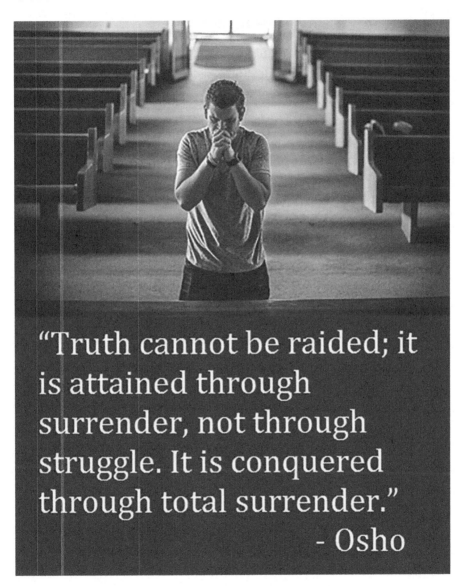

"Truth cannot be raided; it is attained through surrender, not through struggle. It is conquered through total surrender."
- Osho

Surrender to God. HE can do more with your life than you can. An enlightened person is the richest person possible, but his richness comes from *surrender - total surrender.*

Learn to live in total surrender - and you all will see miracles happening every day - every minute - every second! When God steps in - miracles happen! The more aware you become, the more you come closer to the higher realms of consciousness - you start realizing that every moment is a miracle - the breath you inhale is a miracle - the breath you exhale is also a miracle - and you realize how much of miracle is happening all around you - within you - every moment - every minute!

> Miracle happens every day, change your perception of what a miracle is and you will see them all around you.
> **JON BON JOVI**

Come, come you all - let there be no doubts, let there be no questions - just sit down, close your eyes and breathe in and breathe out - focus on your breathing - listen to the rhythm of your breathing - and let there be no thoughts - thoughts are like visitors - they come and go - just don't serve them tea! Stay rooted within yourself - close your eyes and fall in love!

> Remember – the entrance to the sanctuary is inside you....
> **RUMI**

Look within. Meditate.
Jai Shri Ganesha. Jai Guru.

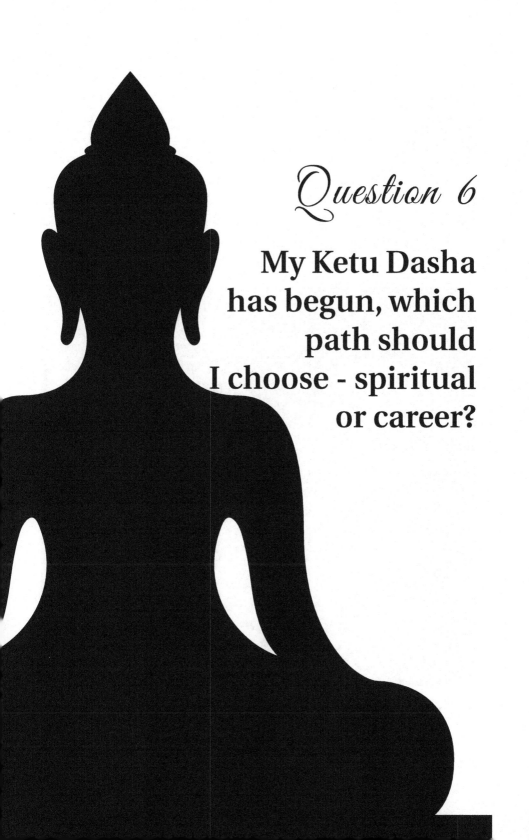

Question 6

My Ketu Dasha has begun, which path should I choose - spiritual or career?

 **"** *F**ollow Me"* - just two words.

Jesus is walking...comes across a fisherman; his name was Peter. And Jesus just looks at Peter - they are meeting for the very first time - and Jesus says these two words - *"Follow Me"* Peter is such a simple man. He is an illiterate man - the most naive and yet he could see something beautiful in Jesus' eyes that nobody else can! He is not even aware of who this young man is - he does not know his name and yet he could feel something moving within his being. Before he could say something, Jesus says, **"I will make you the fisher of men...** *follow me."*

"Come Follow Me"

Jesus

And Peter, the fisherman drops everything and starts following a man whose name he does not know, whose village he does not know, there is NO introduction given and yet he knows that this man is something else - that this is the moment he cannot let go - that this man is saying the TRUTH - I must follow HIM - and Peter simply starts following Jesus - there is absolutely NO CONFUSION - because CONFUSION is of the MIND - Peter is NOT thinking - had he been thinking - he would have asked millions of questions and raised hundreds of doubts - but Peter is a man of heart - he must be like me, he must have been ridiculed by those who were present at that moment - they must have thought - 'what a fool this man is - some stranger is asking him to follow - and this man is following' - they must have made fun of him - they must have laughed at him - but PETER was absolutely sure - there was no question of turning back - he had set on the most beautiful journey of his life - the **journey with Jesus!**

And it is this illiterate Peter, the fisherman - who later became one of the 12 Apostles of Jesus - and is venerated as one of the greatest saints in the Christian Faith!

On the battlefield of Mahabharata - Krishna instructs Arjuna - He says "Arjuna - shoot your arrow on that old man standing before you."

That old man was Arjuna's most beloved Pitashree Bhishma - the man who had nurtured him, educated him, loved him from the day he was born - but NOW Krishna is asking Arjuna to shoot that man - how difficult it must have been - BUT for Arjuna, it was not difficult - there was NO confusion - because there was NO MIND - only TRUST - when you TRUST your LORD - there is no question of any confusion - you simply JUMP - you simply follow His words and Arjuna shoots his arrow...

Arjuna, Peter, the fisherman, and many such beautiful human beings have SURRENDERED to their LORD - the divine master! The moment you truly SURRENDER - the MIND ceases to exist. Understand this and I appeal to all my followers, readers and fellow travellers - understand this - the moment there is absolute SURRENDER at the holy feet of the Master - the MIND loses its strength to enslave you - then the MIND is no more the Master - then you start rising above the MIND - then you become the master of your Mind and once the MIND becomes your SLAVE - the CONFUSION has no place in your life - then you can 'Shoot' like Arjuna - then you can *follow* like Peter, the fisherman, without

thinking much, without bringing up any so-called intellectuality - without bringing up any doubts - any questions!

As long as you remain a slave of your MIND - and I say it to all of you - as long as you continue to follow your MIND - you will remain confused - MIND leads you all to confusion - MIND is Confusion!

"Mind is confusion. Thoughts and thoughts – thousands of thoughts clamoring, clashing, fighting with each other, fighting for your attention. Thousands of thoughts pulling you into thousands of directions. It is a miracle how you go on keeping yourself together. Somehow you manage this togetherness – it is only somehow, it is only a facade. *Deep behind it* there is a clamoring crowd, a civil war, a continuous civil war. Thoughts fighting with each other, thoughts wanting you to fulfill them. It is a great confusion, what you call your mind." - Osho

The MIND creates confusion. Because the MIND thinks - calculates - applies logic. The more you follow your MIND - the more you remain confused - MIND is a monkey - it only will go on and on - confusing you - misleading you - and ultimately leading you to nowhere!

It is only when there is NO MIND - it is only when the MIND dies that 'You' become alive - that 'YOU' are truly Reborn! This YOU is your SELF - it is only when the MIND becomes quiet that your soul speaks - then you get the right direction - then there is no thinking - decisions come spontaneously and you JUMP - you simply JUMP into the unknown!

"A jump is a jump into the unknown - unthought, uncontemplated, unplanned. A jump cannot be planned. You cannot prepare for it, you cannot think about pros and cons. You cannot be the decider. A jump is leaving the ego - doing something which has not been decided by the ego. A jump is allowing the whole to take posession of you. A jump is discontinuos with you; it is NOT a continuity."
- Osho

It is NOT **continuity**. Understand this. Continuity brings MIND into the picture. You are thinking, you are analysing, you are calculating. It is NOT just a one-step JUMP - it has a lot of continuity to it. And it is this

CONTINUITY that goes on CONFUSING you more - because you are trapped in it - you are thinking too much - doubting too much and this makes it difficult for you to DECIDE - to CHOOSE what is good for you!

Peter, the fisherman had no such continuity - he simply JUMPED! And that is why PETER is the most beautiful person that I love, something that every 'individual' who is moving beyond the MIND will love!

For Arjuna - there was no question of continuity - *thinking - analyzing - applying intellectuality* - **NO** - there was absolutely **no** question to any of these plays of the MIND - Arjuna had completely surrendered to HIS master - Krishna! Krishna will direct and Arjuna will simply follow and **that makes Arjuna the most beautiful person** - the greatest disciple - *the most wonderful devotee of Sri Krishna!*

Arjuna - Rama or even Krishna - they never had this question - whether I should choose the spiritual path or career path! Such a question comes because of utter ignorance - the questioner is not to be blamed for this - what he or she do - the society is the reason - the society makes you believe that you can choose one of these - in reality, there is no such thing as if you have to choose either of them - you can choose

both - in fact, the divine masters have always encouraged the common man to practice spiritualism while performing and executing his duties and responsibilities!

"Even in the world, the Yogi who faithfully discharges his responsibilities, without personal motive or attachment, treads the sure path of enlightenment."

- His Holiness Mahavatar Babaji

And so, to all my readers, followers and fellow travellers - I want to insist that there is absolutely NO NEED to leave your house, your wife, your children and go to the Himalayas! Instead - be so pure, so loving, so devotional - that the Himalayas will come to you - that no matter where you are, God comes to you - the divinity comes to you - it is possible - but for that - a certain depth has to be there - a certain understanding has to be there - only then the 'karmic cycle' starts moving in the right direction - then there is a song to it - a music, a beautiful painting - then life is no more a misery but a garden of bliss!

A man who is executing his duties and responsibilities selflessly - AND - at the same time focusing within, turning inwards by being more and more meditative - is for sure on the PATH OF ENLIGHTENMENT! Such a man is the most beautiful person - very rare to find - one in a million - but such a man is on the greatest journey of his life - the JOURNEY with GOD!

> 66 I would like you to become so capable that you can remain in the marketplace and yet meditative. I would like you to relate with people, to love, to move in millions of relationships – because they enrich and yet remain capable of closing your doors and sometimes having a holiday from all relationships, so that you can relate with your own being also.
> **OSHO** 99

Many people come and they come with all kinds of ideas - some ask the same question that the questioner has asked - some go beyond and ask if they should leave their family and everybody and just escape to the Himalayas!

Once a great spiritual master was having a cup of tea. And a young man came. He said, "I am fed up with this material life - I want to go to the Himalayas - meditate there - and live my remaining life in those Himalayan mountains!"

The master smiled and said, "But be careful - because - the enemy country from the other side is always firing...who knows one bullet may just come your way! If not, then there is so much of cold there - that you may just die in a few days!"

The message was simple. There is absolutely no need to go to any mountains and any Himalayas - just be where you are and meditate - just be where you are and turn inwards - just be where you are and let the journey within you begin!

> **"**
>
> The only journey is the journey within.
> **RAINER MARIA RILKE**
>
> **"**

But who wants to listen! People are driven by their MIND.

People go to ASHRAMS and then they think some miracle can happen - miracles don't happen - but love affairs certainly happen, sexual scams certainly happen - political stunts certainly happen! TRUTH is hard. People may condemn me - People may not like me - because the man who speaks the TRUTH is rarely liked! But who cares - a man of awareness is not behind likes - he is behind himself - trying to understand his 'self' - realize his 'self'!

AND I would like you all - to focus on your 'self' - to NOT get fascinated by any ASHRAMS - or the idea of leaving everything and going to the Himalayas - let me tell you all - many have done this and many have failed miserably - nothing has happened out of this foolishness - only miseries and more miseries have come out of this than otherwise!

Buddha renounced in IGNORANCE, and not as a Buddha! Just like anybody - He thought that to experience the 'light' - the 'divine' - he should leave His Kingdom. And He left, He left his wife, his children, his father, his people, and the whole kingdom…

But after 12 years, Gautama Buddha decided to return to His Kingdom.

And He came, the Buddha came… People rushed, the whole kingdom welcomed Him - but not his wife, she remained in her palace.

Buddha said to Ananda, "I must go to the palace and meet my father - he must have become very old, and my wife and my son - Rahul."

And so Buddha went to the palace. He was a totally changed man. He went to meet his ailing father - and the father was very angry, but Buddha stood in silence. When the father said all that he wanted to say, when all his anger was stormed out on Buddha, he looked into Buddha's eyes - and he could see that Buddha was unaffected. There was no reaction - he knew his son, he always used to react, he was a very hot-tempered young man but this man seemed to be a changed man. There was no anger, no reaction - he could see his son standing before him, in deep silence.

His father said, "Say something, I have been saying so much to you, abusing you, but you remain quiet, now please say something. I have not heard your voice for the last 12 years…and I am waiting for you to speak…please speak something…"

And Buddha spoke, for the first time, after 12 years, his voice was heard in the palace. Buddha said:

"You are unnecessarily being angry with me. I am not the same person who left the palace. I am a new being, with 'eyes' to see. I have achieved the ultimate. Just look at my face, my silence; look into my eyes and the depth of my eyes. Don't be angry, I have just come to ask your forgiveness that I had to renounce the kingdom. But I have brought a bigger kingdom of the inner, and I have come to share it with you, and all."

Buddha went to his wife's royal abode and his wife was naturally very angry. She belonged to a much larger kingdom, she was the daughter of a great warrior. After 12 years, she was meeting her husband - Gautama Buddha and she too burst out on him with anger. She said, *"I am not angry that you renounced the kingdom. I am angry that you did not say anything to me when you left. Do you think I would have prevented you?* **I am also the daughter of a great warrior…"**

Buddha felt very sad. He had never thought about it. Her anger was not that he had renounced the kingdom. Her anger was that he did not trust her, her love and thought that she would have interfered in his renunciation. **She was NOT that type of ordinary woman**; *she would have rejoiced that he was renouncing the kingdom.*

Buddha had to ask for forgiveness. He could see the state of his wife. He could see that in spite of leaving her for 12 years - still, the love had not faded away, in fact, it had become much deeper than it was.

His wife – Yashodhara said, "For these twelve years **I have been carrying only one question to ask you.** And that question is: whatever you have attained – and it is certain that you have attained something. I can see it in your eyes, on your face, in your grace. My question is, *'Whatever you have attained, was it not possible to attain it in the palace, in the kingdom? Was renunciation necessary?'*"

Gautama Buddha looked into Yashodhara's eyes – and the answer he gave – is something that you all should meditate upon – **it is one of the most beautiful revelations.**

Gautama Buddha answered – he said:

"At that time, I thought so because for centuries it has been said that unless you renounce the world, you cannot find the ultimate truth. But now I can say with absolute certainty, whatever has happened to me could have happened in the kingdom, in the palace; **there was no need to go anywhere.**"

And that is the answer to your question – and to all my followers, readers and fellow travellers. **There is no need to go anywhere** – Wherever you are – whatever you are doing – execute your duties and responsibilities – and while you do so – let there be 'GOD' within your being.

There is no need to create 'compartments' between spiritual life and career life! Your whole life is spiritual – that is how it is meant to be! Human beings are spiritual by nature – it comes naturally to them – but what prevents them from experiencing the spirituality within them is their utter IGNORANCE! The unending desires – LUST, SEX, POWER, MONEY keep them away from experiencing the beauty within them – the spirituality within them!

I appeal to all my followers – never fall for renunciation – unless you know what renunciation is! And the moment you know what renunciation truly is – the very thought of leaving everything will never come to you!

What is renunciation?

It is not about leaving this material world. It is not about leaving your position. It is not about leaving anything – it is simply being more and more detached – it is simply DROPPING THE NATURE OF CLINGING.

We are taught to cling. The master is helping you all to get over this nature of clinging. Understand this - this can help you in many ways.

When you read about Buddha renouncing his kingdom - Mahavira renouncing his kingdom - you just look at the outer circumstances. You miss going deeper. And the deeper you go - you would realize that Buddha DID NOT renounce His Kingdom - he simply renounced HIS HOLDING on his kingdom - there was no more clinging - he just left. On a dark night, he just left to explore the beyond - just to realize later - that even this was not required - he could have stayed without holding - without clinging and attain what he had attained outside his kingdom!

Mahavira also renounced - but you see that he renounced his palace, his pleasures, his luxuries - in the deeper sense - in the real sense - he had renounced his clinging, his holding to these material worldly things.

Understand the fact that the KINGDOM was there - it had been there from ages - even when Buddha was not born - Mahavira was not born - the kingdom was there - even when they renounced the kingdom - it still remained with someone.

Buddha did not renounce a kingdom - he renounced HIS CLINGING to the kingdom.

"Renunciation means to drop the hold, to let go of the hold; and the other meaning is, not to hold on in the first place, to know that what is NOT yours is NOT yours."
- Osho

But people have some fancy ideas about renunciation. A man says, "This is my money and now I have renounced my money, my wealth, my properties!"

So you see - until this 'MY' remains - until this 'I' remains - no matter how much you leave behind and how much you travel to the Himalayas - nothing - and I say it again and again - in the larger interest of all my genuine readers - NOTHING ever can be attained - you just remain the way you are - there is no growth - real growth to your being!

TRUTH is hard and I cannot help, than to share the TRUTH with you all. Understand the fact that the greatest ENEMY of yours is not on the OUTSIDE - but very much INSIDE you - and that is 'I'.

This 'I' is our EGO. Our EGO is our greatest enemy - around the world, every minute millions and millions of love relationships, marriages, friendships, families are broken just because of this 'I' - the ME factor!

As long as the 'I' remains - the nature of clinging remains!

One has to understand that who is this 'I' - this 'ME' that you all carry on with you?

It is your MIND. The nature of the MIND is to CLING. That is how 'MOON' (MIND) and RAHU (Clinging) are related to each other. RAHU is the north node of the Moon! So as long as the MIND is there - the nature of CLINGING (RAHU) remains!

The moment the MIND is dropped - is merged with your heart - the 'I' starts fading away...that is why every religion encourages you to go beyond this 'I' - the MIND!

The Bible has a beautiful verse.

HE must increase but I must decrease.
JOHN 3:30, BIBLE VERSE

Only when 'I' no longer remains - does the mind cease.

> ❝ It is easy to give up money, it is easy to give up position, it is easy to give up attachment to the mind, BUT it is the most difficult task to break the attachment with my very Self, with my very Individuality, with my very Existence. But as soon as this is broken, the mind is annihilated.
>
> **OSHO** ❞

One of the closest disciples of Buddha - Sariputta - came and asked, "How to attain liberation (moksha)?"

Buddha said, "I cannot liberate you from this 'YOU'." Sariputta could not understand, he said, *"Please explain what you mean?"*

And Buddha said, "If you are looking for liberation, *go somewhere else.* But if you want liberation from yourself, **you have come to the right place.** I will make you free from yourself. So do not ask how you will be liberated. You will not survive in your liberation. You should ask how to be free from this 'I' - how to be liberated from this 'I'."

"I" is never liberated. One is liberated from the "I".

- Osho

This 'I' is our EGO. And it is always there - one has to focus within to overcome it - it is a long 'journey', very long, but every journey starts with a small step.

The moment the EGO is dropped - the 'I' (MIND) cannot hold on - so the MIND always feels uncomfortable when you with your consciousness start overcoming the EGO! In the beginning, it is going to be very hard, very difficult but as you FOCUS on the SELF by being more and more meditative, by turning inwards - by consciously focusing on your ROUTINE LIFESTYLE - you can overcome this EGO that the monkey mind goes on feeding for its survival.

The whole purpose of meditation is to help you overcome the MIND. Meditation is not a way to get out of the mind. Meditation says, "Just watch the **mind** and you are out." Just watch when you meditate - just observe the flowing thoughts - just witness and you will be able to overcome the mind - because the mind is nothing but the traffic of thoughts. When you just watch - witness the thoughts - you stop entertaining the thoughts - and then you can concentrate on your self - on your breathing pattern.

> **"**
> Meditation is the state of 'No Mind' – it is not a state of silent mind, not of a healthy mind, not of a concentrated mind, no. Meditation is the state of 'No Mind': no society within you, no conditioning within you – just you, with your pure consciousness.
>
> **OSHO**
> **"**

The questions are of the MIND - because the MIND likes intellectuality - it loves logic, it loves debating - it loves discriminating! The moment you start moving beyond the MIND - there is no intellectuality - you reach the epitome of intelligence - because intellectuality is of the MIND - intelligence is of the HEART!

I, therefore, love people who follow their heart - some people email me asking my fees - and some people simply share their heart with me - and you all know who is going to get my response - only the man - the woman who is simply sharing their heart - who is not bothered about money - I am much interested to help the few - very few men and women of the HEART!

And so to all my followers, readers, and fellow travellers - those who have been touched by my answers and thoughts - I encourage you all to continue to follow your heart. Let me tell you all - no matter what you all are going through - if you are following your heart - if your heart is pure then that day will arrive soon when you will find what you have been seeking!

What you seek – is also seeking You...
RUMI

A truthful man or woman is always victorious - it takes time - GOOD THINGS ALWAYS TAKE TIME! Remember this - BAD things happen quickly - but GOOD things take time. Bad things happen quickly because evil cannot last for long but the GOOD can! This world is beautiful because still GOOD people, men of heart exist! Had this world been of all intellectuals and logical and calculative heads - we would have lost the very essence of life - which is LOVE!

Finally, we all have come to LOVE. But we have forgotten the language of LOVE. The last word of Buddha was 'Samasti' - Remember! Just remember the forgotten language...just remember – 'Samasti'!

Just for a few seconds, sit down with closed eyes to remember, to make a note of where you have been, to what depth you have been able to reach; what is the taste of silence, peace, what is the taste of disappearing into the ultimate. **Remember. 'Sammasti'.**

There is nowhere to go, there is nowhere to choose - you simply be where you are - live your life in total ACCEPTANCE - a man who accepts what life provides with a sense of GRATITUDE becomes a Buddha!

And so to you all my fellows and readers - I tell you - never leave your family, never leave this material world - there is absolutely NO NEED to ESCAPE - only cowards escape.

The courageous men stay where they are and it is there and there itself that they RENUNCIATE - by NOT CLINGING - by NOT HOLDING - and that is the true path - the surest path towards the ultimate consciousness - God-consciousness, Krishna Consciousness.

A coward cannot meditate. Because to meditate - tremendous courage is needed - only *courageous beings* can meditate.

There is a lot of chaos - a lot of noise within you - and so when you sit for meditation - the moment you close your eyes - all of this inside noise - the chaos creates havoc within you - only a COURAGEOUS being can put up with this chaos - this noise and so to meditate - one needs to be courageous, a coward cannot put up with this chaos within - he or she quickly surrenders to the MIND.

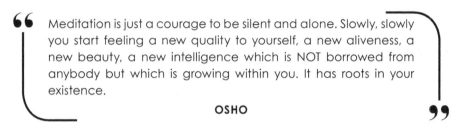

> Meditation is just a courage to be silent and alone. Slowly, slowly you start feeling a new quality to yourself, a new aliveness, a new beauty, a new intelligence which is NOT borrowed from anybody but which is growing within you. It has roots in your existence.
>
> **OSHO**

Meditation happens when there is NO MIND.

> A certain depth of understanding has to be there – Only then the TRUTHS can be given.
>
> **OSHO**

Shallow people cannot follow me, they will only condemn me, ridicule me. And at the most, they will try their best to collapse my answers! That is all they can do, that is all they have been doing.

Only those who are turning inwards, only those few men of the heart can follow me, can understand me and can resonate with my thoughts and my books.

It is your relating that is important - the more you all can relate to me, the more there is a joy to your being. Because it is the WORD of GOD and whosoever relates with HIS word, surely experiences the joy within, the bliss within!

> 66
>
> My words are not important.What is important is your silent listening. What is important is that my words are not coming from the mind, but from my deepest silence.
>
> **OSHO**
>
> 99

So come, come you all, and let's spend some quality time with ourselves. There is absolutely no need to choose any paths - because there is only one path and that is the path of LOVE and DEVOTION.

"Whether we have everything or nothing, if we simply have DEVOTION – we actually have everything!" – Radhanath Swami (ISKCON)

While you walk on this path - continue to carry on with your responsibilities, with your duties. To experience the divine, to experience GOD - you don't have to escape to the Himalayas - because no matter where you go - as long as you remain a slave of your MIND - nothing can help and nothing that is spiritual - can be attained.

By going to the Himalayas or **by choosing a spiritual journey - you don't become a saint or a yogi.** But **by being where you are - by doing your daily duties** - by **executing your worldly responsibilities** - AND WHILE YOU DO SO - trying - focusing - putting efforts towards being more and more meditative - remaining centred - you can certainly evolve into a spiritual being - and that is the real progress - when you attain spiritual heights by being very much among the people around you! That is how real SAINTS are - they don't have to go anywhere - they work - they focus within - and they remain totally surrendered to their Master (Guru) - this is how life blossoms - this is how the spiritual path evolves - this is the way - the way of its happening!

I appeal to you all - especially to all those who are and have been following me closely - let there be so much of love, purity, and consciousness within you - that a day should come when the master comes to you - in search of you!

"
You need not go in search of HIM, HE will come in search of You.
OSHO
"

The master will come - but HE will come only when you are READY.

"
When the disciple is ready – the Master appears.
LAO TZU
"

What does 'readiness' mean? This readiness is the readiness to live your life in TOTAL SURRENDER - to live your life by being more and more meditative - to live your life by taming the monkey mind and overcoming this MIND - to live your life by REACTING less and RESPONDING more - to live your life by balancing the responsibilities of the material world and focussing on your spiritual growth - to live your life by not ESCAPING but by FACING all that life brings to you with a COURAGEOUS HEART - to live your life by NOT following the MIND - but by following your HEART!

When you slowly start following this, you start evolving into a beautiful being. Then, everything around you is the same - but you are no more the same - then something beautiful is happening within you - the bud is blossoming into a beautiful flower - the caterpillar is now no more a caterpillar - it is transforming into a beautiful butterfly. It all happens, but it happens only when you remain focused within and while you do so - you also execute the responsibilities of this material world!

People are running to ashrams, and then what happens? You meet 'someone' there - the grass starts growing. Then one day, you realize that you have become a 'father' or a 'mother' of a child! TRUTH is hard - but to you all, since you all are following me - I want to let you all know that don't run away from life because running away - will only make your life more miserable and the life afterlife even more miserable - unless and until the 'karmic dues are paid off' - there is NO escaping - no matter where you go - you will be caught - and then it will be more difficult than it is NOW!

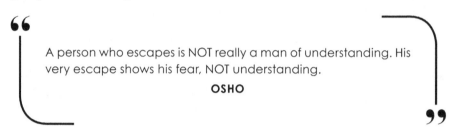

> A person who escapes is NOT really a man of understanding. His very escape shows his fear, NOT understanding.
>
> **OSHO**

Don't escape. The MIND wants to escape - if you remain a slave of your mind, you will continue to escape. That is how people 'escape' - then they become monks, long beards - tilak on the forehead - big talks - but within, there is no silence, there is no peace - in fact, there is this tremendous hunger for SEX, hunger for MONEY, hunger for POWER - understand the fact that they have 'escaped' - because they could not earn or experience any of these desires - so they have just 'escaped'!

BUDDHA has not escaped. All pleasures were at His feet - He was the PRINCE of a wealthy kingdom. Mahavira did not escape. He too was a PRINCE. Jesus, Muhammed - they never escaped - they only left when they were at the peak of their material life - that they have known the futility of this material life but only when they have EXPERIENCED THEMSELVES!

So never escape. Your father, your mother have spent their whole life to prepare you for a great career. Do not hurt them, and do not run away. Do the work, the job that you can and while you do so, spend quality time in meditation. Just 20 minutes every morning and every evening - that is not much, and yet day after day, drop by drop - a beautiful 'lake' is formed - the lake of bliss, of peace, of joy! And then a moment will come when the 'lake' will flow with all its energy, and a beautiful lotus - the ultimate peak of your consciousness is attained - that is the sign of your spiritual growth - that is the start of your spiritual growth!

So come, come you all - and focus within, let the love within you blossom. I know there are people who are negative but always remember, a ROSE is beautiful because it has 'thorns' - a LOTUS is beautiful because it grows in the muddy waters - the negative people around you - should not make you feel low - rather their existence should make you more conscious - move you more towards within - motivate you to look within, turn inwards and work towards real transformation! Real transformation is possible when - YOU get REAL with YOURSELF!

So get real. Rise above the monkey mind and help yourself in every way possible to evolve into a much lovable human being, a much understanding human being!

"True love is born out of understanding" - says the Buddha!

Let understanding be the only law of your life. Understanding is not taught in any college or any school, it has to be earned by being meditative - by turning inwards, by self-inquiring - *"Who Am I?"*

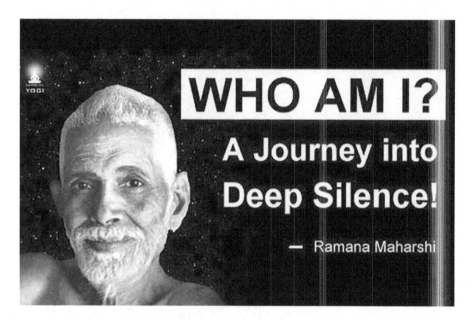

Knowledge is NOISY. And TRUTH can be found only in Silence. Deep Silence.

Silence.

Meditate.

Jai Shri Ganesha. Jai Guru.

Question 7

How bad is Kaal Sarpa Yoga?

One faithful is enough than to have 100 intellectuals. One John is enough than to have 100 Judas. One Peter is enough than to have 100 parrots. One insightful questioner is enough than to have 100 shallow questioners. One devoted seeker is enough than to have 100 intellectual seekers!

Intellect is of the MIND. Intelligence is of the HEART. And only that man - that woman can truly *understand* the essence of the matter - who is not following the monkey MIND but the intelligent Heart!

> **66**
> The heart is always right – if there is a question of choosing between the mind and the heart – because mind is creation of society. It has been educated. You have been given it by society, not by existence. The heart is unpolluted.
>
> **OSHO**
> **99**

A certain quality of understanding has to be there - only then the truth can be given. The reason I accept only a few cases to consult is mainly related to this perspective - if you have the depth of understanding - only then can you understand the 'language' I am speaking. Your money won't attract me - but your faithful heart will - and when it will - all the answers to your questions will be found - the credit is not mine - the whole credit is to your faith - to your depth of understanding. But people are shallow - the majority is shallow - so it becomes difficult to consult everybody - that is not my way - my way goes through your heart - if your heart can connect with me - then you need not speak a single word - your question will be answered.

You don't need a crowd - just one is enough. One man can have the whole universe available if he has found the depth within.

> **66**
> The majority consists of fools, utter fools. Beware of the majority. If so many people are following, that is enough a proof that something is wrong. Truth happens to individuals, not to crowds.
>
> **OSHO**
> **99**

Why do I entertain only a few people? Because the majority is not truly willing to listen to the truth. They come to me - but they want to listen only that they wish to! And to me that is as good as dealing with the 'dead' - the unconscious - the utterly ignorant being.

A man comes and he asks so softly, in a gentle way. People fall for what appears to be - **I can see right through** - your gentle voice won't impress me - I am perfectly aware that *this is not who you really are*. Beneath that gentle voice is an ugly face - an ignorant being. The man asks, **"Should I get a divorce - Should I divorce my wife?"**

Now look at this - this is how the MIND is - now this man is asking his question so softly - so nicely - but you don't know what is going on in his MIND. If I say, "Yes, you should" - this man may like it - if I say, "You should not." - This man will not like it - because he wants to hear what is in his MIND and not what seems to be in his favour. The Mind always distorts things and makes it appear that - which is not the reality.

> Don't waste your time with explanations, people only hear that they want to hear.
> **PAULO COELHO**

This man has come, he is asking a question - but the intent is not pure. If I say 'Yes' - he is going to have doubts. If I say 'No' - he is going to ask ten more questions.

People come but they come with malicious intentions and not with pure and faithful heart. Some people brought a woman to Jesus and said, "She has committed adultery. It is written in the ancient scriptures, that she should be stoned to death. What do you think?"

Jesus was sitting on the bank of a river.

Jesus must have fallen deep in thought: "If I tell them to stone her to death, it will be violence." Then what will happen to Jesus' principle of love? "And if I say no, pardon her, people will be angry. People will say you are speaking against our ancient religion, you are repudiating our ancient scriptures."

In reality, that is what people wanted. They had come just to stone Jesus with these stones if he said to pardon her as he would be speaking in opposition to our religious scriptures. And if he said to stone her, they would kill the woman and ask Jesus: "What happened to your love? To your compassion? Where has your compassion gone? Where has your love gone? It was all phoney talk."

But they did not know what Jesus will answer. Jesus said the ancient scriptures are right. They must be right. Take up stones and kill this woman — but let only those throw stones who have never committed adultery nor who have ever even thought of committing adultery.

And the five who had stood before the villagers, probably all mayors and members of the municipal committee, quickly retreated into the crowd. Who wants trouble? The whole village knew. Everyone's mischief was known. And if they hadn't committed adultery they certainly had thought of it. To find a man who has not thought of adultery is difficult, one who has not been infatuated, who has not been attracted. All quietly moved back. Slowly, the people who had come with stones in their hands let the stones fall where they stood. And slowly people began to disappear.

Evening was falling, the sun was setting. Just as the sun set and it started getting dark, people escaped from there. The woman was left behind, alone. The woman put her head at Jesus' feet and said, "Give me whatsoever punishment you want. I am an adulteress. I accept it. I am a sinner. And your compassion has overwhelmed my heart. Whatsoever punishment you want to give…"

Jesus said, "Who am I to mete out punishments? Who am I to stand between you and your god? You know, you know what you need to do, and your god knows. I am not going to make any judgement. If you feel you have done something bad, then don't do it anymore. And if it feels alright to you then continue. The one to decide is god. The final decision will be between you and god. There is no intermediary. Go now."

Go Now - two words - but those two words transformed the whole life of this woman. She rose to such a height of spirituality - a day came when the same woman became the greatest saint - that the world had ever known!

Everything is possible - the moment the perspective towards life changes - the moment 'consciousness' arrives - the moment you start looking within - you are 'in' for the greatest transformation of life. Real transformation happens within.

Planets falling between Rahu and Ketu - is a sign of this transformation happening – yes, it is going to happen - it happens - gradually - and **when all the planets are in the blanket of Rahu Ketu** - it simply means - that this human life is to PAY for all the misdeeds that one has done in his or her past life.

Life comes in two 'formats' - Paying Back and Receiving End. Understand this - this is of great significance. You are either on the receiving end - OR - you are on the PAYING BACK mode.

When all the planets are enveloped within the RAHU KETU axis - it simply means that this life is in PAYBACK mode. Much has to be paid - much has to be suffered - much has to be realized - and it is through this self-realization that the soul finally achieves liberation (Moksha)!

But people don't get it. Shallow people cannot understand it - they only get engaged when they come across some fancy words like 'KAAL SARP YOG' - then they feel that this is something - then they feel that this is something that has to be overcome - and then they will go to all kinds of temples - and spend thousands - so that they can come out of it.

You won't. The reality is that there is NO SUCH THING as KAAL SARPA YOGA - and when there is no such thing then where is the question of you coming out of it! When you are not locked - then where is the question of unlocking you? But a 'picture' is created - because the Pundits needs money - today thousands and thousands are spent - KAAL SARP YOGA - has become a lucrative business for the Pundits - and if anyone says against these hypocrites - they are badly condemned. But I have no fear - simply because I have no self-interest. And I am here not to make you comfortable - I am here to make you uncomfortable - because TRUTH always makes you uncomfortable - TRUTH is strongly condemned - ridiculed - insulted - offended - and yet it is only the TRUTH that remains - the rest all fades away with time. It is only Jesus that remains in your heart - it is only Krishna that remains in your heart - it is only Buddha that remains in your heart - the TRUTH always remains - and the Truth needs no justification - let this be very clear - the TRUTH needs no justification.

> The TRUTH is like a lion. You don't have to defend it. Let it loose. It will defend itself.
>
> **SAINT AUGUSTINE**

Jesus is remembered. Judas is not. Who is Judas? Judas was very close to Jesus - in fact, he was the only close disciple (Apostle) of Jesus. And it is this Judas who sold Jesus for few silver coins!

What made Judas - the closest disciple - who was really so close to Jesus - to go against Jesus?

It happened so that one day Jesus declared, "Nobody is going to be my successor. I have not come here to create a dynasty, because my kingdom is of the other world. It is the kingdom of God."

And this one declaration from the master caused great pain to Judas who was trying to become a successor to Jesus! That one-foot distance between him and Jesus - became a distance of thousands of miles. The same night, Judas betrayed Jesus. He sold him to the enemies (the Roman Empire) for only thirty silver pieces. Of course, it was done in a very emotional, hasty way - again unconsciously.

This is the trouble with Man. And this is the trouble with you also. **In anger - you lose all your senses - you become extremely ignorant and** you take certain steps that you later heavily regret - but the time has gone - **the damage has been done** - now there is no way out - the arrow has been shot from the bow - now there is no returning - the action (Karma) has been executed - now there is no undoing - you have to PAYBACK - in this life or the life next.

And Judas had to PAYBACK heavily. And you all who have all the planets enveloped within RAHU KETU also have to PAYBACK heavily - that is how the course of life is - that is how the nature of your life is - no matter how many poojas you perform - until you PAYBACK there is no way out. Until you go through the FIRE OF SUFFERING - there is no coming to awareness - The **fire** of suffering **becomes** the **light** of consciousness. Always remember this - yes - Judas committed the greatest sin - out of his desire - his anger - his ignorance - he sold the most innocent man - Jesus for just 36 silver coins. But you still don't know what happened later. The story is still not over.

When Jesus was crucified, Judas was in the crowd with tears in his eyes and he threw away those thirty-six pieces of silver. He had never thought that this was going to be the consequence of an act done in ANGER, RAGE, FRUSTRATION - he was not thinking that this would mean crucifixion.

And twenty-four hours after Jesus' crucifixion, Judas hanged himself from a tree and committed suicide.

Christians don't talk about Judas much. In fact, Judas is not the only one who betrayed his master. It has been happening almost always, with every great master. Strangely enough, those who were very close have gone far away. And those who were far away - had never thought, dreamed, of being very close - came close.

JUDAS maybe an utterly ignorant fool - still, just by being in the presence of the master - had instilled some understanding, some blurred instances of consciousness - and it is this consciousness that finally made him realize his mistake - his ignorance. If you ask me - then before you point your finger towards JUDAS and start accusing him - first ask yourself - how many of you have self-realized and ACCEPTED your mistakes - JUDAS did the cruellest thing - but he also did the most beautiful thing to himself - he **ACCEPTED** his mistake - he accepted how low he had fallen - and this consciousness would not let him live anymore - he finished himself by his own hands - that was the only way he could find - but at least he died in consciousness - and not in ignorance!

Rahu 12 and Ketu 6 - irrespective of what ascendant is - simply is an indicator that one has to get ready to PAYBACK - and because you are not willing to go through what life has to offer - you continue to live in depression. Remember this - nothing comes for free - there is NO FREE LUNCH - if someone is offering you something for FREE - then it is the due of your past good karma - and if you are offering someone for FREE - that is the credit recorded to your future life. Sai Baba at times used to pay a certain amount to some devotees and at times would demand a certain amount from some devotees. The LEELA of the divine masters is beyond the understanding of the common man! And so people would get confused - what is happening - the Lord of Lords - the greatest divine master - Sai Baba - demanding a few rupees - why?

One day, Sai Baba himself revealed the secret - when he demanded 5 Rupees (5 rupees during the British era was close to 10,000) from a gentleman who had just arrived for HIS darshan! Baba said to his devotees, "Last life - this man had not paid me a certain amount that I was to receive from him. Now he has come - and I don't want to leave any balance behind."

How beautiful is this - how deep and how great. Sai Baba - the most compassionate divine master - the world has ever known!

And so the divine benevolent compassionate master - Sai Baba would sometimes demand a certain amount from a devotee - the master can see the PAST and the FUTURE - the ways of the master are beyond the imagination of the common man!

Much has to be revealed - much has to be realized - much has to be experienced but only when you are willing to go with the flow!

Surrender to HIM - surrender to your LORD - to your Master. HE can do more with it - than YOU can! Surrender to HIM - surrender to HIM in totality and then you would experience every moment - a miracle - and the day you start experiencing this - you know, you are on the right track.

When you surrender - life is no more the same - every moment is a moment of a miracle - every moment is a moment of gratitude - every moment is a moment of bliss!

The Holy Name alone is sufficient to take you back home. However to cultivate the mood of surrender, you need a Guru – a master!

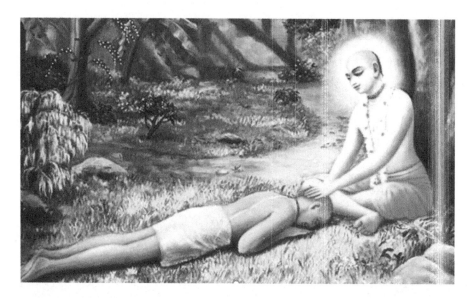

The truth - the answer to your question is very simple.

"Get ready to go through many Ups and Downs of life - and while you go through the many ups and downs - learn to be a witness - do not get attached - do not get entangled - remain on the seashore - while you WITNESS the many HIGH and LOW tides of your life."

Many people suffer - become depressed through this placement - **simply because of their attachments** - when in reality, to overcome the effects of this placement - **one has to become more and more detached** - one has to learn to WITNESS - just WATCH - just OBSERVE - only then can you live through this placement - only then can you become more matured - more evolved through this placement - only then can this placement become a blessing in disguise for you and for all my readers, followers who have their planets enveloped within the axis of RAHU KETU!

> **"**
> You know only two ways: either to be angry, violent or to repress it. You don't know the third way, and the third way is the way of the buddhas; neither indulge nor repress – watch.
>
> **OSHO**
> **"**

Watch. Witness. Don't get attached. Attachments bring miseries. Attachments lead to pain and suffering.

> The root of suffering is Attachment.
> **BUDDHA**

You will go through many pains and suffering - if you remain attached. My Daughter. My Son. My Wife. My friend. This MINE will lead you to many miseries. This MY makes you possessive - and when POSSESSIVENESS comes - LOVE ceases to exist. Love can only exist as long as there is freedom - possessiveness kills love - the moment you get into 'MY' this and 'MY' that - you have killed love with your own hands - remember this -this is of great significance.

Love is non-*possessive* because *love's* very essence is **freedom.**

"If you love a person you would like the person to be absolutely free."
- Osho

When you are near to the woman you love - you are not close. Understand this. Understand the difference. Closeness is not a physical phenomenon, nearness is.

Closeness is a very different thing; you can be near to someone and not close, and you can be very far away from someone and still very close. Closeness is between two beings, nearness is between two bodies, nearness is spatial, closeness is existential.

When you are afraid - you become possessive - you are near to her - but you are *still* not close to her! And to come 'close' - you need not be physically present with her - even from far away distance - closeness can manifest!

For a true spiritual seeker - **closeness** matters and *not* nearness! To the people of Jerusalem - Judas 'appeared' to be close to Jesus - but in reality, he never was 'close' to the master - had he been 'close' - he would not have sold Jesus for few silver coins. Judas was NOT close - Judas was just near to the master - but not close! Understand the difference - unless you understand the difference between closeness and nearness - you would not understand the essence of true love.

Long back - when I was travelling alone through the Bramhagiri Mountains near Nashik - I met a great Yogi. And His aura, His glow, His peace - there was something about this man - and we talked for a few minutes and he was such a gentleman - soft-spoken, long white beard - a glowing face, tall and dressed scarcely - it seemed as if time had paused and as if I should not move beyond anymore - in HIS omnipresence - in HIS compassionate shadow - HIS graceful soothing presence - as if life had come to a standstill.

He asked, "What is it that you would want from your master?"

Unable to control myself - I said, "I would love to meet my master. To have HIM before me."

And the great Yogi said, "Why do you want him to be physically present before you? What is the purpose - do you want to present your wish? Some desires to be fulfilled? If not - then what is the need to have HIM physically present before you?"

What a beautiful, deeply moving answer - only a man who has 'attained' can answer back with such insightful words. That was the day - when I realized - there is absolutely no need to see the master in physical form - or to seek his physical presence - that was the day when I realized that **'closeness'** has nothing to do with physical presence - closeness is absolutely different from being near. You may be near to the master - for several years - you may have seen HIM in physical form for several years - and yet that cannot bring 'closeness' - closeness is an altogether different phenomenon - and only a meditative soul can understand the essence of it.

Being near a master can either become bondage or liberation, it depends. Just by being near, there is no necessity that you will be liberated: you can become addicted to the presence. No, that is not good.

"A separation is needed so that you can come close again. There must be a rythm of being with the master and not being with the master. In that rythm many possibilities open because, finally, you have to be on your own." - Osho

"When the student is ready - the Master appears. And when the student is *really ready* - the master disappears" - says the compassionate divine master - **Lao Tzu!**

In material life - you feel insecure when it comes to your partner - because you have never been 'close' to him or her - you have always been 'near' - and nearness cannot bring you close. To come close - you have to dive within - you have to first realize yourself - only then can you realize the other - only then can the understanding go beyond the mind and reach the heart.

The love that you seek - is physical love - touch is required to express love - that is the base level of love. The highest level is where there is no need of any physical touch - that is the greatest love of all - the love that happened between John and Jesus, Krishna and Jesus, Meera and Krishna, Sariputra and Buddha - the greatest and purest love is the love between the disciple and the master!

So come - come to the truth and the truth is simple. And because it is very simple, **you never look at it.** My answer is also simple - very simple - so simple that only a meditative soul can understand it - because only a meditative man is simple. Simplicity is of the heart - complexity is of the mind. And the journey of every meditative soul is from the mind towards the heart - and so, only those can understand the essence of my answer - who are becoming more and more meditative.

Millions and millions of books will tell you what happens when planets fall between Rahu 12 and Ketu 6 - but nobody is going to tell you how to overcome this difficult placement - it is only your 'self' that can guide you - that can show you the way!

The Self is the Guru - says the divine compassionate master - **Bhagwan Sri Ramana Maharshi** - get back to the source - turn inwards - inquire within and realize your 'self' - there is no other way than to 'self-inquire'!

Your own Self-Realization is the greatest service you can render the world.

SRI RAMANA MAHARSHI

Control your Mind. Your emotions. Your anger. And realize one thing - this life is - a blessing bestowed upon you by providing you with the rarest of rare gift - the gift of 'cleansing yourself - from all the sins - or the mistakes that you had committed in your past life. And that is possible only when you willingly go through all that life provides you with.'

A man who accepts all that life provides with a sense of GRATITUDE - becomes a Buddha! So do not expect an easy life - rather expect a life that has many challenges - because it is these challenges that shape you - that transform you into the 'best'.

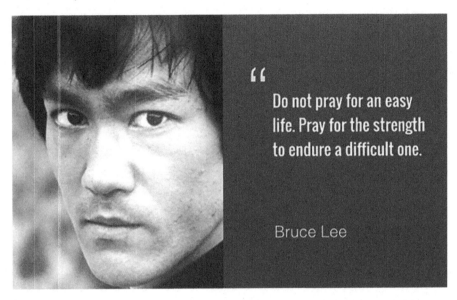

" Do not pray for an easy life. Pray for the strength to endure a difficult one.

Bruce Lee

So let life flow - let the 'river of your life' flow - you just go with the flow - the river is never lost - the river is never left out - someday - it reaches where it has to - the merging happens - it takes time, but it happens - it always happens! You just have to TRUST life - for life is the greatest teacher - you would ever have!

Learn to live in ACCEPTANCE - the more you live in acceptance - the more you would 'evolve' - the journey of each birth - each life that you go through is for you to 'evolve' - to 'mature' - and that is possible only when you go through the fire of suffering - you come to the light of consciousness! And it is this consciousness that leads you to many beautiful moments of life. Life is not remembered by days - life is remembered by moments. You live moment to moment - a man of awareness lives moment to moment - he is not lost in his PAST and he is not worried about his future! He is perfectly aware that NOW is the only moment. If you miss living in the present moment - then you miss your whole life.

Yaoshan Weiyan was a Zen Buddhist monk - the Japanese called him Yakusan. Yakusan says, "Isness is my business." By that he means - To BE HERE NOW - in the present moment is all I teach - is all I share - is all I would want you to know.

And that is my business too - and it should be your business too - to BE HERE NOW - just be here - in this present moment - look outside your window - the trees - the flowers - the birds - they all are HERE - rejoicing moment to moment - so then why can't you? Remember - the PAST is no more and the FUTURE is not yet - all you have got is the present moment. Live the moment - and that's meditation.

> Meditation is to help you get rid of all the hangover of the past, and the projections and dreams of the future so that you can be **herenow** simply spontaneously.
>
> **OSHO**

Don't think about the PAST. The PAST is no more. Don't think about the FUTURE. The FUTURE is not yet. Just BE HERE NOW.

Astrology is not about Future - it has more to do with the PRESENT - if through astrology you have become aware of your present - of your ignorance - of the steps you need to take to bring the desired difference **within you** - then and only then the purpose of astrology is met.

My message to all my readers, followers, fellow travellers and the questioner is to bring you all to the true purpose of astrology - the purpose is not to 'see' in the future - the real purpose is to 'find the present' - by being HERE - in this NOW moment! When you focus on improving the present moment — the future takes care of itself. Astrology is precisely to help you — to be Here Now — by bringing awareness within you. The sole purpose of astrology is to make you aware — to help you to come closer to your 'self' — to help you to become more and more meditative.

> Live each moment completely and the Future will take care of itself. Fully enjoy the wonder and beauty of each moment.
>
> **PARAMHANSA YOGANANDA**

When you focus on every 1% with full attention, you don't have to worry about how the 100% is going to shape up — you don't have to worry about the future — when you live moment to moment— you remain 100% attentive and a man who remains totally attentive is bound to succeed — no one can stop him — and no one should.

The secret to your success is simply in three miraculous words — BE HERE NOW.

be here now

- BABA RAM DASS

Turn inwards. Look within. Meditate.

Jai Shri Ganesha. Jai Guru.

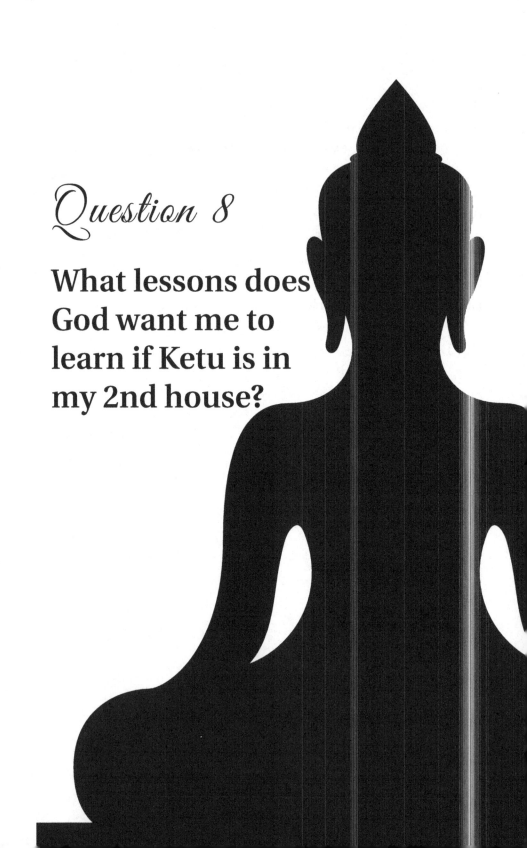

Question 8

What lessons does God want me to learn if Ketu is in my 2nd house?

Where is God? What is God? How to find God? First, you have to find the answers to the above questions, only then you will find the answer to your question.

If you cannot find God within you then - you will not find God in the temple. And if you are able to find God within you - then no matter where you go - you will find God everywhere.

If you are worshipping a plain black stone with utmost devotion - then time would come, a day would come - when the same black stone would transform into a miraculous stone - into the greatest idol! The source is NOT on the outside - the source is within you.

> The Kingdom of God is within you and all around you and not in mansions of wood and stone. Split a piece of wood and I am there, lift a stone and you will find Me.
>
> **JESUS CHRIST**

Jesus says - The kingdom of God is **within you**!

Everything is within you. God is within you. Devil is also within you. Hell is within you. Heaven is also within you. And every day, every moment - you experience HELL and HEAVEN.

Once, the Emperor of Japan asked a Zen Master - "What is hell and what is heaven?"

The Zen Master looked at the Emperor and said, **"You son-of-a-bitch! Have you looked at your face in the mirror lately? I have never seen such a dirty-looking fellow before!"**

The Emperor was enraged! He had not expected such a thing from such a great saint. You don't know great saints! You know only small, puny saints. A real saint is not a cat, he is a tiger!

The Emperor was so enraged that he pulled his sword out of its sheath. He was going to cut the head of the Master. Just as the sword was coming closer, the Master said, *"Wait! You are entering hell. This is the gate to hell."*

The way the Master said, **"Wait!!"** was so powerful that the Emperor's hand was stopped in the middle, and he understood — **"True!"** He threw the sword away, fell at the feet of the Master, and the Master laughed and said, *"This is the way to heaven! You have already experienced both within a single moment. The distance is not far."*

Whenever you are surrendered to existence, whenever you live in trust, love, prayer, joy, celebration, you are in heaven. Love is the way to heaven. Love!

That reminds me of a very old incident - it happened when Buddha was alive. There was a little girl. And she lived in a small village.

Buddha came to her village. And the whole village gathered around Buddha. People waited to hear the golden words of Buddha. Buddha spoke. And people listened. Amongst those people, this little girl was also present. And she could see Buddha - His glowing face, His compassionate eyes, she could hear His soft voice - so much was she engrossed in His words - that when His discourse was over, people started to leave for their homes - but only this little girl remained. Nobody came ahead. But this little girl stepped ahead, she rushed towards Buddha's feet. With her flowing tears, she washed the feet of the Master and then she said, *"Initiate me O Master, initiate me - I have been waiting for you, for many months and years - I have been praying to God to have a glimpse of you - and finally YOU have come...I am truly touched by your omnipresence. Please take me with you, now I cannot live without you."*

Buddha smiled. He raised her up - kissed on her forehead and said, "The road is long and I am getting old. I have come to this village - because I had been receiving your prayers. I could feel your love, your devotion - I have come for you - but I cannot take you with me. I need not be with you in physical form, this physical form is just a dream - do not worry, I am with you."

That night, when Buddha reached the other village, Ananda, his closest disciple asked, "Master, how do you decide your journeys?"

And Buddha looked into Ananda's eyes and said, "My feet move towards that man and that woman who are thirsty for my love, to me - it doesn't matter whether that man or woman is a King or a Pauper - what matters to me - is his Love, his devotion, his faith. That is how my journeys happen - it is not me - it is my devotees that decide the course of my journeys."

There is nothing as high as love!

"Love is a roseflower in your being, but prepare your being. Dispel the darkness and the unconsciousness. Become more and more alert and aware, and love will come of its own accord, in its own time. You need not worry about it. And whenever it comes it is always perfect."

- Osho

Awareness, Consciousness - grows when love grows. And Love grows - when awareness, consciousness grow. It is all linked!

This consciousness is God. In the West - they call it GOD CONSCIOUSNESS, in the EAST - they call it KRISHNA CONSCIOUSNESS!

The essence is the same - just the labelling is different.

God is the ultimate fragrance of your consciousness.

> 66 The Universal Consciousness that some may call 'God' is NOT a separate, superior and condemning entity as most religious institutions claim. It is in fact the core essence of who we really are – which is an all knowing source that is of Unconditional Love.
>
> **OSHO** 99

How can your own consciousness condemn you? How can your own consciousness want to teach you a LESSON? That is not possible.

If you are living your life with consciousness, then you will experience GODLINESS in the temple that you visit. Then you can 'see' Jesus in the Church that you visit. Then you can have a glimpse of Prophet Muhammed when you offer your Namaz!

Whatever is within you - is what you will be experiencing on the outside. Remember this - this is significant. If you are happy - you will find the whole world happier - if you are Godly, then you will find the whole world GODLY!

I had met a very old Fakir in a shrine (Dargah) - and he smiled, and he talked with me - and people were amazed - because the Fakir would never speak much - only occasionally, with a very few men - and some of his words were so beautiful - he said:

"Log Mohabbat Mein Sharabi ban jaate hai; Mujhe Tere Ishq ne Namazi bana diya."

Meaning - *"In love - people become drunkards, in YOUR (Lord) love I have become a prayerful man."*

So what you are, what you love is what you become. Love is contagious. You become what you love! So love something superb, something of higher altitude and you will experience God consciousness.

People have weird ideas about GOD. As if there is a person called God and he has a big staff in his hand and he is giving you lessons of your life! And this is the most foolish - most illusionary thing to believe. There is no GOD waiting to give you lessons - because GOD is not on the outside - GOD is within you.

The Kingdom Of God Is
WITHIN YOU
»»»»»»»»» Find it ««««««««««

The moment you become conscious of *'What am I doing?'* - you are moving away from the darkness of ignorance - and you are coming closer to God consciousness.

But instead of becoming **conscious of what I am doing, what I am talking** - people are happy to find a way that suits them. Then they create illusions that God is watching, God is punishing, God is giving lessons - these all are illusions. Your CONSCIOUSNESS is itself the GOD within you - and if you are not willing to live your life with consciousness then no matter how many temples and how many churches or mosques you visit - you are going to remain as ignorant as you have been from the very beginning of time.

Understand the basics. Only then the beyond - the unseen, the unknown can be realized. God is Consciousness. God is found in every selfless action 'Karma' that you do or you receive from others!

There was a young boy - and somehow he got caught with this crazy idea of meeting God! He said to himself, "I am going to find God. I am going to meet HIM." - And so one hot afternoon - when nobody was at home, he packed his bag, took some lunch - some oranges, some wafers - because who knows - how long it may take to find God! So packed with all his favorite food items, the young boy set out on his journey to meet God. He was too young, must be 12 years old - and so after walking for four kilometers, he became tired. There was a big garden nearby, he thought to take some rest and have his lunch. The garden was beautiful, the young boy found a bench for himself and sat down. He opened his tiffin box - and as he was about to start eating - his eyes fell upon a very old woman. She was sitting alone, just like him - but she had no food - she also looked tired. The young boy called her, "Madam" - he said, "Please come and join me."

The old woman first said 'No' - but the boy won't listen - finally she came, she joined him and the boy shared his lunch with her - they did not speak a single word - the woman looked hungry - the boy was delighted to share his lunch with her - he looked so happy. Never in his life had he felt so happy - so joyous - when the woman finished his lunch - she

145

said, "Thank you" - the boy smiled happily and then they said goodbye to each other.

The boy decided to go back home. When he was back home, his mother asked him, "Where have you been?" The boy smiled and said, "I have been to a garden where I met God. The joy that I experienced in helping an old starving woman is my God – yes, I have found my God."

And, on the other side of the town - the old woman also reached her home. And her daughter asked, "Where have you been?" - And the old woman's eyes became wet - tears could not stop - those tears were the tears of joy - ecstatically she said, "Darling, today I had been to a Garden - and you know what - it was there - in that Garden - I found my God."

You see - this is how it is - so beautiful and so true! God is within us - whenever we are helping someone - God is working through us - Higher Consciousness is working through us!

And so I appeal to the questioner and to all my followers and readers - do not get entangled in the illusions that someone up in the SKY wants to teach you some lesson - there is nobody up in the SKY - it is all within you - raise your consciousness to higher levels and you would never be the same!

KETU 2 brings Rahu in the 8th house! This placement is simply a symbolic representation of your PAST KARMA. Past life - you had focused a lot on your own family - now the in-laws' family demands your focus. Now you have come in this physical form to explore the unseen, the mysterious, the beyond. Now you want to know more about occultism - you are drawn towards black magic, Voodoo spells - either you are drawn or you become a victim of black magic spells. You want to take risks in life - even when you are driving, you are tempted to take risks - to overtake - and so many times Rahu 8 causes accidents. Accidents are caused either through your own ignorance or you simply become a victim of sudden accidents. RAHU 8 wants a deep sexual union - adultery is also seen through such a placement. 8th house is the house of many deep secret sciences - RAHU - here spoils the 8th house. Positive planets like Jupiter, Sun, Moon, Venus - raise the 8th house results to higher levels - but RAHU in 8th - just spoils the essence of the 8th house.

With positive planet placements in the 8th house - you see someone as beautiful as OSHO.

With negative planet placements in 8th house - especially RAHU - you see a black magician, a Vodoo specialist, a spell specialist, a Vashikarn specialist - basically - the energy of the 8th house is diverted by RAHU towards the darker side of the spiritual world. Towards the Aghori!

RAHU 8 - is not that every man is a black magician. If you are not a black magician then chances are that - at some stage of your life - you would be targeted by black magic or voodoo spells or in worst scenario - I have seen many haunted men and women with this placement.

I personally love the 8th house. Look how beautiful Osho was! How deeply spiritual. My father also had major positive planets in his 8th house. And my father was one of the most famous journalists and Editor-in-Chief of a very popular weekly magazine in Mumbai during the 1980s and 90s - and he had a close connection with Osho - had lived with him for a while - and both had major positive planets in the **8th**.

So one has to understand - 8th house is not bad. It is RAHU that spoils the 8th house matters. You place Jupiter, Sun, Venus - and the 8th house is blossoming with its results. The energy of the 8th house is the same - it is highly deep - but how this energy is being utilized is based on the quality of the planet that is placed in the 8th.

RAHU in 8th - gives birth to negative thoughts that can become dangerous if such a man finds the secret knowledge of performing black magic.

And Positive planets in the 8th - give positive thoughts that can become healers if such a man finds the secret knowledge of esoteric sciences.

So there is much to RAHU 8 - and KETU 2. KETU 2 is not bothered about values, family - also has weird eating habits. So basically this is not a placement to rejoice - it has its own challenges - and be aware it is NOT God who has provided you with such a placement - it is your own KARMA of past life that has brought you to this point. Now how to proceed from this point - is totally in your hands - God has nothing to do with it - it is not God's business - it is purely your

"Black magic is nothing but when a man has accumulated thought energy without throwing out his negativity beforehand. And white magic is nothing but when a man has attained too much thought energy and has based his total being on a positive attitude." - Osho

business of which way to choose - LOVE or HATE. IGNORANCE OR CONSCIOUSNESS. What you focus on GROWS. If you are focusing on RAHU - which seems to be the case - else you would not have asked a question specific to RAHU - then RAHU is going to grow in your life. If your focus is on raising the level of your consciousness - then you will start focusing on Jupiter - then you will focus on the positive side of your life - your perspective decides the course of your thoughts - and your thoughts ultimately decide the future destiny of your life! Only human beings are blessed with the WILL to raise their consciousness - only human beings are blessed with consciousness - but look at what we are doing to ourselves – the whole life we spend - looking on the outside - and the 'inside' is ignored - the 'inside world' is totally forgotten and that is RAHU - RAHU is extrovert nature - you have to move inwards - else nothing is going to happen out of this human life - at the most - you will sleep with many beautiful women and have plenty of sex, at the most you will drive millions of cars and build hundreds of bungalows - but in the end - you will die as a beggar - because nothing is going to come with you - in the next life, you will be again chasing like a beggar - more sex, more money, more status - that is how the birth-rebirth cycles happen. And how it happens is very interesting to know.

Birth happens frequently for ordinary souls. How come? Because ordinary wombs are available in plenty! Ordinary souls are very much at the base level - for life after life - they have been in the same level of ignorance - and ignorance leads to base levels of desires - typically - home, marriage, sex, children and that is all. So the ordinary soul comes back quickly on Earth - because they need ordinary wombs - meaning 'mothers' of the same level of ignorance. And such are in plenty - almost in the majority!

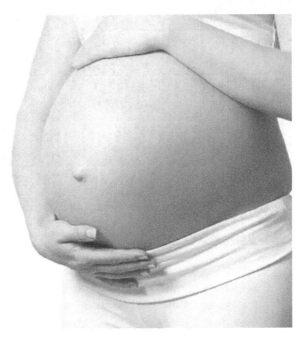

Higher souls have to wait for a long time - because they need **a womb of higher quality** which is very rare and difficult to find. Higher quality womb means - a woman who has a certain quality of understanding, who is spiritually inclined, who has constructive thoughts and moreover - a woman who loves selflessly! A woman who is meditative and has a certain depth.

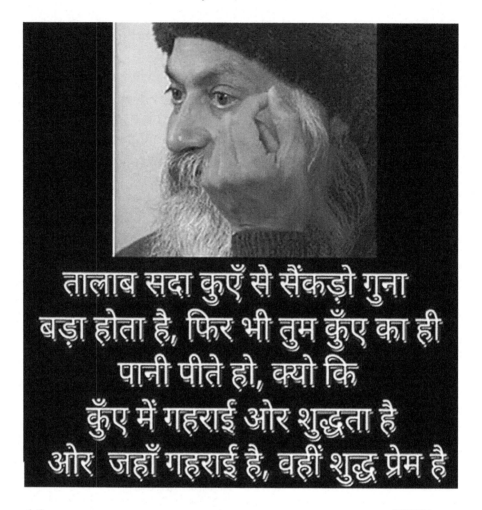

तालाब सदा कुएँ से सैंकड़ो गुना बड़ा होता है, फिर भी तुम कुँए का ही पानी पीते हो, क्यो कि कुँए में गहराई ओर शुद्धता है ओर जहाँ गहराई है, वहीं शुद्ध प्रेम है

> " A lake is hundred times larger than the well. And still, you drink the water of the well because the well has depth and purity and true love exists only where - there is a certain depth of understanding.
>
> **OSHO** "

True love is found only in that man or woman - who has a certain depth of understanding and purity of mind.

So, many higher souls generally do not take rebirth again - for hundreds of years! Between this birth and the last birth - the distance is almost of many hundred years! And higher souls are also not in a rush. Because they are almost desireless! They are almost pushed to human form by the higher masters - because a certain purpose has to be met and the purpose is always in the general interest and well-being of the masses. It also happens that many of the higher souls who cannot find a womb of higher quality - are being pushed for birth on other planets! The legendary book **"Autobiography of a Yogi"** written by Paramhansa Yogananda throws more light on this. This is the only book that I have in my library - a book that is close to my heart. A book that has sold millions of copies all over the world - the only book that has been written by an enlightened Yogi of this millennium - Sri Paramhansa Yogananda! My salute to HIS Holiness.

Live quietly in the moment and see the beauty of all before you. The future will take care of itself.

PARAMHANSA YOGANANDA

The future will take care of itself - just learn to *BE HERE NOW.*

Yoga is the science to be in the here and now.

OSHO

A man of awareness is living moment to moment - he is not thinking of the PAST and he is not worried about the FUTURE. Look at the bird - outside your window - you will see the birds flying - look how happy they are - if you ask them - "What is your PAST?" - They will be confused!! Because they simply don't have anything to do with their PAST. And if you ask them, "HOW do you plan for your FUTURE?" - They will laugh at you! Because the birds are simply in the NOW moment - they are not stuck in their PAST and they are not worried about their Future - they are simply HAPPY TO BE - here - in this NOW moment!

Be like a bird. Be a man of awareness - for a man of awareness is always found to be happy - because he is neither in the PAST - nor is he in the FUTURE - he is very much here - in this NOW moment.

When you are HERE & NOW – not jumping ahead, the miracle has happened. To be in the moment is the miracle.
OSHO

The day you will BE HERE NOW - you have truly begun - your spiritual journey has begun - meditation has begun and you are 'in' for the greatest transformation of your life. Do not get trapped in Rahu 8 and Ketu 2 - there is more to life - turn inwards, discover your true self - **meditate.**

Jai Shri Ganesha. Jai Guru.

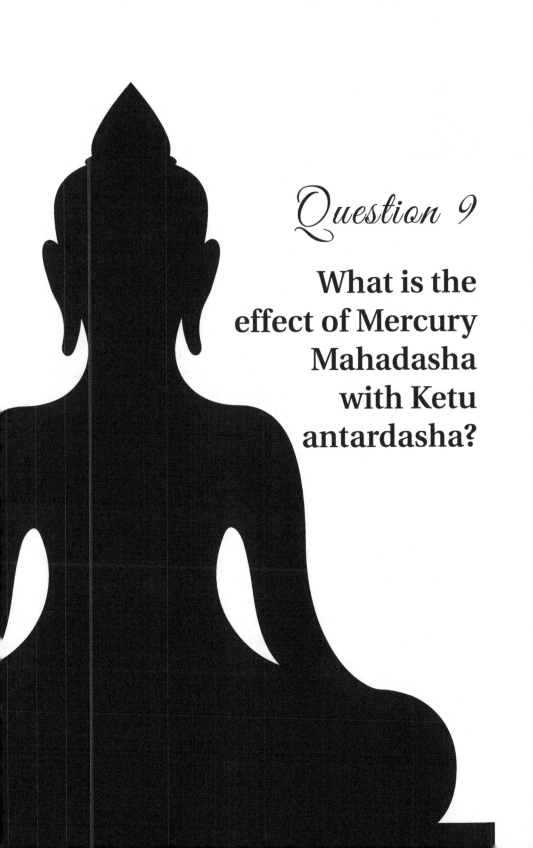

Question 9

What is the effect of Mercury Mahadasha with Ketu antardasha?

M apping.
Life is not about mapping. Life is all about Loving! The Mind goes on mapping. The heart goes on loving. We all are born out of love. Love is our Mother, says the Sufi Saint Rumi!

Love is eternal. We exist in time but we all belong to eternity.

There was a young man and he would always come to bow before the master. Every morning he would come, bow before the master and sit on the ground, looking at the divine master, praying in his heart and then after a while he would again bow before the compassionate master and leave for the day. And this continued for many weeks, always he would sit on the ground, on the hard ground. And then a day came, he arrived as usual, he bowed before the master and as he was about to sit on the ground, the master spoke for the first time, for the first time the divine master's golden words touched his heart, moved his heart. The master said, "Bhola, now don't sit on the ground. The days to sit on the ground are gone. Now take that chair and sit."

And it is said that exactly after this, within a couple of days, Bhola got an appointment letter for a top position in a private company!

Times change, days change but the question is - Are you all willing to be patient? Are you willing to be faithful? Are you willing to stay positive?

Many women and many men come to me and they all are impatient - When will my boyfriend return? When I will get married? When will I get a job? Why God is not listening to my prayer? Many such questions come and the answer to all these questions is in one word - IGNORANCE.

You cannot murder a person and then expect something good to happen in your life. You cannot hurt a person and then expect something beautiful in return. You cannot play politics and then expect saintly response.

Life halts - job is not found, marriage is not happening, husband is not good, wife is not good, children are not having any sense of responsibility - all and all such matters happen in your life - only because of your KARMA.

God has nothing to do with your life, you are the sculptor of your life. You make or break your life through your own Karma.

Tell me - what does your FATHER have to do with your affairs - be it love affairs or work affairs or to simply put it - your own life affairs?

The role of the father is to stand behind you and guide you, provide you with the strength and spirit to get on with your life. That is what God is for you. The Holy Father - God is totally detached and yet his Love towards us is beyond the power of words.

God Loves You. And His Love is detached and unconditional.

One man wrote an email to me. He wrote that he does all kinds of things to appease God, reading scriptures, poojas, rituals and what not. And then he asked me – Why is God not listening?

You see - this is the greatest joke and also a tragedy of ignorant human beings.

LOVE HAS NO EXPECTATIONS.

REMEMBER THIS AND I APPEAL TO ALL MY FELLOW READERS AND FOLLOWERS, remember this.

When you are doing something out of expectation - NOTHING EVER IS GOING TO FRUCTIFY.

To expect anything in return is not LOVE but a well-planned market DEAL.

KRISHNA says to Arjuna, "Just surrender to me. Do what I am telling you to do and do not think of what is going to come your way. Just follow me!"

But ignorant men and women cannot understand this. You know why? Because they are totally enslaved by their MIND. And the MIND is cunning, the Mind will never understand love, will never realize the beauty of unconditional selfless love! And so I ignore answering such people - even Jesus cannot answer them, not even Krishna, then who am I!

My doors, therefore, are open only for those who are turning inwards. They can understand my words, they can resonate with my words - and then there is a certain level of understanding - then there is a certain transformation happening.

People keep scratching their heads on what dasha, what planet, what star and the list continues…

This house and that house - and I am insisting and encouraging all of you to come out of all these houses and experience the beyond, the unseen, the unknown!

I am sharing with you all the nectar and you all are asking for a cup of 'coffee'! And that is the greatest irony of human life - the mind likes calculations, mathematics, complications, the more the complexity, the more the mind is happy to solve. You see - and so then you all are in a deep mess!

On a simple note - just remember that every planet when it comes on the ground - it plays its shots. So it does not really matter to what house and what nakshatra and what sublord it belongs to. If it is Tendulkar and it is coming at the right time, it will play its natural game. So in this case, if it's Ketu, it will play its natural game. Now how the opposition will respond or let's say existence will respond - is totally based on the nakshatra, house and sign it relates to.

But the modern astrologer always makes this - the other way round. He first makes the existence so much important that the actual player is minimized to a mere puppet. And I am totally against this, and I don't care what anybody says or does but just out of love, through your question - I am sharing this for the sake of all my followers, readers and fellow travellers.

Always first focus on the player (planet in dasha/antardasha/pratyantardasha). The planet is not a puppet - it also has its own dignity. But unfortunately, the astrologers have reduced a planet to a mere puppet.

Pray. Eat. Sleep. But while you do so, do not expect anything in return. Love HIM, Love your LORD and when your past KARMA is cleansed and nullified - you will see miracles happening in your life! But who wants to listen?

People are behind DEALS. People are interested in DEALS. IF YOU LOVE ME THAN I LOVE YOU- people make deals and LOVE cannot be experienced through deals, love can only be experienced when there are NO DEALS!

In life - you, I - we all make so many mistakes and yet God never breaks up with us. Imagine what will happen if God does a breakup with us! But you all are crying because either your GIRLFRIEND or

BOYFRIEND breaks up with you! It is okay, if one goes - somebody new comes in - but GOD...there is simply no alternative!

Ignorant men who follow their mind never understand the essence of life. They just come, drive few million dollar cars, have sex with a few women and then spend their last days in hospitals and then finally they leave - just to restart from where they have left.

Paramahansa Yogananda shares a beautiful revelation. The great Yogi says that your next life is based on the point where you left!

Understand this - this is of great significance. That is why the last moment of your life is as much important as your first moment. The DEATH CHART is as much important as the BIRTH CHART.

Neem Karoli Baba- for whose Darshan, the Apple founder Steve Jobs had come all the way from the US – says, "If at the last moment you desire to eat a mango, you will be born again as an insect who thrives on the mango!"

Whatever is your GROWTH STAGE at the last moment of your life - you continue from that stage towards new life - the new rebirth!

And real growth starts from within. That is why I insist to all my followers, readers and fellow travellers to spend some quality time with yourself. Enclose yourself in a quiet spot - I know India is too crowded but that is good, you are getting more trained to face the worst - so find out a quiet spot - and meditate. The mind wants friends, clubs and restaurants and all kinds of social events, because the mind cannot stay alone! A man who is enslaved by the mind, cannot stay alone. Then he tries to find a partner - that is merely an escape route.

> **"** Your relationship is fake if you cannot stay alone. The capacity to be alone is the capacity to love
>
> **OSHO** **"**

Only that man and that woman can truly love - who has the capacity to stay alone!

The Mind feels lonely. The Self feels blissful in its aloneness.

"Aloneness is blissful. Loneliness is of the mind."

Look at a yogi. A true yogi is happy to be alone. He finds abundance of peace in his aloneness. Look at a real video of Bhagvan Ramana Maharishi on YouTube and you will understand what I am saying.

Always remember- God loves you. But because you follow the monkey mind, you cannot relate to His love. You are singing your song when God wants you to listen to His Song!

And those who were able to listen to HIS melody, have turned out to be the greatest saints that the world has ever known. And yet it is this same world that initially had labelled these men of heart as MAD and INSANE fellows!

> And those who were seen dancing were thought to be INSANE
> by those who could not hear the music.
> **FRIEDRICH NIETZSCHE**

So come, come you all and drop all the mathematics and the calculations and come closer to your hearts - for your heart is the source of all your answers, come and embrace your heart - dive within, jump within and meditate...

Time is never the same. On my LinkedIn profile, you will find no title but just a message and the message is in plain words - NOTHING LASTS FOREVER!

Life is a flux, a flowing river. Change is constant. Except change, everything else changes! So why you worry, the Dasha is in itself a sign of how life keeps changing. Just because you had sex with a woman for many years - she is not going to be static - and with you forever! People think that physicality bonds you - and that is the greatest joke. It never does. Hearts can bond and stay for a while together but bonding of two human bodies through SEX cannot assure a long-lasting bonding or a long-lasting relationship!

Rise. Rise above physicality. In the beginning, the curiosity of the opposite sex is natural but if you continue to remain on the same stage then you remain a kid, you never grow up! And the core essence of Dasha is to not just map your timing or phase of life but to help you evolve as you move on from one stage (Dasha) to the other stage of your life. And the core essence of my answer to your question and through your question - to all those followers and readers who have loved me - is to help you all - GROW

There are many ways to reach God. I choose Love.
RUMI

So come, let us all rejoice in love. Who is free from problems, pains and suffering- nobody, not even me, not even you - but still our focus must be on the path of love, of positivism, of goodness! For what you FOCUS on - GROWS!

So let us all focus within, let us all meditate.

Aum.

For more spiritual insights and motivation - you all can avail my published books - 'How to overcome Rahu' & ' Gift of Consciousness' on Amazon. Print book copies are shipped across all geographies.

Jai Shri Ganesha. Jai Guru.

Question 10

What are the results when Saturn and Ketu conjunct?

KETU has immense potential to help you move beyond the mind. But when Ketu is with Saturn – it is like a sanyasi (monk) – is with a politician!

Once it happened – a great mystic (Ketu) heard that one of his friends had become the Prime Minister of the country. They had played together when they were kids, they had spent time together in the same school, same college – it is just that one became a great mystic and the other became a politician. And now the politician had become the Prime Minister. So the great mystic thought that he should visit his old friend and congratulate him. And so the mystic embarked on his long journey – he had to travel through the mountains – he had to climb down the mountain – it was very tiresome journey but just for the love of friendship – just because he loved his politician friend – he kept walking… through the mountains, the forests… towards the capital.

Ketu is like this – once decided – he can jump into the unknown. He loves, but his love is DETACHED. That is how a great yogi is – that is how this great mystic is… and so he kept walking. After many days, he reached the capital. In the capital city, a few people helped him reach the Prime Minister's residence.

The Prime Minister was getting ready for a couple of meetings. It was election time. So, he had no time to spare! When the great mystic came, he recognized the mystic – he recognized that his old friend had come to meet him, to congratulate him….but a politician is after all a politician! The head is more, the logic is more, the calculations are more – and so he said to the great mystic:

"I am happy to see you after such a long time. But I have many appointments lined up – you know now that I have become the Prime Minister, my schedule has become busier than it was. Why don't you come with me, on my way, we can talk and remember our childhood days? I would love if you can come with me."

The great mystic was such a simple man. With great powers, with great insights, with great understanding and yet he was such a humble man. A tree loaded with fruits always bends – is always humble! And so the great mystic looking into the eyes of his old friend said, "How can

I come with you? You are the Prime Minister of this country. Look at me, I have come all the way from the Himalayas and you can see my clothes – they are all in dust, also torn at some places. It would not look good for me to accompany you."

The Prime Minister – a seasoned politician (Saturn) said, "You don't worry, I have a very expensive overcoat. I have never used it, it was gifted to me by the Queen of England. I will give you the coat. You just put it on, it will cover your ragged clothes, the dust and everything."

The coat was given to him.

The Prime Minister's election campaign began. They went to the first house – they entered the house. The Prime Minister introduced his friend, "He is a great mystic. He lives in the mountains. Everything that he has is his own, **except the coat — that is mine**."

The mystic could not believe it, "What kind of stupidity is this?"

Even the family was shocked, to insult the mystic in such a way.

Once they were out of the house, the mystic said, "It is better I do not accompany you. You insulted me. *What was the need to say that it is your coat? They were not asking.*"

The Prime Minister said, "I am sorry, forgive me. And if you don't come with me to the next appointment, I will think you have not forgiven me."

The mystic was a simple-hearted man. He said, "Then it is okay, I am coming."

Entering the second house, the Prime Minister introduced him, "He is a great mystic who lives in the mountains. **Everything is his — even the coat is his!**"

The mystic *could not believe that this man had any intelligence at all.* Outside the house he simply refused, "I cannot go to your third appointment. This is too much."

But the politician said, "I have said that the coat is yours!"

The mystic said, "It is unbelievable how unintelligent a man can be. Your *assertion, emphasis,* that the coat is mine, creates suspicion: there is something you are hiding. ***What is the need to mention the coat at all?*** I don't see the point that in any introduction coats need to be introduced."

And the politician (Prime Minister) said, "Forgive me, but if you don't come to the third appointment, I will never forget that I have hurt you. Please, there is only one more appointment, and I will not say that the coat is yours or the coat is mine. Don't be worried about it."

The simple mystic, innocent, agreed to go with him. At the third house, he introduced the mystic in the same way, "He is a great mystic from the mountains. All the clothes are his, **but as far as the coat is concerned, it is better not to say anything!**"

A politician is a politician. A Saturn is a Saturn. Saturn wants credit for every small thing! A mystic is a mystic. A Ketu is a Ketu. Ketu is simply not bothered about any credit – any name – any fame – it is just happy to BE – happy to offer his love – unconditionally! The mystic had come all the way – just to congratulate his friend who had become the Prime Minister – the mystic was such a simple man – he had absolutely no idea that the man whom he loved – is not leaving even him – to get some credit – to do some politics – to show people how good he had been to him by offering the expensive coat! The great mystic was not disappointed but when he returned back – before leaving he said, "I had come out of love, but you made even this moment of our coming together – a 'medium' for your political gains! You kept on bragging about the coat that you offered me to all the people that we visited – What was the need? You have changed and nobody can now help you. You were talking of that one coat – let me tell you – that my Guru can create hundreds of Prime Ministers in such coats – what to say about the coat then! I am going now, but you please become aware. Else you will be soon in trouble."

And the great mystic left, never ever to come back in this 'world of politicians'! He said, "I am happy in my own bliss, and the bliss within is so beautiful, so divine, so pure that nothing can stand before it – it is the ultimate joy of my being – the love of my Guru, my beloved Master!"

And so he never came back in this world – he was never seen again.

Ketu knows nothing of politics but love. Saturn knows nothing of love but politics. These are two opposite poles – the mystic is the North Pole, the politician is the South Pole – and they can never coexist – Buddha cannot live with Hitler – and Hitler cannot live with Buddha!

A politician is not an intelligent person. He may be intellectual – but certainly not intelligent! A man of heart is intelligent – he can feel the love of his friend – he can be more receptive, more understanding – more willing to go out of his way. An intelligent man is deep in his heart – he can vibrate to the love – he can understand you – he can relate with you – he can feel love because he thinks less and feels more.

But an intellectual man is trapped in his head – in his logic – he cannot feel love – because he feels less and thinks more. A politician is always in his head. Logic is his way – the only way. He knows only calculations – and 'calculations' have nothing to do with intelligence.

> The politician is not the most intelligent part of humanity. Otherwise there would not have been five thousand wars in three thousand years. The politician has destroyed, but has not created anything. It is the politician who is creating the atomic weapons, the nuclear missiles. With what face can he make the people of the world aware that the future is dark, dismal?
>
> **OSHO**

The idea of becoming a HERO is very different in a politician's dictionary. Adolf Hitler in his autobiography writes: **"If a politician wants to be a great hero, a great historical figure, then *the only way* is to create a great war. Without war, you don't have heroes."**

And Adolf Hitler is saying the truth. Because if you all look back into the history of this human world – you will realize that all those politicians who have fought wars – great wars have actually become HEROS!

Alexander the Great, Napoleon Bonaparte, Nadir Shah, Tamerlane, Genghis Khan, Joseph Stalin, Benito Mussolini, Adolf Hitler, Winston Churchill… And what have these people got, except that they lived at the time of a great war?

> It is the War that brings the Politicians to the pinnacle of their glory. And your whole history is full of such 'Politicians' who have become HERO by making millions of innocent men, innocent women and children suffer, die and bleed…
>
> **OSHO**

Politicians have no mercy. Saturn has no mercy. Saturn is a seasoned politician. Therefore, Saturn is a great friend of Mercury – because Mercury gives strength to its power of judgement. Mercury brings abundance of 'LOGIC' and Saturn loves Logic! Mars is in total contrast – there is absolutely no logic to Mars – just energy – pure energy. And so Saturn has a strong dislike towards Mars.

SATURN is highly material by nature. And so, Saturn loves Venus (Bhogi) and Saturn loves Mercury (Logic, Calculative, Pragmatic).

Saturn dislikes all that has NO LOGIC.

MARS has no logic. Just Pure Energy.

KETU has no logic. Just Pure Detachment.

GURU has no logic. Just Pure Righteousness.

SUN has no logic. Just Pure Consciousness.

MOON – Just Pure Emotional. And Saturn knows nothing of emotions!

Saturn has no emotions. Let this be very clear. Because emotions can become a hurdle when it comes to applying logic and making good decisions and judgments. And so, Saturn is very practical and pragmatic. It considers only facts and figures. That is why in companies, generally those who reach higher positions (authoritative) have a strong Saturn in their birth charts because without Saturn, how can they effectively measure the performance of the company? So generally, successive leaders and top executives have good Saturn placements in their birth charts. You will not find Ketu or Rahu associated with their Saturn by any means.

The so-called 'EMOTIONAL INTELLIGENCE' that now is being discussed in the boardrooms of executives across the Western countries – happens when SATURN comes in a positive aspect with JUPITER – then Jupiter's intelligence drives Saturn in managing emotions intelligently.

Emotional intelligence is your ability to recognize and understand emotions in yourself and others, and your ability to use this awareness to manage your behaviour and relationships.

TRAVIS BRADBERRY & JEAN GREAVES

That is why, I personally love the conjunction of SATURN + JUPITER. It brings a certain depth, a certain quality to the individual. It is a great combination especially for spiritual progress – if other placements are favourable.

There are only two planets who are *'dealers'* – MERCURY and VENUS. Venus is a selfish planet. BHOGI by nature. MATERIAL by nature. These two planets bring the best out of Saturn – bringing the spirit of entrepreneurship and if other aspects support, then success in business is guaranteed.

MERCURY and VENUS – both are the only *natural* 'friends' of Saturn. A successful businessman always has a positive placement of MERCURY, VENUS AND SATURN! Once this 'party' of three favours you – you become a good 'dealer' – so one side of your life – 'money' and 'pleasures' are taken care of. What suffers is then the other side – the lack of peace within, bliss within, the missing of joy within – the missing of happiness – the inability of coming to the state of consciousness!

Understand the fact and I insist to all my followers, readers and fellow travellers – Saturn CANNOT LET GO. Revenge is impossible to deny. A Saturnian person is revengeful – he or she – **cannot let go**. They *cannot* forgive. They *cannot* understand. Only a man who CAN understand, can forgive.

To understand everything is to forgive everything.
BUDDHA

Saturn has no space for understanding – an eye for an eye – is the only answer that Saturn knows – and so WAR is impossible to avoid – WAR becomes the only answer. Revenge becomes the only answer – Punishment becomes the only answer. And so Saturn is feared.

But everything in the world can be transformed – GOD's creation never goes waste IF it comes in contact with something/someone who can transform it to its benefit – someone who can uplift it to higher realms of consciousness!

So, let us see who can transform Saturn's qualities to attain the higher realms of consciousness!

That is Shri Guru. Jupiter. And the holy conjunction of SATURN + JUPITER.

Now –

Let us see who can transform Saturn's qualities to attain a well-settled love relationship!

That is the ever-green romantic Venus. The sweet conjunction of SATURN + VENUS.

Let us see who can transform Saturn's qualities to attain pragmatic higher business goals!

That is the logical, calculative Mercury. The calculative pragmatic conjunction of SATURN + MERCURY.

SATURN is fine-tuned as long as it comes in conjunction with the above three planets.

The moment SATURN comes with MARS - Saturn loses its potential to give good results. Somewhere the KARMIC cycle of the native (past births) had NOT been that great. ENERGY is now slowed down. Sexual energy – sexual bliss – comes under the 'control' of Saturn. The free flow of energy – to fight, to voice out, to have a great sexual life (Mar's energy is required in the actual ACT of SEX) is now damaged. On the other side – the pragmatism of SATURN is hampered by MARS. So both damage each other's qualities – leading to havoc in the native's life.

The moment SATURN comes with SUN – consciousness is blocked. The native commits many mistakes because consciousness is missing, ignorance is more. Therefore, his or her life is filled with more tragedies than otherwise. Many losses, many hardships – this happens because, understand the fact, this life is the outcome of previous life where the native had committed many acts out of ignorance – so now God is giving him or her a second chance – through the hardships, through the sufferings. If they can realize – if they can turn inward, if they can embark on the Journey beyond Mind, if they can meditate – then the next life comes with a better Saturn, a better Sun placement.

The moment SATURN comes with RAHU – a cursed life. Such a person is cursed. And the source or the reason for this curse – is DESIRES. Such a person has done certain sinful acts due to the absence of consciousness in the previous life – just to achieve certain desires – certain pleasures – certain goals. But while doing so – such a person has caused much pain to others – and those people have cursed him or her. This curse manifests in the form of SATURN + RAHU. With this combination, the person feels lost – now desires are not fulfilled – and even if they fulfill – the 'party' does not last for long! So, such a soul remains unsatisfied – it is one of the most unholy combinations. A very unfortunate state – it is better that I don't say much – because TRUTH is HARD.

The moment SATURN comes with MOON – it leads to a highly political person. Cunning. Pragmatic. Moon is like water – whatever color you mix in water – water turns to that color! Mughal Emperor Aurangzeb had this placement – Kritika Moon with Saturn in Taurus Sign. And history is witness to the fact that how cunning, cruel and political Aurangzeb was!

But it is not just this one placement that makes Aurangzeb a highly cunning and political person. There is one more aspect to his chart and that is his Ascendant (Aquarius) Lord – Saturn is Retrograde.

Aurangzeb is a good example of SATURN+MOON conjunction.

Saturn is not happy with MOON – Saturn ensures that MOON comes in its total control – and so all qualities of SATURN (good/bad) penetrate into the MOON (MIND) and the person becomes SATURN. Such a person is too cold-blooded – even if angry – does not express openly.

The other side of this placement is that REPRESSION is seen more than EXPRESSION. Many times – if other aspects are not supportive – people with this Saturn combination often commit suicide – are prone to committing suicide.

REPRESSION is something that goes on killing you. You want to have 'experiences' – sex, love, joy, bliss, peace – you want all kinds of experiences but when you REPRESS your desires, your feelings – you don't move ahead – and unless you move ahead – SELF-LEARNING is not possible! And when there is absolutely no SELF-LEARNING – how can you progress in true sense? How can you grow in the real sense?

REPRESSION blocks your growth – never REPRESS your feelings, if you LOVE someone – step ahead and EXPRESS. Expression is Life. Repression is Suicide!

> 66
> Repression is the pitfall for all those people who want to transform their lives- they have to avoid repression. Indulgence is not so bad because indulgence can one day bring understanding but repression can never bring understanding.
> **OSHO**
> 99

A person who has been eating non-veg for many years – at some point, may realize that he must slow down – and shift his gears to vegetarian food.

A person who has had plenty of sexual experiences and pleasures – at some point may realize that he should stop monkeying around – enough is enough – now it is time to experience something that is far beautiful, far blissful than SEX.

A person who has been running behind money and accumulating his whole life – comes to the realization that enough is enough – now it is time to do something for the nation – for others – for those who are still struggling to earn!

So you see – it is only when you EXPERIENCE – that you can UNDERSTAND – and it is only when you understand that you can REALIZE! And so in my life – I respect every man and every woman who has been through all kinds of experiences – because such a man – such a woman CAN move on to the next level – the spiritual level – and only such men and women can become YOGIS and YOGINIS in the true sense. I may be condemned by certain pundits, certain intellectual folks – but who cares – TRUTH never cares for what is going to happen – TRUTH is simply happy to share what *is* – and what is – *is*! Truth remains while the rest, sooner or later, gets dissolved with time.

The whole purpose of meditation is to help you to remain in the *is* – there should be no 'was' and no 'will' – just 'is' – because life is in this moment – and only a man who lives moment to moment is a man of awareness! Isness is his way of life – Isness is my way of life and Isness should be the way of your life!

Yakusan says, "isness is my business."

That is my business also. That has been the business of the buddhas – a single business, bringing people to isness, to here and now.

OSHO

SATURN is all about being REAL. Understand this – and I appeal to all my followers, readers and fellow travellers. SATURN is being REAL. And Life *is* flowing now – NOW is the REAL MOMENT! Whenever SATURN comes in trine (triangle) aspect with SUN – it is a beautiful development. The 'Consciousness' (SUN) now helps you to BE HERE NOW – in the REAL MOMENT (SATURN).

Whenever spiritual planets come in contact with Saturn – Saturn transforms to an altogether different level – now the same material SATURN helps the native to progress in his or her spiritual journey.

To attain something that is far beautiful – far blissful – one has to let go – drop certain aspects of his or her life! And so when SATURN comes in contact with SHRI KETU – two things can happen:

1. Either you remain confused – that leads to material loss
2. Either you rise above the material world – and experience the spiritual bliss within

Now the first possibility is seen when the other Kundli apsects are such that the native is pure material (BHOGI) by nature. In such a case – the first possibility is prominently seen – there is no success – no stability – no peace – no prosperity.

The second possibility is seen when the other Kundli aspects signify a spiritual inclination – that the native is originally a YOGI – and spiritual by nature. Then there is a song to it – a dance – then such a combination brings an altogether different level of spiritual experiences.

In general, the first possibility is seen because the majority are BHOGI by nature. So, this SATURN KETU conjunction becomes a challenging position for many people. Here KETU nullifies many of SATURN's positive qualities. Specifically, this is NOT a good position for authority figures – and the fact is that with this kind of placement – rarely does an individual become an authority figure or a top executive!

To become a top level executive – the C-class executive – it is necessary that Saturn is NOT with Ketu!

A political leader, a government executive or a top executive (SATURN) of a private company will find it difficult to make decisions if there is always a SANYASI (KETU) sitting on his head!

Nehru and many other political leaders were finding it very difficult to tackle the political issues with Pakistan – just because there was always the Mahatma Gandhi (Ketu) sitting on their head! It was only after the Mahatma left this world that Nehru and his government (Saturn) could make some hard decisions.

SATURN wants POWER. REAL POWER. And KETU is absolutely disinterested in POWER POSITIONS. Tell me – and I insisit to all of you – tell me – how can this 'marriage' work? One has no interest in POWER. And the other is very much interested in POWER.

Wherever there is a desire to have power over another person, it is politics.
Power is always political.
OSHO

Therefore, whenever SATURN KETU come together, the desire for POWER is **less**.

And whenever SATURN RAHU come together, the desire for POWER is **more.**

See how beautiful the art of astrology can be! Astrology is not alien – it is very much within us – it is a play of qualities, of energies, of vibrations, of nature, of relating!

Whenever there is 'relating' – there is a 'spark' – the very base of FRIENDSHIP is relating! Arjuna could relate with Krishna. Peter could relate with Jesus. Ananda could relate with Buddha.

Relating is beautiful than *Relationships.* When you are relating – you are simply relating – there are no expectations – but in relationships – there are expectations!

When in relationships – expectations come, these expectations lead you to the road of many miseries! Because you expect something – you are dependent – you become dependent – there is no independence – you are locked in a relationship. Relationship closes the door to Freedom. And love ceases to exist, the moment there is no freedom!

"The moment love becomes a relationship, it becomes a bondage, because there are expectations and there are demands and there are frustrations, and an effort from both sides to dominate. It becomes a struggle for power..."
                                                              - Osho

Relationships cannot give you absolute freedom. Relating can!

When it comes to RELATING – where is the question of dependency? You are simply relating – resonating and that is beautiful.

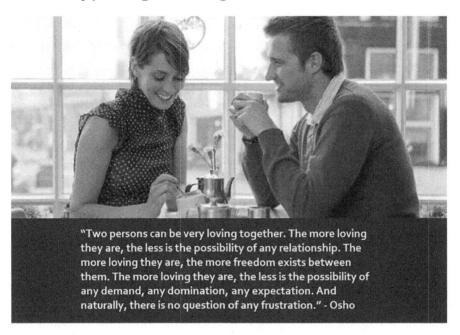

"Two persons can be very loving together. The more loving they are, the less is the possibility of any relationship. The more loving they are, the more freedom exists between them. The more loving they are, the less is the possibility of any demand, any domination, any expectation. And naturally, there is no question of any frustration." - Osho

When 'Relating' happens between two individuals, between two planets – then there is a song to it – music, melody and love is all over!

This kind of 'Relating' does not happen between SATURN and KETU. They are two polarities – one is Hitler and the other is Buddha! And so comes the complacency.

Complacency means a *feeling of contentment or self-satisfaction*, often combined with the lack of awareness of pending trouble or controversy. This unawareness comes because of KETU. KETU creates many clouds of confusion in your mind – then what 'APPEARS' seems to be the REAL – but in reality it is not.

In short, **the realism of SATURN** is damaged by the association of KETU.

Whenever KETU comes in contact with a planet – it brings distortion – and so what is real – is never realized!

KETU – SATURN = No realism. Distortion of reality.

KETU – MOON = No emotional intelligence. Distortion of emotions. Emotionally unstable.

KETU – SUN = Unfortunate conjunction. Consciousness is distorted. Person spends his life in more ignorance than consciousness.

KETU – Jupiter = A good conjunction for spiritual progress – Here Guru channelizes KETU's distortion – nature of detachment to the native's progress.

KETU – VENUS = Damages the sexual/marriage prospects. Person suffers through relationships. KETU's energy is against Venus who is a BHOGI – pleasure-seeking.

KETU – Mercury = Logic is less – hampers the logical ability of the native. But if the native is on a spiritual path – this can be a blessing in disguise – because in God's kingdom – logic has no place – LOVE has! And where there is NO LOGIC – LOVE is! So this can be a boon or a curse – depends on which path the native has been from past birth and rebirths.

Let me tell you all – KETU is gracious to all those individuals who are set on their spiritual journey! And the same KETU can play havoc for those individuals who are simply clinging to material pleasures – sex, money, wealth, properties, power.

That is why the energy of Shri KETU is totally against the energy of RAHU.

RAHU wants SEX. KETU is not interested in SEX. RAHU wants POWER. KETU is disinterested in having POWER. RAHU is highly political. KETU is such a simple being – just like the great mystic who comes all the way to congratulate his politician friend.

Every person's birth chart is either under the realms of RAHU or under the influence of Shri Ketu. It depends on what 'path' the soul has embarked upon for many lives after lives.

SHANI KETU or SHANI RAHU - is also a sign of being victim to certain negative energies (spells, etc.).

In life - especially in human life - I have seen many people becoming a victim of such negative energies - and there are remedies for the same - because GOD LOVES EVERY INNOCENT MAN AND WOMAN. So where there is a problem - there is also a SOLUTION. But such solutions are not generic - they vary from person to person and so I cannot mention them in this book.

It is difficult to stop people - how many people you will stop - each one of us has enemies - open and secret! So it is better that instead of focusing on our enemies, we focus on our SELF GROWTH!

Hence, I insist and encourage you to meditate. To pray. To read the holy scriptures of your faith - everyday. All of these bring good, positive vibrations to your being and when you remain positive - then no matter how many on the outside try to throw negativity on you - you can always survive happily!

That is the beauty of faith - beauty of meditation - beauty of praying and living your life without fear - without bothering of who will say what!

Always remember - if you remain GRATEFUL - if you remain THANKFUL - nothing ever will go wrong in your life - no matter how many times life knocks you down - you will RISE - you will SUCCEED. The key is to remain grateful. The key is to remain THANKFUL.

Your whole life can become a garden of bliss – if the only prayer you say is 'Thank You'!

> If the only prayer you ever say in your entire life is Thank You, it will be ENOUGH.
>
> **ECKHART TOLLE**

It is not Happiness that brings Gratitude. It is GRATITUDE that brings happiness in our life! A man or a woman with a grateful heart is always a blessed person. Such a grateful person goes a long way – then no matter how life is – no matter how difficult life is – such a person is always THANKFUL to God – because he realizes the fact that LIFE in itself is the greatest blessing!

It happened that a young man was very upset. Nothing was happening in his life. So, he went to his master.

He said, "Master – nothing is happening in my life – you always say – celebrate life – but what is there to celebrate?"

The master laughed – a loud belly laugh and said, "Mohan, come here, come closer..." And the master put his hand tightly on Mohan's face – Mohan could not breath…he struggled… The master removed his hand and Mohan took a deep breath. He felt better, his eyes twinkled as if life was back and Mohan smiled.

The master looked into Mohan's eyes and said, "Now you realize – every moment is a celebration – be grateful to God that you are alive – life is precious – and one who realizes this – *celebrates life* – no matter what!"

Value LIFE – because LIFE is the greatest journey you will be ever on!

"Celebration is the foundation of living - not renunciation but rejoicing. Rejoice in all the beauties, all the joys, all that life offers, because this whole life is a gift of God." - Osho

Our whole life is a gift of GOD. Let us celebrate, let us be THANKFUL, let us be grateful for all that we have – no matter how much! Then there is a certain fragrance to your life – then there is a song to it, a dance, a music!

So come, come you all – sit with your closed eyes, and meditate on the Holy Lord's name – just the name of the Lord can take you to many places – because the strength is in your FAITH – the beauty is in your FAITH, the power of possibility is in your FAITH!

Be thankful and keep walking with FAITH in your heart.

When you become more and more meditative – your heart becomes a portable paradise.

"Practice meditation. You'll find that you are carrying within your heart a portable paradise."

~ Paramahansa Yogananda

Let us continue to meditate – every day minimum 20 minutes, morning and evening – without bothering what planet is doing to you – without bothering which house is what planet – without bothering about anything in this world – let there be 100% focus within your being – breathe – breathe in and breathe out while you focus on the Lord's name – the whole story of human life is between two actions – breathe in and breathe out – and one who has realized this – has realized the whole essence of this human life!

My blessings and love to you all. Life is short and active years of life are even shorter – so wake up and let the journey beyond Mind – begin.

Love is possible, love can be experienced only when you start moving beyond Mind. Only then there is a song to your life – only then there is a certain fragrance to your being – the whole purpose of this human life is to embark on the Journey beyond MIND – and it is only when you move beyond MIND that the fragrance of true LOVE can be experienced.

Love is the Goal. Life is the Journey.
OSHO

Mind is logical. It cannot feel the essence of love. To love, first you have to go beyond MIND- only then love is possible, only then the joy of living is possible.

Mind has reasons. Love has no reasons. Love is unreasonable – and yet Love has all the answers to all your questions.

So, let love become the ultimate path of your spiritual journey. The more you start moving beyond MIND, the more you will experience the true essence of love. And then life is no more a problem but a beautiful song, a melody, a dance!

Love is the only language that can move the whole universe - what to say about you or me! No matter how much 'noise' is there on the outside, you always make sure that there is abundance of love and understanding inside you - within you.

ALWAYS remember love is the shrine - the only shrine that can show you the way towards your real growth - the growth within.

Jai Shri Ganesha. Jai Guru.

Question 11

What significance does Ketu has in one's life?

Many times, people want answers - **they want to know the TRUTH** - but the real question is - are they *willing to ACCEPT the truth?*

> People see what they want to see and what people want to see never has anything to do with the truth.
>
> **ROBERTO BOLANO**

Many women come and they want to know if their boyfriend is going to be with them and is going to marry them or not! And so do many men who are desperate to know if their girlfriend is honest with them or cheating them on their back!

Now if I tell them the truth - they cannot digest it - because the mind is the monkey - and the mind is elusive and the mind would never want to ACCEPT the truth - the mind loves to live with its own illusions!

> People don't want to heart the TRUTH because they don't want their illusions destroyed.
>
> **FRIEDRICH NIETZSCHE**

A husband believes that his wife is honest with him - but in reality, she is caught up with someone else! Not that she does not love her husband but she also cannot let go of her lover!

So many such cases are happening around us - millions and millions of stories are developing every moment - every second - and so to know the TRUTH - first you have to PREPARE yourself to DIGEST the TRUTH - to ACCEPT the TRUTH!

Six months ago, you saw a man and a woman - all entangled with each other and six months later - you see the same man and the same woman waiting to kill each other!

You see - and I say to you all - anything can happen anytime - LOVE can transform into HATE and HATE can transform into LOVE!

A young man once asked, "Why is it that I am so much in misery? Why is it that I cannot find peace within?"

And the master smiled and said, "Because you go on clinging to everything that you come across - so many attachments are in your life - you cannot let your WIFE have any freedom - you cannot let your children have any freedom - because you want to control them - you have ATTACHED yourself SO MUCH to your wife - your children - that you have closed all the doors to freedom - you are totally blocked by your own nature of clinging."

This nature of clinging is the nature of RAHU!

The young man said, "BUT I love my wife, I love my children..."

The master said, "This is NOT LOVE. This is being POSSESSIVE. And the moment there is possessiveness - LOVE ceases to exist - love is possible only when there is absolute FREEDOM. You think it is LOVE - but it's no more LOVE - it has become a POSSESSION."

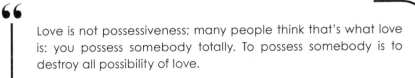

> Love is not possessiveness; many people think that's what love is: you possess somebody totally. To possess somebody is to destroy all possibility of love.
>
> **OSHO**

If you LOVE your wife - let HER have absolute FREEDOM. If you LOVE your girlfriend - let HER have absolute FREEDOM. If you LOVE your husband or boyfriend - let them have absolute FREEDOM.

If there is DOUBT - then LOVE has not yet become a full moon! Love has not yet blossomed to its totality. There is still some space - else DOUBT cannot penetrate into the monkey mind!

The ugliest nature is the nature of **being DOUBTFUL!**

There was a young man - his name was Hertz. He was the son of Baal Shem. Baal Shem was a mystic, a highly spiritual man - many believed that HE was a messiah! And Baal Shem lived his whole life serving the poor - the sick. Now he had become very old. He said to his son, **"Hertz, today at midnight I am going to die. You take care of yourself."**

Hertz was a doubtful man. You can say - he was like those white-collared intellectual heads - he doubted if his father was REALLY going to die! He doubted whether this man's words were really true!

You see - the majority of those who come to me - are like Hertz - they are filled with doubts and doubts. But that is how the majority of this planet is! You can't help!

So Hertz doubted his father. He was aware that his father is not a common being - that his father is one of the greatest lovers of God - and that whenever he would say something - it would always manifest. But *still* he doubted and so he went to sleep at night - but at MIDNIGHT - suddenly he woke up - as if someone had come to wake him up and he opened his eyes and went to his father - he was shocked - **his father was dead.**

Hertz burst out with a big cry - he started crying, weeping. He had missed the greatest opportunity to have the last word with his father - his father - the Great Baal Shem had informed him that he was going to die at midnight - Hertz could have remained awake near his father - but Hertz doubted - he doubted the words of his father and now he was at a great loss - he could not control himself, he kept crying - there was no one to give him a hand - it was midnight hour - and Hertz just broke out - he could not understand what to do - his father was dead and Hertz was in deep shock.

Understand the fact - and I appeal to you all - understand the fact that Hertz never doubted his mind - he doubted his father - Baal Shem! Baal Shem had said, **"Hertz, today at midnight I am going to die. You take care of yourself."** But Hertz did not believe in his father's words - he believed in his mind - he doubted his father - but he did not doubt his mind! And that is the whole tragedy of human life - you would doubt the other person - but you would NEVER doubt your MIND!

Hertz was crying - there was no one - but the body of his dead father - Baal Shem. As he was crying he remembered his father's words - Baal Shem! Baal Shem would always say to him, "Hertz - come to me."

But Hertz would always say, "Yes, I will come but there are many other important things to do first…"

And this is what happens with you all - the Master says, "Come to me."

But you all say, "There are more important things to do first - I will come when I am done with all those things."

And the TRUTH is - you never come - because the things that you think will be over - never are over - after one desire - another desire is standing in a queue - you remain stuck - while the master waits for you!"

Baal Shem was such a beautiful person - a great master with a compassionate heart that he could not see the miserable state of his son - even when dead - Baal Shem appeared before Hertz and said, "Hertz - come to me."

Hertz was crying, he heard his father's voice but again the DOUBT came! "What does he mean when he says come to me? He is dead and he wants me to die. Is he asking me to commit suicide?" - Hertz thought.

In reality, Baal Shem was asking his son to drop the MIND and come to him - to the source - the self - the reality!

But DOUBT once comes - blocks the very source of your consciousness - you can't understand a single word of the master - Hertz could not understand - he said, "I will think over it."

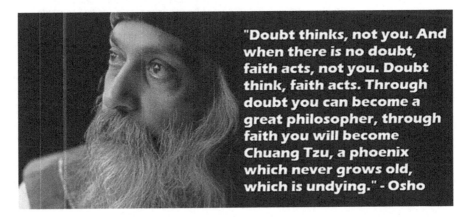

"Doubt thinks, not you. And when there is no doubt, faith acts, not you. Doubt think, faith acts. Through doubt you can become a great philosopher, through faith you will become Chuang Tzu, a phoenix which never grows old, which is undying." - Osho

Whenever you say **"I will think over it"** - you have started doubting. Then the whole essence is lost - the beauty is lost - then there is no love but only doubt and **DOUBT is DEATH!**

To love - there is no chance to think - when you love, you simply love!

Only a man of the heart can love. Only a woman of the heart can love. And it is only these followers of heart that can relate to the words that I share, that the master shares - the rest will continue to 'think' - while those who are followers of heart - will continue to absorb the words of the master - the greater the capacity to absorb - the greater is the possibility for you all to grow!

The MIND obstructs you from absorbing - letting the words of the master penetrate into your being - your heart. There are two types of listeners - the first listen by his or her mind - the second type is the one who listens by his or her heart!

I am all for the second type - they are in minority - it always happens - TRUTH can only be accepted, absorbed and realized by the minority - because men of the heart are few - very few! We have more intellectual HEADS and hence the misery, hence the suffering is more than otherwise!

Kabir was a great saint - and Kabir always loved those who listened by their heart - and NOT by their mind!

"Kabir says: Please don't agree and disagree with me. Just listen. Listen attentively, totally. Kabir says: Please don't be in a hurry to decide and conclude. I am not preaching anything here. I am simply saying something that has happened to me, that has grown in me, that I have experienced, I am simply singing my own song.

All agreement, disagreement, is foolish, stupid. When truth knocks at your door you will simply be suddenly silent, unmoving. And that is real agreement - which is not of the intellect, not of the mind. That is not from you; that is from such a depth in your being that you can almost say it is from God."

- Osho

It brings great joy to me - when I come across such men and women, they are absolutely a joy to meet - pure hearts - lovable people - innocent people - to such people GOD comes - to such people - the Master comes - because GOD is interested to know the **state of your being** - and NOT of your mind! No matter where such people are and no matter what condition they are in - they always rise - they always attain success because there is something beautiful within them - and that is they THINK LESS and they FEEL MORE!

RAHU creates many doubts - the 'darkness' will lead you to many doubts and worries and malice in your mind. RAHU corrupts the Mind. You become attached. You start clinging. You become possessive. You become selfish. And then you come and ask, "Why is my life a sea of miseries - why am I miserable?"

KETU helps you to get over the nature of being doubtful. How?

Because KETU is DETACHMENT. And it is only when you can DETACH yourself from everything that you can stop doubting - and start experiencing happiness within!

Detachment is not that you should own nothing. But that nothing should own you.

ALI IBN TALIB

There is ABSOLUTELY no problem in having a GOOD bank balance, a few cars, a few properties - let it all be there - that is what you have been wishing for since many births and NOW you have been blessed with it - so let it be there - the MAIN POINT is YOU should not get ATTACHED with all that you HAVE!

It is a typical INDIAN MINDSET that to be spiritual means you have to live as a poor man - that is not required. You can drive a Mercedes and you can be a truly spiritual man! Spirituality has ABSOLUTELY nothing to do with WHAT YOU HAVE or WHAT YOU DON'T

HAVE - Spirituality has MORE TO DO WITH HOW MUCH YOU ARE DETACHED WITH WHAT YOU HAVE!

It happened once. A king loved his people and so every night, he would disguise himself as a common man and take a ride around his capital town. Every night, he would go around the town and observe a young man sitting below a huge banyan tree. Many nights he passed by the tree and the young man - half-naked - was seen in a deep meditative state. The king became curious. He said to himself, "This man must be something. I must step down and have a word with him."

So one dark night, the king stopped at the banyan tree. He stepped down from his horse and walked towards the young man - his eyes were closed, there was a certain lingering fragrance around him and there was so much of peace - the king felt good within, he came closer to the young man and said, "Master..."

The young man opened his eyes - and the king was taken aback. How much of bliss - how much of peace - how much of love was flowing through the young man's eyes. The king said, "Sorry, you are meditating and I disturbed you."

The young man smiled and said, "I am not meditating, I am meditation."

The king bowed before the young man and said, "Master, will you come to my palace? I truly wish to have you in my palace."

The young man said, "Why not! Let's go."

The king was happy to know that the master had agreed, but somewhere the MIND created a doubt. How come such a spiritual man agreed so quickly to come to the palace?

You see - this is how the MIND is. But the king welcomed the master to his palace. For the next six months - the king offered a huge royal abode to the master - with all its frills and fancies. Beautiful maids. Many servants. Royal bed. Royal food. Everything that one could imagine!

And the master lived in his own bliss.

One evening as the king and the master were having a walk in the royal garden, the king said, "Something has been keeping me awake for many nights."

The master smiled and said, "What is it?"

The king said, "I have been thinking that I am living a royal life - have the pleasures of the royal palace. You are also living a royal life like me - then what is the difference between you and me?"

See how the MIND is! It was the KING who had invited the master to stay in his palace, and then from last many months this is how the KING was doubting the credibility of the master - just because he had agreed to come - agreed to stay at his palace!

But the master was truly an enlightened man. Looking at the king, the master smiled and said, "You should have asked me this question earlier. Why did you spend so many sleepless nights? I will let you know the difference - but not here, you have to come to the boundary of your kingdom."

The king agreed. At the boundary of his kingdom, there was a flowing river. The master crossed the river, went to the other side of the river and said, "See - I have now left your kingdom, your palace and I am on my way - **Are you coming with me?**"

The king said, "How can I come? I have my palace - I have my wife - I have my children - I have my wealth - I have my treasures…"

The master smiled and said, "So did you now get your answer? This is the difference - I am absolutely detached - I was as happy under that banyan tree as I was happy in your palace - I am as happy as I am on the street as I am in your royal abode - there is absolutely no attachment - whether you put me in a prison or in a garden - whether you put me in a royal abode or under a tree - my bliss remains as is - it doesn't matter what is on the outside - what is in the inside - remains as is!"

The king started crying…he realized his mistake of doubting a great master. He said, "Please forgive me for doubting you - please come back."

The master said, "I can come back but I don't want to hurt you because then you will again start thinking why I came back. So now let me go my way, under that same tree from where you had invited me. You remain in your palace, I will remain in my own bliss!"

And the master left, the king could not control himself, he burst out in tears, but now there was no coming back - the master had left.

Doubt is death. The mind creates many doubts and these doubts lead you to many miseries! The mind makes you believe that the doubt is real - and then you yourself destroy your life. This is how the mind is - be aware of your mind.

Mind is a beautiful servant – but a dangerous master.

OSHO

LOVE has no doubts. Understand this, this is beautiful. When you truly love your wife - there is absolutely no doubt - even if your wife may cheat on you - still your love is so innocent that a day may come when your wife may realize her mistake and then there is no limit to her love towards you - understand the fact that LOVE has the power to forgive and forgiveness has the magic to ***transform!***

But people don't really love. They say they love but behind this so-called love is a doubtful mind that is NOT WILLING to FORGIVE!

Always remember - LOVE and only TRUE LOVE can FORGIVE!

And I tell you all - that such a woman who truly loves and CAN forgive, such a man who truly loves and CAN forgive - is ONE in a million!

> There is no love without forgiveness, and there is no forgiveness without love.
>
> **BRYANT MCGILL**

A man of awareness can forgive. He can let go. Because he is perfectly aware that the way ahead goes through the act of forgiveness!

It is only when you can forgive - that you can move on with your life. And it is only when you move on with your life - that you can progress in your life. The key is to FORGIVE!

To understand everything is to FORGIVE everything - says the Buddha!

If you can love and forgive, nothing else is needed. If you cannot forgive, you cannot love; if you cannot love, you cannot forgive.

"Only great love knows how to forgive, and only great forgiveness knows how to love, otherwise everybody has limitations. Everybody commits mistakes; to err is human, to forgive is divine. And the more you forgive, the more you start moving towards the divine; you start transcending humanity. And the higher you reach, the more love becomes possible." - Osho

In life - you all may have been hurt. Many of you may have been cheated. May have been looted. But still, I insist on to you all - FORGIVE.

Because unless you forgive - there is no way out. By taking REVENGE, you are simply digging your own grave. The way out - the way towards bliss is to first ACCEPT life in totality and once you ACCEPT - only then you can FORGIVE!

So come - come you all - I see a lot of possibility in you all - that you can progress - that you can transform into a much more beautiful being - it is good that people are trying to understand what is Rahu and what is Ketu - somewhere the 'movement' within has begun - somewhere the effort to know what lies beneath has begun - somewhere the 'process' of self-inquiry has begun - it is a good progress - the moment you start asking basic questions - there is every possibility for your progress as an individual - the beauty is always in the basics!

Always.

> Sometimes when we lose our way, we must return to the basics.
> That's where the beauty lies.
> **RODRIGO DE SOUZA**

Come back to the basics. The mind is always coming in between - trying to keep you away from the basics. But I am encouraging you all to come back to your basics. What am I doing? What is my daily routine lifestyle? How much time I am spending with myself? How much I am meditating on the Lord's name? How much I talk and how much I remain silent? How much I eat and how much I drink? How much I have sex and how much I maintain balance with my sexual and spiritual life?

Many such questions can help you all to come back to basics, to work on the basics. It is only when the basics are rectified that a 'beautiful shrine' can be built upon it. It is only when the 'foundation' (basics) is strong that a strong and a tall 'building' can be built!

Following me is difficult because understanding me and my answers is very difficult. Only someone who has a certain depth to his understanding can understand me - then there is no difficulty but total simplicity.

Only those men and women will continue to follow me - who themselves are progressing - within! Who themselves are meditating - putting efforts to **turn inwards** - and realize the true essence of this human life!

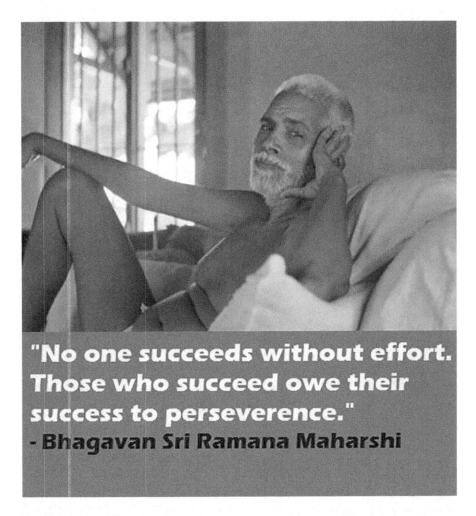

"No one succeeds without effort. Those who succeed owe their success to perseverence."
- Bhagavan Sri Ramana Maharshi

We all have to remain conscious of what is happening in our MIND - what thoughts are coming to our mind, and we have to tame this monkey mind - and I know - I know that many of you are putting your efforts in overcoming the monkey mind!

Sri Yukteshwar Giri - the Guru of Paramhansa Yogananda had once said that **a certain book is destined for certain readers only! So true…**

A beautiful picture of Sri Yukteshwar Giri in a meditative posture. Salute to His Holiness.

Meditate.
Aum.
Jai Shri Ganesha. Jai Guru.

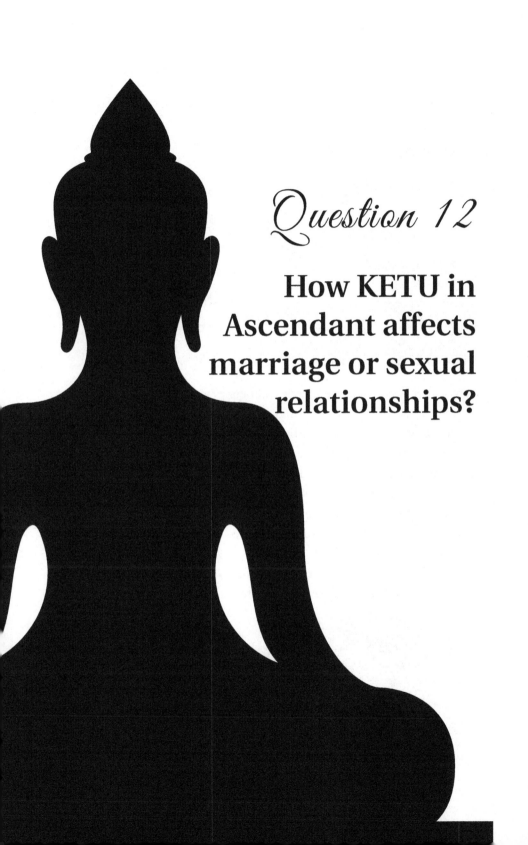

Question 12

How KETU in Ascendant affects marriage or sexual relationships?

Opposites attract. A man is attracted to a woman. A woman is attracted towards a man and that is very natural. Every man wants to be a *woman's first love* and every woman wants to be the *man's last romance!*

"No man understands the woman; no woman understands the man and that is the beauty of their being together."
-Osho

Ketu 1 and Rahu 7 native marries someone who is the exact opposite to her nature! 360 degrees. And that makes the bonding stronger - that is the beauty of their being together!

7th house is the house of 'mating' - in plain words - sexual relationship. The quality of 'mating' is based on the quality of the lordship of Rahu and Ketu. When the seventh house lord is placed positively - sexual pleasures and satisfaction - are guaranteed. Rahu 7 native is sexually very active. 'Too much sex' is the outcome of Rahu 7 - while 'too less sex' is the outcome of Ketu 7.

Rahu 7 is direct sex. Rahu is not going to wait - he is going to jump in the bed and *just do it' - there is more of sexuality in Rahu 7 - than real love.*

"Love is the real thing and when SEX happens without any sexuality in it, it is divine."
- Osho

But for RAHU 7 - there is more of sexuality than real love!

Marriages fail, relationships face challenges when RAHU KETU capture the 1st and 7th house or vice versa.

The primary reason for failure is **lack of understanding.** Here - relationships are formed - but they are more based on 'passion' - 'sexual attraction' - than real love! And so many times - with Rahu 7 - marriages struggle - and with KETU 7 - marriages fail.

The question is not how a marriage can succeed - because there are millions of couples **who are not sexually satisfied *by*** their marriage partner and **yet they would not break their marriage.** Simply to maintain the so-called status of marriage.

No matter what the fake hypocrite society say - but the key to a successful marriage is based on the depth of sexual union. If sexual life remains great - then marriage stays - then relationships remain stronger. RAHU 7 provides the sexual power - but it is too much - and if the partner is unable to 'respond' - then the marriage or relationship fails.

The most commonly striking feature of this placement is - DIVORCE.

Love marriages are the most vulnerable to the possibility of a DIVORCE. And that is the reality of today's world. *Why love marriages fail more than arranged marriages?*

For the simple reason - you have fallen in love without bringing the head (RAHU) in between. This love of yours is initiated by your heart. The heart is not stable - it keeps *wavering* - because you are still to meditate - still to stabilize the heart. And a heart that is not stable - can CHANGE at any time - and this is the greatest RISK of any love marriage.

Stability of the HEART is *only available* to those who **meditate.** To those who are turning inwards. Always remember - in your love story - LOVE is the FIRST STEP - but after LOVE - friendship should take place - else relationships can break.

People move into love with such great enthusiasm, with such great hope and fantasy. With high hopes, they enter into love and **within days it is gone!** In fact, the **honeymoon is not over** and *the love has gone.* What is happening? And then, the whole thing becomes a drag — dragging, ugly, and one somehow manages, pretends… hypocrisy.

Once love has failed once, twice, thrice, one starts feeling hopeless, one starts feeling that it is all nonsense, just a dream. It doesn't happen, it is not real, it is not true - a hallucination or an autohypnosis but nothing more.

"Love is not an hallucination, it is a moment of high passion, but one cannot remain on the high moment forever. One has to cool down, come back to earth, that's where life exists. You can fly high in the sky for a few moments but then you have to come back to earth. Before you come back to the earth create friendship because that will last. So love, love as much as possible, but always remember that love has to give space to friendship." - Osho

To create friendship - Rahu 7 native has to become more understanding. And to bring a certain depth of understanding - Rahu 7 native should meditate - turn inwards - only then the possibility of saving the marriage or relationship is possible. Ketu 1 makes the native ignorant of his or her health. The native's identity is, moreover, through the Rahu 7 - a certain obsession towards the life partner is seen through this placement. Native becomes possessive of the partner - and that brings along many miseries that, ultimately, if not addressed with maturity - can lead to divorce or a breakup or separation.

But when will the 'lovers' meditate? They have no time to look within - they are madly in love with each other - the hearts are dancing, the hearts are singing - the hearts want to become 'one'! The urge to connect 'sexually' is so much that it all becomes too fast - and many times, the native feels cheated.

If there is no direction to the heart - no meditation – someday, the heart is going to CHANGE - boredom is going to strike - and with boredom comes the risk of a breakup - a divorce!

So, love marriage can last only **if the lovers become more and more aware.** If they bring a certain **quality of understanding within.**

True love is born out of understanding - says the Buddha! And understanding comes only through 'awareness'.

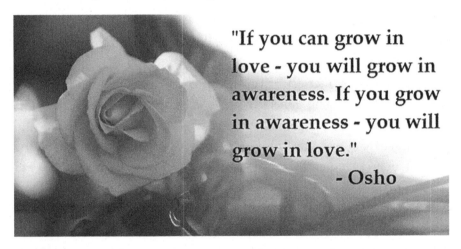

"If you can grow in love - you will grow in awareness. If you grow in awareness - you will grow in love."

- Osho

Arranged marriages are far easier to survive. Simply because they are not born through the heart - but through the HEAD (RAHU).

Rahu 7 generally finds herself or himself in an arranged marriage.

And the HEAD (Rahu 7) is super-calculative. The intellect is of the head - and the intellect has logic and mathematics, and it has a stability that is available to everybody. That is why intellect can be trained - there are schools and colleges and examinations for it - but there are no schools for the heart, no examinations. The heart cannot be trained. You have fallen in love - but you haven't yet dissolved your EGO! For a while, the warmth of love - the madness of love 'covers' this EGO - but after a while, the EGO pops up and it is this EGO that eventually destroys your 'love marriage' - love is killed by EGO. Love and EGO cannot go together for long. They cannot keep company.

You can love - only if you become a 'Nobody' - if you remain a 'somebody' - then love cannot happen.

> " Love is a dangerous path and only those who have courage can travel it. To love means to drop the Ego, to drop yourself, love means – Not To Be!
>
> **OSHO** "

When you love - surrender not to the person whom you love - but **surrender to love!** And then the possibility of a successful love marriage is guaranteed.

RAHU 7 is highly calculative when it comes to finding a life partner. Such a woman or man generally settles in an arranged marriage setup. This is a marriage arranged by the society - experience, calculation, and know-how are all used for this kind of marriage. Things are more lasting in such an arrangement. It is true that the height of love marriage is not touched, but at least the feet stay planted firmly on the ground. There will be no great showers of bliss as it is during love marriage - but a little trickle of happiness and unhappiness continues. And those who desire for showers of bliss, generally get lost in the desert of misery - that is what happens with many love marriages. Arranged marriage remains on the moderate pace - moving ahead with little happiness and unhappiness - but not touching the heights of bliss and heights of misery - something that love marriages experience!

RAHU 7 is for an arranged marriage. Generally - if other aspects are supporting and RAHU's house lord is well-placed - then such arranged marriages survive through many thick and thins of life. Remember - arranged marriage is neither born out of love nor will it collapse through the disappearance of love. Because such a marriage is not created out of love, the question of love disappearing does not arise at all. Arranged marriage is a social institution, based on the experience of thousands of years, and this experience gives the heart no chance; the whole matter is decided by the intellect.

Marriage is one thing. And Love is another.

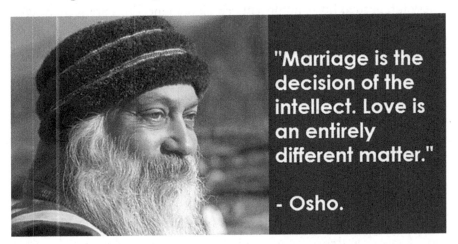

"Marriage is the decision of the intellect. Love is an entirely different matter."

- Osho.

Love has no relation whatsoever to the intellect; it is quite unconnected to the thought. Just as meditation is thoughtlessness; so is love. And just as meditation cannot be managed by the intellect, so it is with love. Meditation and Love are two names of almost the same experience. When meditation happens through contact with another person - we call it love. And when love happens in a person without any contact with anybody else - we call it meditation.

Love and meditation are two sides of the same coin. Meditation and Love are names of the same door seen from two different places. Seen from the outside, the door is called love. Seen from the inside, it is called meditation. If you arrive from the outside, the label is love; if you arrive from the inside, the label is meditation.

RAHU 7 is never confused when it comes to selecting his or her marriage partner. They are very much in the HEAD and generally marry in an arranged marriage setup. Much of the native's energy is spent on the marriage partner. The marriage partner or the sexual partner becomes the 'center point' - and the life of the native continues to revolve around this 'center'.

KETU 1 in MAGHA signifies a native - who is spiritual by nature - but falls in love or marries a person who is intensely material by nature! Opposites attract. Rahu in Aquarius sign in its own nakshatra provides a very intellectual husband or wife. Foreign connections are seen. Magha and Satabhisha - are totally opposite polarities - attraction is natural and differences in the thought process are also natural.

The partner is highly sexual by nature - demands more sex and the native - if falls short of sexually satisfying her partner - then many times, adultery is also seen through this position.

Rahu Ketu in the 1/7 axis is generally not a good placement. The person lacks clarity of vision - is generally chased by the opposite sex - if a woman has Rahu in 7 - then she is followed by strangers - has to face certain challenges when dealing with the opposite sex. KETU in Ascendant - generally spoils the health - native is not bothered about her health - she is more focused on the 'other' person in her life - the life partner.

KETU spoils the ascendant - the base of the whole chart.

RAHU fuels the house of sexual union - which is the base of marriage life. Here sex is demanded - and the demand never ends. And if the demand is not met - then either the native or the partner starts 'looking out' for possible new companionships.

The person becomes helpless. And if the ascendant lord is weak - then it becomes more difficult! After all, who would want to have a 'shadow axis' (RAHU-KETU) - right on your head when you are born?

Wearing the gemstone of the Ascendant lord is a must - but one has to see if it is truly beneficial by observing all possible dimensions of the ascendant lord.

Rahu 7 is very much interested in sex. Rather obsessed. Sex before marriage is many times seen through this placement. Because Rahu loves to do all those things that are against the social norms! And since we all are living in a RAHU AGE (KALI YUG) - in the coming years - it is going to become very difficult to find a virgin man or a virgin woman for marriage!

The idea of marrying a woman who has never been 'touched' or a man who never had any sexual relationship is going to fade away with time.

Ketu 7 denies sexual pleasures or sexual satisfaction. But RAHU 7 provides a highly passionate sexual life - so much - that the person 'wants' sex until the very late years of his or her life.

RAHU KETU become more intense and decisive when they fall in the Kendra houses - 1, 4, 7, 10 - and so the results of RAHU and KETU are more intense for the native. Rahu Mahadasha or Ketu Mahadasha grills the native - so much that many have committed suicide!

RAHU KETU in 1/7 axis - in some unique cases - also affect the sexual organs. Many times the functioning of the sexual organs is affected in some way or the other. Diseases related to sexual organs are also seen.

Basically, it is a shadow - the shadow of denial (KETU) Ascendant and the shadow of desires (RAHU) - Rahu in 7th - means a native who is 'looking' out for sexual union to which we call marriage or a relationship. Rahu 7 is desirous of having an intense sexual relationship with the opposite sex - in plain words - someone who is 'SEXY' - and is born to finish her or his unfinished business of satisfying his or her sexual desires (Rahu 7).

Marriage becomes the focus point. Either you are entangled in your marriage life because of your obsession towards your partner or because of the problems created by your partner. But either way - the person's energy is spent largely on and around the life of the marriage partner.

Either your life partner becomes a friend or the worst enemy - depends on the placement of other planets.

There was a man - he had many sexual affairs - then he came back to India - *pretended (Rahu)* as if he is such an innocent virgin man. Then he 'chose' a perfect bride - who would follow his orders. Marriage happened. The bride realized what a cheat this man was (Rahu 7) - and from day 1 - this man, his sister, and his mother - they all started harassing this poor bride. After one year - a baby boy was born - but the man would not spend much time with his wife - he would pay more attention to his sister, his mother - and one day a small fight took place - and the man kicked this woman (his wife) out of his house. After 2 years of intense court fight - finally, the woman filed for a divorce. And the woman made this man so miserable - that she claimed his property, big fat alimony and basically stripped this man's wealth. This man had Rahu in 7th house. As mentioned earlier - trouble from life partner is seen - if the 7th house lord is not positive. Here - his 7th lord - Moon was placed in 8th house. And 8th house lord (sun) was placed in 8th from 8th - 3rd house! The main reason for his divorce turned out to be his sister (3rd house - 8th from 8th)!

So many terrifying marriage stories are heard when RAHU is placed in 7th. But at the same time - when RAHU's Nakshatra Lord, House Lord is placed well - **many stories of a successful marriage are also heard.**

Woman with RAHU 7 are highly attractive and attract many men - which at times can also become a problem.

A man with RAHU 7 also has a magnetic personality and generally, women are attracted to him.

In case of divorce scenarios-

KETU 7 - Divorce happens generally because of the partner - who is engaged in an extra-marital affair.

RAHU 7 - Divorce happens generally because the native himself or herself is engaged in an extra-marital affair. Or is not understanding towards the life partner. Brings ignorance to the marriage life - leading to sudden upheaval in marriage life.

But there is always a catch:

1. If RAHU KETU is moving in Chalit Chart - then I have seen couples with this placement - having successful marriages
2. If RAHU KETU is aspected by Lord Jupiter - not much damage is seen to the marriage
3. If the Lord of 7th house is positive - and if RAHU's nakshatra lord is also positive - then a highly passionate marriage is seen - which lasts longer than expected.

In this case - RAHU KETU being at home (in its own nakshatras) - the damage is less than it would have been.

KETU 7 - generally delays marriage. Love marriages are seen more with KETU 7 than with RAHU 7. Marriage happens generally after the 30s.

Rahu 7 - Since the birth itself has been with the desire to get into a deep union - which is marriage - marriage generally takes place without delay. Before the 30's - the person is found to be married.

The native with this placement generally lives with a 'No Head' and follows either the life partner or some 'other' person's advice.

Now if the life partner turns out to be a good match - then the native's life is all set for many wonderful moments - so this is a placement that can either make the native's married life heaven or hell. There is no middle ground - you are either in Hell or you are in Heaven - when Rahu Ketu hover over your 1st and 7th or 7th and 1st cusp.

Yesterday, a man asked, "Does marriage destroy LOVE?"

The question is wrong. The real question should be "Do you destroy love in marriage?"

And the answer is 'Yes'. Because you fail to become a great lover. Understand this - this of great significance. You are so much in a rush that you meet a **woman** — the canvas is there. You immediately become a lover — you start painting. And she starts painting on you. Of course, you both prove to be foolish — painted fools — and sooner or later, you understand what is happening. But you never thought that *love is an art*. You are not born with the art, it is nothing to do with your birth. You have to learn it. It is the most subtle art. **You are born only with a capacity.** But first, you have to become a great lover. Only then your love can last - only then your marriage can last - only then there is a possibility of celebrating love.

Learn to love. Don't be in a hurry for marriage, learn to love. First, become a great lover.

Love means giving unconditionally.

And what is the requirement? The requirement is that *a great lover* is always ready to **give love** and is not bothered whether it is returned or not. It is always returned, it is in the very nature of things. It is just as if you go to the mountains and you sing a song, and the valleys respond. Have you seen an echo point in the mountains, in the hills? You shout and the valleys shout, or you sing and the valleys sing. Each heart is a valley. If you pour love into it, it will respond.

The first lesson of love is not to ask for love, but just to give. Become a giver. And people are doing just the opposite. Even when they give, they give only with the idea that love should come back. It is a bargain. They don't share, they don't share freely. They share with a condition. They go on watching out of the corner of their eye whether it is coming back or not. Very poor people… they don't know the natural functioning of love. You simply pour, it will come.

And if it is not coming, nothing to be worried about — because a lover knows that to love is to be happy. If it comes, good; then the happiness is multiplied. But even if it never comes back, in the very act of loving you become so happy, so ecstatic, *who bothers whether it comes or not?*

Love is not what is ordinarily understood by the word. Ordinary love is just a masquerade; something else is hiding behind it. Real love is a totally different phenomenon. Ordinary love is a demand, real love is a sharing. It knows nothing of demand; it knows the joy of giving.

You CAN love - only when you turn inwards, when you meditate - when you bring spirituality to your life - only then can you realize the true meaning of love - only then can you realize the true essence of SEX.

> 66
>
> Sex should be accepted as a normal, natural thing in life – just as sleep, as hunger, as everything else. Furthermore – Sex can be joined with meditation, and once sex can be joined with meditation its whole quality changes. Sex without Meditation can only reproduce children. Sex with meditation can give you a new birth, can make you a new human being.
>
> **OSHO**
>
> 99

In ancient India - sex was **not** a taboo - it was a very natural way of life. During those times - sex was not condemned - how can you condemn sex - the very source through which we all are born into this physical form?

The New Age - forces you to suppress sex - and that gives birth to perversion. In the very ancient times - during the Age of Rama and Krishna - you were free to express sex. The many sexual scandals that you read in this AGE - are because of the suppression of sex - even sexual education is denied in schools - when in reality, it would have helped the young generation in so many ways.

> " If you supress sex it becomes sexuality; if you express sex it becomes love. And through sexuality you cannot reach the divine. It is a perversion. But through love you can reach – it is a natural growth.
>
> **OSHO** "

Rahu 7 is more of sexuality than real love. Rahu is ignorance that gives birth to a specific desire. When Rahu is in 7th - the house of sexual union - the desire to have sexual pleasure is more. But through sexuality, you cannot realize the higher self - you will continue to enjoy sex - but that is all. It is only when you become meditative - then the quality of your sexual life changes. Then sex is no more just a physical exercise - it has a certain 'depth' to it - such meditative sex can give you a new birth, can make you a new human being.

Certain so-called monks, nuns practice CELIBACY. But this CELIBACY is out of negation, denial. The CELIBACY that goes through denial is perverted; your mind will be filled with sexuality. The real CELIBACY that happens gracefully, through alertness, through acceptance, becomes a grace. The CELIBACY that comes through self-realization - understanding the FUTILITY of the sex life - such celibacy has a beauty of its own, and by and by it goes beyond itself. Then it is love. Then it is prayer. And the love that was flowing toward the opposite sex starts flowing towards the divine - the same love, the same energy!

RAHU 7 - this life moves you through many sexual encounters - but if you remain satisfied with just the sexual experiences then there is no further growth to your 'self' - if you bring awareness through meditation - then there is a possibility that a time would come in your life - when you would say, **"I had enough of sex - now let me 'see' what goes beyond sex!"**

Then you are truly growing inside-out - then you can live a life of a celibate - then there is a certain fragrance of TRUTH in your actions - then there is harmony is what you think - what you say and what you actually do! And when you walk the talk - life is no more the same - you are no more the same - then there is a song to it - a poem, a beautiful painting, and life becomes a garden of bliss!

If you have RAHU 7 - satisfy your desires - you are born to satisfy your set of desires - but also remember the fact that after one desire is satisfied - the next is always in waiting!

So, one has to **know** - when to STOP - for Lao Tzu - the divine master says, "TOO MUCH - is the only SIN."

This 'knowing' comes only through self-realization. And self-realization comes only through 'meditation'. A time comes in life - when an **evolved soul** realizes the **futility of SEX** - this realization is the turning point in his or her life - then there is no looking back - the sky is clear and you are ready to fly!

But unless you experience sex with **awareness** - *how can you realize its futility?* So instead of condemning sex - one has to experience sex in all possible ways - through marriage, or through relationships. The great saints and yogis - you see today - **do you think they never had sex in their past lives?**

They must have had - but they brought awareness to their life - so much so - that in this life, **they are totally free of any sexual desires** - the MOON has become FULL - and now there is no moving back.

So do not condemn anything in life - everything at some point of life is necessary **for you to realize *what is* Real Gold** - and *what is* Fake Gold!

Jai Shri Ganesha. Jai Guru.

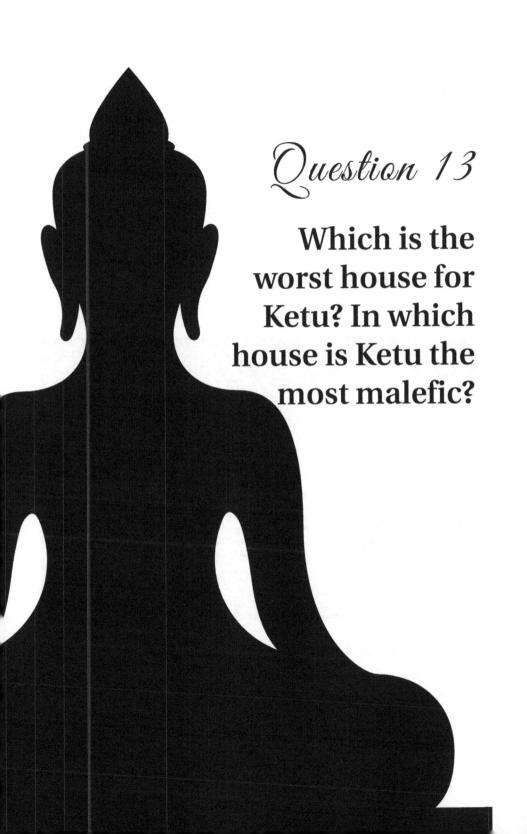

Which is the worst house for Ketu? In which house is Ketu the most malefic?

The doctor is never harmful else he would not have been a doctor! The Master is never malefic - else he would never have been a Master. The Yogi is never going to cause you harm - else he would never have been a Yogi!

Understand the fact - there is absolutely NOTHING wrong with anything - with any energy that this whole universe is made of.

"There is nothing wrong with God's creation. Mystery and suffering only exists in the mind." – Bhagavan Ramana Maharshi

Albert Einstein is probably the only scientist who has so beautifully mentioned about the significance of ENERGY.

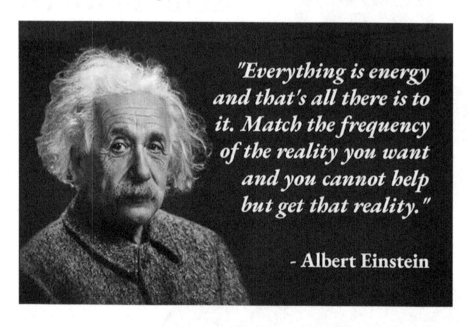

"Everything is energy and that's all there is to it. Match the frequency of the reality you want and you cannot help but get that reality."

- Albert Einstein

The whole universe is nothing but ENERGY - and let me tell you and through you and your question - to all my readers and followers - that the ENERGY is never ever the reason for causing any damage - because understand the fact that even to generate ELECTRICITY - along with the positive - the negative is also required!

> " You cannot create electricity with only the positive pole; you will need the negative pole too. Only with both the negative and the positive pole you can create electricity.
> **OSHO** "

The negative is not absolutely negative. It is complimentary and so it is not against the positive.

So, when people ask such questions - they are missing the whole essence of realizing the fact that it is NOT Ketu or RAHU or Saturn - that is malefic or bad - it is HOW YOU HAVE BEEN USING THE SPECIFIC ENERGY of these entities from the many past births and rebirths - if NEGATIVE energy has been used for POSITIVE PURPOSE - constructive purpose then even the NEGATIVE turns out as a Blessing in disguise!

For a benevolent YOGI - there is absolutely NO BAD HOUSE or GOOD HOUSE - you cannot make him HAPPY and you also cannot make him unhappy - he is in his own bliss - you may go on pressing all the 'buttons' that you have known - but he will not move - he will not be disturbed - he remains engrossed within.

Once it happened - Buddha was passing through a village of Brahmins. And the Brahmins have always been against Buddha - because Buddha objected to the Caste System - the Manu system. And that made the Brahmins very insecure - this man is a danger - he is passing knowledge to everyone - a day may come when our importance will be lost - and so he must be condemned - he must be stopped - he must be ridiculed - and so the Brahmins gathered to insult Buddha.

It happens. It has always happened - the man who is saying the truth, sharing the truth - is ridiculed - is condemned - is insulted...

Buddha was also insulted. He listened silently. They pushed and pushed on the usual buttons but nothing happened. There was absolutely NO reaction from Buddha - he continued to listen silently with absoluteLY no expressions. Now the Brahmins became worried - restless, this man is not reacting. They said, "Are you listening? Why are you standing silently? We are insulting you and condemning you. Have you gone dumb? Have you gone deaf? Can't you speak?"

Buddha said, "I can feel. I can see your worries, your embarrassment, but I am sorry. You should have come ten years ago if you wanted me to react. Now it is too late. *Now these buttons don't work.* **I have gone beyond.**"

Read HIS words again - HE says, "It is too late - I am finished with it - I HAVE GONE BEYOND."

You cannot disturb the BUDDHA. You cannot disturb the benevolent KETU.

The state of BUDDHA is of KNOWING. The REAL KNOWING happens when you start *transforming within.* Until then, you only KNOW - you have been gathering knowledge from all over the world - but you missed the most important thing - and that is KNOWING YOURSELF.

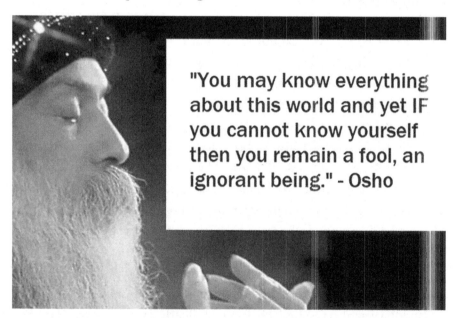

"You may know everything about this world and yet IF you cannot know yourself then you remain a fool, an ignorant being." - Osho

This KNOWING YOURSELF comes through the benevolent energy called KETU.

KETU is *TURNING IN*. RAHU is **TURNING ON.**

The real 'journey' begins when you **no more** turn on - but *you start* **to turn in**.

Buddha's whole message was to TURN IN. The Brahmins could not understand Buddha - they continued to condemn him.

By birth, I belong to the caste of Brahmins. So if you are a Brahmin - there is no need to feel low - or to get furious at this answer - because I am also a Brahmin by birth.

One has to ACCEPT the shortcomings of our community - the idiocy of our community. So, even though by birth I am a Brahmin - still I am sharing the truth - only a man of awareness - only a man who is turning inward - can openly discuss the shortcomings of his caste - his religion - his country - his state - and the state that Buddha travelled - which is now called Bihar - never accepted Buddha in totality - until he died, he left this planet - until he was no more in human form.

The whole of Bihar condemned him. Now the name Bihar is because he walked there. Bihar means: where Buddha walks.

OSHO

The most beautiful man walked on this planet and his name was Buddha, **Gautama Buddha!**

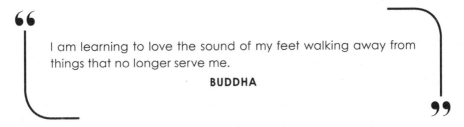

I am learning to love the sound of my feet walking away from things that no longer serve me.

BUDDHA

TURN IN - is the message of the master - of the Buddha. KETU is also saying the same to each one of you - TURN IN - in whatever place/house - KETU is simply asking you to TURN IN - the matters that are related to that house, that sign, that nakshatra.

Mohan is also a Brahmin by birth. He felt sad that the men of his community condemned someone as beautiful as the Buddha. He came to me and said, "I feel low to know that the Brahmins ridiculed the Buddha."

I said, "You come here and sit and listen…"

I shared an incident with Mohan - about a young man who was going the wrong way…and one day, this young man comes to the Master and says, **"I have been such an IDIOT all my life."**

The master smiled.

The young man said, "But now tell me when will I start walking on the right path?"

The master again smiled and said, **"Right now** - the moment you SELF-realize your idiocy - *you are set on **the right path.**"*

> Knowing yourself is the beginning of all wisdom.
> **ARISTOTLE**

But the majority is doing the exact opposite - they are trying to KNOW the OTHER - and in the process are losing the rarest of rare opportunity - time - to known themselves.

Shallowness has become the way of life - and so RAHU is on the rise - Ketu is ignored and then such question of what is worst and what is not - arises - DEFAMING the REAL - the TRUTH - the DIVINE - becomes the fashion - the routine in this world of shallowness - the human world has always been condemning KETU - they have CRUCIFIED KETU - they HAVE ridiculed KETU - they have INSULTED KETU - and yet KETU remains unmoved - you can CRUCIFY JESUS - you can ridicule MAHAVIRA, you can INSULT the BUDDHA - but you cannot get rid of them - you can NEVER get rid of the TRUTH. The TRUTH remains.

And the TRUTH is that there is absolutely NO HOUSE that is WORST for KETU.

For the simple reason that KETU is NOT BOTHERED about the OTHER. The OTHER is the WORLD. KETU is disinterested in the affairs of the WORLD - but KETU is extremely interested in the WORLD WITHIN. You place a YOGI in a palace or you place him in the most difficult place - the dirtiest place and yet you will not find him disturbed. You will find him in his joy, his bliss - then you may also ask him like the Brahmins had asked Buddha, "Are you deaf, are you crazy - don't you feel anything?"

And Ketu would reply in the same way what Buddha had said, "Now it is too late. Now these buttons don't work. **I have gone beyond.**"

KETU can't be turned on. You cannot TURN ON the BUDDHA - you cannot TURN ON the benevolent KETU - you may try to press all the 'buttons' that you have known - you may try to play all the moves that you have known - AND yet you cannot DEFEAT KETU - simply because KETU is not interested to WIN.

"You CANNOT defeat me - simply because I am NOT interested to WIN!" - Osho

There was one great Monk - and he was also a great Astrologer - but not of the books - of the SELF! And he had a large monastery - located somewhere in the north of Japan. Many would come to become his disciple but he would let in only a few - a very few. In fact, the count of his disciples would not be more than seven. Every year - only seven men or women were let in - while the rest of the monastery was filled with a large number of devotees.

Once it happened, a young man who lived at the far east of Japan - came to know about the great Monk and he came all the way to meet him - to become his disciple - but the Monk won't let him in.

The young man said, "Master, you tell me anything and I will do it - but don't reject me - I have been praying all my life, all my way to become your disciple...please test me - please give me one chance..."

The Monk said, "Fine. But you have to know the rules of the game."

A Big Chess Board was brought before the young man. The Monk said, "In this monastery - there are only seven disciples - one of my disciples will play CHESS with you. But remember - if you WIN - you will STAY. And my disciple will leave. If you lose - then you will LEAVE. And my disciple will stay."

The young man agreed. He was a good chess player. In fact, his whole life he had been a great chess player - nobody had ever defeated him in the Game of Chess.

And so, confidently he sat before the chess board - waiting for the other player to arrive.

And the other player arrived - he was such a sweet young boy - deep eyes, calm posture, he came - he bowed before the Master and then sat down to begin with the game.

And the game started. The Master was watching - the devotees were watching - and the young man was playing very well. Move after move - he was becoming more and more aggressive - more offending - and the young boy was struggling and slowly the fight began - it was becoming difficult for the young boy to stop the young man from playing his game - and the MOMENT came - the MOMENT to CHECKMATE the young boy came - and now it was just a matter of one move and the game was going to get over - the young man was going to WIN - everything was going to be AS HIS WISH - but suddenly, something moved within his heart... his heart won't let him make the final checkmate move - somewhere his consciousness won't let him - he said to himself, "If I WIN - I will get the place of this young boy and then the young boy would have to leave this monastery - Where will he go? Where will this innocent boy go? I have many bungalows and properties - but where will this young boy go - he will have no home - he will have to face depression - he will have to go through so many hardships - I CANNOT LET THIS HAPPEN TO THIS YOUNG BOY - it is better that I lose than Win..."

AND THE YOUNG MAN started making the wrong move - letting the young boy WIN. The whole monastery was surprised - the young man was winning - then WHY DID HE LET THE YOUNG BOY WIN?

The Master got up...went to the young man...gave him a HUG and said, "NOW YOU ARE WELCOME."

The young man started crying...the master looked into his eyes and said, "This game was just to test your HEART. The Moment you started THINKING ABOUT OTHERS - the moment COMPASSION arose in your heart - you had started to WIN my heart - you LOST the GAME on purpose - and it is this purpose that I wanted you to make - for the life that is yet to come."

And it is said that the young man not only became the disciple of the Master but he was the only one who cried that whole night when the Master was no more, when the Master had left his human form.

"YOU CANNOT DEFEAT ME - because I am NOT interested to WIN."

How beautiful is this - the young man must have had the same thought - when he gave up on WINNING - and chose to live to the Higher Purpose - the higher realms of consciousness!

KETU is also NOT interested in WINNING - so you cannot defeat KETU - you cannot defeat a Yogi - you cannot defeat the Buddha.

WINNING is the game of RAHU.

LETTING GO is the way of KETU. The way of the BUDDHAS.

When KETU is in a specific HOUSE - he has **gone beyond the matters related to that house** - so no matter what you do - the house he is placed in - brings NIL results - SHUNYATA - EMPTINESS. Whereas the house opposite to KETU - gets ACTIVATED - FIRED UP - because RAHU is on the OTHER end.

FIRST HOUSE KETU - the focus is on the OTHER (7th). Self-realization becomes difficult because the whole focus - obsession is about the OTHER - it is, therefore, an unfortunate placement - NOT for KETU - but for the NATIVE who has never ever paid attention to channelizing the KETU energy towards self-realization and he or she continues to go on and on and on…they KNOW a lot - but KNOWING is missing - they become SCHOLARS but they can never become the BUDDHA - unless they stop focusing on the OTHER and start focusing on the SELF.

SECOND HOUSE KETU - the focus is on hidden secrets, in-laws, debts, magic.

THIRD HOUSE KETU - the focus is on religion, higher education, sister/brother-in-law, publications.

FOURTH HOUSE KETU - the focus is on CAREER - obsessed with CAREER. I have met many crazy men and women who would do anything to get to the top of their career.

FIFTH HOUSE KETU - the focus is on networking, social life, benefits, media, a highly extrovert person.

SIXTH HOUSE KETU - the focus is on the BEYOND - the unseen, the monastery, the actions behind the curtains, the spiritual, the Yoga, the meditation.

SEVENTH HOUSE KETU - the focus is on SELF. 'I' becomes greater than the OTHER. Such a man always keeps his wife on the backseat - such a woman always is found to take the front-seat and keep her husband on the backseat.

EIGHTH HOUSE KETU - the focus is on FAMILY, MONEY, POSESSIONS, BANK BALANCE, and building fortunes.

NINTH HOUSE KETU - the focus is on 'doing something', communicating, expressing, siblings - such a person is always restless - this restlessness if gets a positive support then can lead to something unique – it is a good placement for entrepreneurship.

TENTH HOUSE KETU - the focus is on the HOME, the mother, the properties, the urge to be the center of attraction. Material happiness is the focus - no matter how much this person gets - he or she always feels that it is NOT enough.

ELEVENTH HOUSE KETU - the focus is on LEARNING. Such women and men are passionate about LEARNING. And they are also passionate in ROMANCING! LEARNING and ROMANCING - without these two aspects - they feel lifeless. They can become doctors and engineers because learning is more. They also can become good artists - because art and romance and love and poetry and painting and dancing is what is their passion.

TWELFTH HOUSE KETU - the focus is on the daily routine life - service. Such people are passionate about job, they also do well in politics, generally are liked by the society - they also are fitness freaks - many fitness professionals do well with this placement. Because the focus is always on 'Who is my enemy?' and 'How can I defeat him or her?' - they generally defeat their opponents.

Have you seen a see-saw? The one that you see in a children's park. If you sit on one end and a child on the other - what will happen? You will be down and the child will rise up. Ketu always remains on the ground - down - a nobody - while on the other side - Rahu fuels in - and blooms up the matters related to the house in which Rahu is placed.

So as you see - KETU is SHUNYA - and no matter where you place the SHUNYA - the EMPTY - the RESULT always remains the same...

$1 + 0 = 1$.

$1 - 0 = 1$.

ZERO is KETU. The RESULT remains the same - whether you ADD or Subtract ZERO.

BEST and WORST is for someone who is going to GIVE you - PROVIDE you with something.

BEST and WORST are NOT for someone who has ABSOLUTELY NOTHING to GIVE - to PROVIDE - there is absolute NOTHINGNESS. And so how can you expect KETU to give WORST or to give BEST - when there is absolutely NO GIVING - to the nature of KETU - the very essence of KETU is SHUNYA - there is NO GIVING and there is NO TAKING - absolute NOTHINGNESS.

> "
> In nothingness, there is everything, energy. The ending is a beginning.
>
> **JIDDU KRISHNAMURTI**
> "

One day a young man came and said, "I have lost my home, my job, my wife, my daughter, my son - NOW WHAT TO DO?"

The master smiled and said, "Now you have to RESTART AGAIN with strong BELIEF that everything is going to be just fine!"

The young man said, "BUT..."

The master said, "As long as there are BUTs and IFs -you will remain stuck. What has happened has happened - it was your PAST - NOW is your PRESENT and life is flowing NOW - life is neither in the PAST nor in the FUTURE - LIFE IS NOW - so get back to work - always remember - IT IS NEVER TOO LATE."

KETU may bring EMPTINESS - KETU may clear the 'ground' - so that you move to the next level. Many times it happens - you become a loser - so that you GROW double in the years to come! And this is the way of GOD - the benevolent Master - Shri KETU. You may not realize HIS WAY at the moment - but ONE DAY - YOU WILL!

> Jesus replied – "You don't understand now what I am doing; but one day you will.
>
> **JOHN 13:7, BIBLE VERSE**

A RAHU-ish man or a RAHU-ish woman cannot understand the language of KETU. They are the ones who will condemn KETU - who will condemn me. And I can understand their problem - they just can't get away from the - OTHER. They are SO MUCH focused on the outside - that they just cannot understand the language of BUDDHA - the language of MEDITATIVE YOGI - the language of KETU.

Buddha therefore says that - Remember the FORGOTTEN LANGUAGE.

Mohan asked, "What is this Forgotten language?"

It is the Language of Silence. Unless there is SILENCE - TRUTH cannot be realized. GOD cannot be experienced. LOVE cannot be experienced in the true sense. Real communication happens in silence.

Knowledge is noisy. And TRUTH can be found only in Silence. When you meditate - you become SILENT. In that silence - the SELF speaks - the HEART moves, vibrates - and then there is a song to it, a dance!

Expect and you bound to feel frustrated. Cut yourself off from the past and the future live in present, and your life becomes a song a dance.

OSHO

KETU is innocent. He has absolutely nothing to harm - because he simply has NO AGENDA. You become frustrated with KETU - only when you are deep into SEX, MONEY, POWER, LUST, GREED - when you are obsessed (RAHU) with all of these - you will definitely resent KETU. It is YOUR IGNORANCE that becomes the HURDLE - that becomes the CAUSE of the WORST OUTCOMES - when KETU DASHA BEGINS - or when KETU TRANSITS over your SUN or MOON.

Then your mind starts boggling - then you start wondering why everything is losing out from your tight GRIP (RAHU) - then the CLINGING nature is challenged by the LET GO nature of KETU and because you have been habitual of CLINGING - of ATTACHMENTS - you find the KETU period as the most difficult period of your life.

So understand this - for ARJUNA - the years of EXILE were not at all an issue. His nature was NOT OF CLINGING. Krishna would command and Arjuna would simply follow and that was the beauty of their relation - the relation between the Master and the disciple is the greatest love relation - the master stepping towards the disciple - the disciple stepping towards the master - how to express such a divine pure love - ONENESS...I am speechless.

"NO love is so total as the love that happens between the master and the disciple. The love that happened between John and Jesus, the love that happened between Sariputta and Buddha, Gautama and Mahavira, Arjuna and Krishna, Chuang Tzu and Lao Tzu – these are the real love stories, the highest pinnacles of love." - Osho

You can become a disciple only when you can resonate with the energy of KETU. Because the very first step that KETU wants you to take - is to DROP YOUR INTELLECTUALISM - drop your EGO - drop your LEARNING - and become a 'NOBODY'.

People don't understand. The majority is running behind all that Shines - whereas the real remains away from the limelight - because the moment the limelight comes - the danger of getting dragged into the never ending glamorous distracting world of RAHU is always there - the real Yogis, therefore, remain away from the People - though they continue to share their message - their direction through someone who is a 'NOBODY'!

And this NOBODY is KETU - so how can a NOBODY cause harm to someone!

If you place a holy divine Idol on your 'DISCO FLOOR' - it is obvious that you will start going through hardships - the fault is NOT of the IDOL - the fault is in your IGNORANCE - you are so much ignorant that you DON'T KNOW WHERE TO PLACE WHAT - it is like a BLIND MAN who just plays with the REAL DIAMOND - and then SHOUTS TO THE WHOLE WORLD that "I AM STRUGGLING _ I AM POOR!"

And so - to all my fellow travellers, followers and readers – FIRST, you have to UNDERSTAND KETU - and to understand KETU - you have to FIRST VISIT HIS WAY - and HIS WAY is INWARD - TURNING INWARD!

So, come you all - let us meditate - let us go again and again to that inner space and experience the PEACE, the JOY, the ABUNDANCE of LOVE within. Always remember - you can love others only WHEN YOU CAN LOVE YOURSELF! The first ripple of love has to be around yourself - only then can the love reach the farthest shores, only then can your love heal those who are suffering, only then can you comfort those who are in trouble. But it all has to first start from YOURSELF.

> 66
> You must love yourself first, then you create a ripple of love that will touch everyone's lives. You have the power within you. Make a start and heal yourself first.
>
> **LEON BROWN**
> 99

KETU is the KEY to HEAL yourself first! And you all can do it. Those who have been following me - must be something because following me and reading my thoughts, my answers is not everybody's potential - very few, only the chosen ones can relate to my sharing - in fact, it is HIS sharing, I am just a medium, just a servant.

Mohan always asks, "When will my master find me? Should I go in search of my master?"

The answer is - NO.

> You need not go in search of the Master. The Master will come in search of you.
>
> **OSHO**

The child seeks the mother. But the child misses to realize that the mother too is waiting to meet her child! Your first birth is through the mother - your second birth is through the Master. The Master is equal to your mother - HE surrounds you like a Mother. The Master is your spiritual mother. The Master is more like a mother than the father. The Mother can understand you more than your father.

Always remember - what you seek is also seeking you! There is absolutely no need to go anywhere - just be where you are and focus WITHIN, turn inwards, and move towards total SURRENDER and then when your SURRENDER is TOTAL - when you are a NOBODY (KETU) - when you have dropped everything that no longer serves the higher purpose of your life - ONLY then the Master will come - only when you **100% Ready.**

When the disciple is ready - the master appears, says the divine master Lao Tzu.

And when the disciple is really ready - the master disappears - says Lao Tzu. Because a true master would never want his disciple to remain dependent on HIM - he would never want his disciple to remain attached - because the very essence of spiritual life is to become detached - more and more detached!

KETU is the very source of DETACHMENT. KETU enables you to CUT all those things that have become useless to your REAL GROWTH - the SPIRITUAL GROWTH!

So KETU is beautiful. KETU can HEAL. KETU is NOT for those who have lost their 'eyes' (Awareness) - they can never relate to KETU and in the process will continue to live in the 'ILLUSION' that KETU is causing them hardships. Let them live in those illusions - while you all - my fellows - you all continue to focus WITHIN - take a deep breath - and MEDITATE. Morning and evening - whenever you have time - MEDITATE. I have seen many people living in riches and yet in the end what comes to their share is - MISERY and just MISERY.

BUT YOU ALL - you all can turn the tables - you all have still got time to turn inward - while the majority of this human world is concerned with TURNING ON - you all can focus more and more and more on TURNING IN!

The whole essence of this human life is to TURN IN. And that's KETU. That's Meditation. And that is the surest way to eternal happiness.

> **"**
> When you give up thinking of outward objects and prevent your mind from going outwards & turn it inwards and fix it in the Self – the Self alone will remain.
> **SRI RAMANA MAHARSHI**
> **"**

To realize the SELF - you have to reach the state of NO MIND - and the way towards NO MIND goes through KETU - if you cannot walk the KETU WAY - you really cannot attain -you remain in the grip of Rahu - you remain in the grip of miseries.

You have to make a choice - you have to begin with meditation - this can be your last chance - this can be your first chance - you don't know, I don't know, nobody knows - what is going to happen after this human birth - all you have got is this moment - the NOW moment and the more you can BE HERE NOW - the more you can progress spiritually. The key is to BE HERE NOW - to live without regretting your PAST and without worrying about your FUTURE - PAST is gone, FUTURE is not yet - NOW is the moment - BE HERE NOW. Meditation happens only when you are able to BE HERE NOW.

A young man had once asked, "What is the easiest way to BE HERE NOW?"

The master had smiled and said, "LOVE."

When you are in LOVE - you are 100% able to BE HERE NOW! And this is the beauty of LOVE - so let there be LOVE within you - no matter how many times you have been ditched or missed on LOVE - always remember LOVERS fail - LOVE never fails - LOVE remains and it remains forever - you are born out of LOVE - we all are born out of love - LOVE is our mother, says the divine Sufi Saint Rumi!

And so when you meditate - meditate with love - with devotion - with your whole being surrendered to HIS love - God's Love and then you can see the miracle happening - it happens - it always happens - this is the way of its happening - the larger question that you all should ask yourself is - Are you ready for it?

Love brings you HERE and NOW and then there is no looking back - the sky is clear and *you are ready to fly.*

To be in the moment – is the miracle. Learn to BE HERE NOW - and only then you can appreciate KETU - only then you can realize the essence of meditation - only then you can experience the greatest miracle of your life - the miracle of *transforming your life from the inside-out.*

Jai Shri Ganesha. Jai Guru.

Question 14

When KETU is in the 7th house, out of community marriage happens?

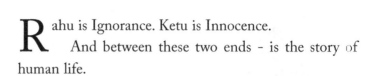

R ahu is Ignorance. Ketu is Innocence.
And between these two ends - is the story of human life.

Desires continue to hover over your mind as long as there is ignorance (Rahu). And the moment you turn inwards, the moment you look within, the moment you are willing to ACCEPT all your mistakes, ACCEPT all that life provides you with a sense of GRATITUDE - you become a Buddha (Sri Ketu)!

RAHU is rebellion. KETU is going with the flow...

> Let Life Flow;
> don't interfere.
> **OSHO**

A man of awareness goes with the flow of his life. He is living in total acceptance - to the Buddhist - such a man is Tathagata! Tathata means 'suchness' - such are the things - such is life - such is HIS wish - suchness!

And a man who lives in 'suchness' - is always found to be in peace. He is a deeply meditative man - no more is he meditating - he is meditation!

> A state of meditation is an innocent, silent state. You are blissfully unaware of your awareness. You are, but you are utterly relaxed. You are not in a state of sleep; you are fully alert, more alert than ever. Rather, you are alertness.
> **OSHO**

Through KETU - you can experience this innocent, silent state of meditation. But when? Only when you have had enough of SEXUAL EXPERIENCES - so much of sex you have had in your past lives, this life - that now you have realized the futility of this 'physical ecstasy' which lasts only for few hours! Now you are searching for something that would last forever — something of higher nature, something that can help you to be in the higher state of ecstasy where the need for other person doesn't arise - you alone can celebrate the joy of ecstasy by being rooted within your 'self'.

When there is a 'cause' - there is dependence. Your freedom is lost. Your happiness is based on the other person's actions/reactions!

Buddha says - The 'Sage' **alone** is happy. Only the person whose cause for happiness is within himself is happy, who does not depend on something outside, who is not holding his hands out to anyone for his happiness, who has found the well where a continuous stream is *easily flowing within himself. And that is how Ketu in 7th is. But only for an evolved soul!*

Ketu 7 to a conscious evolved soul - steadily leads to the beyond, to the unseen, to the state of transcendence. BUT ONLY TO A SOUL OF HIGHER REALMS.

To a commoner - KETU 7 - leads to the feeling of not being satisfied in sexual experiences - the person is either married late - or even after marriage - somehow sexual life is not that great. Such a man falls short in satisfying a woman sexually - or - if it is a woman - then she is a bit disinterested in having prolonged sex. Either way - sexual happiness or sexual satisfaction becomes a point of regret with KETU 7! And the reason is simple - here KETU is asking the native to give up the craving for sexual desires or sexual happiness and LOOK BEYOND! But to a soul which is not evolved - this placement seems to be a challenging one - instead of listening and understanding the message of Sri Ketu - the person just goes into depression. Marriage, sex life, physical ecstasy - becomes challenging with KETU 7 - BUT ONLY FOR THOSE SOULS WHO ARE YET TO EVOLVE.

For an evolved soul - KETU 7 is a perfect placement - he can now focus beyond the physical (sexual) desires - he can now 'use' this placement to expedite his spiritual journey by being more and more meditative!

The message of KETU 7 is getting over your desires for sex, this desire for sex is your ignorance - you think that you will find happiness through sex - but how long is this happiness going to last? After a while, this human body is going to become old - awaken and arise! But only evolved souls can learn their lessons through KETU 7 - the rest of the majority continues to follow desires and in turn, continues to live an utterly miserable life - a life that may look glamorous from the outside - but is totally broken from the inside!

Your DESIRES (RAHU) create your FUTURE. And that is why the AXIS of RAHU AND KETU is immensely critical in the science of astrology and the pattern of life!

Remember - for desires - future is required. For life - there is no need of any future. For life, this present moment is enough. Right now I am alive - right now you all are alive. For living - why do you need tomorrow - future? But for desires - tomorrow is necessary - future is required because desires are many - how can today - you can fulfill all of these desires? Tomorrow is needed - Desires create future and not life.

For material men - KETU 7 - can lead to out of community marriage - for the simple reason - that here KETU is not much worried about what caste, religion or background - the 'partner' is coming from. KETU is 'NO HEAD' - so many times KETU in 7 - leads to Love Marriage - because to love - you need NO HEAD - NO LOGIC. KETU 7 in a way is the only man or woman who can TRULY FALL IN LOVE! Because love happens only when there is absolutely no logic!

230

Love and Logic never meet, cannot meet. Logic means the outward journey. Love means the inward journey. Inward journey is possible with KETU - and only with Sri KETU!

True love is possible only through detachment. This state of detachment can only be experienced through Sri KETU! That is how deeply KETU is connected with the source of LOVE. And there is nothing higher than LOVE!

So, KETU 7 can marry a woman - outside his community - but NOT RAHU 7!

KETU 7 man or woman - just JUMP - there is no HEAD, but only the HEART! And the Heart is innocent - it knows no other language than the language of love! And so KETU 7 can either succeed in their love or face many failures or cheatings in their relationships - because like an innocent baby - they continue to fall in love - whether they succeed or fail - is totally based on the other aspects.

RAHU 7 - will usually never marry outside his community. He is shrewd. He is a calculative man when it comes to marriage. NOW - you have the HEAD in 7th - only the HEAD! So, this man is never happy with his marriage. But here the reason is different - with KETU 7 - the problem was not getting enough sex - here the problem is different - here sex is available in abundance and still the man is not happy! The more sex he gets, the more he craves for! He has an 'intellectual' wife - a 'sexy' wife - but still, he is not happy. RAHU 7 is always 'looking out' - to add some 'spice' to his sex life. Here 'love' has no place - but only hard sex, here 'feelings' have no place but only 'hard head' - logic rules over - and not love and so the end result is always - **misery.**

A great mystic once had said - The dead are Unhappy - the living are unhappy! Rahu 7 are unhappy with their married life. Many times you would find people with RAHU 7 saying - **that it would be better to be dead.**

There is an old story:

A woodcutter was returning from the forest. He had become tired, he had become old and tired of life - always carrying wood, day after day. Many times, he thought, it would be better to die.

One day, a strong feeling arose in him, "What is left in my life? I gain nothing, every day I carry wood, go home, eat food, go to sleep, wake up in the morning again. My hands have become feeble and shaky, I cannot even manage to walk, my eyes cannot see properly - what is the point in continuing to live? I have found nothing in life. I got nothing when I was young, what can I get now?"

He heaved a sigh and said, "DEATH! You come to everybody. You have taken away those who were born before me, you have taken away the young people - why are you leaving me here? Why are you torturing me? Take me with you. Come now!"

Usually, DEATH does not listen to anybody, but something happened that day - DEATH must have been around somewhere - it came. The woodcutter had become so sad that in his sadness he dropped his load of wood, sat down and said, "You come now" - and DEATH came! When DEATH stood in front of him, even his old eyes could see him, he asked: "Who are you?"

Death said, "You have called me. I am DEATH. I have come."

He was at a loss. His heart trembled. He thought, "I called you in my sadness. It does not mean that I REALLY want you to come."

A man can say this sometimes, in some weak moment. You are also like this woodcutter - out of sadness - out of ignorance - you ask for something - you ask for more and more sex, you want all the women of this world - this is all madness - but RAHU 7 cannot understand - they continue to live in ignorance - leading them to many miseries of life.

A woodcutter is also an ignorant man - he asked for DEATH (too much sex or the desire to have too much of sex also leads one to his or her spiritual DEATH) - and DEATH appeared before him - and now what to say! So the woodcutter says, "Yes, I have called you out of my ignorance. I am old and I have no one to help me lift up my load. Please help me to lift up my load. Thank you!"

When he saw DEATH - he again picked up the load that he had dropped.

> You are unhappy while alive, you think many times about dying, but if death comes then you tremble and you don't want to die.
>
> **OSHO**

Always remember - a birth chart - is just a representation of certain planetary placements. Every minute - millions and millions of babies are born - maternity clinics - across the globe are filled with joy - every minute - every second - birth continues just the way death continues. So practically, you are getting photocopies of birth charts - every minute, every second!

And so, every birth chart may appear as a duplicate - to someone in this world! So one has to first observe - the evolved stage - of the soul whose chart you are reading.

RAHU KETU 1/7 AXIS for an evolved soul - a meditative soul - will be totally different from a soul who is yet to be evolved. For a material man - RAHU KETU 1/7 AXIS - is a pain when it comes to health, marriage, sexual union, or sexual satisfaction. But for someone like Kabir - this is a perfect placement - yes, he would be bombarded with the same pains and challenges - but since HIS perspective towards life is different - he accepts all those pains, failures with a sense of gratitude and realizes the FUTILITY of this human life - and then like Prince Siddharta - he is on the greatest journey of his life - to know his 'self'!

So always remember - every minute - a baby is born - the birth charts are going to look similar - it is like a CAR - of the same model - they all look the same - but WHO DRIVES THE CAR - matters the most - that decides what, where and how the native is going to live his life!

Recently, a beautiful advertisement for **Volkswagen Passat** was broadcasted. And it is worth watching - serene mountains, a luxury car driving through the rough roads - and finally reaching the peak of the mountain - and the car door is opened - and you see a young man dressed as a monk - gets down - locks his car and moves towards the mountain peak to **meditate!**

Beautiful! So you see - how you use the 'car' (planetary placements) is based on the individual who is DRIVING the car!

The same 'car' (planets) could have gone to a disco bar and the same car (planets) also can go to the highest peak - and meditate!

Sai Baba once was seated in his Dwarka Mai - and a young man along with a sexy woman came - his intention was to distract Sai Baba. But who can distract the Master! The young man said, "This woman is a great dancer, she would like to dance before you."

Sai Baba smiled. He said, "Who am I to stop anybody?"

The woman started dancing and the winds started blowing, the trees started shaking - and suddenly she fell on the ground. She looked at Sai Baba but she could not see him - then she folded her hands - rushed towards Sai Baba and touched his feet - she said, "Forgive me."

The young man who was a well-known singer also rushed towards the Master, bowed before HIM and asked for mercy.

Sai Baba looked into the young man's eyes and said, "How beautiful it would be if you start singing in Lord's praise."

And it is said that from that moment - the young man, who was a great talented singer, was transformed - from that moment he sang only in the praise of Sai - in the praise of the Lord!

With divine intervention - the SAME qualities (PLANETS) can be lifted up to new heights - so, results for a specific placement vary based on the state of consciousness of that individual.

A prostitute can become a great saint. A prostitute can be saintly. A priest can become a rascal. A priest can be evil. There is every possibility to transform a given placement of planets - remember this - this is of great significance. With the arrival of consciousness - a thief can transform into a Saint. Ratnakar became Saint Valmiki. Saul becomes Saint Paul. And with the arrival of ignorance - a Saintly man, a priest also can go to the lowest corrupt levels.

Once a rich, young man from Iran came to Basra. He asked people, "Is there anything that is out of the way, something special here?"

"Yes," they all told him. **"We have the most beautiful woman of the world!"**

The young man naturally became interested and he asked, "Where can I find her?"

And they all laughed and said, "Well, where else?… in a **brothel."**

That repulsed the rich, young man, but finally, he decided to go. And when he got there, the matron asked for an exorbitant fee. He paid the fee and was ushered in. There, in a silent and simple room, a figure was praying. What beauty she had! He had never seen such beauty and grace, not even in his dreams. Just to be there was a benediction, and the prayerful atmosphere started affecting him. He forgot about his passion. He was entering into another kind of space. He was drugged. **He was turned on to God.**

An hour passed and he intensely felt he was in a temple! **Oh, such joy and such purity!** He went on feasting on her beauty. But it was no more the beauty of a human being – **it was God's beauty.** It no more had anything to do with the body – **it was utterly other-worldly.**

And then Rabia opened her eyes, those lotus eyes, and he looked into them, and there was no woman in front of him – he was facing God. And this way the whole night passed as if it were only a moment.

The sun was rising and its rays were coming through the windows, and he felt it was time to go. He said to Rabia, "I am your slave. Tell me anything, anything in the world that I can do for you."

She said, "I have only one little request."

He asked, "What is it?"

Rabia said, "Never tell anybody what you have seen and experienced here. Allow the people to come to me – this beauty is nothing but a trap set for them. I use it as a door for them to enter God. Please, promise me that you will never tell others what you have experienced here tonight. Let them come to a whore and a brothel because otherwise, they will never come to me."

"Oh!" he said, "So this is the secret of this city. The whole city clamors after your beauty, yet nobody tells me about his experience."

Rabia laughed and said, **"Yes, I extract the promise, this promise, from all of them."**

Rabia used her beauty as a trap. Buddha used his words as a trap. Krishna used his flute as a trap. Meera used her dance as a trap.

You have to be trapped. And you can only be trapped in ways that you can understand. You have to be taken from the known into the unknown, but the beginning has to be in the known.

You understand passion. **The young man was not in search of God,** but he became interested in a beautiful body, in a beautiful woman – and was trapped. He had gone there because of his passion. **Once he was there in the presence of Rabia,** the passion started changing – *it became prayer.*

And this is exactly what I would want all my readers to understand. Passion can become Prayer. Ignorance can be replaced by Consciousness. Ugly can become beautiful. RAHU KETU 1/7 can become a blessing in disguise - only if YOU are turning inwards, only if you are motivated to look within and to move beyond the unending desires - only if you are becoming more and more meditative!

Rabia of Basra also known as Rabi'ah al-Basri is considered to be the first female Sufi Saint of Islam, the first in a long line of female Sufi mystics. She was born and lived most of her life in Basra, a seaport in southern Iraq. When Rabia was a little girl - Prophet Muhammad came in her father's dream and said, *"You have been blessed with a daughter **who will be a great saint**; her intercession will be wished for by seventy thousand of my community."*

Certain truths cannot be expressed through words! And yet words have to be used - because you can understand words - that's why all the Buddhas have used words, knowing perfectly well, saying again and again, that the truth cannot be expressed in words. But you understand words and truth cannot be expressed in words, then how to communicate? The journey has to start from where you are. The Buddhas have to speak words. Words will bring you closer to the Buddhas; words will not give you the truth, but they will bring you closer to the Buddhas. Once you are close to them, you will start forgetting the words; you will start falling into **silence**. Successful people have two things on their lips - Smile & **Silence!**

My words are simply to bring you closer to your 'self' - my answer is simply to motivate you to come out of the dry logic arid land of astrology and realize the true essence of human existence. Astrology is not to be learnt - Astrology has to be **self-realized!** And the irony of this mad world is that everybody wants to learn astrology but nobody really wants to 'know' astrology!

The difference is vast - learning & knowing. Learning means you are just accumulating knowledge from all the books of astrology written under this sky - nothing ever is going to be revealed! You will just become a trained 'parrot'! And that is what the world has become - it has more trained parrots than real astrologers!

To become a real astrologer - you have to drop all the books of astrology, all the scriptures - all the learning. But who wants to listen? Shallow people and shallow life. It is a sad scenario - out of millions - only a few could become astrologers - because the majority is simply caught in parroting the books of astrology!

Astrology is not 2+2 - else all mathematicians would have become astrologers. Astrology is beyond mathematics, it is beyond the self - it is a highly spiritual science - where MIND has no role to play - but only the HEART!

Words cannot express truth, but they can bring you close to a Buddha. Buddha is not a name - it is a title - a state of higher consciousness.

Your state of life can change when your level of consciousness moves towards the higher altitudes.

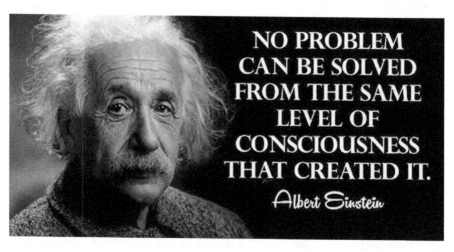

When you are turning inwards, when you learn to introspect, when you start meditating - slowly the **nature of your receptiveness** towards the results of your negative planets changes - you become more understanding, you become less reactive - and through these transformative changes - you overcome the negative MAHADASHA/

TRANSITS. But people are shallow, they move like herds - they want something magical - they want to change their life - except they don't want to change themselves! And this is the greatest irony of this human life. Unless you change yourself - life is not going to change - let this be very clear. You will run across the globe - you may visit hundreds of temples and still nothing is going to change in your life - because the real change has to happen within you - and for that, you have to look within - **meditate.**

CHANGE THE FOCUS; RETURN TO YOURSELF.

Dive within - look within - and you will start having glimpses of your pure being. That's what I call meditation. Once tasted, it transforms forever!

Come, let us all meditate. Let us all drop all that has been holding us - let us learn to live in a LET-GO - for once you have LET GO everything - all your PAST and all your worries of the FUTURE - you find yourself - HERE - in this NOW moment - and the sole purpose of meditation is simply to BE HERE NOW - only that man and only that woman can progress in life - who *is* living moment to moment - for 'isness' should be the way of our life - to still the mind - and once the mind is stilled in the present moment - you are 'in' for the greatest transformation of your life! PAST is no more, and the FUTURE is not yet - just be in the present moment - watch, witness, and stay 'awake' - then life can change, then you can change. The first step towards change is to 'surrender' - the old cannot change itself - to change - you have to allow change to happen - you have to 'surrender' to your Lord - your Master - then the ring starts moving in the right direction - then you are no more the same - then everything around you is the same - but you are no more the same - then there is a song to it - a poem, a beautiful painting, and life is no more a problem but a garden of bliss!

Love knows no communities and no boundaries. Love is willing to take the risk, it is only Love - that can JUMP - it is only LOVE that can bring joy to you, it is only LOVE that can transform you inside-out - come fall in love with yourself, let love be the anchor of your soul.

"DROP ALL FEARS AND MOVE INTO THE WORLD OF LOVE. THIS IS THE VERY SHRINE OF GOD. THIS IS THE ONLY SHRINE."

Osho

Only when you are in love with yourself - can you love others! The first step towards love is to first love yourself! And you will be able to love yourself - only when you realize your 'self'! So focus within - there is much to be revealed - there is much to know - there is much to discover - and it is all within you - so why not look within and rejoice in bliss?

For more spiritual motivation- you all can avail my published books - 'How to overcome Rahu' & ' Gift of Consciousness' on Amazon. Print book copies are shipped across all geographies.

Jai Shri Ganesha. Jai Guru.

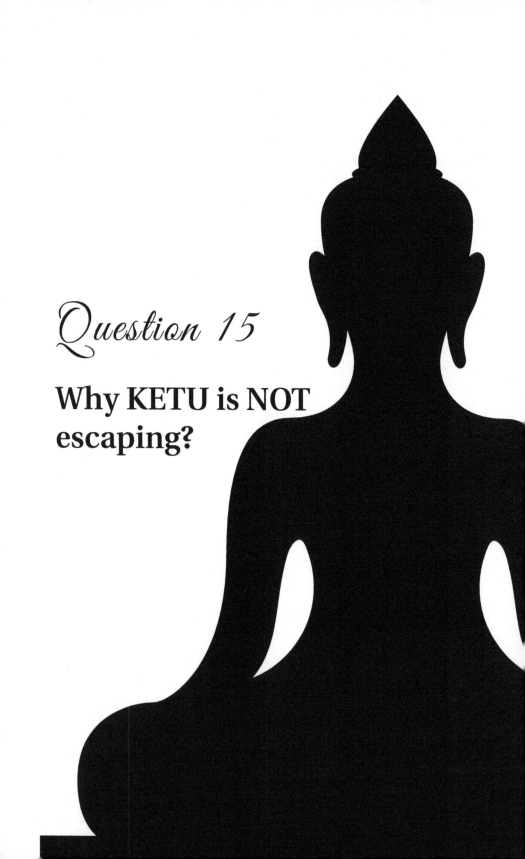

Question 15

Why KETU is NOT escaping?

There was a man. And he too was fed up with his life. The nagging wife, the irritating, arrogant children, the miserable office life - the unending politics that continued to block him every day - he was getting suffocated - life was becoming painful and miserable and so one dark night - when everybody was asleep - he left his house forever! Forever - he left all his people - his wife, his children, his father, his mother - he left them all - boarded a train to the Himalayan region.

After two days - he reached the Himalayan Mountains, he decided to live in a small village - located at the footsteps of the Himalayan Mountains. He dropped all his clothes and became a monk. He found a small place near a huge banyan tree - and started living his life - an ascetic life.

But the life of a monk is not easy - there were rats - and the rats started eating his clothes - one by one - and he would see big holes in his underwear - he had just two underwear and now the trouble was - how to fix this problem.

The villagers noticed his problem - they said: "Why don't you keep a cat? The cat will take care of the rats - she will kill them and your clothes will be safe."

The man agreed. And so a cat was provided. But now another problem arose - how to feed the cat - she needs some milk…and so the man started collecting some milk from the villagers. Every day in the cold morning hours, he would go door to door - just to collect a bowl of milk. It was becoming difficult - and so the village chief came up with a solution - he said, "Why don't you keep a cow? She will give milk and you don't have to roam around the village. One of our wealthy villagers will donate you a cow."

And so a cow was donated. Now the man had a cat and a cow. And life was sailing smoothly but somebody had to take care of the cow - cleaning the cow, giving her food - taking good care of her so that she continues to give a good amount of milk - Who was going to do all of this? After a few days - the man became tired - the villagers noticed his hardships - somebody said, "He is so young and alone…we should do something."

And so a very old woman came up to meet - she said, "We see that you are a very young man. We know you are a monk - but even a monk needs some help. There is a suggestion or rather a proposal from us - just at the back of my house - there is a young widow - she lives alone. We would ask her to join you - so that she can take care of your cow."

The man agreed.

And now the woman came in. And life started sailing smoothly - the cow was happy, the cat was happy, the man was happy - the woman was also happy - and grass started growing - green pastures - it all grows on its own - until one day - the woman became pregnant and she gave birth to twins! And the man said to himself, "O my God - what have I done? I left my wife, my family to renounce this material world - to escape from the pains of the material world and look where I have fallen - I have again started back from where I started!"

And this is what happens when you try to escape! Escaping is not the solution. Facing life the way it is - accepting life the way it is - that is the solution.

People want to escape - but escape is not the solution. The more you escape, the more you will be chased by your KARMA! Let it be very clear - the answer to your misery is not in escaping but in facing life the way it comes!

> Don't escape from any situation — if you escape, then something will remain missing in you. Then your bodhi-chitta (consciousness) will not be that ripe, will not be that rich. Live life in its multidimensionality.
>
> **OSHO**

What will you escape from? People come to me - and they ask the same question - How to escape from all our troubles and miseries? - But the question is, **"What will you escape from?**

Sexual needs? - You cannot escape from your sexual needs - they are deeply embossed in your DNA.

Food? - You cannot escape from your food - because without food - you cannot survive.

Anger? - You cannot escape from your anger - because anger is not behind you - anger is within you.

Material world? - You cannot escape from your material world - your wife, husband, children, friends - because of your ATTACHMENTS.

Desires? - You cannot escape from your desires - because it is YOU who are the source of your desires - until you stop giving birth to desires - there is no escaping.

Whatever you are trying to escape is WITHIN you - how are you going to escape?

And that is how millions and millions of Monks, Sadhus - you will see with long beards roaming around the Himalayas and yet they all are trapped in their desires - they 'look' ascetic - but inside they are still not free from their sexual needs, anger, spiritual 'ambitions' - you see and that is how there are hundreds of SEXUAL SCAMS around these so-called CELIBATES/MONKS/SADHUS - because just like your question - they too have found their answer in ESCAPING and ESCAPING has made their life more miserable than otherwise!

Repression is SUICIDE. Expression is LIFE.

People escape - they become MONKS - in turn, they have repressed their sexuality - understand this - I appeal to all my followers and readers - understand this - this is of great significance.

Repressing sexuality - repressing desires - and you are sitting on an atom bomb - someday you 'move' a little bit and the bomb of immense suppressed desires EXPLODES! And you then read the news of sexual scams - property scams - money scams - because the DESIRES were always there - the sexual need was always there, the obsession towards money was always there - it is just that all these desires were SUPPRESSED and you had escaped by becoming a MONK - but that never helps - it has never helped anybody – instead, it has made your life more miserable than otherwise!

Real 'Vairagya' - (renunciation, detachment) has to be from the very core of your inner being. You don't need a LONG BEARD, you don't need SAFRON CLOTHING, you don't need all sorts of PAINTINGS on your FACE - to show off that you are some kind of Monk or SADHU - you can be in plain clothes, well-shaven - modern and yet you can be the REAL SAINT - the true meditative person who is focusing on **OVERCOMING** the many desires - within and NOT escaping. Because a man of awareness is perfectly aware that ESCAPING IS NOT THE SOLUTION - OVERCOMING is.

24 hours you are FASTING and if you're always thinking of FOOD then what use it is - what is the value of your FASTING?

24 hours you stay away from women - you *act* as if you do not think of women, you do not think about SEX, and in reality if every minute and every second you are thinking of WOMEN - of SEX - of PLEASURES - then what is the use - what is the value of your MONKHOOD?

And this is exactly what is happening and it has been happening from the very beginning of time. Millions and millions of women, young girls are made VICTIM of the REPRESSED SEXUAL NEEDS of these so-called MONKS and SADHUS. Why does this happen? Because they all had the same question - how to escape from the challenges of the material world? And the answer they found was in growing long beards, applying thick Tilaks on their forehead...

Recently, a woman had asked a similar kind of question - and there are hundreds who come to me with the same question - they want to leave everything - they want to become a monk - they want to have peace - and the most idiotic thing is that they all think that by becoming a MONK - or by escaping - they all would find peace and happiness and joy!

JOY. PEACE. HAPPINESS - it is all within you. AND IF YOU CANNOT FIND IT WITHIN YOU THEN YOU WILL NOT FIND IT ANYWHERE - let this be very clear - to all my readers, followers - I insist - there is no need to go anywhere - there is no need to go to the HIMALAYAS - find your peace - find your happiness within you and then wherever you are - you become the HIMALAYA! That is the stage of a true YOGI - he needs no long beards, and no tilaks and no fancy dresses - wherever HE is, the HIMALAYA is - that is how SAI BABA is, that is how Bhagwan Ramana Maharishi is - that is how the great MEHER BABA is - that is how OSHO is. They have not escaped - they have lived very much within us and realized GOD. They have not escaped - they have lived within us and realized their 'self'!

And that is the message of Shri KETU - to all evolved souls who are reading this - let it be very clear that is the message of Shri KETU - **there is no need to go to the Himalayas** - *there is no need to go anywhere…*

> " The very idea of going somewhere is basically wrong. Nothing is going anywhere. Existence is now-here; it is moving towards a particular destiny. There is no destiny, there is no ultimate purpose. But we have been taught for centuries that existence is moving towards a certain goal and we have been also taught to live ambitiously, to prove that you are something, somebody: 'Reach somewhere'. But existence is absolutely purposeless. Its significance is not that of the marketplace. It is a totally different kind of significance: the significance of a roseflower, the significance of a bird on the wing – it is an end unto itself.
>
> **OSHO** "

But because you are being ignorant - you are not able to listen to what life is saying to you - what Shri Ketu is saying to you. Listen to life - FLOW WITH YOUR LIFE - but you don't believe in yourself, then how can you TRUST the flow of your life? You are always thinking that life may drag you somewhere - but Life is the greatest teacher - it never will drag you - it will always give you experiences that IF you take it positively - you will GROW as an individual - you will become MATURE as an individual. But you are turning a deaf ear to KETU - and so you will continue to suffer - NOT because of Shri KETU but simply because of your utter ignorance. Ignorance of not living in total acceptance.

> " Don't be angry at life. It is not life that is frustrating you; it is you who are not listening to life.
>
> **OSHO** "

Shri KETU wants you to listen to what your life is saying. ACCEPT all that life is providing you with a sense of gratitude and you will find peace within. But your expectation is huge - the MIND is always restless - and Shri KETU staunchly is against the MIND! The more you follow the monkey mind - the more you would find yourself in utter depression. Remember - the way is to reach the NO-MIND stage - and that is precisely what meditation is all about!

The mind is the world and the no-mind is freedom from the world. The mind is misery and no-mind is the end of misery and the beginning of ecstasy.

OSHO

Remember - We all are born as a NO-MIND - Let this sink into your heart as deeply as possible because, through that, a door opens. If you were born as a no-mind, then the mind is just a social product. It is nothing natural, it is cultivated. It has been put together on top of you. Deep down you are still free, you can get out of it. One can never get out of nature, but one can get out of the artificial any moment one decides to.

Meditation is a state of no-mind! You can not find meditation through the mind .. because mind will perpetuate itself! You can find meditation only by putting the mind aside, by being cool, indifferent, unidentified with the mind.

OSHO

And, NO-MIND is exactly what SHRI KETU is! Whenever KETU DASHA begins - and I share this with all my followers and readers - just put aside your mind - the message of SHRI KETU is - sit down and meditate - turn inwards, look within - BUT you suffer because you are focused all the time on 'what is happening outside' - who is doing what - who is going where - who is saying what about me - the whole time - your focus remains on the outside and if you continue to do so - you and all those who are going through KETU DASHA - are going to find life as hard as the mountain rock.

But the same life can become as soft as a cotton pillow - when you start turning inwards when you learn to OVERCOME the monkey mind.

"If you turn inward, you will find a space where there is a solution for everything." - Sadhguru

If you are a RAHU-ish (extrovert) person - you will find KETU dasha very difficult.

If you are a KETU-ish (introvert) person - you will excel - you will grow - you will transform inside-out during Shri Ketu Mahadasha!

Shri Ketu represents Lord Ganesha! Have you seen the idol of Lord Ganesha? You must have 'seen' millions of times. But have you ever observed? Observe. And if you observe - you will realize that Lord Ganesha has no head - no mind! The head that you see - is of the Elephant! And why Elephant? Because Elephant is the wisest being on this planet! And so it is a perfect representation of a GOD who is totally engrossed within - where the MIND is not at play - where the 'self' is constantly meditated upon! How beautiful is this representation of the greatest God of all - Lord Ganesha!

Whatever you worship on the outside - is what you become from the inside!

That is how 'idol worship' was introduced by the ancient seers and sages!

But in some parts - in Europe, in the Middle East - idol worship became a business of many priests and pundits - and so someone as great as the Prophet Muhammed, Jesus Christ, Gautama Buddha had to come in human form - to eliminate idol worship - and that is how Islam, Christianity, Buddhism came into existence - else the whole Middle East, the whole Europe worshipped idols of various Gods and Goddesses just like the Hindus worship idols! Whenever things go out of hand - become corrupt - divine interference is executed - that is how the cosmic law works - everything is watched - and action is also initiated - but only when the time is right!

There are instances where idols of Lord Ganesha have been found in the Middle East, South America and the Far East!

When you are running through KETU MAHADASHA - visit Lord Ganesha temple every Wednesday or Sunday. Worship Lord Ganesha - eat non-spicy food, if possible be more and more vegetarian - do all that your life demands - your survival demands - but bring God to your life, introduce God to your life - and be more and more meditative. While you work - remain focused within - to be meditative is not to sit for a few minutes and then forgot everything. To be meditative is to continue to work with your hands while you remain focused within!

> **66** Once you turn in, meditation has started. Meditation means the capacity to be joyously alone, the capacity to be joyously alone, the capacity to be happy with yourself. To be with yourself is meditation. The joy of aloneness, not the misery of loneliness, is meditation.
> **OSHO** **99**

To be with yourself is to be in harmony with Shri Ketu! To be with yourself is to be in meditation while you perform your daily activities!

Escaping is not the answer. A man who is not getting any success - escapes and becomes a monk - a man who has never tasted sexual bliss - runs away and becomes a monk - a man who is an utter failure - escapes and finds comfort in becoming a monk - but all of this is SHORT LIVED – someday, he gets back in the SAME TRAP that he had so cleverly escaped!

You will never become a Buddha - you will never attain spiritual liberation - you will never find happiness until you realize the basic truth - that it is not ESCAPING but FACING your own KARMIC DUES - that can truly liberate you from the unending sufferings of the birth and rebirth cycle.

Spiritualism is experienced - only when you have everything that you had wished for - and yet you drop all the pleasures - you have opted for monkhood NOT by chance but by CHOICE - you have millions of opportunities to enjoy sex - and yet you are no more interested - you have millions of opportunities to exercise power - and yet you are no more interested, you have thousands of treasures - and yet you are no more interested - you have all the happiness you had wished for - and yet you are no more interested - BECAUSE you have realized the truth - that all these are not going to LAST forever - that is how Prince Siddhartha realized - he was the greatest Prince - all pleasure was at his feet and yet one night, he left it all - not because of pain and suffering - not because of any failures - not by chance - but BY CHOICE! And that is how Prince Siddhartha was transformed into the greatest saint that world has ever known - **Gautama Buddha!** The most beautiful enlightened man who walked on this planet!

He did not escape because of any pain - he had all the happiness and pleasures - and yet he opted out - he renounced the material world - that is when real spiritual experiences are observed - but who wants to listen? People are shallow - and shallowness leads you to nowhere!

Happiness is within you. The key to success is also within you. The key is your 'quality of understanding' - the greater the quality, the greater is the understanding and it is only understanding that can help you sail smoothly through the many difficult times of human life!

Let 'understanding' be your only law!

And my goal is to help all my followers and my readers to simply 'understand'.

Understand the depth of life - and you will be able to do so - only when you overcome your MIND - for the MIND is shallow - but your heart has the depth - and meditation is simply a journey from the Mind to the Heart - from the shallowness to the depth of your inner being!

Shri KETU loves all those beautiful souls who are turning inwards - who are taking the efforts to look within - to introspect - to 'self-realize'! And so the answer to your question is in two simple words - 'Turn inwards' - meditate.

It is going to be difficult - it is difficult for a Rahu-ish person to turn inwards - but it is not impossible! So try to control your Mind - work towards overcoming your MIND and then there is no need to escape - to go anywhere - you simply would find your answers - at the same place where it all had begun!

Look within, meditate - that's the message of Shri Ketu - the enlightened Lord! To meditate is to have no thoughts - when there are thoughts - it is a distraction, when there are no thoughts - it is meditation - says Bhagwan Ramana Maharshi! Don't just meditate - be meditation!

> When all thoughts cease – there is nowhere to go – you simply are at home. This at-homeness is meditation.
> **OSHO**

Suffering is of the MIND. But because you become the MIND - you suffer! Remember - the nature of the MIND is to wander - YOU are not the mind.

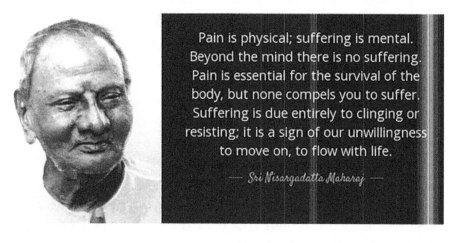

Pain is physical; suffering is mental. Beyond the mind there is no suffering. Pain is essential for the survival of the body, but none compels you to suffer. Suffering is due entirely to clinging or resisting; it is a sign of our unwillingness to move on, to flow with life.

— *Sri Nisargadatta Maharaj* —

Shri Ketu is all about being DETACHED! The Shri KETU DASHA is a signal that becomes more and more DETACHED - but how will you become detached? You are so much attached to everything that is in your life! Your wife/husband, house, family - and it is this attachment that brings miseries.

Buddha says "the root of suffering is attachment."

People who are very much attached - who have the typical nature of Rahu - that is to go on clinging - suffer at the hands of KETU - not because of KETU - but because of their nature of clinging - *it is ignorance that pulls you towards attachment and it is consciousness that moves you towards detachment!*

Buddha says - you only lose what you cling to!

And then comes the pain, the suffering - it is all of the MIND - it is all at the mental state and it all happens because of clinging, because of attachments!

Shri Ketu wants you to become more and more detached - for real love blossoms only through detachment! Love is not attachment. Love knows no attachment, and that which knows attachment is NOT love. Love blossoms only when there is no attachment,no posessiveness - when love is detached.

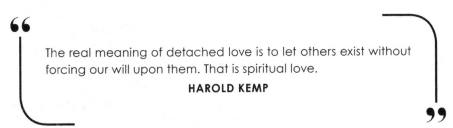

> "
> The real meaning of detached love is to let others exist without forcing our will upon them. That is spiritual love.
> **HAROLD KEMP**
> "

Let detachment be the answer to all your miseries - to all my readers and followers - if you are going through Shri Ketu Mahadasha - learn to become more and more detached and you would be able to do this - only when you overcome your Mind - for the MIND is habitual of clinging - but the heart is like a flowing river - never attached - and yet filled with abundance of love - focus on your heart - focus within - that's the message - the only message of Shri Ketu!

Escaping is easier. But escaping is not the solution. Let this be very clear. The only way out is through facing your difficulties with deep faith and understanding. To understand everything is to forgive everything!

Let understanding be your only law.

Jai Shri Ganesha. Jai Guru.

Question 16

When Rahu and Ketu are at 29 degrees in a particular house, what happens?

This is the beginning of a new story - good story/ bad story - but a new story is in the making - when RAHU is at 29 degrees - an absolutely brand new story - story of new desires - story that has begun because the soul in its journey - has finished with the previous desires and has 'arrived' on this physical plane to begin with a totally new set of desires related to the house it is placed in!

So a new story has begun and you are asking - previous house stories to be re-wound? Re-played? - That is not the reality - the past desires of the past house have been fulfilled - and now a new story of new desires has just begin!

This one life may fall short - to satisfy - to complete the new story of desires - may be a couple of births and rebirths until the whole 29 degrees are covered by RAHU - the significator of your desires!

Somebody had asked why RAHU KETU are always retrograde - why they move behind - and the answer is - because your shadow always moves behind you and not ahead of you!

And so at 29 degrees - which is a degree of great significance - RAHU has just moved in a new house - he is coming from behind - he is your shadow - wherever you move - he is following you – "Be aware of your shadow" were the words of a great Sufi saint - "Be aware of your shadow!" How deep are these words - only a man of awareness can realize the depth of it - be aware of your shadow - the shadow is nothing but the shadow of your desires - and so be aware of your desires - for they may drag you to the most miserable situations - and so the great Sufi saint says, "Be aware of your shadow!" beautiful!

A man was reading a story. He was alone on a farm in a small hut, in deep darkness of the night. The story said that shadows are ghosts. He became so frightened that he looked at his own shadow, and started running. Again, he looked and the shadow was there. The natural logic was that he was not running fast enough, so he started running faster and faster. The faster he ran, the faster the shadow followed him.

And this is how the faster you run to satisfy your desires, the faster the desires (shadow) follow you! You think that by satisfying a desire you would overcome the desire - but that is a myth - the more you fall for your desires, the more you would be chased by your desires!

So, the man became very tired, so much so that he could not run anymore and just sat under the shadow of a tree. And the moment he sat under the shadow of the tree, his shadow disappeared.

Now look at this - this is of significance and this is so beautiful - the moment he sat under the shadow of the tree - his shadow disappeared! - The moment you sit down - the moment you surrender to your master - your lord - the shadow of desires no more exists - it starts evaporating!

> 66
> You must surrender your judgement to the Lord, then the Lord will assume full responsibility and be the guardian, guide and motivating power.
> **SAI BABA**
> 99

But who wants to surrender? And who wants to stop, pause and turn inwards? - People are running after desires - one desire ends and a new begins - you are always found in the queue of desires - a queue that just never ends!

The moment the man stops running, and sits down under the *tree* - the *shadow of the tree* fades away the shadow of the man! You see - this 'tree' is the holy divine master – SadhGuru - the Lord of lords! And when you are coming - surrendering yourself in totality - to the *shadow* of the Lord (tree) - where is the question of you chasing your desires, and making your life miserable? You have finally arrived - you have finally found peace in the holy presence of the Lord, your master!

The way to get rid of your shadow is not to run away - is not to escape - but to look into its 'eyes' and defeat it! Don't run away from the problem - focus on the problem and you will find a solution.

The moment you realize what is RAHU for your 'self' - what it means as far as YOU as an individual - you are slowly coming to the 'light of consciousness'!

It is good that people are looking at astrology - What is astrology? It is a science that is bringing you closer to the 'light' of consciousness - at least, you are becoming aware - of the *state* of your planetary positions - even though this awareness is just a tip of the iceberg - it is good to see you becoming conscious - though very much on the outer circumference - but still, it is good when I see some genuine followers of astrology - who are not just interested to know what I am going to be - but are more interested to know 'who am I'!

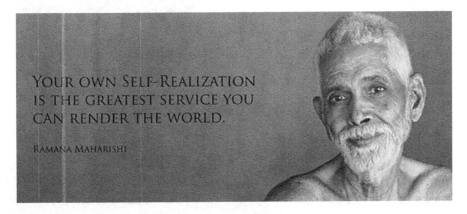

YOUR OWN SELF-REALIZATION IS THE GREATEST SERVICE YOU CAN RENDER THE WORLD.

RAMANA MAHARISHI

I am for all those fellows who have certain depth - who are not interested in debating or correcting or showing off their intellectualism - but who are purely living and following their hearts - such are the people whom I welcome - the others - I always excuse.

Rahu when at 29 degrees is extremely powerful and such a man should be careful - for at 29 degrees, Rahu is empowered with 'too much' energy to spoil the game.

Lao Tzu - one of the greatest spiritual masters puts it - "TOO MUCH - is the ONLY sin."

So my suggestion for an individual with 29 degrees Rahu - is - "Be aware of your shadow - be aware of indulging in - Too Much."

Jai Shri Ganesha. Jai Guru.

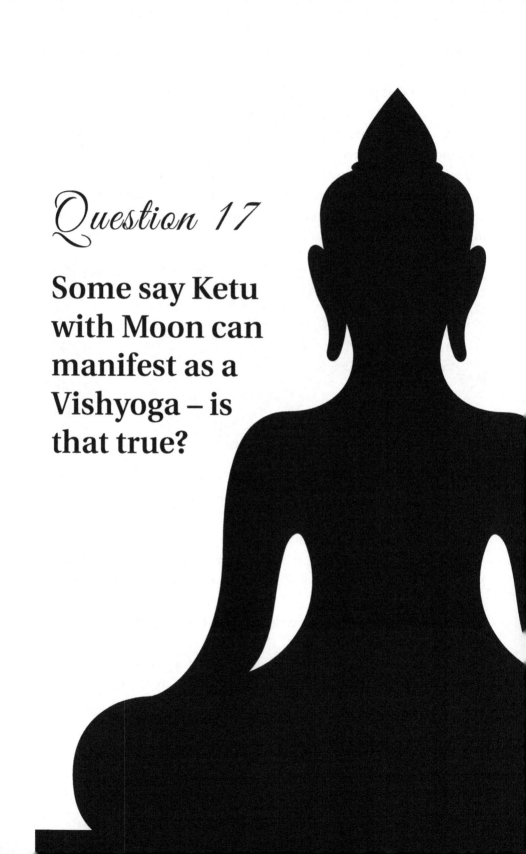

Question 17

Some say Ketu with Moon can manifest as a Vishyoga – is that true?

KETU is a healer. And so, KETU + MOON is **NOT** a Vishyog – **it is a SHIVYOG!**

It is very unfortunate that people are defaming KETU – but till I am ALIVE, till my fellow travellers are ALIVE – we will ensure that nobody defames KETU – till the last breath of my life – I will keep saying AGAIN and AGAIN – that KETU is absolutely HARMLESS – it is the greatest irony of this KALI YUG that the **one who is a provider** is *being labelled as a Killer!*

In D9 or any 'D' chart – the conjunction of MOON + KETU is definitely a BLESSING IN DISGUISE!

KETU distorts the MIND – KETU makes the MIND disappear, and it is only when there is NO MIND – that meditation is possible, spiritual progress is possible. With MIND – meditation is NOT possible, with NO MIND – meditation manifests!

For spiritual life, for spiritual progress – KETU is necessary.

For material life – RAHU is necessary.

Moon coming in contact with KETU – followed with a beautiful positive aspect with JUPITER is the most fantastic placement for spiritual upliftment.

KETU – the focus is on TURNING IN.

RAHU – the focus is on TURNING ON.

KETU MOON – is a strange guy. He may have sex but if a time comes in his life then he may simply drop the idea of having SEX – forever – and that leads him to SANYAS – a life of celibacy, a life of an ascetic.

RAHU MOON – is a very sexual person. He goes on having sex, many sexual fantasies – he gets TURNED ON very easily – in fact, for a woman to attract a MOON RAHU man is pretty easy. RAHU MOON man is too weak when it comes to the opposite sex, they fall easily to their temptations! RAHU MOON men, therefore, become easy victims of sexual relationships.

But MOON KETU – is a man without HEAD. Just a positive guidance – and he never ever goes back to sex – he has moved beyond sex – he has embarked on the journey beyond!

> 66 Sex is a meeting of two bodies - the most superficial meeting. Love is the meeting of minds - deeper than Sex, but yet not very deep. Prayer is the meeting of Beings - but still two remain two. Meditation is the ULTIMATE MEETING - the two disappear, only ONE remains.
>
> **OSHO** 99

Just for my close followers and readers, I am sharing a wonderful experience in relation to this beautiful MOON KETU conjunction – and it is so wonderful that it touched my heart – it may also touch...

On a beautiful evening, I was reading about a man who went on to become a great healer – a Yogi! I found his birthday and birth-year. Just casually, I cast his horoscope and voila – there it was – a MOON with KETU in the sign of Pisces!

And the best part is that I had a definite hunch before casting his horoscope that his MOON must have some connection with KETU – and it was – it really was, and it was in PISCES – the 'marriage' of Moon and Ketu had happened in his PISCES sign!

And because KETU is exalted in PISCES (the 12th sign and one of my favorite signs of all 12 zodiacs) – KETU proved extremely beneficial for him – his KETU with MOON in Pisces worked great wonders – spiritual wonders for him!

One has to realize what does EXALT in reality mean.

Mohan, one day, asked me, "What is this thing called EXALT in astrology?"

I said, "Mohan – you have asked a beautiful question…"

Exalt is the state of MATURITY. What happens when you MATURE – what happens when your bonds mature?

When a savings bond matures, you get the principal amount plus all of the accrued interest.

Similarly, when a planet comes to its EXALTATION point – it means it has MATURED – now it is READY to PAY you all that you have invested (GOOD KARMA) along with the INTEREST (Benefits).

In the unending cycle of BIRTH and DEATH – every individual goes through 'births' in which a certain planet is either at inception level (debilitated) or maturity level (exalt state).

A man with EXALTED planets generally has many good qualities – so he or she lives by following certain ETHICS and principles. It is obvious that such men of ethics earn less – because in the AGE OF RAHU – VALUES have taken the backseat and GREED has taken the front-seat! The DO MORE is in ACTION – ethical people cannot DO MORE – they believe in DOING based on the NEEDS and not WANTS.

A man with DEBILITATED planets generally has qualities of lower nature – so earning plenty of money in this RAHU AGE becomes easy for HIM – because he has absolutely NO VALUES, NO ETHICS, NO

PRINCIPLES and there is nothing that could STOP him from earning MONEY – for such men and women – the saying:

BAAP BADA NA BHAIYA – SABSE BADA RUPAYA (- बाप बड़ा ना भइया, सबसे बड़ा पैसा) goes well. In fact, they have been believing in this philosophy for many births and so they carry on – with their stupidity – earning millions of rupees/dollars. It is a different story that they are NEVER happy with what they have – the feeling of dissatisfaction continues to HAUNT them – they die in utter misery – pain and dissatisfaction.

Exalted planets may not make you RICH or a Millionaire – but they will certainly bring an abundance of wisdom, love, satisfaction and happiness, joy to your life.

One has to understand – how a MATURED being will behave and how a novice would!

A matured being is aware of the FAKE GOLD that the world is running behind.

A novice – a not-so-evolved soul keeps running behind money – his focus is on MONEY. A matured being's focus is on SELF GROWTH! He understands the fact that when SELF GROWTH happens – money comes on its own – you don't have to chase money!

One has to understand maturity in depth. KETU is a highly matured being – a meditative being.

It is difficult to find a mature person. Because every person – you come across has some desire – either the desire is to have money – or the desire is to have moksha. Either the desire is to have power – or the desire is to experience GOD. The desire is there – and a MATURE person – is a person without any desire – HE is the BUDDHA!

If you meet BUDDHA – you will find HIM with absolutely NO DESIRE. He is totally RELAXED. You may provoke HIM – you may go on pressing all the 'buttons' that you have known – but you cannot disturb the Buddha – you cannot make him angry and you cannot make him happy – HE is relaxing with the WHOLE – your words won't affect HIM.

> Maturity is Not to desire things – maturity is Relaxing with the Whole. Immaturity is conflict, struggle, the part fighting with the Whole. The part coming in tune with the whole, coming to a harmonious settlement with the whole – not in defeat but in understanding – is maturity. To realize that nothing can be done is Maturity.
>
> **OSHO**

NOTHING CAN BE DONE. And that is the whole message of KETU – of the divine masters – that you simply have to go with the flow – you have to simply go on ACCEPTING – living with ACCEPTANCE!

The central concept of Buddhism and Buddha is of TATHATA! Tathata is living with suchness. Such is the situation – such is the happening – it is RAINING – you cannot do anything – you simply live in the suchness – TATHATA!

Understand the fact that MOON KETU conjunction is a beautiful conjunction that provides you with all the qualities that can help you to LIVE YOUR LIFE IN ACCEPTANCE.

For a matured person – there is NO goal. To have goals is like having toys! The matured person is perfectly aware that there is no need to have any toys (goals) – there is no need to go anywhere – to seek anything on the OUTSIDE – all that is – is WITHIN – you just have to come to it – realize it by TURNING INWARDS.

> Drop the idea of becoming somebody because you are already a masterpiece. You cannot be improved. You have only to come to it, to know it, to realize it.
>
> **OSHO**

Moon when comes with KETU – what happens?

Moon – the MIND is now under the command of KETU! But this conjunction becomes more matured from spiritual perspective when MOON and KETU not only conjunct but fall in the SAME NAKSHATRA! Then the 'honeymoon' truly takes place – and then through this honeymoon what comes out – what manifests is – deep meditation and it is beautiful!

Nowhere to go...just in....

OSHO

Just in...just turning inward – that's KETU and it is this KETU that can bring a great transformation within you – and real transformation happens only when it moves you from the INSIDE!

The whole story of KETU – is the INSIDE STORY.

The whole story of RAHU – is the OUTSIDE STORY.

As long as you remain stuck in the OUTSIDE STORY – you remain miserable.

The moment you sit down – close your eyes and start exploring the INSIDE STORY – you start slipping out of the MIND (Moon) – and the moment there is no MIND – there is no misery – you become FREE – you experience FREEDOM for the very FIRST TIME in your life – for the REAL FREEDOM comes only when you slip out of the MIND.

> 66
> Mind is your prison. No-mind is your freedom. Mind is your ignorance, no-mind is your enlightenment. Move from mind to no-mind. This is the whole path, this is the whole religion.
> **OSHO**
> 99

KETU unlocks the 'Prison' (MIND) – it is KETU that leads you to the final LIBERATION (moksha) – KETU, therefore, exalts in the 12th sign of Pisces – the 12th house of the KAALPURUSH – 12th – the house of liberation – END – end of the cycle of birth and rebirths!

And LIBERATION comes only when the SOUL has overcome the MIND – it is a MYTH that liberation comes after death.

Liberation of the state of total freedom (MOKSHA) comes to you when you are very much ALIVE in human form. The great Yogis experience MOKSHA very much when they are alive. Jesus, Muhammed, Mahavira, Buddha – and the many divine masters attained liberation when alive and NOT after death.

KETU MOON can JUMP into the unknown – it brings COURAGE – it brings INTELLIGENCE – it overcomes INTELLECTUALISM which is a poor substitute for INTELLIGENCE!

A KETU MOON man or woman is not to be taken lightly – a tremendous energy is within them – how they use it – depends on the sign in which this conjunction happens and the aspects that influence this HOLY CONJUNCTION!

KETU MOON is one the best conjunctions – in fact, it is even better than MOON JUPITER!

MOON JUPITER brings EGO – it brings more strength to the MIND – the MIND becomes powerful – this is a good conjunction from material perspective – but from spiritual perspective – it often becomes a hurdle – such a man or woman is obsessed to DO GOOD – doing GOOD is good – but getting obsessed to do good often boomerangs and leads them to depression.

The whole essence of MEDITATION is to drop the MIND – to overcome the MIND – and who can be the most suitable than Sri KETU – one who has NO HEAD, NO MIND. Ketu can then take MOON under its control – it is a beautiful conjunction that helps you to CONTROL YOUR MIND. Mind is a beautiful SLAVE – but a dangerous master!

When MOON KETU – MIND can be enslaved.

When MOON RAHU – MIND makes you its SLAVE.

And Buddha says:

"RULE YOUR MIND BEFORE THE MIND RULES OVER YOU."

The MIND is restless – the nature of the MIND is being restless. A man or woman ruled by the MIND is always restless – but if you watch – if you observe the Buddha – a meditative being – HIS MIND IS STILL – HE is not restless – HE is not worried – HE is not disturbed – HE is no more meditating – HE IS MEDITATION!

> No thought, no mind, no choice – just being silent, rooted in yourself.
>
> **OSHO**

That is how a meditative being is – deeply rooted within.

A woman – a man with MOON KETU conjunction should worship Lord Ganesha – should meditate on HIS name – Aum Gam Ganapataye Namaha.

Many times – almost all times – a person having prominent KETU is often a devotee of Ganesha or Shiva!

It is through the worship of Ganesha and Shiva – that you will be able to STILL the wavering MIND – and once the MIND becomes STILL – overcoming it becomes far easier than otherwise!

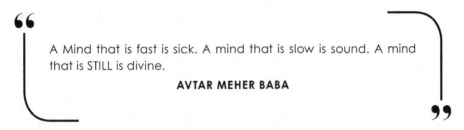

A Mind that is fast is sick. A mind that is slow is sound. A mind that is STILL is divine.

AVTAR MEHER BABA

The conjunction of KETU with the MIND (Moon) – is a signal that the 'potential' to transcend – the 'potential' to progress spiritually is there – IF support of positive energy (Jupiter drishti – 5, 7, 9 or aspect with Jupiter – Trine) exists in the birth chart. If not, then it can go waste – leading to many depressions and frustrations.

Because KETU wants support of GURU – when GURU stands with HIS GRACE (Drishti) on this beautiful conjunction – then you are meeting a man who is going to change – going to transform – going to be a BUDDHA!

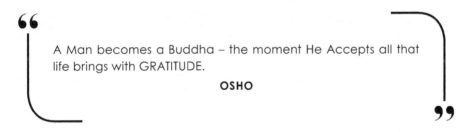

A Man becomes a Buddha – the moment He Accepts all that life brings with GRATITUDE.

OSHO

And you will be able to ACCEPT only when the MIND becomes NIL and it becomes NIL only with the arrival of KETU! KETU, therefore, is a great blessing in disguise – it is natural that the process is painful – the process of enlightenment is always painful – because it brings the destruction of the elusive MIND!

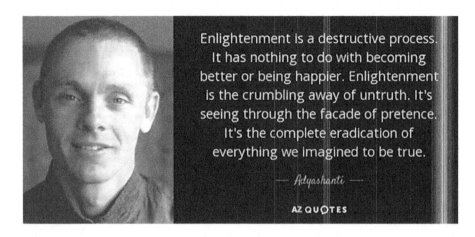

Enlightenment is a destructive process. It has nothing to do with becoming better or being happier. Enlightenment is the crumbling away of untruth. It's seeing through the facade of pretence. It's the complete eradication of everything we imagined to be true.

— *Adyashanti* —

AZ QUOTES

All the illusions that you imagined to be TRUE – are burned up – so as to bring you FACE to FACE with the TRUTH – the ultimate TRUTH.

And TRUTH – you can face only when the MIND is no more.

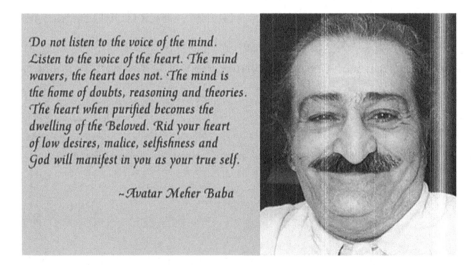

Do not listen to the voice of the mind. Listen to the voice of the heart. The mind wavers, the heart does not. The mind is the home of doubts, reasoning and theories. The heart when purified becomes the dwelling of the Beloved. Rid your heart of low desires, malice, selfishness and God will manifest in you as your true self.

~Avatar Meher Baba

One of the greatest saints – Meher Baba – the man who transformed many mad men into enlightened beings! And he travelled across the world – millions and millions followed him – but he rarely would talk with anyone – for the major part of his life – he would simply write – if someone would come to seek His darshan – Meher Baba would write – BLESSINGS.

And that's all – but even those written words would move – would transform the person in totality!

MOON KETU can make you a man of heart – a woman of heart and a heart-full man or woman is beautiful. Such a man – such a woman can RELATE to the words of the master – such a man, such a woman can progress in the true sense!

Realize – and I have been insisting to all my followers, readers and fellow travellers – that REALIZE is the word – and realization happens through the HEART and not the MIND. Realization happens through INTELLIGENCE and NOT intellectualism.

But who wants to listen? Shallowness has taken over this world – but among these shallow men and women – there are a few who can arise above the monkey MIND – my answers are for those selective beings – beings who are followers of the HEART and NOT of the MIND!

Let the MIND evaporate – KETU can do it – the question is whether you are willing to do it by realizing the many benefits of KETU – by having a positive perspective towards KETU – towards life – towards yourself – because it is only when you are POSITIVE – you can appreciate all that is positive – when you LOVE yourself – you can love others – when you are happy – you can spread happiness around – so FIRST, the focus has to be on – YOU!

To focus on yourself is NOT selfishness – it is simply BEING YOURSELF!

Be Yourself. People don't have to like you, and you don't have to care.

You don't have to do anything special to get LIKES – you just have to Be Yourself – those who can vibrate with your thoughts – with your sharing will come – will be pulled towards you – because always remember. there is always somebody out there – WHO UNDERSTANDS YOU – who resonates with you!

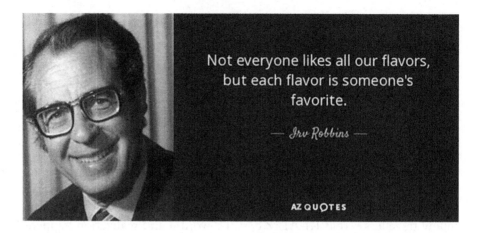

Not everyone likes all our flavors, but each flavor is someone's favorite.

— Irv Robbins —

AZ QUOTES

So come – come you all and focus WITHIN. Spend every day – a few minutes in a closed room with your 'SELF' – meditating – breathing – breathe in – breathe out and focus on the name of the Lord. While you do so – there is absolutely no need of any techniques – techniques are of the MIND and the moment you start seeking techniques to meditate – you are bringing forth the monkey mind – nothing is ever going to manifest – so no techniques – just FEELING – just LOVE – just the nectar of your DEVOTION and that is ENOUGH – to take you towards the higher altitudes of Consciousness!

People like to talk a lot – but talking takes you away from your 'Self' – by talking, you may make many 'connections' – these 'connections' may help you to prosper in life – but from within, you become poorer – you move away from your SELF – you get into a lot of 'noise' – and then you wonder "What is going wrong in my life?"

Nothing is wrong in your life – but everything is going wrong WITHIN you – the way is to COME BACK HOME – the way is to RETURN to your SOURCE and the SOURCE is WITHIN you – so close your eyes, and start moving back towards the SOURCE – towards the 'SELF' – only then there is a possibility to experience PEACE – only then there is going to be LOVE, JOY and HAPPINESS in your life.

It all begins WITHIN and KETU's message, therefore, is in just two words – ***TURN IN.***

"TO TURN IN MEANS
ALL THE TWENTY-FOUR HOURS...
Go on turning in.
Whenever you find a moment to turn, turn.
And it is such a simple act to turn within –
nobody's help is needed.
No ladder is needed,
no door has to be opened.
Just close your eyes and look in.
Sitting in a bus, traveling in a train...
you can do it any time,
and slowly slowly
you don't even need to close your eyes.
The remembrance simply remains, of its own
accord." - OSHO

Meditate.
Jai Shri Ganesha. Jai Guru.

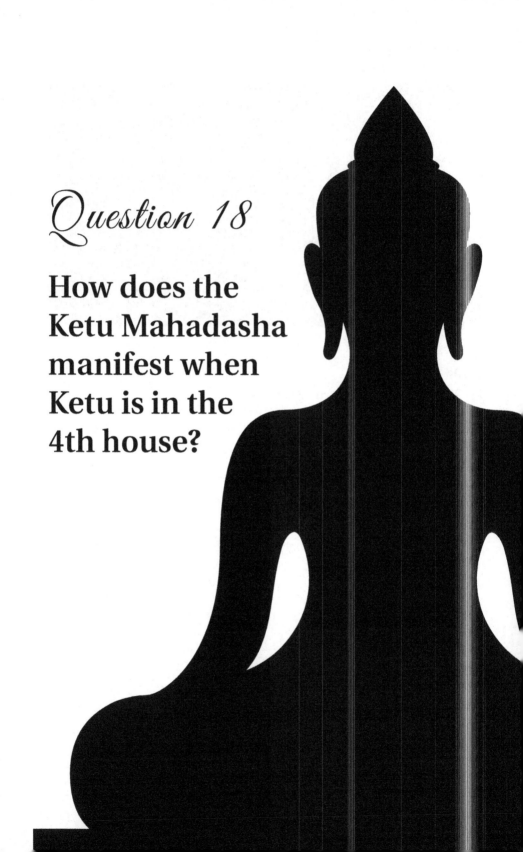

Question 18

How does the Ketu Mahadasha manifest when Ketu is in the 4th house?

If you cannot understand the message of Sri Ketu, then you will suffer. If you can understand what Ketu wants you to do, then you will find bliss!

Ketu in the fourth house brings Rahu in the tenth (obsession with career matters). Such a man or woman is very ambitious by nature. Ambition makes you run and run and run until a day comes when you cannot run anymore, and then comes the frustration. Then you start assuming that it is because of Ketu. The problem is NOT Ketu - the problem is your ambition.

66

Ambition is a poison, but the label on the bottle says - it is pure nectar.

OSHO

99

So Rahu in 10 - people make their life a mess by being too ambitious, and then they ask, "Why am I so miserable?"

Ketu is the opposite of Rahu.

Asexual is Ketu. Sexual is Rahu. Forgiving is Ketu. Revengeful is Rahu. Selfless is Ketu. Selfish is Rahu. Being content is the nature of Ketu. Being ambitious is the nature of Rahu. Do as much is needed is the slogan of Ketu. DO MORE is the slogan of Rahu.

Rahu is doing too much.

66

Too much is the only Sin

LAO TZU

99

The hurdle that you feel is of the MIND. The MIND wants too much whereas Ketu is saying Slow down. Then you feel it is a hurdle - in reality, it is not. When your job goes away - when you are fired - when you become unemployed - it is the message of Ketu that you have been running a lot - now is the time to sit back and recharge yourself by turning inward and realizing your shortcomings.

But people take it otherwise. They start shouting and screaming. Once it happened - a young man was shouting, "GOD, WHERE ARE YOU? GOD, I WANT MY ANSWER. GOD, HOW CAN YOU BE SO IGNORANT?"

Now GOD thought this must be settled for once and all. So God came and said, "How old are you and how many years have you been working?"

The young man said, "I am 37, and I have been working for the last 13 years..."

God said, "Then those 13 years - who was taking care of you?"

The young man said, "YOU were taking care of me."

God said, "Then you forgot those 13 years, and for just 13 months of unemployment, you are screaming and yelling at me! Who is ignorant-you or Me?"

And this is what happens - people forget.

And that is the whole message of Buddha - in one word "SAMMASTI" - Remember.

For 40 years, Buddha moves around the land that is now Bihar, and all he does is to help the IGNORANT MEN to REMEMBER.

Sammasti means Remember. Just remember all that you have been blessed with, and the moment you remember - you become GRATEFUL.

AND the moment GRATITUDE comes in your life - you start surrendering to the existence, to the Almighty!

And this state of surrender is what Ketu loves. Meditation happens only when you live your life in total surrender.

Ketu is ZERO. And the human being is running to become a Hero.

Ketu is saying - Enough. But the human being is not willing to listen.

Ketu is saying - find a balance in your life - along with your sexual and material desires, let there also be an essence of spirituality in your life. But people who are not willing to listen become frustrated - it is not life that is frustrating you, it is you who are not listening to life.

Ketu is connected to Goddess Saraswati. And those who have been following me closely on various forums can very well understand how it is all related. Ketu represents Shri Ganesha, and Saraswati (Vidya) relates closely to Shri Ganesha. So, KETU Mahadasha is always good for all kinds of studies - higher, lower, medium - simply because the whole message of Ketu is to raise your awareness, and on a material level, one can raise his or her awareness by educating themselves with the subjects of their liking.

So, definitely Ketu Mahadasha is good for higher studies. The whole message of Ketu is to focus on your self-growth. Earning money is not Ketu's domain, but there is absolutely nobody as wise as Ketu. Wisdom comes only when Ketu supports. Buddha is least interested in money - a meditative man is least interested in money. Buddha may not give you money but wherever Buddha walked - prosperity showered and it showered so heavily that the world was moved - the whole villages and towns were moved, and yet Buddha never cared...because to even think that something good is happening because of ME leads one to Ego and then this Ego becomes a hurdle!

So, Ketu is not the source of hurdle - Ketu is simply helping you to relax - to slow down but the RAHU within you always makes you restless...and then the same story repeats and this is how life after life, the same story goes on repeating - the pattern remains the same - just the design keeps changing.

Jesus says to a wealthy merchant - He has come for the very first time to the merchant's home and Jesus says, "Share your wealth with the poor who are waiting at your door."

And the merchant happily shares his wealth with the poor! Now to an ignorant man - Jesus would appear as a hurdle - as a pain. But for a conscious person - Jesus's message is a blessing in disguise!

This is deep, and time is short. But through this answer - I want to again make all my readers, followers and fellow travelers aware that you will feel frustrated during Ketu Dasha if you are too ambitious and too ignorant and too focused on the outside. But the same Ketu Dasha can become one of the greatest periods of your life - one of the greatest blessings of your life, if and only if, you turn your focus from the outside towards the inside.

If you can sit down. If you can self realize that it is time to slow down and focus on your self-growth then and only then, Ketu can transform your life into a beautiful poem. Then life will be no more the same - then life will be no more misery, but a garden of bliss. Then you can transform, you can change, and then this change will lead to prosperity in your life when Venus Dasha begins!

The period of Ketu Mahadasha is to sow the seeds of success that later in Venus Dasha start blossoming into a beautiful flower.

Jai Shri Ganesha. Jai Guru.

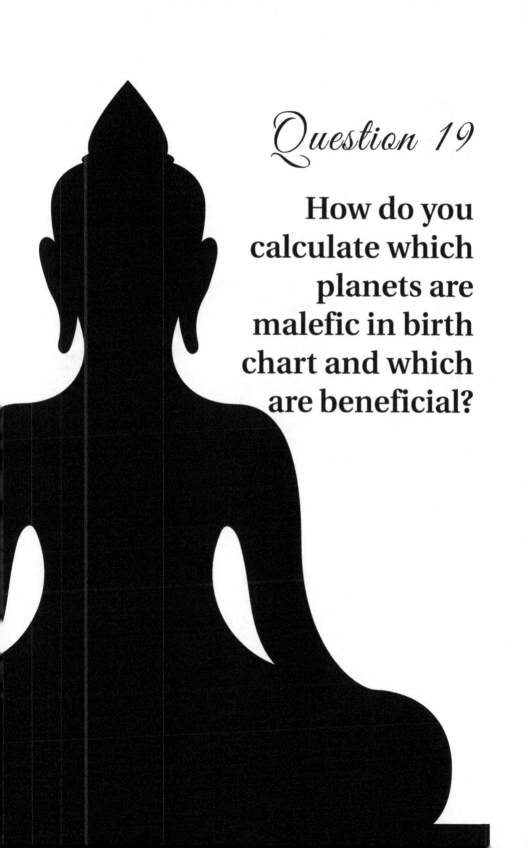

Question 19

How do you calculate which planets are malefic in birth chart and which are beneficial?

 The ancient Indian food was, in reality, a reflection of our galaxy!

The 'thali' or 'Indian Lunch-Plate' was filled in such a way that it represents all the planets and the SUN of our galaxy!

That is how advanced and rich our ancient culture was – it respected each and every planet of our galaxy. There was no discrimination – the ancient seers were perfectly aware that it *is* not the 'planets' that are good or bad – it is the 'receptive' power of individuals that decides what is good and what is bad for him or her.

If your 'antenna' is not receptive to a certain channel (planet) – or is not able to smoothly display the 'signal' of the channel (planet) – your television screen (life) would mess with the display (effect) of the channel (planet).

Who is to blame? The channel (planet) or the 'antenna' (you)?

Sugar is sweet. But for a diabetic person, it is a sweet 'poison'! Who is to blame – who is bad and who is good in this case – sugar or the diabetic person?

Bitter gourd or Karela is extremely bitter in taste. Commonly, not many can eat it – for many, it is not a much-desired vegetable – but for a diabetic person – the same much-hated bitter gourd is a life-saver! Who is bad and who is good here?

No planet in any birth chart is malefic or benefic – it is human beings who have the habit of discriminating – in reality, every planet in your birth chart has come with a 'message' – because you fall short of 'receiving' and 'understanding' the 'message' – you end up asking which planet is causing you trouble and which planet is rewarding you with goodies!

In reality – the trouble is not caused by any planet – and this is of great significance. The trouble is caused because from many past lives – you have been messing up with the 'energy' of that planet – and due to over-messing – now in this life – you aren't able to receive the 'energy' of the same planet in harmony, in full form.

So, the planet has nothing to do with your good or bad – all it has to do with is how you have 'evolved' as an individual – how fine-tuned your 'antenna' is!

> **"**
>
> If you suffer it is because of you, if you feel blissful it is because of you. Nobody else is responsible – only you and you alone. You are your hell and your heaven too.
>
> **OSHO**
>
> **"**

But people don't get it. How can they? When the astrologers themselves have been categorizing planets and stars in the good and bad list. When 'ignorance' becomes your guiding force – you would find yourself in utter darkness – and the height is – when you start believing this darkness as the truth!

And that is what is happening. Astrology has become a Business of FEAR. Create fear, and then start looting. Fear sells faster than FAITH! This is the outcome of this Kali Yug (Dark Age) – Age of Ignorance!

> "
> Everything is perfect in God's creation. Ignorance and suffering exist only in the minds of people.
> **SRI RAMANA MAHARSHI**
> "

One who speaks the truth is violently opposed, ridiculed, offended. Truth is very hard to digest. Millions of them who want to hear the false will oppose you - you will be labelled as a fool – but don't get lost, don't give up.

Once, the divine master said to the young man, **"You will be rejected several times, but don't give up."**

The young man bowed before the master and said, *"Why more rejections and less acceptance?"*

And the master smiled – looked up and showed him the highest mountain – then he said, **"How many would accept the challenge to reach the peak of that mountain?"**

And the young man said, *"Very few."*

Then the master asked, **"How many would reject the challenge to reach the 'peak'?"**

The young man said, **"Many."**

The master smiled, raised him up, he looked into the eyes of the young man and said, "You are that **'peak'** – so you would face more rejections and less acceptance."

The more you move towards the 'peak' (truth) – the more you would be facing more rejections and less acceptance. More dislikes and fewer likes. Sounds hard? But that is how the truth is – very, very hard. The truth isn't always beautiful and beautiful words aren't always the truth.

> 66
>
> Truth is not always hard to find; it is often staring you in the face. The problem with truth is that it is hard to believe. It is even harder to get other people to believe.
>
> **WALTER DARBY BANNARD**
>
> 99

The willingness to hear hard truth is vital not only for CEOs of big corporations but also for anyone who loves the truth. Sometimes the truth sounds like bad news, but it is just what we need.

— *Bill Gates* —

And the TRUTH is – that no planet is good or bad. You will find millions of books on how to find malefic or benefic planets – but no one is going to tell you why they 'become' malefic and how to transform these so-called malefic into benefic planets.

I don't believe in 'parrot-talk' – I believe in 'self-talk'. By reading the books, you will talk like a parrot – you become a 'limited version' – someone who can travel from A to Z – then the doors close – then there is no further going! And that is how the majority of astrologers have become – 'limited versions'!

> 66
>
> Logic will get you from A to B. Imagination will take you everywhere.
>
> **ALBERT EINSTEIN**
>
> 99

But I would want all my followers to become – 'UN-limited versions' – someone who can go beyond the set boundaries – someone who would follow his or her heart, someone who has a certain depth of understanding!

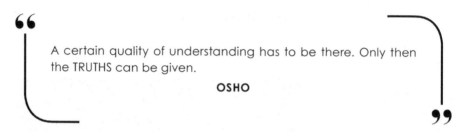

> A certain quality of understanding has to be there. Only then the TRUTHS can be given.
>
> **OSHO**

People approach me with questions like "What is the purpose of my life?" – They want me to read their birth charts to find the purpose of THEIR life! And this the height of IGNORANCE! No astrologer or no man can TELL you the purpose of YOUR life – you have to find the purpose of your life – through your own 'self' – meditate, introspect – look within, turn inwards – but nobody wants to do the real thing – they want everything – READYMADE – and so I ignore such men, what else can be done! It is sad to see the current state of things.

People have fancy ideas about finding the purpose of life! I have met people across the world and they all have different ideas – but my answer to all my followers who are unnecessarily putting a lot of stress on finding the so-called purpose of life is in the following quote of His Holiness – The Dalai Lama.

> Our primary purpose in this life is to help others. And if you can't help them, at least don't hurt them.
>
> **DALAI LAMA**

Further, to get a deeper understanding of the purpose of human life – the following quote of the Dalai Lama, throws more light:

I believe that the very purpose of life is to be happy. From the very core of our being, we desire contentment. In my own limited experience I have found that the more we care for the happiness of others, the greater is our own sense of well-being.

— *Dalai Lama* —

But common men are not bothered to go deeper. They are happy to live a shallow life – happy to derive some shallow meanings – something that they can digest. And thus the categorization of planets, stars – continues… when in reality – neither RAHU is bad, neither KETU is bad, neither SUN is bad, neither MOON is bad – no planets are bad or good – they are simply here – in a certain 'situation' (placement) because of your PAST KARMA. Improvise, focus on raising the quality of your KARMA and then you would never have to face with a question of how to find malefic or benefic planets – even if you find – what are you going to do? The only answer is in focusing on your ACTIONS (KARMA) – but people are not comfortable with the truth – that makes them uncomfortable – they are happy when someone gives them something that they can digest, that they can play around with!

But I am here not to entertain you and make you comfortable – for TRUTH is never going to make you 'comfortable' – TRUTH is here to make you uncomfortable – because it is only when you become uncomfortable that you wake up – you become aware – and it is only through more and more awareness – that you can progress in life – that you can experience the 'real growth' – astrology is not a parrot talk – it is to 'move' you from inside-out – so that you come face to face with reality – so that you grow – inside out.

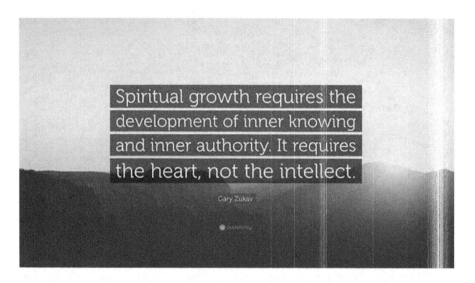

I encourage all my followers and readers to focus on your spiritual growth – I would want you all to become more and more meditative.

There is no other miracle in the world than meditation. It is the only science of transforming you into a new man.

OSHO

Real transformation is your inner transformation. Focus on your 'self' – meditate.

Jai Shri Ganesha. Jai Guru.

Question 20

What are the remedies for strengthening Ketu in a horoscope?

The very thought of asking such a **beautiful question** is in itself a wonderful sign that you are on the right path, you are moving towards the right direction.

The questions that are born within you - signify the direction you follow - the growth, and the state of awareness within you! When you ask about strengthening someone as meditative as Ketu, **you are already becoming meditative!**

It is also a wonderful question in many ways because a very few would ask such a question when the majority is behind strengthening the qualities of material planets - Bhogi, pleasure-seeking planets.

Much derives from the questions one asks. Your question reflects - WHAT YOU ARE!

> It is NOT the answers you give, but the questions you ask.
>
> **VOLTAIRE**

Your question itself is a sign that 'KETU' - the **meditative quality** is strengthening within you. You do not have to take any special efforts because the blossoming is happening within you - naturally! And what happens naturally is beautiful. The moment you are *natural* - you look beautiful, and then you need no make-up - you simply look beautiful!

> Nature leads to God because God is hidden in nature. First, be natural. Then you will be flowing in the river of the natural. And one day the river will fall into the ocean of the supernatural.
>
> **OSHO**

Remember the fact that **each one of us** at some point and in some previous births and rebirths was RAHU-ish. But as we all moved on with our journey of birth and rebirths - slowly we started moving from **being**

Rahu-ish to *being Ketu-ish*! It is a PROCESS. And we should trust the PROCESS.

Every saint has a PAST - He may have committed certain mistakes out of ignorance - but what made him RISE above the miseries of life is HIS **turning inward (KETU).**

Every sinner has a FUTURE - He may have committed certain acts out of ignorance - but what CAN transform HIS LIFE is His **turning inward (KETU).**

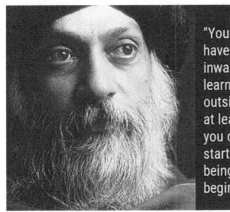

"Your kingdom is within you. You just have to learn to close your eyes and look inwards. A little discipline, a little learning not to remain focused on the outside continuosly, but to turn inwards at least once or twice a day whenever you can find time...slowly, slowly you start becoming aware of your eternal being. And the transformation begins..." - Osho

Birth happens out of DESIRES. Rahu represents these desires. Rahu is the very reason for our birth. Desire is the very reason for our birth. To execute the desires - **action** is needed - this action is seen through the 3rd house. Rahu, therefore, is very active in the 3rd house.

Liberation or Moksha happens out of DESIRELESSNESS. KETU represents this wonderful yogic state of desirelessness. Ketu is the very reason for our liberation - moksha. 12th house - the house of liberation is, therefore, the home of Ketu. It is here where Ketu liberates you. The moment there is no desire for any action - liberation happens.

The whole journey of the soul is from Rahu to Ketu. Desire to Desirelessness.

It is necessary for you all - to realize that DESIRES remain. Because the moment DESIRES are finished - you are liberated - you attain MOKSHA. You remain no more on this planet - you transcend to the Beyond.

So DESIRES remain. It remains in a common man, and it also remains within a YOGI - the difference is the QUALITY OF THE DESIRE - the difference is WHAT YOU DESIRE!

Desire has not to be destroyed, desires has to be purified. Desires has to be transformed. Your very being is desire; to be against the desires is to be against yourself. Desires are NOT bad. And Desires cannot be dropped. But DESIRES can be RAISED to **a higher level of consciousness** and then the whole essence of life, the whole meaning of life is changed - then you no more are what you are, you transform into a *beautiful person!*

When a beautiful woman comes before you - there are **many dimensions** of desires **that can arise within you.** Either you would want to have her. Or you would simply wonder *if my mother would have been so beautiful* like her or *if my sister would have been so beautiful like her.* Or **if you are a meditative Yogi** - you would simply fold your hands *to appreciate her beauty* - because through her beauty, you see a glimpse of the Goddesses that dwell in the heavens - Laxmi, Saraswati, Durga!

So you see - one beautiful woman and many dimensions or levels of desires *based on your state of awareness!*

A meditative man **also has desires.** But his desires are of experiencing God. His desires are of experiencing Love - pure unconditional love. His desires are to HELP people. So you see, **desires are there** but now the whole dimension, the whole essence has changed - it is no more physical, **it is all spiritual!**

Once it happened. **Gautama Buddha and his disciples** were staying in the capital. And in that capital lived the **most beautiful woman,** and her beauty was beyond the power of expression. Even priests and pundits would forget the scriptures and the holy sermons when she would appear before them! Kings and wealthy merchants were slaves of her beauty. She would just lift her finger, and people would fall at her feet. She was born beneath a mango tree, and so her name was Amrapali! And Amrapali was the Goddess of beauty. There was not a single woman or queen who could match her beauty - she was the most beautiful woman that the world had ever known.

One day, Amrapali was standing in her balcony when a disciple of Buddha came to her notice. And the disciple was a very handsome young man. There was a certain glow to his whole being. He was feeding the birds, and Amrapali could not get her eyes off him. '**What a handsome young man**' - she thought.

Rainy season was about to start. Amrapali went and met the young disciple of Buddha and said, "*Monsoon is going to start. You are a monk and monks need shelter during the monsoon season. Why don't you come and live with me? I can provide you shelter for four months of monsoon in my house.*"

The young disciple was a meditative disciple. He said, "**I will ask the Master. And if he permits, I will come to stay with you.**"

The young disciple went back to Buddha - bowed before the Master and asked for permission.

Buddha smiled and said, **"You can go and stay with her for four months."**

The other disciples of Buddha were shocked. *How come the Master agreed.* Some of them also became **JEALOUS.** How come this young man is getting a chance to live with the most beautiful woman of the kingdom - they felt jealous within! You see the most insecure men - the most ignorant men feel JEALOUS. They could not stand this idea; some even thought - *why not me!*

Buddha said, **"Let him go. And let us wait until he comes back."**

But some said, "Master, *what if he does not come back?* **What if that woman gets him?"**

The Master said, **"Be patient** and don't jump to conclusions. Wait and watch."

The young man joined Amrapali at her residence. And days passed by. The monks and the disciples of Buddha started gossiping. Some said,

"That man is gone. It is foolish to even expect him back when the Goddess of Beauty is with him."

Some said, *"That woman will never let him return. She has got him."*

Days and months passed. And after four months, **Amrapali** herself came and fell at Buddha's feet.

Buddha was in deep meditation. He opened his eyes and said, **"For what have you come? What is it that you want from me?"**

And Amrapali started crying. Her whole being was moved…looking at Buddha - she said, **"I want to be your disciple.** *I want to follow you.* Because **if your disciple is so great so pure so loving** then I can understand **how pure and how great you must be!"**

Buddha took her hands in his and said, "Let all my disciples who are present here, let them all know *what happened during these four months?"*

Amrapali said, "I tried in every way to attract your disciple, but he simply was never attracted towards me. I tried to distract him by undressing myself before him and he would say, **'What are you doing? You will catch cold.'** I have seen people - great kings and merchants waiting eagerly to see me in the most sensational postures - **but this man was a totally different man.** And through his presence, through his pure love - **I changed. My thinking changed.** He would sleep alone on the hard ground of my palace, and yet he would take care of me. **Like a child, he would take care of me.** He cooked for me. He guided me. **But he never touched me; he never showed any interest in my body.** I just could not imagine this - I just could not imagine someone like him could also exist on this planet - when the whole world had been behind my body, my beauty....he never was distracted to my physical beauty - I thought of changing him **but he has changed me...**And now even I want to become your disciple...Buddha O master, please take this sinful woman under your wings..."

The whole group of monks and disciples were moved by this unique incident...**from behind came the young disciple** who had stayed with Amrapali. He came and bowed before the Master and the Master smiled and said, **"Son, welcome back."**

The greatness is of the MASTER - whose teachings, whose sharing enabled the young disciple to overcome the trap of beauty - of physical attractions. But the young disciple did not just stop here - through his understanding, through his compassion - he also CHANGED Amrapali - and Amrapali became one of the greatest disciples of BUDDHA - without AMRAPALI - the story of Buddha is incomplete. Amrapali completes Buddha - in a subtle way!

It is NOT that the BAD can always influence and impact the GOOD - the GOOD have more power to change the BAD into GOOD - always believe in the GOODNESS of this human world - this WORLD exists because there are GOOD people. There is no quality or energy that cannot be diverted toward good. Always remember that which can become bad can always become good; that which can become harmful can always become helpful.

> **"**
> Helpful and Harmful, good and bad are directions. It is only a question of transforming by changing the direction and things will become different.
>
> **OSHO**
> **"**

Amrapali was desirous for **the young disciple.**

The young disciple was desirous of **experiencing GOD.**

Desire remains. **But the QUALITY OF DESIRE matters,** and **it is this QUALITY OF DESIRE** that goes on shaping *your present and your future.*

Why is reading Holy Scriptures helpful? Why is chanting the name of God helpful? Why is meditation helpful? Because in some way or the other - they all help you to RAISE THE LEVEL OF YOUR AWARENESS, and when AWARENESS GROWS - The QUALITY OF DESIRES ALSO MOVES TO HIGHER ALTITUDES. Then the journey from **SEX to SUPER-CONSCIOUSNESS** begins!

Every man and every woman should go through the basic need - basic pleasures of human life. SEX, therefore, is extremely important because unless you realize the futility of SEX - you cannot rise above sex. And to realize its futility - it is necessary that **first, you go through the many experiences of sex.**

Repressing your desires of having Sex - is like committing SUICIDE. Repressing is NOT the way - you can only come out of SEX when you have gone through the many experiences of SEX.

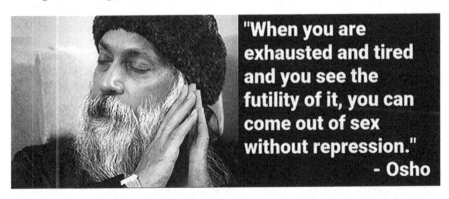

"When you are exhausted and tired and you see the futility of it, you can come out of sex without repression."
- Osho

A man who has had SEX - and **had it enough** - can move much smoothly *towards the beyond* - simply because he had it and he has realized the whole futility of it - he has realized that **there is something far beautiful than Sex** - that there is something that can stay on for a longer time - than Sex and that is the beautiful state of meditation. So now, such a man

DESIRES - but HIS DESIRE has been uplifted to the higher realms - the higher altitudes of human life - the desire to meditate and self-realize!

> Your own self realization is the greatest service you can render the world.
>
> **SRI RAMANA MAHARSHI**

Self-realization is a process that begins with the question - WHO AM I? - but ends with the dissolution of the QUESTIONER himself - who was asking - WHO AM I?

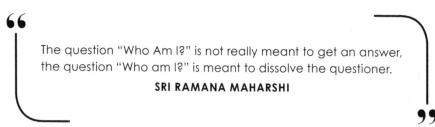

> The question "Who Am I?" is not really meant to get an answer, the question "Who am I?" is meant to dissolve the questioner.
>
> **SRI RAMANA MAHARSHI**

And the moment the questioner dissolves - ONENESS is experienced (ADVAIT) - in that state of ONENESS - TRUTH is realized, and it is beautiful!

As your meditation becomes deeper, as your identification with the head and the heart starts falling, you find yourself becoming a triangle. And your reality is in the third force in you: the consciousness. Consciousness can manage very easily, because the heart and the head – both belong to it.

Certain AVATARs are born for a special purpose- **they often don't marry** and **or have sex - because they are Avatars** - they have come for a special purpose, and they leave **when the purpose is met.**

And then there are certain Men and Women - who are also AVATAR - but they have to GO THROUGH MARITAL LIFE - just to become an EXAMPLE for those who are married - who have certain material worldly responsibilities. Through their AVATAR life story - they pass on the message that EVEN THOUGH you are married - even though you are living a material life - you can also become a YOGI. In fact, to become a YOGI by going through the material life is far difficult than to just RENOUNCE and become a YOGI.

And always remember - I specifically say this to those who are seeking spiritual journey - that SANYAS or ASCETIC life has nothing to do with HOW YOU APPEAR ON THE OUTSIDE - it has more to do with WHAT LIES WITHIN!

"Sanyasa is taken from within, not from without."

- Bhagavan Ramana Maharshi

Buddha had a wife. Her name was Yashodhara.

People talk a lot about Buddha **renouncing everything and becoming a monk**. But *do you know what happens when Buddha comes back to his capital* - his kingdom?

Buddha arrives. With him is Ananda. And the whole kingdom comes to welcome them, but **Buddha›s wife remains in her Palace.**

Buddha reaches her palace. He asks Ananda to stay outside the palace. And Buddha goes to meet his wife - **Yashodhara**.

Yashodhara is boiling with anger. Looking at her husband returning after so many years- she says *"WHY? Why you never told me before leaving? Do you think I would have stopped you? Do you think I was so ignorant that I would not have realized your thirst for the divine? WHY? Why you did this to me?"*

And Yashodhara broke into tears. Her cry was so loud that the whole palace was moved. Buddha was also touched. Taking her hands in his - Buddha said, **"Look at me Yashodhara, look at me."**

And Yashodhara looked at Buddha's face. And something moved within her whole being; the Grace. The compassionate eyes, the glow... she could see that this is not the man who had left her...this is a man who has transformed into a beautiful person. After a decade, she was meeting her husband, and she could sense that this man is something.

Buddha said, "Something beautiful has happened within me - look at me, and I have come to help you experience the same beauty within you. And now I have realized that there was absolutely NO REASON and NO NEED to renounce and leave you or this palace - even here in this palace - I would have attained ENLIGHTENMENT - there was absolutely no need to go away from you..."

Yashodhara could not control herself....the voice, the feeling, the aura - she could feel God's presence. Now instead of resentment - love started welling up in her whole being...she fell at Buddha's feet and said, "...take me under your wings...be my master and let me be your disciple."

Buddha smiled. He initiated Yashodhara, and Yashodhara became the disciple of Buddha! One of the greatest events happened - an event that can move your whole being if you can relate. Only **Buddha could do this** - it is pure love and compassion of Buddha that can even melt the heart of his angry wife and **a wife becomes a disciple of her husband** - one of the most unique and unimaginable events took place - something so enlightening - something so moving that is beyond the human imagination!

Anger can transform into Love - just a touch of awareness and Yashodhara's **anger transforms into love** - so much so that she is no more just in love with her husband - **she becomes totally devoted to Him.**

Devotion is love overflowing!

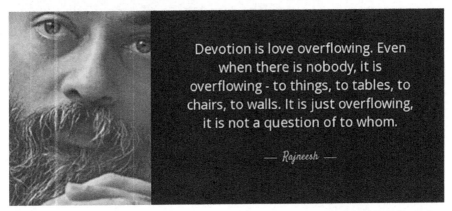

Devotion is love overflowing. Even when there is nobody, it is overflowing - to things, to tables, to chairs, to walls. It is just overflowing, it is not a question of to whom.

— *Rajneesh* —

It is not a question to whom - and when Buddha is standing before you - and if you are a man of heart - it is natural to melt - it is natural to cry... it is natural to let the tears flow...for that is the only way you can express the inexpressible!

"Never be ashamed of your tears. Be proud that you are still natural. Be proud that you can express the inexpressible through your tears."
- Osho

Only a man who cries his heart out - only a woman who cries her heart out is the most beautiful being - they are men and women of heart - they melt - they cry - they love and they are simply beautiful!

You will cry - when you have the heart to cry! And you will feel your HEART when you overcome the chattering HEAD - the intellectualism - the monkey MIND.

And it is here - where KETU comes to your HELP. KETU rescues you from the tight clutches of the MIND - KETU helps you to move beyond the mind - and it is only when you move beyond the mind - that ALL CALCULATIONS STOP - and REVELATIONS BEGIN - because the moment you reach the HEART - the HEART starts revealing the many TRUTHS that you never had known - because you always have been in the tight clutches of your MIND!

Ketu represents the following qualities:

- Becoming meditative and turning inwards
- Becoming selfless
- Becoming detached

- Letting Go
- Forgiving
- Loving unconditionally
- Living with ACCEPTANCE
- Living your life in TOTAL SURRENDER

SURRENDER is the ANSWER to your QUESTION. YES - this is the ANSWER, and through this question - I would like my readers to realize that the only way you can strengthen the qualities of KETU within you is by slowly SURRENDERING yourself to GOD - to the existence!

The moment of surrender is NOT when life is OVER. It's when it begins.

Krishna says to Arjuna - "Surrender - And I will take care of YOU in totality."

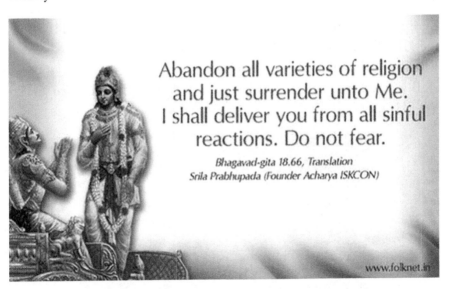

Abandon all varieties of religion and just surrender unto Me. I shall deliver you from all sinful reactions. Do not fear.

Bhagavad-gita 18.66, Translation
Srila Prabhupada (Founder Acharya ISKCON)

www.folknet.in

A man who lives his whole life in TOTAL SURRENDER to his LORD - always comes out of difficulties - it may take some time, but in the end, he always wins. Always!

The only REMEDY for strengthening KETU is to go back to your SOURCE - WITHIN - by becoming more and more meditative.

"Love deeply, Love
without Jealousy, Love
blissfully & Help each
other to be more
Meditative."

\- Osho

Always remember - and I say it specifically to all my readers - that all remedies are precisely to bring CHANGE WITHIN YOU! When you do a remedy - donating food to poor - a certain joy wells up in your being - you see - the remedy is happening on the outside - but the effect is happening WITHIN!

Lord Ganesha is the only LORD whose whole appearance is spiritually inspiring - look closely - Lord Ganesha has NO HEAD - the HEAD that you see is just a representation of WISDOM - because ELEPHANTS are the wisest animals!

But in reality, Lord Ganesha has NO HEAD - HE is deeply engrossed WITHIN.

What you WORSHIP on the OUTSIDE is what you BECOME WITHIN!

And so one of the most effective remedies of strengthening KETU is to worship LORD GANESHA - because the message of KETU is to LOOK WITHIN, and the message of LORD GANESHA is also - to LOOK WITHIN!

WITHIN is the word - and KETU simply wants you to LOOK WITHIN. The best remedy is, therefore, to spend quality time - by focusing WITHIN. Help others - donate - share - but while you do so - do not forget to come back to your SOURCE!

SAMMASTI - that was the last word of Buddha. For forty years, he traveled all around the place which is now called Bihar, and all he did was to help those who had forgotten the language - the language of Silence! SAMMASTI means REMEMBER.

The whole story of our life is based on this one miraculous word - REMEMBER!

Remember the forgotten language of silence. Remember to go back to SILENCE - remember the language of Meditation - remember - just Remember!

The more you meditate - the more you would remember the significance of SILENCE.

In silence, you can find the TRUTH—the cosmic origin of things that are beyond the mind, the words, the intellect.

Real communication happens in silence.

Let us all remember the most beautiful man who once walked on this planet - Gautama Buddha and **let us meditate** on His words - on His message of Love, of Devotion, of remembering the forgotten language - the language of heart - the language of Silence. When you start moving towards your heart - in deep meditation - you will experience the SILENCE WITHIN - then you all will realize KETU - then you all will realize the beauty of meditation - and a time will come in your life when you will no more meditate - you will become 'meditation'!

Our whole effort should be to remain calm, peaceful even though from the outside, negative people try to offend you, disturb you, insult you. That is what Buddha is - a SILENCE - and that is what each one of you can become - a SILENCE!

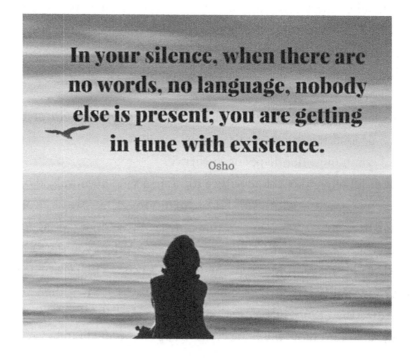

In your silence, when there are no words, no language, nobody else is present; you are getting in tune with existence.

Osho

Nothing is more ALIVE than SILENCE - let Silence be your language. This is the language that Buddha preached all his life - this is the language that Meher Baba emphasized all his life - this is the language that Mahavira shared all his life, and this is the language that can bring a great transformation in your life.

The moment SILENCE comes - the cosmic dance begins - then there will be joy - then no matter how much noise is on the outside - the dance within - the song within will continue, and you will say - ***"It is beautiful!"***

Come, come to the most miraculous state - the state of meditation - close your eyes, breathe in, breathe out - focus within and quieten the chattering mind.

When the Mind becomes quiet - the soul speaks.

Let the soul within you - speak. And the soul speaks only when there is SILENCE - within.

Silence is the language of the Soul. Silence is the language of God. Silence is the language of the Buddha.

Let there be - Silence, **within.**

Meditate.
Jai Shri Ganesha. Jai Guru.

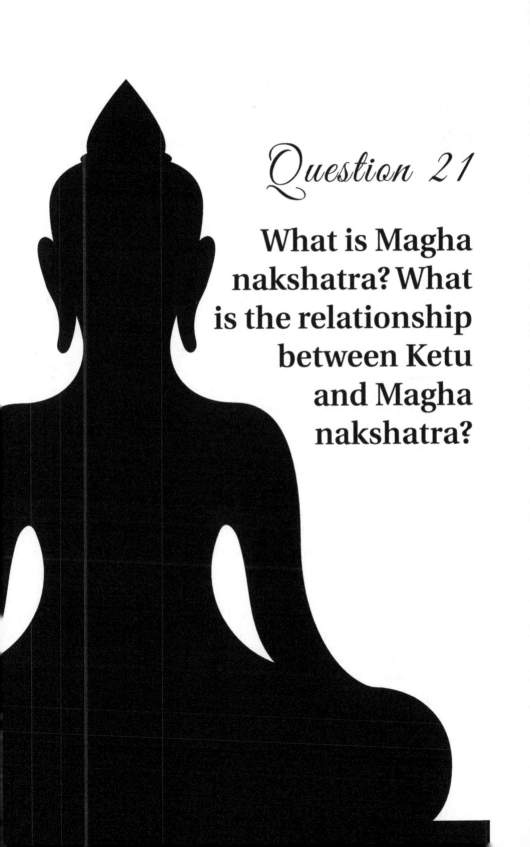

Question 21

What is Magha nakshatra? What is the relationship between Ketu and Magha nakshatra?

shwini. Magha. Moola.

The journey of KETU begins from Ashwini - Ketu is at its peak in Magha, and in Moola, the same Ketu brings a great transformation through certain pain and sufferings!

Moola - the source of destruction - the energy of SHIVA - the Lord of destruction!

Through destruction comes the state of enlightenment - and it is beautiful!

> 66 Make no mistake about it – enlightenment is a destructive process.It has nothing to do with becoming better or being happier.Enlightenment is the crumbling away of the untruth. Its seeing through the façade of pretense. It's the complete eradication of everything we imagined to be true.
>
> **ADYASHANTI** 99

Life begins with ASHWINI (Aries). Life dissolves with REVATI (Pisces).

From NOTHINGNESS - (KETU) the Zodiac begins (Aries) and goes back to NOTHINGNESS by 'dissolving' back into the cosmos (Mercury).

NOTHINGNESS is the basis of everything. KETU, therefore, is of great significance - one who can understand KETU - can understand the many depths of this human life.

From where does the tree, the flower, the fruit come? From where does all that exists in and around us come? What is the SOURCE of existence?

The answer to these questions is found in the **Chandogya Upanishad.**

In one of the chapters, a wonderful incident is illustrated in which the great Sage Uddalaka reveals the very source of existence to his son - **Svetketu.**

The great Sage asks his son, Svetketu, to bring a fruit of the Banyan tree. Svetketu is an obedient son. He quickly brings the fruit of the banyan tree.

"Here it is Father, I gave got it."

Sage Uddalaka says, "Break it."

"It is broken, Father."

"What do you see there?"

"There are many seeds, plenty of them, almost infinitesimal."

"Break one of them."

"It is broken, Father."

"What do you see there?"

"NOTHING - Father - absolutely NOTHING!"

The father said, "My son, that subtle essence which you do not perceive, of that very essence this great banyan tree exists. Believe it, my son, that there is this subtle essence in all things that are existing. That is the truth. The real truth."

The banyan tree is a huge tree. The father asks for a fruit, Svetketu brings it. Fruit is the thing that has flowered, fruition has happened. The father says, "Break it."

Svetketu breaks it - millions of seeds are seen inside the fruit. The father says, "Choose one seed, break it too." He breaks the seed. Now there is nothing in the hand. Inside the seed - there is NOTHING.

Sage Uddalaka says, "Out of this NOTHINGNESS comes the seed. Out of the seed comes the tree. Out of the tree comes the fruit. But the basis is NOTHINGNESS, the SILENCE, the EMPTINESS - the FORMLESS, the un-manifest, the beyond - the transcendental."

This FORMLESS - this SILENCE - this BEYOND, this NOTHINGNESS is KETU. In deep state of meditation - the Yogi experiences the state of nothingness - emptiness - Shunya. No thoughts. No MIND. No Head.

Everything has come from - 'NOTHINGNESS'!

> **"**
> Scientists have known for centuries that 'NOTHING' is the key to understanding absolutely everything, from why particles have the mass to the expansion of the universe – so without 'nothing' – we would be precisely nowhere.
> **JEREMY WEBB**
> **"**

From this NOTHINGNESS - (KETU - ASHWINI NAKSHATRA) evolves the world.

It is energetic - the sign of Mars (Aries) gives it a perfect stage to bring ENERGY - bring LIFE to this world!

Have you seen an ASHWINI NAKSHATRA man or woman?

They are very lively - very energetic - in fact, they have so much ENERGY of MARS (ARIES) that they simply LOVE TO START - to INITIATE (evolution is the essence of KETU's ASHWINI).

ASHWINI - that's its beginning! And so people born on ASHWINI are competent enough to become great ENTREPRENEURS - because KETU's ASHWINI is a good starter - the very nature of this NAKSHATRA is to GET STARTED and they succeed in initiating new enterprises - new companies - new ways of living - all that is NEW - FRESH.

After ASHWINI - comes the next NAKSHATRA of KETU - **MAGHA!**

And what a beautiful NAKSHATRA is this - how to express it - language is really poor - words cannot suffice!

MAGHA is where the BEGINNER (KETU from ASHWINI) comes to EXECUTE its duties - now KETU is no more just a BEGINNER - but a real TASKMASTER!

MAGHA becomes the SEAT OF KETU - where He sits and does what He does at His BEST - the evolution of SPIRITUALISM! Here the SPIRITUALITY of KETU EVOLVES - MAGHA brings a certain INTELLIGENCE.

LEO is a sign of INTELLIGENCE. AQUARIUS is a sign of INTELLECTUALITY.

In the SIGN of LEO - KETU's nakshatra - MAGHA is found. The SEAT OF INTELLIGENCE. And one who is INTELLIGENT is the real KING.

In the SIGN of AQUARIUS - RAHU's nakshatra - Shatabhisha is found. The SEAT OF INTELLECTUALISM. And one who is INTELLECTUAL - remains far away from the TRUTH - the ultimate consciousness!

Intelligence is of the HEART - LEO is the sign of HEART, and it is in LEO that KETU has a very prominent role to play - through HIS NAKSHATRA - MAGHA!

Intellectualism is of the HEAD - AQUARIUS is the sign of HEAD, and it is in AQUARIUS that RAHU has a very prominent role to play - through HIS NAKSHTARA - SHATABHISHA!

The BEGINNING happens through ASHWINI.

The REAL WORK (SPIRITUAL PROGRESS) happens through MAGHA.

The ultimate self-realization - the ultimate peak - the state of BODHISATTVA happens through MOOLA.

First - you have to be born - evolve (Ashwini)

Then - you have to become 'intelligent' - (MAGHA)

And then – finally, you have to DIE (MOOLA) just to be REBORN - MOOLA. The death that Moola brings is the death of all your illusions (Maya), Ego, preconceived notions and learnings. Unless you become EMPTY - the divine cannot fill you. The cup becomes useful only when it is Empty! Moola brings along this emptiness, and it is beautiful.

How beautiful is all this - how deep and how enlightening astrology can be! Only specific meditative souls can relate to this beauty - only those who have a certain depth of understanding can resonate with the beauty of the cosmic play that KETU so wonderfully brings along!

MAGHA represents the BANYAN TREE!

And it is the BANYAN TREE that has been a 'home' for millions and millions of Yogis - one of them was Buddha - the most beautiful man who once walked on this planet - **Gautama Buddha!**

When he left his kingdom - Buddha was just a PRINCE - Prince Siddharta.

But when he was enlightened - he remained no more a prince - but became a KING - the REAL KING.

MAGHA has all the ingredients to help you evolve into the greatest KING - a KING who has absolutely NO PALACES - NO LUXURIES - NO PLEASURES and yet HE is the most wonderful man you would ever meet - a MAN who can GIVE AWAY - everything - a MAN who has NO ATTACHMENTS - a MAN who has gone beyond the MIND - a MAN who has CONQUERED himself!

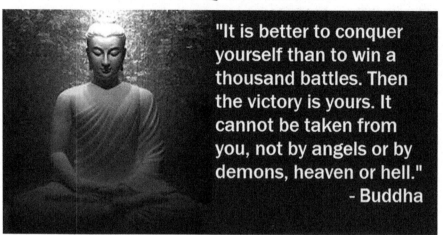

"It is better to conquer yourself than to win a thousand battles. Then the victory is yours. It cannot be taken from you, not by angels or by demons, heaven or hell."
- Buddha

Millions and millions of KINGS and QUEENS have come and gone - but the only KINGS - that the world remembers and will remember - are the KINGS who have CONQUERED themselves. The world remembers the BUDDHA, the world remembers JESUS, the world remembers MAHAVIRA - they were the greatest 'KINGS' who had absolutely NO PALACES and NO POWER TO CONTROL LANDS - but they ruled the HEARTS of millions - many will come and go but the names of these real KINGS will always remain in our hearts - always!

MAGHA represents such KINGS - who have conquered themselves - and so the ancient seers have mentioned MAGHA as a ROYAL SEAT - on which the MASTER sits and DIRECTS the world through HIS divine MESSAGES - through HIS divine WORDS and WISDOM!

Paramhanasa Yogananda - the man who moved millions of hearts across the world - was one such 'KING' who was born on MAGHA NAKSHATRA (Ascendant)!

When I was in college - the only book that I read was "Autobiography of a Yogi" and for many nights, I used to cry - those tears were the tears of joy - tears of devotion and then there was no looking back!

Always remember - NAKSHTRA is to be seen from the ASCENDANT and NOT the MOON SIGN.

MOON (MIND) is a monkey - even if you are born with LEO MOON SIGN in MAGHA NAKSHATRA - it is just going to provide you the qualities of KETU from the MIND LEVEL - and whatever happens from the MIND LEVEL makes no sense - you just 'THINK' - and THINKING is not a REALITY.

REALITY is WHAT YOU ARE. And it is the ASCENDANT that tells you what you are!

MAGHA on ASCENDANT makes you a real YOGI - or has the potential to help you evolve to the state of a YOGI.

MAGHA on MOON SIGN level - is just a thought pattern and not a reality.

REALITY IS YOUR ASCENDANT and never go by the MOON SIGN NAKSHATRA - that will only give you the idea of the MINDSET - but the NATURE is to be found from the ASCENDANT, and it is the NATURE that matters and NOT the MONKEY MIND.

Paramahansa Yogananda had his ASCENDANT in MAGHA and also MOON in MAGHA - so the very NATURE (ASCENDANT) and MINDSET (MOON) were influenced by MAGHA, and that helped HIM to come to the state of TOTALITY - he became a YOGI in totality - one of the greatest YOGIS of the modern times.

Here in MAGHA - KETU is at WORK. So now the NATURE of LETTING GO is more pronounced - more seen - than in ASHWINI.

Here in MAGHA - KETU is working to help the individual understand the significance of DETACHMENT.

Here in MAGHA - KETU is working to help the individual to realize the significance of FORGIVING.

So you see - MAGHA is the 'WORKPLACE' of KETU where KETU has much to do - much to offer - for the overall GROWTH of the individual!

Did I say 'individual'? YES - one of the most beautiful qualities of MAGHA is that KETU brings forth - the INDIVIDUALISM within you, you are no more just the MASK (personality) - you drop the personality and embrace your INDIVIDUALITY!

In MAGHA - you get the confidence to say, "I AM HAPPY TO BE MYSELF."

Only a KETU-ish man or woman can live by 'BEING YOURSELF'!

A RAHU-ish man or woman is always focusing on the MASK (Personality) - they FEAR to SHOW their REAL FACE - the INDIVIDUALITY - and so they strengthen the MASK - PERSONALITY.

A MAGHA ASCENDANT PERSON - KETU-ish person works around to STRENGTHEN HIS INDIVIDUALITY.

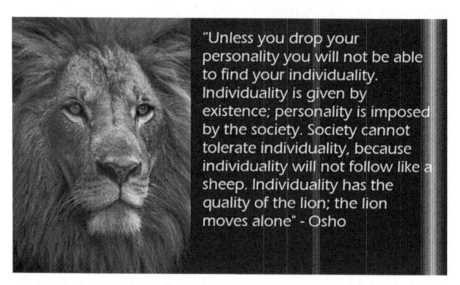

"Unless you drop your personality you will not be able to find your individuality. Individuality is given by existence; personality is imposed by the society. Society cannot tolerate individuality, because individuality will not follow like a sheep. Individuality has the quality of the lion; the lion moves alone" - Osho

The lion is one of the most intelligent animals on this planet. Leo is one of the most intelligent signs among the 12 zodiac signs!

And it is because of MAGHA! The very start of LEO sign is with MAGHA - first comes the INTELLIGENCE - and then follows the 'manifestation' which is seen through VENUS's nakshatra - PurvaPhalguni! The whole sign of LEO is based on these two NAKSHATRAS - MAGHA (KETU) and then PURVAPHALGUNI (VENUS) - and just the end of LEO begins with SUN's UTTARAPHALGUNI - it is the beginning of coming to the state of consciousness - through which the 'knowledge' of literature, arts, practicality comes - which later is seen in VIRGO - the sign that succeeds LEO!

312

So the whole 'homework' is done in LEO - it is HERE - where the foundation is built!

And my Master always used to say, "If the foundation is good then you can always build a good building upon it - the point is - that the foundation has to be good!"

And KETU does the job very beautifully - in MAGHA - the native gets all the ingredients to first focus on the FOUNDATION!

So you see:

ASHWINI - KETU BEGINS...

MAGHA - KETU builds upon the FOUNDATION...

MOOLA - KETU matures - now everything is okay to start building the 'TOWER' - the TOWER OF LIGHT - LIGHT of CONSCIOUSNESS!

Beautiful.

Foundation. Magha!

Once it happened - Buddha had become old - for forty years, HE traveled through the land which is now Bihar and shared HIS divine messages - but now the body had become too old - and so one day HE said to His disciples - "I am about to leave this human body - so IF there is anything that you want to ask - ask. Because once I am gone - there will be no one to answer your questions."

Ananda was the first among all - to burst out in tears - for forty years, he had been *following* Buddha - like a shadow, he had been with Buddha and now when the Master says, **"I am leaving this human body"** - imagine - just imagine how difficult it would have been for Ananda…he couldn't control himself - he started crying……

Buddha said, "Why are you crying? You can cry later when I am gone - right now, ask if you want to ask any question?"

Ananda said, "I am crying because **once you are gone there will be nobody of your stature** to answer my questions - for many decades there will be nobody of your stature - and I am lost at words…but I have one question that I have been trying to hold on, for many years - but now it is time - before you leave, I must ask…"

"Ask," said Buddha. A smile appeared on Buddha's face. The Master always is aware of what is to come - Buddha knew what the question was going to be…

And Ananda asked - he asked a beautiful question - a question that is worth contemplating. Ananda asked, "Many people came to you - and many also became enlightened - but I have been following you for forty years and I haven't yet attained enlightenment - I have been your shadow - and yet I haven't been able to taste that which others have tasted in your omnipresence. Those who came very late - after me - they have become enlightened - but someone like me - who has been with you for many years - still doesn't know even the A.B.C of enlightenment. *Why so?*"

Buddha smiled. And what a smile that was - it moved the heart of Ananda - he could see so much love showering through the Master's eyes. Buddha looked into Ananda's eyes and said, "Because of your Conditions."

Ananda could now remember – yes, the Master was right. When He had come for the first time - he had said to Buddha, "I am your elder cousin brother. So before I become your disciple - I would want you to accept my three conditions."

The whole room was packed with disciples and Buddha was listening - Buddha had smiled and said, "I am listening, you can specify those three conditions."

Ananda had said, "First condition - I will always be with you, and I will be taking care of you - no matter where you go - you have to let me follow you."

Buddha had said, "Accepted."

"Second condition - if I bring along anybody - then you have to solve his or her problem."

Buddha had said, "Accepted."

"Third condition - if I ask you any question - you have to answer - you cannot postpone it - you have to answer immediately."

Buddha had said, "Accepted."

40 years had passed to this incident, and ANANDA could very well remember the conditions he had laid before the Master - Buddha's words echoed in his ears - the Master said, "Because of your conditions."

When you lay conditions - love cannot flow freely - hearts cannot merge - the state of ONENESS cannot be experienced and unless there is ONENESS - unless the DISCIPLE moves towards the MASTER - unless there comes the state of ONENESS - where the DISCIPLE is no more a DISCIPLE and the MASTER is no more the MASTER - ONENESS - how to express such a beautiful state of ONENESS - unless the state of ONENESS comes - ENLIGHTENMENT is not possible.

Ananda could not become ONE with the Master - could NOT melt into the Master. It is only when you go back to the SOURCE (Master) that you are REBORN - that you are TRANSFORMED - and you will be able to go back to the SOURCE (Master) only when there are no CONDITIONS - CONDITIONS become the greatest hurdle that prevents you from moving into the Master!

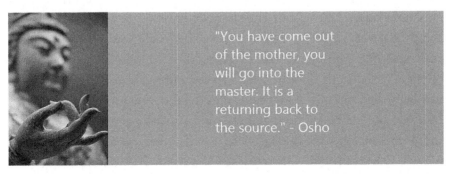

"You have come out of the mother, you will go into the master. It is a returning back to the source." - Osho

Ananda could not return back to the source - the Buddha. His conditions came in between HIM and HIS wish to experience enlightenment!

And so now - when Buddha was about to leave his body - about to embrace Death - Ananda started crying and the Master simply helped him REMEMBER his own CONDITIONS.....

Ananda asked, "Now...*now what is the way*...master...?"

Looking at Ananda - Buddha said, "Now the **only way is my DEATH**. It is only when I die that all your conditions that I had accepted will cease, and it is only when they cease - that you will find the 'road' ahead. It is then that you will be enlightened. Exactly 24 hours after my death - you will be enlightened. Ananda, I have loved you so much but you always missed to relate - but now you will be able to do so - after I die."

And Buddha moves towards the Banyan Tree (Magha) - and beneath the great banyan tree - Buddha leave his body - the whole world comes to a standstill - one of the greatest Yogi that the world had ever know - had left his mortal human body......and Ananda goes back to his room - he locks the room and goes deep into meditation.....and he goes so deep that for next one day he remains in meditation - now there are no conditions - the conditions have evaporated with the Master - the Master has gone and so have all the conditons that he had laid - he could see the road clear - and he moved and he moved within so deeply that exactly after 24 hours Ananda became an enlightened man - he could remember the words of Buddha - Buddha had said, "Exactly twenty fours after my death, you will become an enlightened man...."

Tears started flowing through his eyes - FORTY YEARS - he had been following, but the MIRACLE had happened now - had there been no conditions - had he not laid any conditions - had he realized that 'family relations' have no role to play in the Yogic world - had he been understanding - he would have been enlightened long back - in the very physical presence of Buddha...his tears would not stop - enlightenment had happened but at a 'cost' that cannot be recovered for lives to come - Buddha comes after millions and millions of years - and He had missed - simply missed to realize the significance of Buddha - he remained attached to his CONDITIONS - he remained lost in his IGNORANCE!

Had the foundation been stronger - enlightenment could have come far early to someone as beautiful as ANANDA - a man who was devoted to BUDDHA - but somehow he had been caught up with the idea of laying conditions, and conditions are what made his 'foundation' weak - immature.

MAGHA is the FOUNDATION. KETU works here to help you strengthen the FOUNDATION.

"What is the most significant sign or state of a good FOUNDATION?" STILL Mind.

First, the MIND has to be made STILL. That is the FOUNDATION - the basic FOUNDATION of a spiritual journey.

Once it happened - a young man while travelling through the mountains of Himalayas - met one Yogi. And what a Yogi he was - so much light - so much bliss - so much love showered through his compassionate eyes - and the young man asked, "Will you guide me in my spiritual journey?"

The Yogi said, "Why not! But right now - your CHITTA (Mindset) is wavering. Unless it becomes STILL - the 'motor' cannot operate."

MAGHA (KETU) can be a great motivator and enabler for you to STILL the MIND.

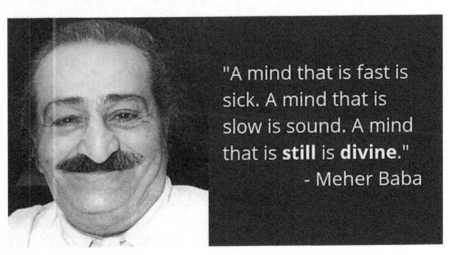

"A mind that is fast is sick. A mind that is slow is sound. A mind that is **still** is **divine**."
                                    - Meher Baba

How to STILL the Mind?

Meditation. It is only through meditation that you can STILL the mind. It is only through chanting the lord's name that you can STILL the mind.

Your nature, and I say it to all - because of your nature of CLINGING - you find it difficult to STILL the MIND.

> **66**
>
> When the mind is left without anything to cling to, it becomes still.
>
> **BHAGAVAN RAMANA MAHARSHI**
>
> **99**

Intelligence comes only when the MIND becomes STILL. And the way to STILL the MIND is to move away from the MIND while focusing on the Lord's name.

Chant Hare Krishna sincerely and all good intelligence, consultation shall come from within. Krishna says that, 'those who are engaged in My service, I give intelligence for his progressive march'.

Srila Prabhupada's letter, Los Angeles, January 1968

MAGHA is beautiful - KETU is beautiful - simply because it is through KETU that the MIND can be dropped - that you can become the MASTER of your MIND - that you can become the DICTATOR of your MIND.

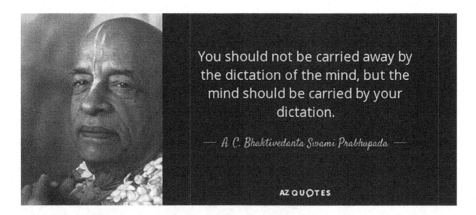

It is okay if you are not yet to the point where you can resonate with the energy of KETU - what is not okay is that when you remain ignorant and continue to SLOG by becoming a SLAVE of your MIND.

And always remember - the MIND is a beautiful SERVANT - but a DANGEROUS MASTER. If you make the MIND as your MASTER - if you continue to be carried away by the dictation of your MIND - you continue to live a miserable life.

Miseries stop when you start DICTATING the MIND - when you - yourself realize that YOU are NOT the MIND - you are the SELF.

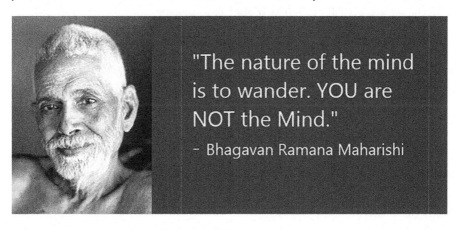

KETU is the only energy - and I say it to all my followers - till the last breath of my life - till blood is flowing though all my veins - that KETU is the only energy that CAN HELP YOU ALL need to move beyond the

MIND - because it is KETU that can make you TURN INWARDS - and REAL LIFE begins only when you start TURNING INWARDS.

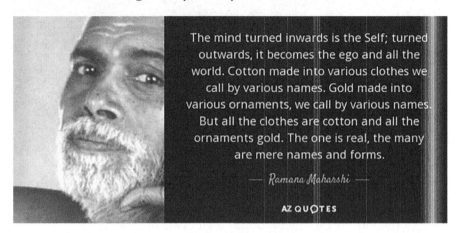

The mind turned inwards is the Self; turned outwards, it becomes the ego and all the world. Cotton made into various clothes we call by various names. Gold made into various ornaments, we call by various names. But all the clothes are cotton and all the ornaments gold. The one is real, the many are mere names and forms.

— *Ramana Maharshi* —

AZ QUOTES

A time should come in your life - when you are no more meditating - you have become 'meditation'! KETU is meditation - deeply engrossed within - always focused within! MAGHA can SPIRITUALLY enrich your life - only if you have the depth to relate - to understand - to realize.

Once it happened - a great Emperor met a monk. And the monk was a very strange man. The Emperor said to the monk, "I need your help."

The monk asked, "What is it that you want from me?"

The Emperor said, "I want to see where this MIND is within me. So I want your help to find the MIND - and once I find the Mind, then you know what you need to do…"

The monk smiled and said, "I know, and I have a big wooden staff in my hand. As soon as you find the mind - I will beat it with my wooden staff."

The Emperor said, "So then when should we begin with the exercise of finding the mind?"

"Tomorrow sharp at 4 AM. And you should come to my abode - ALONE. No bodyguards - no weapons - nothing. Just you – ALONE," said the monk.

The Emperor was taken aback. Nobody had dared to talk in such a way – the whole life he had been the EMPEROR of so many provinces and countries - and yet nobody had dared. But this monk - this old man seemed to be different - he is NOT afraid of me and the depth of HIS voice is such that it is difficult to say NO. The Emperor said, "Okay - I will meet you alone - tomorrow sharp at 4 AM."

The monk left.

But the Emperor could not sleep that night. He kept turning from this side to that side - "Should I go or should I not?" But the words of the monk were so moving, so straight and so deep that the Emperor got up and reached the Monk's abode - it was sharp 4 AM. And the Emperor had come alone - no bodyguards, no weapons.

"Sit down," said the monk. The Emperor found a place to sit.

"Close your eyes," said the monk. The Emperor closed his eyes.

"Now focus on your breathing - breathe in and breathe out, and IF you find that MIND - then tell me, and I will beat it with my wooden staff. But remember, do not open your eyes until you find the MIND - else I will beat you with my wooden staff."

The Emperor quickly followed. *Who knows this man may also beat me with his wooden staff - he is a strange man and so I must not risk myself.* And so the Emperor started moving WITHIN…and slowly he started getting more engrossed within, and he continued to move deeper and deeper within… Cool breeze was flowing, the sun was rising, birds were coming out of their nests…and the Emperor was still deeply engrossed within.

The Emperor had arrived at 4 AM - and it was now 6 AM, and still the Emperor was deeply engrossed WITHIN - the monk was seated next to him - watching him closely - with a wooden staff in his hand - and time went by - one hour, two hours, three hours, four hours, and finally the Emperor opened his eyes and there was so much bliss, so much joy flowing through His eyes. Looking at the Emperor - the monk smiled and asked, "So did you find the Mind?"

And the Emperor looked into the monk's eyes and said, **"There is NO MIND."**

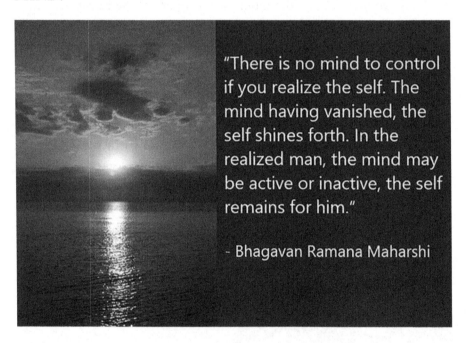

"There is no mind to control if you realize the self. The mind having vanished, the self shines forth. In the realized man, the mind may be active or inactive, the self remains for him."

- Bhagavan Ramana Maharshi

The monk said, "I wanted you to find the answer through your self REALIZATION. And now that you have found your answer - you can go back to your kingdom."

The Emperor went back to his kingdom. But when he went back, he called his minister and said to him, "When I die - I would want you to inscribe the following letters on my graveyard...

"There was a man - a very strange man - and yet through his practical teaching - he made me realize the most beautiful Truth - that in reality there

is NO MIND – the moment you turn inwards – the MIND can exist no more. And I remain indebted to this strange man who although carried a wooden staff in his hand but had a heart of GOLD and I shall remember HIM and remain grateful to Him – for many lives to come."

The moment you turn inwards - the moment you focus on one thought - the MIND starts evaporating.

> **"** When one makes the mind stick to *one thought,* the mind becomes rock-steady and the energy is conserved.
> **BHAGAVAN RAMANA MAHARSHI** **"**

This one thought can be the name of the Lord - the praise of the Lord - the holy words of the scriptures. What is important is that you focus on one thought so that the MIND remains focused - and through this focusing - slowly the MIND becomes STILL - and it is only when the MIND becomes STILL that you can move beyond the MIND - your real 'journey' begins only when the MIND becomes STILL.

This whole process is what KETU brings along – MOON, therefore, hates KETU - and so all those men and all those women who are RULED by their MIND will HATE KETU - will HATE ME - will go on hating all those MEN who speak the TRUTH - because TRUTH is very shattering and the MIND loves to live in illusions!

So, for LEO ASCENDANT - CANCER becomes the 12th house! MOON, therefore, becomes the ENEMY for LEO ASCENDANTS - because MAGHA OF LEO (KETU) is a great danger to the existence of the MIND – It is a great danger to the ILLUSIONS OF the MIND - and so CANCER SIGN people are always a nuisance for those who belong to LEO ASCENDANT (MAGHA)!

It is only when the 'baby' comes out of the 'Mother's womb (MAYA) that the baby becomes independent! Similarly, it is only when YOU ALL come out of the illusions - out of the ATTACHMENTS - out of the CLINGING NATURE - that you will EVOLVE as INDIVIDUALS!

A man who belongs to MAGHA NAKSHATRA (ASCENDANT) is an INDIVIDUAL. He moves ALONE - he stays away from the CROWD - because he is perfectly aware that TRUTH happens to INDIVIDUALS and not to CROWDs.

> **"**
> The majority consists of fools, utter fools. Beaware of the majority. If so many people are following, that is enough proof that something is wrong. Truth happens to individuals, not to crowds.
>
> **OSHO** **"**

An intelligent person is an individual - he is not a personality - he is not a crowd - he is NOT intellectual - he lives by HIS experience and not by theories.

> **"**
> Truth cannot be found by intellectual effort because truth is not a theory, it is an experience.
>
> **OSHO** **"**

Leo is the Mecca of Intelligence. Creative intelligence. And when MAGHA is rising on the Ascendant - only then can you see this creative intelligence at its peak!

The highest mountain peak is the Everest - and the deepest valleys also exist near the Everest! Where the highest mountain peak (success) is seen - also seen are the lowest valleys (failures) - it goes hand in hand - the peak exists where the valleys also exist!

And so MAGHA brings certain failures in life - certain tragedies - certain pain - but this all is to bring AWAKENING within you - because unless the thorn goes deep into your heart - you will not become AWARE - you will not wake up!

And so MAGHA brings a great TRANSFORMATION within you - you go through many pains and sufferings - and by going through all of it - you EVOLVE into a man - who has CHANGED - who has TRANSFORMED into something so beautiful - that it is hard to believe!

KETU brings all the arts of magic, miracles to MAGHA Nakshatra. Many magicians are born on MAGHA!

The nature of Magha is to Help others selflessly! A Magha man or woman is a true friend, and a true friend always attracts true friends.

There is a magnet in your heart that will attract true friends. That magnet is unselfishness, thinking of others first; when you learn to live for others, they will live for you.

— *Paramahansa Yogananda* —

Paramhansa Yogananda's Ascendant was also LEO - MAGHA!

So you see - all spiritual beings are born on Ketu's Magha Nakshatra. Great Healers are born on Magha Nakshatra.

A young man once asked - "I meditate, but why nothing is happening?"

I said, "Nothing will happen because you are meditating with a GOAL in your MIND - and a person who meditates with a GOAL in his or her MIND always fails."

And a person who meditates without having any GOAL - any AGENDA but simply out of LOVE - out of DEVOTION - finds the bliss - the peace - the joy within!

And the moment you are filled with JOY - the moment you are filled with love - the whole universe becomes available to you - then you can FLY - then you can DANCE - then you can SING - that is what GOD always wanted you to be - a DANCE - a PAINTING - a BEAUTIFUL POEM!

But your nature of clinging (RAHU) has spoiled everything in your life - this life and the many past births you have been clinging and clinging, and you have never known that real happiness flows - real joy flows only when you STOP CLINGING and START BECOMING DETACHED!

KETU - MAGHA helps you to become DETACHED. KETU is the very source of detachment and without detachment - you cannot find the way ahead - you remain stuck - you remain where you are!

The moment you start detaching - the moment you start witnessing - the moment you start living your life by LETTING GO - the HEALING begins - and it is only when you can HEAL yourself that you can HEAL others!

Focus on meditation - through meditation, you can HEAL yourself.

And so come, come you all and start meditating. Through meditation, you can overcome the chattering mind. Through meditation, you can find peace within. Meditation is the only miracle that can change you into a new person. KETU is meditation. Ketu is Buddha. And Buddha is a 'PRESENCE' - the Master is no more meditating - HE is 'meditation'.

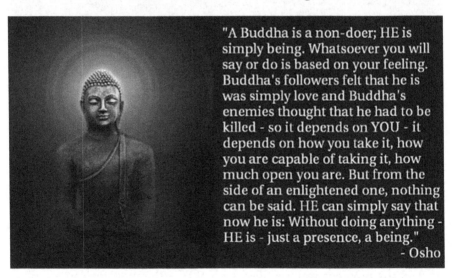

"A Buddha is a non-doer; HE is simply being. Whatsoever you will say or do is based on your feeling. Buddha's followers felt that he is was simply love and Buddha's enemies thought that he had to be killed - so it depends on YOU - it depends on how you take it, how you are capable of taking it, how much open you are. But from the side of an enlightened one, nothing can be said. HE can simply say that now he is: Without doing anything - HE is - just a presence, a being."
- Osho

You all can also become Buddha - you all can also evolve to higher realms of consciousness.

A young man once met a great Yogi and looking at the Yogi, he said, "I feel jealous of you. I have never come across a man like you. Compared to you - all others are subhuman beings. How integrated you are! How beyond the world! Is there any possibility for me to attain such integration, such individuality, such compassion, and such **detachment** to things?

The great Yogi smiled and said, **"It is possible. It is everybody's potential."**

Everything is possible, my fellows - everything is possible - but man is not willing to change - not willing to turn inwards - not willing to meditate!

Man wants everything READY-MADE - he forgets the fact that nothing in this world is READY-MADE - not even happiness!

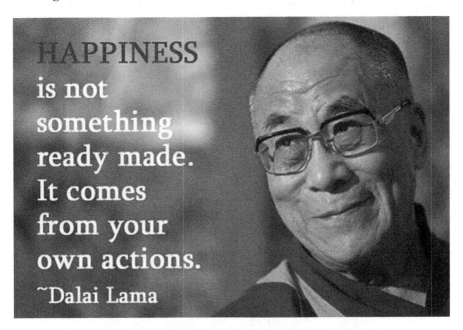

And your ACTIONS will be in the right direction - when you become AWARE - when awareness becomes the torch of your life!

This awareness - this beautiful state of living your life with consciousness comes only when you stop running behind the 'fake gold' and start focusing WITHIN yourself - the 'real gold'!

A fakir once had asked - and his question should be written in GOLD - he had asked, "WHO IS THE REAL KING?"

One who has CONQUERED himself or one who is running to conquer others?

Who is the REAL KING? -

Jesus or the wealthy merchants of this modern world.

Buddha or the men and women who have billions of dollars in their accounts.

Mahavira or those who are falling short of hiding their money and gold and diamonds.

WHO is the REAL KING?

And the question REMAINS. Those who have answered correctly - have gone beyond - they are no more on this planet - they have attained enlightenment.

And those who have answered incorrectly - are still caught up in the many miseries of this human world. They are still counting their money and, along with money, the many miseries of their life.

You all - also have to ANSWER this question - WHO IS THE REAL KING?

The sages and the ancient seers have answered - they have said again and again - it is MAGHA - it is KETU - it is the FAKIR who is the REAL KING!

If you all also can resonate with this answer - then you also can become the REAL KING.

A glimpse of how a REAL KING is! The benevolent Bhagavan - clicked in His natural kingly pose! The whole world is in HIM, and yet HE is not in the world - DETACHED - that's KETU - that's the Master - that is how the LOTUS flower is - rooted in the water - but not in the water! Lotus is ALWAYS seen above the water - the lotus grows - *blossoms above the water...*

"It doesn't matter what you are - rose or lotus - what matters is that you are blossoming..." -Osho

My whole effort is to help you all blossom...

As long as you are *blossoming* - it is enough.

The more you meditate - the more you start turning inwards - the more you start going back to your inner space - the more blossoming will happen - the message of Ketu - the message of Magha is, therefore, in one word - **"Meditate."**

Know meditation. Know life.

Jai Shri Ganesha. Jai Guru.

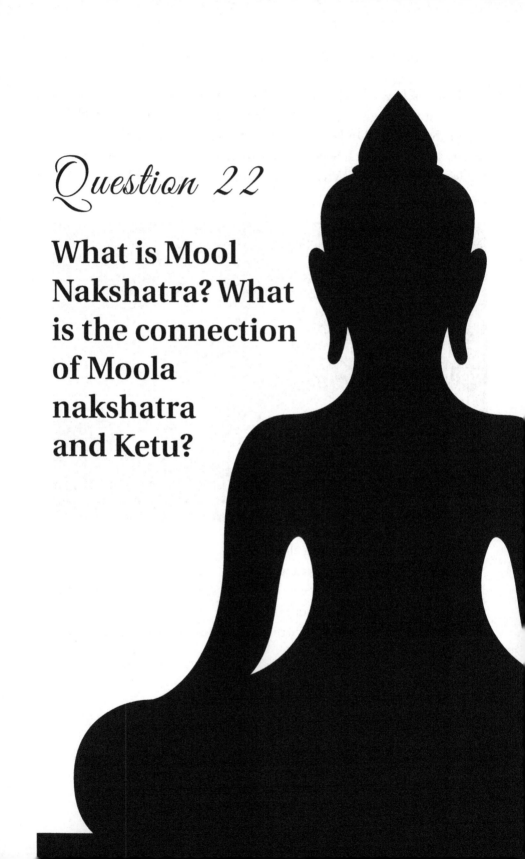

What is Mool Nakshatra? What is the connection of Moola nakshatra and Ketu?

"*First, you have to die - only then can you experience the TRUTH, only then can you experience GOD - only then can you experience true LOVE.*"

That is the message of KETU's Nakshatra MOOLA.

And that was the message of Jesus - *when Nicodemus came on a dark night to meet Jesus.*

And Jesus was sitting beneath a tree. When Nicodemus came - Jesus asked, **"Why have you come to me? What is it that you want from me?"**

Nicodemus is one of the greatest scholars of Jerusalem. Not only he was the wealthiest person but also highly knowledgeable, and yet he had come all the way to meet Jesus on a dark night.

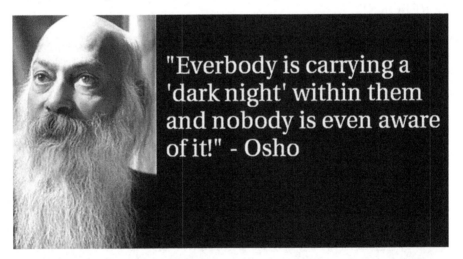

It happened with Nicodemus also - he chose a dark night to meet Jesus, and yet he wasn't aware of the 'dark night' (ignorance) that was within him.

Nicodemus was a very old man - must be in his late eighties - he had been hearing a lot about Jesus - but it was a risk to meet Jesus during the daylight! Because *what would people say? That a great scholar was going to meet a carpenter's son! That was not possible - going in daylight, it was impossible to meet Jesus - and so Nicodemus had come to meet Jesus during the night - a dark night - a no-moon night!*

And Jesus asked, "What is that you want from me?"

331

Nicodemus said, "I want to experience God."

Jesus said, "Even to meet me, you have chosen a dark night - how will you be able to face GOD?"

Nicodemus said, "Then how can I experience GOD?"

And to this - Jesus looked into his eyes and said, "You have to be REBORN."

Nicodemus said, "What do you mean? I should go back to my mother's womb?"

Jesus said, "To be Reborn - you first have to die. This DEATH is not of your physical body - it is the DEATH of all your EGO, your NOTIONS, your IDEAS - unless this DEATH happens - you cannot be REBORN!"

Nicodemus got down on his knees - he started crying – his whole life was spent in gathering knowledge – his whole life was spent in running behind respectability - and now this man - JESUS - had brought a certain light of awareness to his whole being - he started shaking - he touched Jesus's feet - and Jesus blessed Him. With every drop of tear - old

Nicodemus was getting dissolved - and new Nicodemus was taking birth - KETU's MOOLA NAKSHATRA is the state of this DISSOLVING - DISSOLUTION - unless you DISSOLVE - you cannot EVOLVE!

DISSOLVING is the nature of MOOLA - and you will DISSOLVE only when your ROOTS (MOOLA) are SHAKEN! MOOLA means ROOTS - from the ROOT, the 'DISEASE' of ILLUSION (MAYA) should be **DISSOLVED** - that is the whole message of KETU - and that is the whole essence of KETU's Nakshatra - MOOLA!

"The enlightened man, while alive in the body, is *already dissolved.* He knows he is no more, he knows he is a nothingness. The dissolution has already happened." - Osho

PADA is secondary - primary is the NAKSHATRA in itself. The building is important - the apartments within the building make less impact than the building (NAKSHATRA)! And so the focus should be on MOOLA.

Whenever any PLANET falls in MOOLA - the message is simple - DISSOLVE.

7th house planet in MOOLA - Marriage DISSOLVED

4th house planet in MOOLA - Happiness from mother - DISSOLVED

5th house planet in MOOLA - Happiness from children - DISSOLVED

6th house planet in MOOLA - Disputes DISSOLVED (It becomes a blessing in disguise)

8th house planet in MOOLA - Happiness from In-Laws - DISSOLVED

9th house planet in MOOLA - Happiness from father - DISSOLVED

10th house planet in MOOLA - Career Prospects - DISSOLVED

11th house planet in MOOLA - Desires - DISSOLVED (This can become a blessing in disguise if the PATH CHOSEN IS SPIRITUAL)

12th house planet in MOOLA - Loss - DISSOLVED (Again a blessing in disguise)

The larger question is, how this DISSOLUTION helps?

It helps when you raise your CONSCIOUSNESS - when you EXPAND your awareness.

Yesterday Mohan came - he is a man who lost his mother when he was 4.

His FOURTH HOUSE LORD MARS is in MOOLA - Happiness from MOTHER - DISSOLVED!

But GOD wanted something more from Him - and so one afternoon - GOD took away His FATHER! And Mohan was just 15 years old!

Mohan's NINTH house LORD MARS is in MOOLA - Happiness from FATHER - DISSOLVED!

But Mohan had been such a beautiful person - always going with the flow - it is a different story that he had many successes in his life - but whenever anybody would ask him, "What is it that made you so successful?"

He would answer back, "The early DEATH of my MOTHER and FATHER."

MOOLA DISSOLVED HIS FATHER - HIS MOTHER - and through this DISSOLUTION - a new MOHAN was REBORN - a great TRANSFORMATION happened within HIS whole being - HE Was No More The Same Mohan!

TRANSFORMATION is closely related to MOOLA!

FIRST happens the DISSOLUTION - only then happens the TRANSFORMATION!

The old has to be dissolved - only then the NEW can evolve – MOOLA, therefore, is one of the greatest TRANSFORMING ENERGIES - without the DIVINE TOUCH of MOOLA - TRANSFORMATION is not possible - without a SHAKE-UP - transformation is not possible - without a certain PAIN - Transformation is not possible!

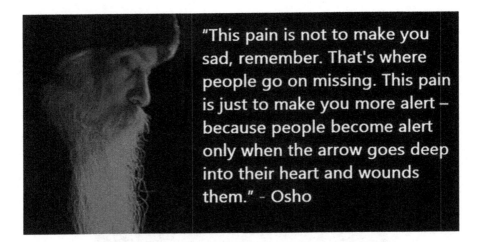

"This pain is not to make you sad, remember. That's where people go on missing. This pain is just to make you more alert – because people become alert only when the arrow goes deep into their heart and wounds them." - Osho

SUN is in MOOLA - the EGO has to BURN - DISSOLVE

MOON is in MOOLA - the illusions (maya) has to BURN - DISSOLVE

MARS is in MOOLA - the nature of FIGHTING, ARGUMENTS, BOSSING over others - ambitions have to BURN - DISSOLVE

Jupiter is in MOOLA - the thought of 'I AM SOMEBODY' has to burn - the verse of BIBLE - "HE must become GREATER and 'I' must become LESS" is what MOOLA means when Jupiter is in MOOLA.

Venus is in MOOLA - You had enough of pleasures - now it is time to give you a nice shake-up - so that you come out of the pleasure-seeking desires and evolve into a much mature person - that is the message of MOOLA.

MERCURY in MOOLA - You had been a hell of a LOGICAL PERSON - now it is time to DISSOLVE the LOGIC and move towards the REAL - LOVE!

Shallow people CANNOT understand the message of MOOLA - they cry - they moan - they make a lot of noise - they even BLAME God - you see - the most IGNORANT person ALWAYS BLAMES others - because that way he finds an ESCAPE ROUTE!

The IGNORANT man's AWARENESS is not yet EVOLVED - he CANNOT understand what GOD is up to. But GOD is perfectly AWARE of what HE is up to.

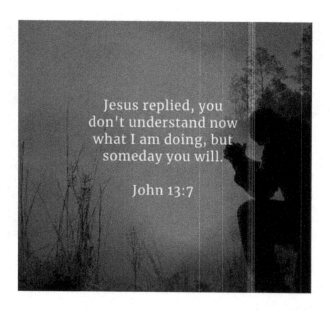

IGNORANT men and women are enslaved by the MIND - they cannot REALIZE - they cannot FIND happiness - even if Buddha, Jesus come to them - it is difficult - because Jesus can take you to the well - but finally, you will DRINK water only if you have the **'THIRST'** - Jesus says - those who thirst for ME - for My Love will be blessed.

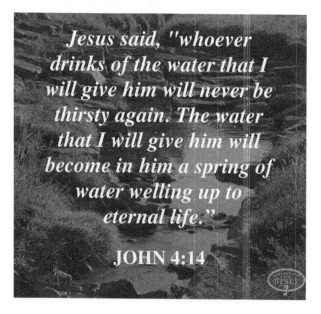

In the Hindu religion - Lord Shiva is addressed as the LORD OF DESTRUCTION!

This DESTRUCTION is of all your ILLUSIONS. This DESTRUCTION is of your EGO. This DESTRUCTION is all of that - WHICH HOLDS YOU BACK FROM EXPERIENCING GOD - FROM EXPERIENCING the DIVINE!

And, therefore, LORD SHIVA is the LORD OF MOOLA - because unless the DISSOLVING happens - unless the DESTRUCTION happens - you cannot be REBORN. That is why Jesus said to Nicodemus, "To experience GOD - to experience the ultimate TRUTH - you have to be REBORN!"

I earnestly bow before the LORD of LORDS - MAHADEV SHIVA!

KETU is SWADHARMA.

And therefore - you all will see KETU's NAKSHATRAS in DHARMA SIGNS -

ASHWINI - ARIES (DHARMA SIGN)
MAGHA - LEO (DHARMA SIGN)
MOOLA - SAGITTARIUS (DHARMA SIGN)
1.5.9. - ARIES. LEO. SAGITTARIUS - these are DHARMA
SIGNS - SIGNS OF SELF NATURE - **SWADHARMA**

"To reach your own self-nature is the ONLY religion. To become that *which you are* - is the only religion. That is why Krishna has emphasized Swadharma, Self-Religion. Self Religion or Swadharma has nothing do with religions. The real meaning of Swadharma is that you settle into your own nature." - Osho

Following your self-nature is **self-religion**. In the Gita - **Lord Krishna** asks Arjuna to follow **Swadharma,** which is **Self-Religion.** Swa - is a Sanskrit word meaning 'Self' and Dharma means 'religion'. Swadharma has NOTHING to do with the religion you follow - it simply has to do with your 'Self-nature'.

When Krishna says to Arjuna - GET UP and SHOOT YOUR ARROW on those who are standing AGAINST TRUTH - he is simply raising AWARENESS to FOLLOW YOUR SELF-NATURE - and if your NATURE is now standing against those who are utterly shameless - utterly sinful - then you don't have to bother if they are your BROTHERS or GRANDPARENTS - you simply have to SHOOT - "SHOOT" - says KRISHNA and ARJUNA shoots - follow SWADHARMA - there is no HEAD, no MIND - only the instinct and the determination to follow SWADHARMA.

KETU is that SWADHARMA - because to FOLLOW your NATURE - you have to keep aside your MIND - your HEAD!

Only then the arrow can SHOOT - only then the GOAL can be attained!

This ARROW - this quality of following the SWADHARMA (Self-Nature) is the quality of MOOLA - among all the three NAKSHATRAS of KETU - MOOLA is the most favorite of KETU - because it is here - that the DESTRUCTION happens - it is here that the DISSOLUTION happens and it is here - through which the NEW WORLD - the NEW LIFE - the NEW MAN is REBORN!

Pain is necessary. Suffering is also necessary. Certain failures are also necessary. Look at the world - today - it is all under LOCK-DOWN - this LOCK-DOWN - this utterly MISERABLE STATE OF THE WHOLE WORLD is a SIGN that a NEW WORLD - a NEW MAN is in the making - POST LOCK-DOWN, you all will see a much HUMBLE, a much WISER population than otherwise!

PRESSURE - MOOLA brings PRESSURE. You all have seen how MOHAN went through PRESSURE - no mother, no father and age was 15. PRESSURE came and through these LIFE PRESSURES - HE CHANGED. HE TRANSFORMED.

PRESSURE - MOOLA - will either force you to DEATH or help you to CHANGE.

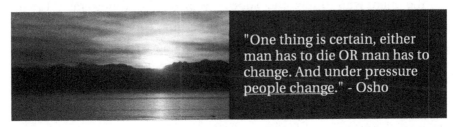

"One thing is certain, either man has to die OR man has to change. And under pressure people change." - Osho

The crop is able to provide quality grains - only when it goes through the pressure of intense heat (sun) - wind and rainfall!

Similarly, every Man and every Woman 'evolves' into a beautiful flower - a beautiful dance - a beautiful poem - when they go through certain pressure - certain pain - certain loss!

MOOLA represents this pain - this pressure - this loss - and it is beautiful!

It is beautiful because through this loss - this pressure - these difficulties - a certain AWARENESS is born WITHIN you and the moment awareness comes to your life - to your presence - a certain glow comes to your living - then even when you are walking - people notice you - even when you are talking - people notice you - even when you are doing nothing - absolutely nothing and still people notice you - because AWARENESS brings a certain GRACE to your being - then you are no more the same - everything around you is the same - but you are no more the same!

Once it happened - a young yogi was giving a discourse. And he was such a beautiful person - full of heart - a song, a dance and he was speaking - sharing - and people were listening - when suddenly a man threw a shoe on him - but the young man was a man of awareness - quickly he caught the shoe that was hurled on him - and with a smile, he asked, "Where is the other shoe? How can I wear only one shoe?"

Now the man who had thrown the shoe was baffled - this was something unusual - he thought the young man would become angry - would start abusing him but nothing sort of that was happening - instead the young man was asking for another shoe! So that a pair is available for him to wear!

The man who threw the shoe - wanted the young man to get embarrassed - but now he himself had become embarrassed - after the discourse was over, he went and met the young yogi and said, "Sorry - please forgive me."

The young yogi said, "Where is the question of forgiving you? - I haven't had any anger towards you - any resentment - any complain - so where is the question of forgiving you?"

But the man took to his heart. He went away, but for the next four months, he would continue to write a letter - asking for forgiveness. The young yogi would find it amusing that when there is absolutely no reason for him to say sorry - then where is the question of forgiving him!

AWARENESS is the key. Once you become aware, then anger cannot attack you - then whenever anger comes - you turn inward and start looking from where the anger is coming. And the moment you start turning inward - the anger cannot haunt you - and you also don't have to control your anger - slowly - you overcome the anger - by turning inward - by becoming more and more meditative.

Moola has immense significance in the whole gamut of astrology and beyond. Through MOOLA - the BEYOND is experienced, and so many YOGIs and SAINTS are also born on MOOLA.

People do some poojas and rituals to bring SHANTI to MOOLA - it is like interfering with NATURE - with the play of GOD - with the existence, and **manipulating is not always an assured solution** - Many times, it boomerangs. Neem Karoli Baba mentions this in the most beautiful way...

"It is very difficult to know exactly what good should come out of a particular situation. To attempt to manipulate circumstances so that *your idea of good* can come about is to <u>let the ego play God</u>-and that, as you know, can and does backfire."

- Neem Karoli Baba

What has to happen, let it happen. Yesterday Mohan said, "My son is born on MOOLA nakshatra - now what to do?"

I said, "There is nothing to do - just go with the flow!"

But people want to MANIPULATE - and then to MANIPULATE, they go on interfering - doing many poojas and rituals - unknowingly they are creating one more circle of misery - because the more you manipulate, the more you try to find an ESCAPE route - the more you will have to come again and again in this HUMAN FORM to FACE that which you have been trying to manipulate and escape!

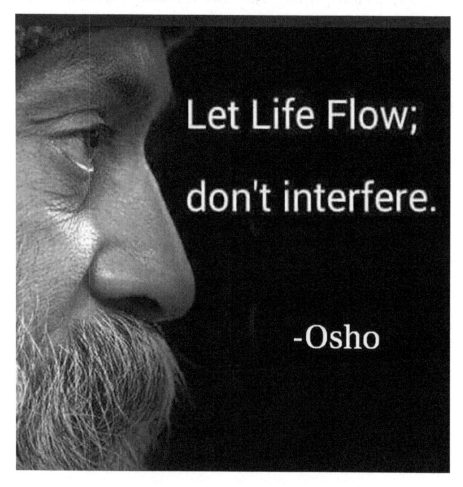

Let Life Flow;

don't interfere.

-Osho

Just go with the flow - let what has to happen - happen - you remain engrossed within - you remain focused within.

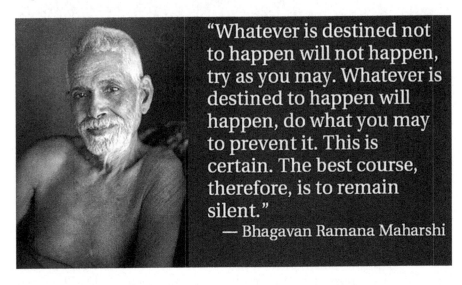

"Whatever is destined not to happen will not happen, try as you may. Whatever is destined to happen will happen, do what you may to prevent it. This is certain. The best course, therefore, is to remain silent."
— Bhagavan Ramana Maharshi

Silence. Silence is the language - real communication happens through silence!

And so let there be more and more silence in your life - in that silence - in that nothingness - you will see the first glimpse of God, and it is beautiful.

KETU has been the most unrealized energy, and yet it is KETU that has brought realization to many!

My new book on Ketu is coming in July 2020. Never had I planned for it - never had I any thoughts about it, but life takes its own course and the compassionate Master - the benevolent Master makes things happen - the DOER is HE - and the moment you come to this realization - a great awakening comes to your being - then there is a song to it - a dance - a beautiful poem!

Life becomes creative when you are in LOVE with LIFE!

"To be creative means to be in love with life. You can be creative only if you love life enough that you want to enhance its beauty, you want to bring a little more music to it, a little more poetry to it, a little more *dance* to it." - Osho

Failures or Success. Pain or Gain - when you remain in love with life - when you are bubbling with energy - then you become a blessing to others - then wherever you go - you bring a glow - you bring a certain fragrance with you - this is how life has to be - this is how you have to be - and this is possible - this can happen only when the DIRT within you is CLEANED - and this CLEANING is done by MOOLA!

So, do not fear the **spiritual cleansing** that Moola brings along - for the '**iron rod**' comes out **shinning** only WHEN IT GOES THROUGH THE FIRE OF SUFFERING!

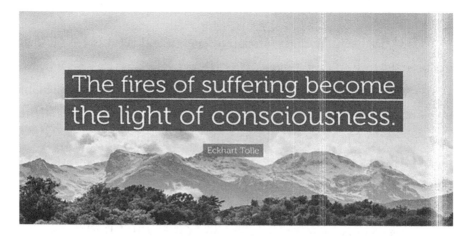

The fires of suffering become the light of consciousness.

Eckhart Tolle

Without the divine touch of MOOLA - consciousness is not possible - GOD is not possible - Love is not possible! MOOLA moves you to the

HIGHEST PEAK OF CONSCIOUSNESS - it has the potential to TRANSFORM you into a NEW MAN.

The more you go through the pressures and sufferings, the more you start turning inward - the more you are blessed, the more you would continue to meditate - and meditation is the only miracle that can and that does transform you into a NEW MAN!

So come - come you all and meditate. 20 minutes every day, you have to find time - because time never finds you! When a person says, "I am just passing time" - it is in reality the other way round - time is passing you - time is moving on - and it is moving very fast - minute after minute - death is coming closer and nobody knows when the last call is to come - it never comes with a fixed appointment - it just STRIKES anytime anywhere!

And so, BEFORE it STRIKES - start turning inward - start looking within - that is the whole essence, and that is the whole purpose of MOOLA - (KETU) to help you come back 'home'!

Nobody can push you - nobody can make you walk - I can show you the way, Buddha can show you the way - the Master can show you the way - but finally it is YOU who have to WALK.

Buddha says, *"I can show you the way, **but you will have to walk.** I cannot walk for you.»*

Walk your way HOME. Come back 'home' (Center of your heart). Come back to your ROOT (MOOLA) - when *you* come home - you come home - and the whole 'world' (MIND) disappears, and then you find your peace.

The key is to come back home.

Be in the world but don't let the world to be in you - stay DETACHED - MOOLA is detaching you - if you can listen to MOOLA - you will find the greatest gift and if you cannot then you will find the deepest misery - the whole essence is in understanding MOOLA - understanding KETU - understanding SHIVA!

Meditate.
Jai Shri Ganesha. Jai Guru.

Question 23

What leads to your birth in a specific family?

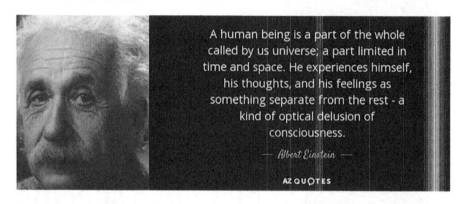

Birth happens. How does it happen? What leads to your birth in a specific family?

What is a family?

Family is a group of souls that in some way or the other have been on the SAME LEVEL OF CONSCIOUSNESS.

> A human being is a part of the whole called by us universe; a part limited in time and space. He experiences himself, his thoughts, and his feelings as something separate from the rest - a kind of optical delusion of consciousness.
>
> — *Albert Einstein* —
>
> AZ QUOTES

Mohan asked, "But sometimes a man or a woman leaves the family and sets on his or her own way..."

That is right - it simply means that NOW his or her CONSCIOUSNESS level has either risen above the consciousness level of his family or has FALLEN below the consciousness level of his family - in both situations, such a man or woman can no longer stay with the family - they move out...

It is the state of CONSCIOUSNESS - that decides the whole course of your birth and rebirths.

Choice always comes your way; you have to make a choice. Every choice that you make - goes on shaping your destiny. To make a good choice - you have to raise your Awareness - consciousness.

> "I want human beings to understand that they have the capacity to fall in their consciousness to the lowest level or they can rise to the highest pinnacle of consciousness." - Osho

You may leave your family - if your consciousness level has risen above the level of your family members AND you may also leave your family - if your consciousness level has fallen below the consciousness level of your family members.

One is a positive development. The other is negative.

A soul takes birth based on his or her consciousness level. There is nobody in the cosmos who directs the soul to take birth in a specific family - the soul finds its own way based on its consciousness level - it selects or is dragged or moved towards a certain family - a certain womb!

So everything happens naturally based on the stages of consciousness. The soul comes exactly into a family whose ISHTADEVTA - the soul has been worshiping for many past births!

Accidents happen. Similarly, accidental births also take place where the ISHTADEVTA of the family and the ISHTADEVTA of the soul happens to be different- in that case as mentioned above - when TIME comes - the individual moves out on his own - his understanding and his consciousness are not in match to that of his family!

Many such real-life scenarios are in existence. One is of PM Narendra Modi - who moved out of his family and went to the Himalayas.

Swami Vivekananda also left his family to seek the spiritual path.

Souls/individuals who leave their families to seek the TRUTH - the ultimate consciousness - God Consciousness - such souls or individuals evolve into beautiful beings.

The negative are those men and women who moved out of their families out of IGNORANCE, EGO - their AGENDA or Purpose of leaving the family is their own selfishness/greed and the lust for more and more material benefits. Such men or women generally fall from Grace.

But those souls or individuals who have simply stepped out of the family to SEEK SPIRITUAL PATH - to EXPERIENCE GOD - to find answers through which they can SERVE the PEOPLE - selflessly - such souls and they are beautiful souls - such souls are blessed with GRACE - they keep moving on until their journey becomes the destination!

Once it happened, I was travelling through the Mountains of Sahayadri when I met a very old man - a Yogi, and he was seated beneath a tree - I went to him, bowed before him. We talked for a while. The old man seemed to have liked me; he said, "I will tell you a story - my life story..."

I said, "I will be blessed to listen to your life story...please..."

The old Yogi said, "I was born in a very wealthy family. I was doing my engineering when I met Shreedhar Swami (the disciple of Samarth Ramdas Swami). Shreedhar Swami was a great Yogi - a man of miracles. And His peace, His bliss, His joy - His smile - the very first time I met him, I lost myself - I completely lost myself - I decided to spend my whole life at His Feet. My family members were also His devotees - my father, my mother - they also loved Him. But I was the only son - the only heir to their 'empire of luxuries and many pleasures and so they wanted me to marry..."

"Then...then what happened?" I asked.

The old Yogi smiled. He said, "I told them, I will not marry, I don't want to marry...I have taken to celibacy - and I have started fasting on every Ganesha Chaturthi - now don't force me into marriage."

"So did they agree?" I asked.

The old Yogi smiled and said, "Do you think they would give up so soon?"

I asked, "So what did they do?"

"They went to Shreedhar Swami - and started complaining about my attitude towards marriage - my decision of not indulging in marriage."

Shreedhar Swami smiled at them. Swamiji's way of speaking was very gentle and soft - but his words were so powerful that they would move the mountains!

And so Swamiji looked at my father and mother - and said, "Your son has taken to celibacy for the betterment of the people - if you force him into marriage - you will be responsible for your debacle and then even I would not be in a position to help you. Let him do what his heart wants to - I cannot stop him; you also should not stop him."

"After that day," said the old Yogi, "nobody stopped me - I left all those riches and pleasures and moved away from them - towards my master... I never met them again - I don't even remember what happened to them, I was so much engrossed in my penance...but wherever they are, they must be in good shape."

When the consciousness is no more the same as of your family - when the consciousness has risen above - you will move out of your family - to seek that which cannot be bought in the market - to seek that which cannot be earned - cannot be stolen - cannot be shared - but can only be realized through your own self-realization!

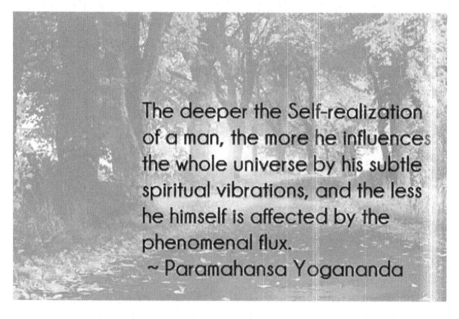

The deeper the Self-realization of a man, the more he influences the whole universe by his subtle spiritual vibrations, and the less he himself is affected by the phenomenal flux.
~ Paramahansa Yogananda

Astrology cannot help, but it is your self-realization that can help you to identify with your ISHTADEVTA.

Generally, the ISHTADEVTA of the family - happens to be the ISHTADEVTA of the individual who is born in that family.

That is the reason that I always emphasize on focusing on the Family Deity - KULDEV AND KULDEVI.

Samarth Ramdas - the Guru of Shivaji Maharaj, has specifically mentioned that every individual should first worship and remember his or her family deity - KULDEV and KULDEVI.

But people don't get it. They run from one temple to the other. Many are not even aware of their family deities. Some know the God but don't know who the Goddess i! Some know the Goddess but don't know the God.

Before the British rule, Hindu families all over the Indian subcontinent were aware of their family deities - God - KULDEV and Goddess - KULDEVI.

But then came the British rule and the changing lifestyle and demands created a GAP. Today, this gap has become the primary reason for many families who are lost - simply lost. They don't know their family deities - they keep visiting hundreds of temples, but nothing happens for good!

How will it happen? When you are knocking on the wrong door - when you are dialing the wrong number.

The right door is the door of your family deity. The right number to connect is your family deity's number.

But people are shallow. People are relating everything with Astrology, and that is where they go on missing. I would not want my followers to do this mistake else, they too will get trapped in astrology!

Astrology should not become a trap. Should not become a blockage to your FREE WILL. But that is what is happening, and it is very unfortunate- very tragic.

God cannot be found by your logic. God cannot be realized by your astrology. God cannot be understood by your calculations.

"If you really want to understand God, then life has to be loved because it is divine. Life has to be affirmed with your total being because God is hidden in it. God is another name for life, another name for love. Life is to become your God. Then whatever life implies becomes divine." - Osho

And so I appeal to all my followers, fellow travelers and readers that STOP identifying everything through the narrow glasses of astrology - let your vision be wider - throw away those narrow glasses and look up in the SKY (consciousness) and the solution, the answer will be found.

Identification or identifying is totally based on your perception - the deeper you move within - the more you can identify with the real problems of your life - the real hurdles to your growth.

Krishna has provided with the most significant 'key' that can help every conscious individual to attain self-realization. What is the 'key'?

Swadharma (स्वधर्म)

Following your self-nature is self-religion. In the Gita - Lord Krishna asks Arjuna to follow Swadharma, which is Self-Religion. Swa - is a Sanskrit word meaning 'Self' and Dharma means 'religion'. Swadharma has NOTHING to do with the religion you follow - it simply has to do with your 'Self-nature'.

"To reach your own self-nature is the ONLY religion. To become that *which you are* - is the only religion. That is why Krishna has emphasized Swadharma, Self-Religion. Self Religion or Swadharma has nothing do with religions. The real meaning of Swadharma is that you settle into your own nature." - Osho

Self-Nature - your nature, your consciousness becomes your ISHTADEVTA - your RELIGION - your GOD - and it is this consciousness that finally leads you towards the beyond - the unseen - GOD.

CONSCIOUSNESS is the greatest ISHTADEVTA. But human beings need some support of the 'Idol' - of a certain 'God' who himself has become the ultimate consciousness - KRISHNA CONSCIOUSNESS, JESUS CONSCIOUSNESS, SHIVA CONSCIOUSNESS - you see - that is how GOD becomes the BRIDGE for you to move towards CONSCIOUSNESS - because GOD is the ultimate fragrance of your consciousness!

For many, the family deity is itself the Ishtadevta. You are born into a family that worships the God or ISHTADEVTA that you have been worshipping in your past births.

So the first step is to first worship the family deity (KULDEV and KULDEVI). Then, the way ahead manifests before you when the time is right.

Many times, when the soul has accidentally taken birth in a family whose family deity is not matching to his or her ISHTDEVTA then when they continue to worship the family deity - someday, at some point in their life - they themselves self-realize - who is their ISHTADEVTA.

But in general, the family deity is the ISHTADEVTA, and even if you continue to worship the family deity - it is more than enough.

Astrology is not the way to identify with your ISHTADEVTA. Through ASTROLOGY - people are finding GOD! And that is the greatest irony of this human world.

And GOD is laughing - because through CALCULATIONS - through the futile exercise of finding the ISHTADEVTA through this house and that house of birthchart - you can never find the ISHTADEVTA.

You can find the ISHTADEVTA - the one who benefits you - only when you start turning inward - when you start meditating - when you start looking within.

But people are shallow. They like to entertain their mind - their intellect - they like calculations, and the height of their stupidity is that they BELIEVE that TRUTH can be found through Calculations!

And I am a totally different kind of man - I know nothing - I am a total ZERO - if you ask me calculations - I will show you the door because you are using your MIND and I have no mind - How will you relate to my answer? You are in your HEAD, and I am in my HEART - disconnection is inevitable!

The connection is only possible when the language that I speak is the language that you speak. And that is what Buddha has been doing His whole life - trying to make people REMEMBER the forgotten language - the language of the heart.

The last word of Buddha was "SAMMASTI" - meaning REMEMBER. Just REMEMBER the space WITHIN you - just REMEMBER to come back to yourself - AGAIN and AGAIN until you are deeply rooted within - then nobody can disturb you - nobody can steal away anything from you - then you remain unmoved - you remain just a 'presence'!

The divine master is just a 'PRESENCE' - you may insult him, you may love him, you may try to harm him, you may try to appease him - all that is happening is from YOU - the Master is not affected by any of your actions - the Master is just a presence - a pure omnipresence.

With our love, hate is inevitably present. If you love someone, you know hate will be there. If someone loves you, you will expect both - love and hate. Hate gives a passion to love; an intensity. But what happens in a *Buddha-like Consciousness* - when love and hate both disappear? In that state - you cannot feel love, and you cannot feel hate. But whosoever is around you feels a deep love flowing...through your whole being - that is the state of a true master. Buddha cannot feel love or hate. The polar opposite disappears - and simple presence remains. Buddha is a 'presence' - not a mood. We are moods - not a presence. And we remain 'moods' as long as we remain trapped in the MIND - the moment you start slipping out of the mind - you start slipping out of the 'moods'.

"Sometimes you are hate, one mood, sometimes you are love - another mood; sometimes you are anger - another mood; sometimes you are greed - another mood. You are moods, you are never a pure presence, and your CONSCIOUSNESS goes on being MODIFIED by your MOODS. Each mood becomes the master. It modifies the consciousness, cripples it, changes it, colors, deforms it." - Osho

Many were AGAINST Buddha - many tried to KILL Him - it all depends on YOU - You can either become a friend, a lover or an enemy - depends on you, on your sensitivity, on your mind - how your mind feels. It all DEPENDS on YOU. Buddha will NOT react, you may go on pressing all the 'buttons' that you have known - but you cannot disturb the one who is enlightened. If you HATE - that is your take. If you LOVE - that is your understanding. The master remains unmoved - undisturbed - you cannot make Him happy, and you cannot make Him unhappy - He is not a 'mood' - He is a 'Presence' - a conscious presence.

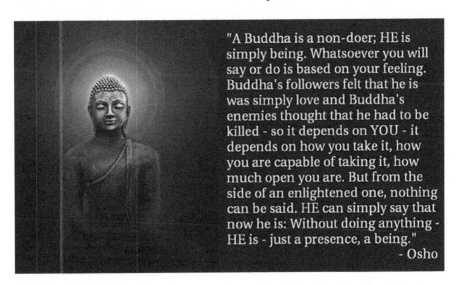

"A Buddha is a non-doer; HE is simply being. Whatsoever you will say or do is based on your feeling. Buddha's followers felt that he is was simply love and Buddha's enemies thought that he had to be killed - so it depends on YOU - it depends on how you take it, how you are capable of taking it, how much open you are. But from the side of an enlightened one, nothing can be said. HE can simply say that now he is: Without doing anything - HE is - just a presence, a being."
                                                                    - Osho

To be with the master is to be with a 'presence'! To be with the master is to BE HERE NOW. And to BE HERE NOW - in this MOMENT is MEDITATION!

And so when you are with your master, when you are REMEMBERING HIM every minute of your life - every breath of your life - then where is the need to take any special efforts to MEDITATE? Meditation happens on its own - everything starts happening on its own - the ISHTDEVTA is also found in His PRESENCE - then all the GODS and GODDESSES are also found in His PRESENCE!

Once it happened - Sai Baba was alone in Shirdi, and a very close devotee remained with Him. Sai Baba said, "Why you stayed behind when the whole village has gone to seek the blessing of Lord Shiva?"

The devotee's eyes were filled with tears - looking at Sai - he said, "Baba - my Shiva is YOU - I could see HIM in your PRESENCE - I could FEEL HIM in your PRESENCE - then what is the need to go anywhere???"

Sai Baba smiled. Lovingly he nodded his head - and a certain fragrance emerged through His Presence - the devotee said, "These are the same incense sticks that I had given to the villagers to instill at the Lord Shiva's temple!"

Incense sticks were instilled and burned 1000 miles away from Shirdi and yet its fragrance was coming through the omnipresence of Sai!!!

How to express such a beautiful incident - language is really poor, words cannot suffice!

One has to go through all kinds of experiences that life provides with. It is through experiences that you evolve - so never be afraid of any experiences.

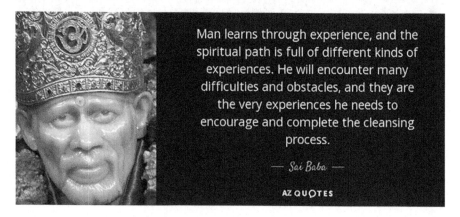

Man learns through experience, and the spiritual path is full of different kinds of experiences. He will encounter many difficulties and obstacles, and they are the very experiences he needs to encourage and complete the cleansing process.

— *Sai Baba* —

AZ QUOTES

The greater the cleansing process, the greater is the GROWTH WITHIN!

Family changes from birth to birth - because as the state of level of your consciousness changes - so do your birth destinations! When you spend your life with more IGNORANCE and less consciousness - your next birth is of inferior level - when you spend your life with more CONSCIOUSNESS - and less ignorance - your next birth is of a superior level!

And so based on the state of your level of consciousness - your father and mother, your wife/husband, your friends, your overall quality of life keeps changing from birth to birth - but what remains the same is your ISHTADEVTA - your GURU - your LORD!

In simple words - if you fail (IGNORANCE), you remain in the same standard, if you pass (CONSCIOUSNESS) - you move to the next standard - this cycle continues - many have FALLEN and many have 'GRADUATED' and those who have GRADUATED have become the greatest SAINTS that the world had ever known!

But people are shallow - they say, "Those men or women who became Saints, Yogis - they all must be extraordinary."

Shallow people categorize the evolved beings in a 'Separate Category'!

"That is what we have done with Buddha, Mahavira, Adinatha, Patanjali, Kabir : we have put them in a separate category. They are special people, we are ordinary people. But they were also ordinary before they took the jump. It is the jump that has made them extraordinary, not that there were extraordinary - hence they could jump. The reality is *vice-versa*." - Osho

The evolved beings were also at some point in their life - as ordinary as you and I are! But then what transformed them from ordinary to extraordinary??

COURAGE. COURAGE to JUMP into the unknown!

Worshiping Hanuman brings courage - AND it is this courage that enables you to 'JUMP'- to 'RISK'!

The most beautiful way to worship Hanuman is to recite the HANUMAN CHALISA!

"Every line of the Hanuman Chalisa is a Mahamantra."
- Neem Karoli Baba

Hanuman Chalisa - It is a miraculous devotional hymn (stotra) written in praise of the Monkey-God - Hanuman! And it is written by one of the greatest saints in the Indian civilization - Saint Tulsidas.

His divine words have touched the hearts of millions - and continue to inspire. I humbly prostrate before one of the greatest devotees of Lord Hanuman - Saint Tulsidas.

The beauty of the divine devotional verse of HANUMAN CHALISA is that - it brings great courage to you - you suddenly become very courageous and strong like the monkey god Hanuman who carried a mountain in his hands!

And COURAGE is very important. You cannot propose a girl - if you have no courage. You cannot propose to God - if you have no courage! The door to LOVE opens only when you have courage to express your love - the door to GOD also opens only when you have courage to MEDITATE and express your devotion!

Meditation is possible only when you are courageous. Only a courageous man, a courageous woman can meditate.

When you sit with closed eyes - what happens? Millions and millions of thoughts engulf you - create a lot of noise - you feel as if thousands of bees are buzzing all over your head - now tell me, can a coward continue to sit? He or she will quickly get up - they will never dare to meditate again!

But a courageous man, a courageous woman - they will not give up - they will let all those thoughts come and go - they will treat those thoughts as VISITORS - they will NOT entertain those thoughts - they will show tremendous courage by IGNORING the thoughts and FOCUSING on the BREATHING - by FOCUSING on the GOD's name.

And so to meditate - one needs to be courageous and to be courageous - one needs to be TRUTHFUL!

You see - how all is inter-connected! And unless you understand and self-realize the inter-connections - you will not realize the way it all happens - everything is interconnected - this whole universe is interconnected - the only difference is that the SWITCH is not on - the moment the SWITCH is on - you too will start realizing the interconnection - you too will start realizing that you are NOT separate from this Universe - you too will start realizing the ONENESS (Advait) - that everything is ONE - ONE PARMATAMA - ONENESS!

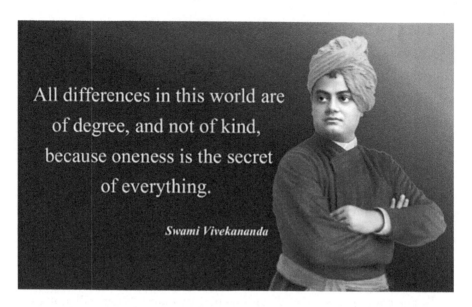

All differences in this world are of degree, and not of kind, because oneness is the secret of everything.

Swami Vivekananda

ISHTDEVTA or KULDEVTA - all the DEVTAs and all the Gods are simply to help you move towards ONENESS. And always remember, before the GOD comes first the GURU!

Through the GURU, all the Gods of this whole universe can be experienced. But before all the Gods comes first, the benevolent compassionate Guru.

"If here before me stand both- my Guru and Govind the almighty, I'd first prostrate my Guru. because it is He, who revealed to me, the Govind." - Sant Kabir

Gods will come - only when you have the blessing of the Guru, the benevolent master!

Without the Guru, nothing is possible. With the Guru, everything is possible!

The first birth is through the mother; the second, the true birth, spiritual birth to which Jesus calls 'Reborn' - is through the master.

And it is only when you are REBORN - that God can be experienced, TRUTH can be experienced, LOVE can be experienced!

The way towards the beyond - the journey within begins only when you are blessed by the benevolent compassionate Guru.

You never have to find your Guru - the Guru finds you. It is the Guru who chooses his disciple. When you live with faith, with love, with compassion and when the 'thirst' to find HIM grows within your whole being - so much so that you cannot remain without HIM - He comes... when you are 'ready' - the master will come.

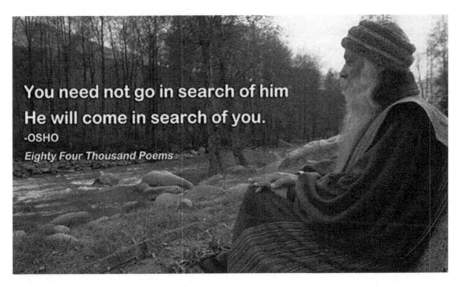

You need not go in search of him
He will come in search of you.
-OSHO
Eighty Four Thousand Poems

Peter, the fisherman never had to go in search of Jesus. Jesus came to him. Arjuna never had to go in search of Krishna. Krishna came to him. Sariputta never had to search Buddha, Buddha came to his town. The master comes, when you are 'ready' - when you have become a full moon - when you are willing to surrender yourself - when you are ready to live your life in total surrender!

That is the word - a miraculous word - SURRENDER. Unless there is surrender - there is no coming to the truth - there is no coming to the master. The whole story of your life swings from one point of EGO to the other point of total SURRENDER - you all should ask yourself, on which side you are - the side you decide to be with - shapes your life. What you choose is what you become. What you follow is what you become. It all begins with YOU - it is the conscious choices that you make in your life - that matter!

Choose wisely. Choose consciously.

A life lived by choice is a life of consciousness - and a life worth living!

Meditate.
Jai Shri Ganesha. Jai Guru.

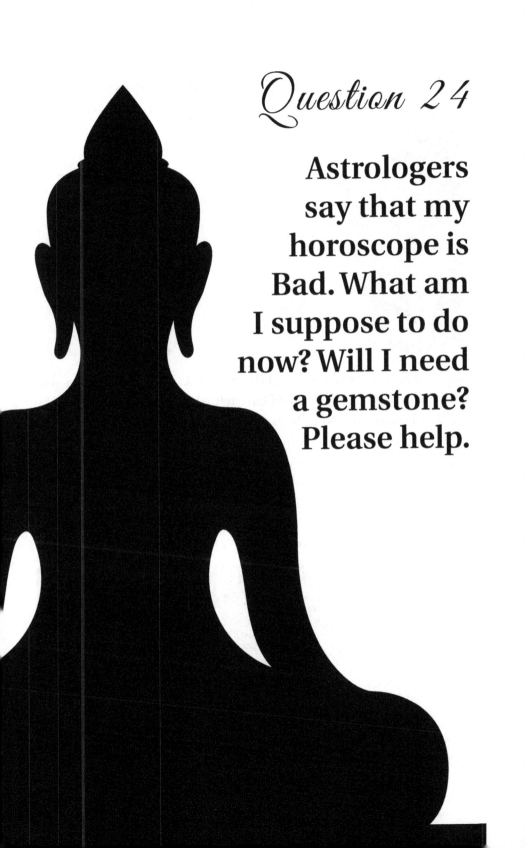

Question 24

Astrologers say that my horoscope is Bad. What am I suppose to do now? Will I need a gemstone? Please help.

No horoscope is bad. And no horoscope is good either! Good and Bad is the play of the Mind. And the MIND is a monkey.

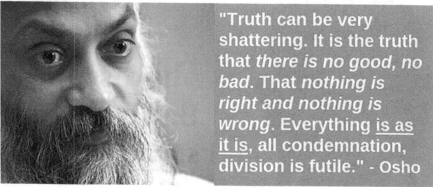

"Truth can be very shattering. It is the truth that *there is no good, no bad*. That *nothing is right and nothing is wrong*. Everything is as it is, all condemnation, division is futile." - Osho

Always remember, you are the CHILD OF GOD. And God loves You. **I can understand how you would have felt** when you were humiliated **by people who said your Kundli (birthchart) is bad - very bad.**

But don't worry, such men and women are fast asleep, and those who are asleep cannot help you with the TRUTH. And the Truth is that **every Kundli comes with a certain purpose** – something has to be done – some unfinished business has to be finished – you are NOT born accidentally - the UNIVERSE has a purpose to be met through YOU! So then, how come you become useless? How come you become bad?

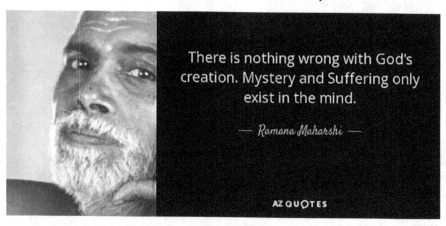

There is nothing wrong with God's creation. Mystery and Suffering only exist in the mind.

— Ramana Maharshi —

AZ QUOTES

Good or Bad – is totally based on **situations**! If a KNIFE becomes your shield – and you can save yourself – protect yourself, then the KNIFE becomes your savior! And if the KNIFE is used to harm you – then the same KNIFE becomes your killer. Now if you ask me –Whether a KNIFE is good or bad?

The answer is impossible – a conscious person would never LABEL anything or any person as GOOD or BAD – he is perfectly aware that it all depends on what PURPOSE is – if the purpose is GOOD – then even a KNIFE becomes GOD, if the purpose is GOOD then even the most condemned man or woman can prove to be a great savior of mankind!

Once it happened – a young man and what a man he was – simple, hardworking and always helpful to all the people of his village. One day – he lost his wife; **she died in an accident.** After a few days – **he lost his daughter.** She fell sick, and he was short of money, the doctor won't come – and the only daughter that he had, took her last breath at midnight when the whole village was fast asleep. She was only six years old, and now the young man had to take her dead body all the way to the graveyard – all alone. Now there was nobody in his life – everything was lost – everything was gone. People started gossiping – 'this man must have done many sins in his past life.' – some would say 'this man must be a curse to our village' – some said 'how ill-fated this man is' – and slowly all the villagers started condemning him – they started maintaining distance from him. Now the young man left out by all – took to drinking. He became a drunkard.

And every day he was found with a bottle in his hand, swinging around, walking through the narrow lanes of the village. The villagers decided to kick him out of the village but they couldn't – law would not let them do so...

And so, they all would try by every means and ways – to ridicule him, to insult him – to treat him like an animal – and the young man would laugh – he would simply laugh – and move on.At times, a few villagers would beat him – and he would start bleeding – and yet he would not say anything – he would just slip out and keep moving from one place to the other...

One day – it started raining, and the rains were so heavily showering that the village was flooded with rain water – the rains were not stopping – many houses were flooded, people became homeless – the crying of the women, of the children – the havoc all around…and the young man could not control himself…he could not see dying children and the plight of the women of his village – and so for the first time in his life – he looked up in the sky and said, "GOD – if you stop the rain, I will stop drinking. And that is my word."

And the miracle happened – the rain stopped! God said, "If by stopping the rains – one good thing is happening – if one man is waking up from his 'sleep' – then it is worth it."

And the rains stopped – and the man started crying – he became one of the greatest lovers of God that the world has ever known – the villagers came and said, "You saved our lives – you please stay with us – we will help you in every way we can…"

But the young man was fired up – he was no more the same – he said, "I am leaving now – the call from the mountains has come – God has chosen me and my 'journey' has begun!"

And it is said that the young man went on to become one of the finest Yogis that the world has ever known! A man who was condemned – a man who has beaten to bleed – a man who was LABELED as BAD – becomes the finest YOGI – everything is POSSIBLE – and I say it to all my readers – everything is POSSIBLE – only if your HEART is pure – only if you are a man of HEART and not of HEAD.

People are shallow. The majority is shallow – they are quick to Judge – rarely they can observe – and observation without evaluation is the highest form of INTELLIGENCE!

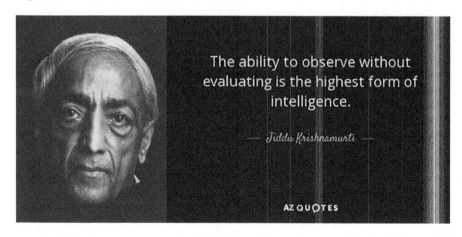

The ability to observe without evaluating is the highest form of intelligence.

— *Jiddu Krishnamurti* —

AZ QUOTES

Observe. A very deep word – the Yogi only observes – deep observation. The Yogi will never label you as BAD – he will simply observe. Through this observation – he may feel sorry for you – he may feel compassion for you – he may try to HELP you and NOT condemn you.

But astrologers are quick to condemn – quick to LABEL someone as BAD, and that is the greatest tragedy of this human world. It is shallow – so shallow that the real Yogi is, therefore, not found in this crowd – HE moves as an INDIVIDUAL – because he is perfectly aware that TRUTH happens to an Individual and not to a crowd.

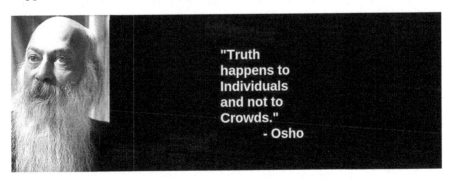

Your MIND is made to **believe** that your horoscope is BAD. The second question about finding a gemstone is a *by-product* of **your belief,** and it is **belief** that becomes the greatest hurdle between YOU and your PROGRESS.

"Belief is PURE POISON. Never believe a thing. Experiment, live it thoroughly so that you can say on your own authority that it is true." - Osho

An intelligent man never believes – HE experiments – and then, based on his experiments – HIS OWN EXPERIENCE – he comes to the TRUTH of the matter. It is HIS experiences that make him a REAL MAN – an INDIVIDUAL who never believes but always experiments and enriches his life with experiences.

Belief is disastrous because it closes your MIND – once you believe that 'Cutting your hair on a certain day is bad' – then no matter what – you will never cut your hair on that specific day! Now there is NO proof of anything bad happening – but just because you have come to believe – you have simply closed your mind. Now even if Jesus comes – Krishna comes – Buddha comes – Mahavira comes – nobody could convince you – because you have simply closed your mind by BELIEVING that hair should not be cut on a certain day – else GOD will get angry at you!

Now what GOD has to do with what you do with your hair! There are millions and millions of people on this planet, and God certainly has much better things to do than to watch who is cutting when!

But people fall for beliefs – and that is how they go on missing the many opportunities that God brings on…

"If you have a belief and you come against an experience which the belief says is not possible, or - the experience is such that you have to drop the belief, what are you going to choose - the belief or the experience? The tendency of the mind is to choose the belief, to forgot about the experience. That's how you have been missing many opportunities when God has knocked at your door."
- Osho

There are women who are approached by men who are simply awesome – and yet the women go on rejecting them because they are MANGLIK!

There are men who are approached by beautiful, well-cultured women, and yet they go on rejecting because they belong to different community and marriage with somebody who is outside the community or caste is 'believed' to bring miseries to the family!

So you see – BELIEF plays a major role in people's lives – they are well-educated but what they follow is BELIEF, and NOT experience and that keeps them away from the TRUTH – from LOVE – from GOD!

A young man was in love. It happens – love happens at the most unexpected moment, and you can't help – you just can't! You cannot 'manage' love – it is not politics!

And so the young man fell in love – and what a beautiful woman she was! Her glow, her smile, her grace – her soft voice, her understanding – the young man could not stop himself from falling in love! He was a meditative man...he was aware that he is falling in love – but still he could not stop himself! Love is very powerful – more powerful than electricity!

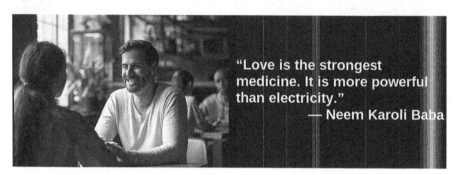

"Love is the strongest medicine. It is more powerful than electricity."
— Neem Karoli Baba

And so love blossomed – he fell madly in love with that woman. Love is alchemist – you become what you love! And the woman was a strong believer of astrology! The young man also started believing in astrology. And then one day – something strange happened...

The young woman came and she said, "We need to break up."

The man was shocked. He said, "What happened? Did I do anything that made you upset? Please tell me – you are breaking my heart..."

The woman said, "There is nothing wrong with you – in fact, I have been dating with you for the last 10 months, and you have been such a gentleman..."

"Then why are you breaking up?" asked the young man.

And the woman said, "Because my astrologer has said that your HOROSCOPE IS BAD and it is so BAD that it should be thrown away in a dustbin."

The man fainted. She had to call an ambulance – but that was the only day when she met him – they never met again. Never.

You see – she says 'you are a gentleman – you have been such a gentleman…all the time we were together…..' – her EXPERIENCE says that the man is a real gem of a person – but it is HER BELIEF that overshadows the EXPERIENCE – the FACTS!

The man went into a trauma for the next six months until he was finally out of it!

It is a MYTH that it is only WOMEN who become victims of LOVE and RELATIONSHIPS – the majority is of MEN who suffer more than the WOMEN! On this planet, there are more men – who take pills at night to overcome their breakup trauma and depression than the women!

BELIEF plays a role – a major role and not the experience. You can easily come out of the BELIEF that your HOROSCOPE is BAD – only when you put aside the monkey mind and start turning inward! Just look inward and you become aware of the TRUTH. Then you don't ask for beliefs. Blind people believe in light. Those who have turned inward – have the 'eyes' and they don't need to believe in light – they simply see it.

But there was one blind man – who believed that there is NO LIGHT. And he was very good at logic. He was a very logical person – and the villagers were fed up of him because he would argue that to experience light – either he has to FEEL the light – smell the light or touch the light!

Now light has no smell, and you cannot feel the light – neither can you touch the light! And so the blind man would laugh at them and say, "There is no such thing as light – you all are blind like me – and you all are just fooling me – there is no light."

The villagers had no answer. But one day – Buddha was passing by – and the villagers thought that now the moment has come – only Buddha can answer this blind man – and so they took the blind man to Buddha. They said, "This blind man is a logical man, and through his logic, he has been denying the fact that there is 'light' in this world – now only you can help us – please help us."

Buddha said, "The blind man is right – and you all are wrong. What he needs is eyes to see and not argumentation. You have come to the wrong person – he needs a physician – take him to a good physician."

The villagers asked, "Do you know any good physician – because we don't have anybody in our village who can cure this man's eyes?"

Buddha said, "You can take him to my personal physician."

A great King had provided a personal physician to follow Buddha – just so that he can take care of Buddha's body. And so the blind man was brought to Buddha's physician and Buddha left the village.

After a few months, the blind man's eyes were cured. It was not that he had lost his eyes – it was just some severe infection that had brought a certain blindness to his eyes, and now his eyes were cured. The blind man was no more blind – his joy knew no bounds – the first thing he did was to ask, "Where is Buddha? Where is the man who has given back – my eyes? I want to meet him….please tell me where is Buddha – where is the master?"

Nobody could give him the address of Buddha because Buddha never lived at one place for more than a month. And so they just showed him the road through which Buddha had walked – that was the only time when they had seen the Buddha walking out of their village! And the man took to the path of Buddha – he searched and searched and he would ask everybody at every village – every town – "Did you see my master – did you see the Buddha?" And people would just show him the way…they would say, "That was the road we had seen him walking…"

For many days and weeks, the man searched until one day while walking through a forest – he dropped down, he was thirsty and somebody came from behind and said, "Take some water…you must be thirsty…" And the voice…the voice moved the man's heart – he remembered the voice, it was of the Buddha – the same conviction – the same depth – the same love – the same care – the man turned around and his eyes were filled with tears – he started crying – he couldn't control himself – looking at the Buddha, he said, "Master…O master, I have been searching for you…look, look at my eyes – they are yours – they are a gift of yours – how should I thank you – because of you I got back my eyes and to meet you – to share this joy with you, I have been searching you all this while."

Buddha said, "Look now, I have come – now you can relax. Whenever my devotee thirsts for me – I come – my legs move towards those who are deeply in love with me – who are thirsty for my love – you relax, now I am with you."

And the man relaxed – he relaxed so much in the existence that he went into a trance – he transcended the moment Buddha touched him with His 'Presence' – the man became one of the greatest lovers of

Buddha and whenever anybody would ask him, "What is the reason you love Buddha?"

His would answer, "Experience."

Experience matters – not belief. The man experienced the compassion of Buddha. Buddha provided his personal physician to treat the blind man – who would offer his or her personal physician to a complete stranger? But it was Buddha's compassion – HIS love – HIS grace that moved the blind man – to him – BUDDHA was GODLY – and Godliness is **not** something that can be proved or disproved by your logic. Godliness is something that can only be EXPERIENCED!

And so before you start BELIEVING that what has been told to you is the TRUTH – my appeal to you and through your question – to all my readers, followers and fellow travelers is that – instead of believing – instead of falling prey to your belief – turn inwards – and EXPERIENCE *who you really are* by being more and more meditative!

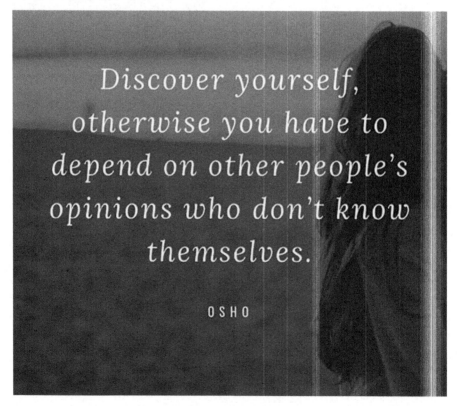

Discover yourself, otherwise you have to depend on other people's opinions who don't know themselves.

OSHO

Once you become a meditative man – you don't have to rely on what others say about you – then there is a certain depth to your life – a certain music to your life – then everything around you is the same but you are no more the same – then the 'noise' on the outside remains but the peace within you remains undisturbed by the noise on the outside – then you are truly transforming – then you are in the true sense – PROGRESSING – GROWING – for the real GROWTH is the GROWTH WITHIN!

When your BELIEF drives your life – you become a coward – you become a closed mind – you become fearful – and then **this fear compels you** *to find some SUPPORT* to comfort you! The gemstones that you seek are an outcome of the compulsion that is born out of fear!

And the more you go on believing – the more you would destroy all the possibilities to LIVE YOUR LIFE TO THE FULLEST.

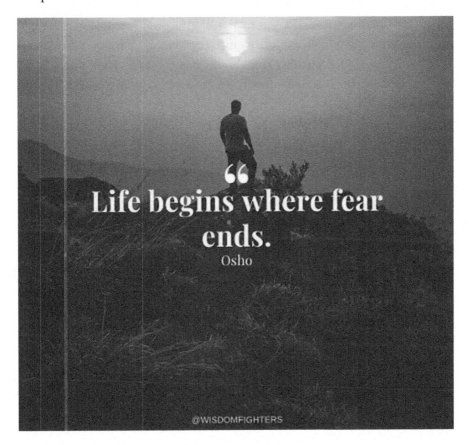

> **Life begins where fear ends.**
> Osho

@WISDOMFIGHTERS

My whole message through this answer to you and to all my readers, followers, and fellow travelers is that FOCUS ON YOUR OWN EXPERIENCES and DROP ALL YOUR BELIEFS – only then a beautiful person within you will evolve – only then, there is a possibility for you all to live a joyous, happy life!

And that is what we all are here for! To live a happy life. But it is our ignorance – our beliefs that come in the way, and then you wonder, "What is wrong with my life?"

Nothing is wrong with your life – if at all there is anything WRONG then it is WITHIN YOU and unless and until you start turning inwards – unless and until you start meditating – you will continue to live your life by relying on others. You will continue to focus on the outside – and you will continue to miss the fact that NOTHING on the outside can be controlled – but only from WITHIN!

Just watch. Someone today is a friend, tomorrow becomes a stranger. Someone today likes you, tomorrow dislikes you. Someone you have been trusting betrays you someday. **You should never rely on that which is on the 'outside' – you have absolutely no control on that which is on the 'outside'** – *people change, situations change, life goes on changing, people come and go* – and **there are many who will come and go...**you just have to Watch – by being a 'witness'.

"Meditation is witnessing. To meditate means to become a witness."

"Watch from your inner sky and let the clouds float. Become just a watcher. And remember, clouds will come and go, you can remain *indifferent*."
- Osho

Remain indifferent – remain unmoved – and you will be able to do so – only when you turn inwards – when you meditate.

And so come – come you all and sit down and meditate – what happens when you start meditating – millions and millions of thoughts start creating a lot of noise within you – and while all this happens – what you are supposed to do?

WITNESS. Just WITNESS the many thoughts that come to your mind – you don't have to entangle your 'self' in those thoughts – you don't have to entertain any of those thoughts – you just have to treat all those thoughts as VISITORS – and visitors should not be served with TEA! And so never entertain the thoughts when you meditate – the very base of meditation is the WITNESSING – the more you become a WITNESS – the more you will be able to focus on the SELF without getting distracted by the THOUGHTS. When there are thoughts – it is a distraction – when there are no thoughts – it is meditation, says the Bhagavan. Bhagavan Ramana Maharshi!

The key is to WITNESS while you meditate! And the same key also enables you to overcome the many challenges of material life as well.

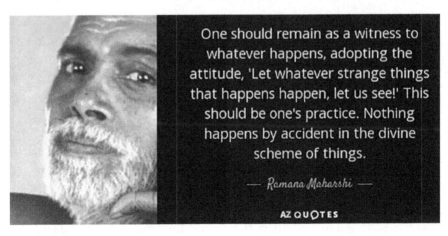

One should remain as a witness to whatever happens, adopting the attitude, 'Let whatever strange things that happens happen, let us see!' This should be one's practice. Nothing happens by accident in the divine scheme of things.

— *Ramana Maharshi* —

AZ QUOTES

Always remember – that nothing is bad, and nothing is good – it is your perception that you go on labeling people as good or bad – in reality, there is nothing that can be said as good or bad. It is your INTERPRETATION – you see a flower outside your window – and you say, "How beautiful is this flower." Somebody else who is walking on the road looks at the same flower and says, "Looks like a boring flower – no colors, plain white."

Now the flower exists there in its own **authenticity. It has nothing to do with what OTHERS have to say about it or are saying about it!**

Be like that Flower! Be engrossed in your **authenticity – and then millions and millions of people may go on INTERPRETING you as GOOD or BAD and yet it will not make any difference to you – you will become a dance – dancing in the breeze –** *just the way the flowers dance and swing in the breeze!*

Be a flower – be a dance – let the belief *drop out* and let your **experience** become your guide and then the whole universe will be available to you – then nobody can disturb you – then you no more remain a limited version – you become unlimited – then you start resonating with the higher realms of consciousness – then you get the 'wings' to fly – and then there is no looking back – the sky is clear, and *you are ready to fly.*

Astrologers say that my horoscope is Bad. What am I suppose to do now?

Meditate.
Jai Shri Ganesha. Jai Guru.

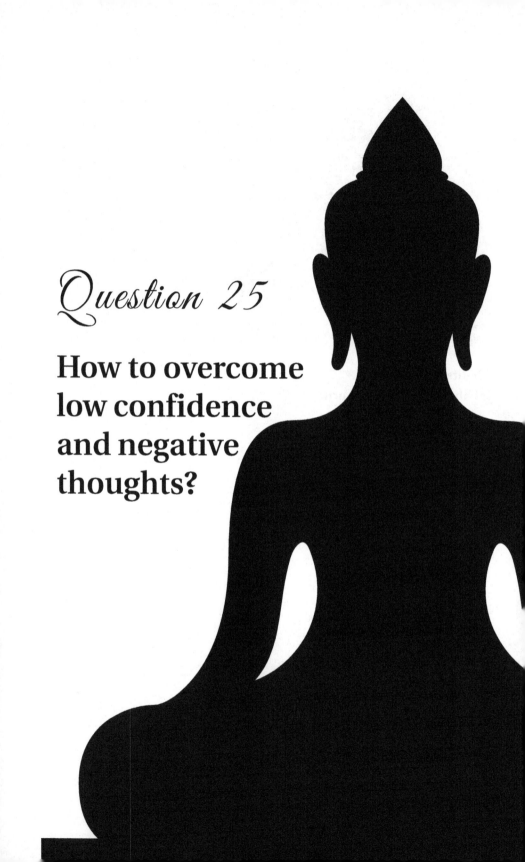

Question 25

How to overcome low confidence and negative thoughts?

C onfidence comes when you focus on the SELF.
SELF is represented by the SUN. SUN is the source of consciousness – the greater the consciousness, the greater is the realization of the SELF.

Consciousness is within all of us – the SUN is within all of us!

> There is a Sun in every person.
> **RUMI**

Righteousness is represented by JUPITER. It is through the planet Jupiter that you come to the realization of **WHAT IS GOOD and WHAT IS BAD** *for you*. **People who make wrong decisions** – often have an **afflicted Jupiter** in their birth charts – simply because they cannot realize what is truly good to their progress in life. They generally make wrong decisions in the early stage of their life – but with time – they mature and start making decisions that are well-balanced.

> Truly successful decision-making relies on a balance between deliberate and instinctive thinking.
> **MALCOLM GLADWELL**

COURAGE is represented by MARS and KETU. It is through MARS and KETU that you are able to show COURAGE and LEAD the pack. COURAGE comes only when you have CONFIDENCE in your 'SELF'.

> Believing that you're enough is what gives you the courage to be authentic.
>
> **BRENE BROWN**

SELF is at the root of one's confidence. So, SUN is the key – the essential key to – confidence.

Low confidence and negativity have to do more with what path you choose to walk upon. A truthful man or a truthful woman has nothing to FEAR – for many births and rebirths – such a soul has always been walking on the PATH of TRUTHFULNESS – such a man – such a woman is beautiful – they never have to fear – they don't know what fear is – they remain strong when the 'tide' is low – and they remain humble when the 'tide' is high!

Once you start following the TRUTH – once you start becoming a part of the TRUTH – then – CONFIDENCE comes, then the whole world is available to you – then you are no more the same – you have TRANSFORMED into a beautiful butterfly – the ugly caterpillar has TRANSFORMED into a beautiful butterfly!

But a question may arise – How to get started?

And the answer is simple – get started with 'Friends' who LOVE the TRUTH!

COMPANY matters. With whom you are – matters and it matters significantly. SANGHA – or – SATSANGHA enables you to gain confidence. Listening, reading the words of TRUTH – the WORD of GOD – following the light of consciousness – bring tremendous change and a push to your confidence level. Then you start realizing that – YOU TOO CAN CHANGE – YOU TOO CAN EXPERIENCE THE HIGHER ALTITUDES – that YOU TOO CAN LISTEN to the melodious 'MUSIC' of this wonderful journey called – Life!

Many times, alone you may not be able to gather that much courage, alone you may feel hopeless. But when you see many people dancing, singing, rejoicing in their 'journey' – great courage arises in your heart, great trust, confidence arises in yourself. You become confident that it is possible in this life to be a Buddha.

Only a man/a woman who is following the WORD of GOD – can live his or her life with confidence, with dignity, with love.

> In the beginning was the WORD and the WORD was with GOD, and the WORD was GOD.
>
> **JOHN 1:1, BIBLE VERSE**

A woman who has been cheating her husband/lover – cannot gain confidence – she may move around with fake confidence – like a 'sheep' in the disguise of a lioness – but she is not the real lioness – the confidence of a 'LIONESS' never exists in her – it never can!

A man who has been fooling around the town cannot gain the confidence of a LION – he too is a 'sheep' that roams in the disguise of a lion!

CONFIDENCE COMES ONLY WHEN THERE IS ABSOLUTELY NOTHING TO FEEL ASHAMED OF – NOTHING TO HIDE – NOTHING TO MANIPULATE! YOU simply are as you are – you have ACCEPTED yourself in totality. And only a man - who ACCEPTS himself – becomes beautiful! He is NOT afraid of his reality – he is not hiding anything – he lives his life with absolutely no regrets – such a man always wins in the end – such a man is the real man – the real being – he is an 'individual' and not just a personality!

> My whole love and respect is for the person who accepts himself totally, as he is. He has courage. He has courage to face the whole pressure of the society which is bent upon splitting him into divisions – into good and bad, into saint and sinner. He is really a brave, courageous being who stands against the whole history of man, of morality, and declares to the skies his reality, whatever it is.
>
> **OSHO**

One day, a young man came and he said, "A girl loves me – but today she told me everything about her past – she has a 'past' and I got to know about it when she told me everything…"

I told him, "She *is* the girl that you should not let go – because she loves you, she has shown the courage to tell you the truth – and a person who is truthful – is rare to find. She is worth it. Do not let her go – let her become a part of your life and your life will definitely blossom into a beautiful flower…"

To be with a truthful woman, a truthful man – is what can make your life a garden of bliss!

And TRUTH requires tremendous courage. The FEAR of losing is always there – the nature of clinging prevents you from being truthful – but then what is the value of such a life – a life lived with lies and fear?

FEAR exists – LOW CONFIDENCE exists – when you are TRYING TO BECOME – when you are NOT happy of BEING YOURSELF.

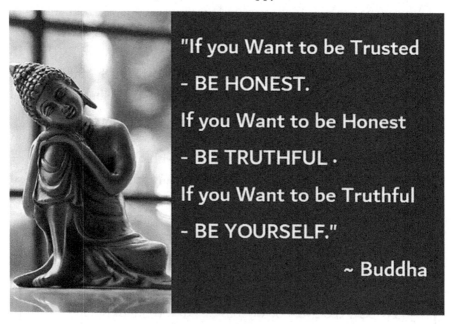

"If you Want to be Trusted - BE HONEST.

If you Want to be Honest - BE TRUTHFUL.

If you Want to be Truthful - BE YOURSELF."

~ Buddha

The first step towards gaining CONFIDENCE is to declare to the skies – your REALITY without feeling ashamed of anything – without hesitating to open up in totality.

Only an open man can be truthful – a closed man is a man of many lies – he is a man who goes on suppressing his feelings, the truths and in the process becomes more miserable than otherwise.

You have to be with an open man – a man who is moving towards the beyond – but such a man may not be appealing to a woman – who is yet to meditate – yet to turn inward!

Once it happened – a young man, a meditative man, fell in love with a beautiful woman. And love happens – you cannot help. It happened with this young man but after few days, he came to the master and said, "My Girlfriend says – I am cold. I am not hot. She says, 'I don't know anything about love.' She may be right. But please guide…"

Now read those words again – the young man is concluding – he says, "She must be right."

The master smiles and says, "She is NOT right, because you are not cold, you are COOL. And it is NOT true that you don't know love. But people are accustomed to a Hot Love, and in their mind there are only two possibilities – either you are hot about them, or you are cold. They cannot relate to the balanced state – they simply miss."

"A man of meditation - a man of awareness NEVER becomes cold and never remains hot either: he becomes cool, calm and quiet. His love takes a totally new dimension, which will appear to ordinary people as *indifference*. To those who understand, his love becomes less noisy, less stupid, less retarded, less biological, but starts having a flavor of spirituality, which needs an understanding otherwise the other person - your partner or lover is bound to think you have become cold." - Osho

Why the Girlfriend of this young meditative man thinks that 'he is cold'?

Because the young man has gone way ahead – through meditation he has moved on to the higher altitudes of love – while his girlfriend has been left behind! She is not growing in meditation – the young man is growing and so the 'distance' is growing between them – either the girlfriend has to catch up by being more meditative or the distance can eventually lead to a break up – because when there is NO RANGE – the 'call' always disconnects!

But the matter does not END here – because the young meditative man had said that 'Maybe she is right.'

It seems that the girlfriend has become more powerful in making him think – that she is right – it is indeed a very unfortunate situation for a man who is growing in meditation but is giving up to a woman who knows nothing about meditation!

Now either he can help her to move into meditation or else she will destroy him in totality. And convincing her to move into meditation is not an easy task – every woman – every girlfriend in the very beginning throws many tantrums – she will throw pillows on you – she will try to disturb your meditations because she understands that you are slipping out of her hands – she cannot possess you anymore – meditation has given you a freedom that is beyond her understanding and she just can't stand it – Socrates's wife also used to disturb Socrates when he used to teach his students. Socrates was a meditative man, deeply meditative. One day, his wife poured boiling water on his face – and burnt his half face for his whole life. He was teaching his students – and you will now understand what 'coolness' is – he simply wiped the water from his face and continued with what he was teaching.

Now the students who were witnessing all of this were shocked – they thought – how can this woman behave like this? And even if she had to – she must have done it when we were gone – at least not infront of us! So, now all the questions that they had come up with were forgotten and the only question that remained in their head was – WHY? WHY the master – Socrates – such a great wise man has not taken any note – of this strange behaviour of his wife? Why has he not reacted or responded? Why and how can he be so COOL?

And Socrates smiled and said, "Whatever she is capable of doing she has done. And whatever I am capable of I am doing. Our capacities are different – this is nobody's fault."

Socrates is not angry with his wife, on the contrary he is very compassionate.

He further says, "Any woman would have done the same – because I am continually concerned with my students, with philosophers coming from faraway places to visit me, and I am discussing things in which she is not interested at all. Sometimes the whole day passes and I don't have any time for her. She is a poor woman and she is behaving just as any unconscious human being is supposed to behave."

It happens. It always happens – when the partners are not at the same level of consciousness – the friction happens – and it is always one-sided – because the other side – is always COOL – compassionate and understanding!

But when both the partners – the husband and wife or the girlfriend and boyfriend are meditative beings – then the BALANCE blossoms – the relationship becomes more beautiful – then there is a song to it, a dance, then life becomes a garden of bliss!

When you and your partner grow together in meditation – then it has a beauty of its own. No conflict is seen. When couples grow together – hand in hand, dancing the same dance – singing the same song – as they grow together, the understanding also grows – then there is no trouble. But IF they both are not growing together then the one who is left behind feels offended – then he or she goes on creating troubles.

The young man realized his mistake. At least he should have tried to help his girlfriend grow along with him – at least he should have helped her to initiate meditations – because when you are in a relationship – you should try to see there is a BALANCE – and BALANCE is possible only when you and your partner – both meditate – both self-realize the significance of meditations!

When you become meditative, when you become a prayerful man or woman, when you devote a certain time to your daily meditations and when you remain FIRM on the path of TRUTHFULNESS – Confidence comes naturally – the greater the willingness to remain DETACHED – the greater is the depth of SELF-CONFIDENCE.

It is only when you remain ATTACHED that you FEAR of losing – and this FEAR then prevents you from BEING TRUTHFUL – and once you move away from the path of truthfulness – you start losing on confidence – and your body then starts attracting negativity.

Always remember – Life is a flow. In this flow – one comes across many experiences – one goes through many relationships – many people – many situations – DO NOT SUPPRESS those experiences – Suppression is Suicide – Expression is Life.

When you express yourself freely – when there is absolutely no HIDING – then LIFE is STRAIGHT – and a STRAIGHT PATH always makes everything STRAIGHT in your life!

A young woman had been through multiple relationships – they all failed – but she remained open – she would not hide her past – only that woman hides her past who is NOT willing to FACE and ACCEPT her failed relationships. She is afraid of sharing her failures and so she goes on suppressing herself – which in turn impacts her confidence levels.

A woman who has ACCEPTED her PAST – has nothing to HIDE – she opens up – she looks confident – there is absolutely NO GUILT – such a woman understands life – she succeeds in her life because whatever she has been through – she never REPRESSES – she never HIDES – she ACCEPTS – and only a person who ACCEPTS her or his PAST can move on – and it is only when you move on that you can progress in life with confidence.

It all begins with being TRUTHFUL. If you have done certain mistakes – so what? You simply accept your mistakes – learn from them and move on...

"To commit mistakes is NOT wrong - commit as many mistakes as possible, because that is the way you will be learning more - you will evolve. BUT don't commit the same mistake again and again, because that makes you stupid."
- Osho

By being TRUTHFUL to yourself – you are able to be TRUTHFUL with others and that makes a huge difference in your life – a significant positive difference.

People are looking into horoscopes to find out the REASON for their LOW confidence – their NEGATIVITY – and this is the GREATEST IRONY of mankind.

Horoscopes are nothing but a REFLECTION of WHAT YOU ARE. Horoscope is just a representation of – WHAT YOU HAVE BEEN DOING FROM MANY BIRTHS AND REBIRTHS – repeating the SAME mistakes again and again and again – until a day comes in your life – when you start turning inwards – when the divine intervention of the benevolent master – brings AWARENESS to your being – then – only then the repeating cycle of mistakes stops – the vicious cycle of IGNORANCE is finally brought to end – and with this end – the new beginning – the new sun rises – the new direction to your life comes and then there is no looking back – the road is clear and you are ready to walk the talk.

Once it happened, a young prince came all the way to meet Mahavira. And Mahavira used to live in a forest, beneath a tree – and there was no question of having any clothes because he roamed naked. There was no question of food because a little help from the forest trees was enough to take care of his body. And there was nobody with him, he lived alone...nobody knew about his whereabouts – but the young prince had found the way, it happens, it always happens – when the master wants you – you find HIS way! And so the young prince had found the way towards the master, he came, he bowed before the master and said, "I have renounced everything – now I have decided not to go back to my palace – I have left behind all the luxuries of the palace, all the pleasures...I have left forever...now please don't let me go back, I don't want to go back, I had enough, now I want to live the rest of my life at your holy feet...Master..."

Mahavira was listening but his eyes were closed. A certain fragrance lingered around Him...his glow, his peace...his aura – the young prince was deeply touched by just being in the omnipresence of the Mahavira.

Mahavira smiled. He said, "If that is what you want then be it so. You can stay with me."

The young prince's joy knew no bounds – there was nothing else that he had wished for. His wish was granted, he was let in.

But life in the forest is not an easy one! In that forest, the young prince somehow spent the first two nights. But it was becoming difficult – sleeping on the hard ground – and there were mosquitoes – many mosquitoes! And in the night, the fearful voice of the wild animals…that was too scary…

After spending four sleepless nights – the young prince started missing his luxurious life, the beautiful maids, the servants, the royal bed…

On the fifth night, the young prince could not control himself – he got up – he decided to leave the master…and as he was about to leave – suddenly the master – Mahavira – appeared before him…

The prince was taken aback – he wondered how the master came all of a sudden! He bowed before Mahavira and said, "I cannot live such a difficult life…master…I came to stay with you…but now I want to leave…"

Such was the state of his being that his eyes became wet – life in the forest is indeed a very hard life – especially for someone who has been living a luxurious life.

Mahavira smiled, it was understandable. Mahavira also had been a Prince – A prince of a very rich kingdom. He could understand. HE touched the young prince – just a soft touch on the forehead and then left.

The next morning, when Mahavira was seated beneath the tree - the young prince came rushing towards HIM. The prince fell upon the feet of the master and started crying…

Mahavira – the master asked, "Why you cry? You haven't yet left?"

Upon listening the words of the master – the prince said, "How can I leave you? How benevolent you are, how compassionate…yesterday, with your gracious touch – I went into deep trance and in that state I went through my past births and then I realized that in my past birth also I had left you – because I wasn't able to live the forest life. For luxurious life – I left you last time and this time also I was about to leave you —— but it was your divine intervention – your compassion that prevented me from committing the same mistake again. How can I thank you? Even if I give my whole life to you, still it will not be enough…master…all I am, all that I have – I lay them down before YOU. I will never ever leave you again. Never." And the young prince never left the master. It is said that he went on to become one of the greatest saints that the world has ever known – AWARENESS can CHANGE YOUR LIFE. It always can.

Life goes on repeating like a WHEEL – unless you become aware – unless you become conscious of your actions.

You have to raise the level of your consciousness by being more faithful, more meditative, and more truthful.

Horoscope is simply the naked truth of all that you have been doing in the last births – this birth and the many births to come.

Horoscope is just a medium that lets you KNOW about your Journey so far and the journey beyond this human life.

The word is – KNOW. Remember this and I appeal to all my readers – remember this – the word is – KNOW. Whenever you KNOW something – it is known through Knowing.

It is through KNOWING that you KNOW. And so KNOWLEDGE has three dimensions – KNOWER, KNOWN, and KNOWING.

You are standing before a rose plant. You are focused on the rose – you are able to KNOW the ROSE. But it is one-sided – the focus is only on the outside – the focus is only on the ROSE – you may succeed in KNOWING the ROSE – but you remain unknown to your SELF – as long as you remain pointed towards the outside world – the rose – you may know the world – you may know the rose – but that will not help in letting you know about YOUR SELF.

Knowledge reveals only the Known. The knower (yourself) remains unrevealed.

And the whole essence of meditation is to help you know the knower (yourself)!

The Buddha way is to forgot the 'rose' and focus on the 'knower' (yourself)!

When you look at the rose – you REMEMBER who is looking at the rose. And when you start remembering your self – the focus on the rose changes from outward to inward – and when you turn inwards – a time comes when the KNOWING (rose) is forgotten and the KNOWER (yourself) is also forgotten and that is the ultimate stage of Buddhahood – a deeply meditative state of experiencing ONENESS – advait!

Buddha encourages this way of meditation – in the modern world, it was re-introduced in the form of 'self-remembering' – when you remember yourself – the focus changes from KNOWING to KNOWER and that is the real beginning of your spiritual journey – that is when the 'buds' within you start flowering – start blossoming...

Like the rose – your focus is too much on your HOROSCOPE. And that is where you all go on missing. The focus should change from KNOWING to KNOWER – and that is YOUR SELF! The focus should be to look within – because what is on the outside is NOT REAL – what is in the inside is REAL and my whole effort is to help you all bring face to face with the REAL – YOUR 'SELF'.

> **"**
>
> Without understanding yourself, what is the use of trying to understand the world?
>
> **SRI RAMANA MAHARSHI**
>
> **"**

But people don't get it. And the majority is shallow. They keep on emailing me asking about this house and that house – why this house and why that yog. They are simply focused too much on the ROSE (Horoscope) – they are focused too much on 'KNOWING' – and in this futile process of 'knowing' they have completely missed to KNOW THE SELF – themselves! And they should not be blamed for this – because nobody has ever let them realize the fact that KNOWING is secondary – REALIZING THE SELF – is primary! So, they have been following the ROSE – and have completely lost the TOUCH – with themselves – now tell me and I ask to my readers – tell me – how can I respond to their emails – they will not understand my language.

But to you all – my close followers, readers and men of meditation – to you all – I say and I say it again and again that the FOCUS should not be in KNOWING – the FOCUS should be on the KNOWER – that is YOUR SELF.

The human world has always been focusing a lot on the logical mind – the conscious mind – the intuitive mind is always ignored. It becomes a headache for me when people with razor sharp logic come to me and start analyzing everything with their sharp logic – the essence is lost – it is simply lost.

With their RATIONAL MIND – they go on dissecting every part and parcel of astrology – of human life – of religion – of spiritualism and then they ask, "Why am I not getting the 'answers'? Why am I not being able to experience GOD?"

How will you? When your whole life you have been spending on rationalizing everything – analyzing everything...

> **"** The intuitive mind is a sacred gift and the rational mind is a faithful servant. We have created a society that honours the servant and has forgotten the gift.
> **ALBERT EINSTEIN** **"**

You miss to realize the GIFT of GOD – the gift of consciousness and you go on focusing on the OUTSIDE – how will you ever be able to realize the TRUTH – there is absolutely no chance – because the way is not on the outside but inside!

So come you all – come and focus on the inside – real growth happens always when you focus WITHIN – when you start turning inwards – when you start meditating – when you start transforming into a prayerful person – then everything comes your way – then you are no more interested to KNOW the horoscope placements and what is good and what is bad – then you are simply interested to KNOW yourself – then you are simply focused in knowing the knower – and that is YOU – your SELF!

How beautiful is all this – life is short – and with days passing by – it is becoming shorter – do not let this life pass by focusing on the outside world – by focusing on the planets and the yoga and what not – mind is super calculative – but I am for the HEART – the HEART is beautiful – your heart is also beautiful – everybody's heart is beautiful – what comes between you and your heart is the MONKEY MIND – the DIRTY MIND – the CUNNING MIND.

So, I am for all those who think less and FEEL MORE, you cannot deceive a man of heart – he quickly realizes who is REAL and who is FAKE!

And the whole story of this human life is to SELF REALIZE THE REAL. And the REAL is within each one of us – the more you 'swim' within – the more you would become REAL and the society always dislikes the REAL – because the REAL can make you wise – and the society would never want to have wise men and wise women – because then how can they exploit you – how can they loot you?

> **❝**
> Before Buddha, the religious search was not concerned with the within but with the without; it was extrovert, and when the religious search is extrovert it is not really religious. Religion begin sonly with introversion, when you start diving deeply within yourself.
> **OSHO** **❞**

Always remember – there is no teacher and there is no student, there is no teaching.

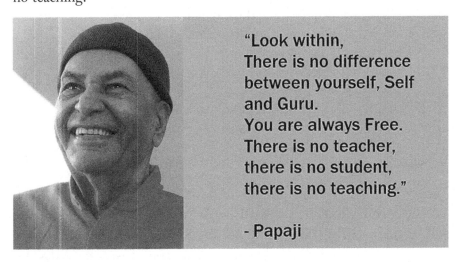

"Look within,
There is no difference between yourself, Self and Guru.
You are always Free.
There is no teacher, there is no student, there is no teaching."

- Papaji

I am not here to teach anything – I am here to simply share something beautiful that which has happened with me – those who can relate – can benefit – those who cannot – will continue to condemn me – it is the old tradition of this human world – the TRUTH has always been condemned – though it is only the TRUTH that has remained.

The 'SELF is the GURU' says the Bhagavan – Bhagavan Ramana Maharshi. This SELF is consciousness – and the divine master is also the CONSCIOUSNESS! The moment you realize the SELF – the CONSCIOUSNESS – you connect with the master. THE SELF is the GURU – beautiful – as always the compassionate master shares one of the rarest of rare diamonds with us and it is truly beautiful! Touched.

People want the TRUTH – but when the TRUTH is shared, they CANNOT digest it – because their MIND won't let them. TRUTH needs NO INTELLECTUALISM – it simply needs a HEART that loves – a HEART that drives the MIND – and the HEART is intelligent – it can FEEL – and it is only when you FEEL that you start transforming into a beautiful flower!

No thoughts. No thinking. No Mind – and then you can FEEL.

You are TOO MUCH into your head – and I am saying this to all my followers – you have been taking everything that you come across – with so much of seriousness that you have forgotten the fact that life is not static – it goes on changing – CHANGE IS CONSTANT. Unburden yourself – breathe – just breathe and enjoy the moment – because life flows through moments – you always remember the moments and not the days!

> Absorbed in this world you have made it your burden. Rise above this world. There is another vision.
>
> **RUMI**

The WORLD is nothing but an EXTENSION OF YOUR MIND! YOUR MIND IS YOUR WORLD. Rise above your MIND and you will be able to RISE ABOVE THE WORLD – then there will be no burden – because the very feeling of being burdened is of the MIND – overcome the MIND – and you find your freedom. Then you will be able to FEEL more – and it is only when you can **FEEL** that you can relate to the Master. If you go to a master with all kinds of thoughts, those thoughts will function as Walls and not Bridges. To connect with the master – you need to build bridges and not walls – as long as you think too much – you may go on missing. Only those who feel can connect. And once the contact starts happening, then it takes you on the greatest journey of your life – the greatest adventure – the greatest ecstasy. And it is beautiful…

> 66 Move from thinking to feeling – it will be enough. Then from feeling to intuition – it is very easy. The relationship between the master and a disciple is NOT a rational thing. It is more of feeling than of thinking. Those who think too much may go on missing. Only those who Feel – can connect with the Master.
>
> **OSHO** 99

Life always gives you a CHOICE – you can either be like Judas or you can either be like Jesus! You can either go on THINKING and THINKING and putting your HEAD in every matter of life – OR – you simply go on feeling – vibrating with the existence!

When Marry Magdalene pours the most expensive perfume on Jesus's feet – Judas objects. He is a man of intellect – he cannot understand – he cannot relate to the deep love that Marry Magdalene has for Jesus! He argues with Jesus – he says, "The money from this expensive perfume would have fed the whole town."

Jesus says, "In deep love, she has poured the perfume on my feet – I cannot stop her – I couldn't stop her. The town will be there even when I am gone – but I will not be in physical form forever – in deep love – not finding a way to express her love – she has expressed it by pouring this perfume – I could not stop her."

Jesus could feel. Judas could not. This human world is divided into two parts – Jesus and Judas! And it is up to you all to decide on which side you are! What you choose is what you become!

Meditation is the journey from the Mind towards your heart. It begins from the MIND – the mind should be turned inwards and then slowly the mind merges with the heart and then the work is over – it is a long journey – the journey from the Mind to the Heart – someday it has to begin – millions and millions of souls are born every moment around this world – and millions die without knowing the essence – the true purpose of this human life. Even one in a million WAKES UP – it is enough – even one 'candle' is enough to bring 'light' to other 'candles' that are yet to be en- lightened!

Always remember – the cause of your miseries is your FEAR. This FEAR goes on killing you every day. FEAR kills. You have not lived until you have overcome the fear that is within you. It is a chain, a vicious chain. Fear comes due to the nature of clinging. Attachments. Then this Fear gives birth to Doubts. And Doubt is Death. Life begins where Fear ENDS. How will this Fear end?

By letting in more FAITH.

The Greater the FAITH – the lesser the space is for any fear!

Let your FAITH become GREATER than your fears. Let there be more love than doubts. Only then there is a possibility to experience God – only then there is a possibility to live life with self-confidence.

Confidence comes, positivism comes, love comes only when you learn to live your life by being TRUTHFUL – by walking on the path of TRUTH.

> **66**
>
> God is TRUTH. And you begin in LIES. Life is TRUTH and you begin in HYPOCRISY. If you go on missing, it is no wonder.
>
> **OSHO**
>
> **99**

When you walk the talk – when you live by following the TRUTH – when your communion is with those who love God, who are truthful beings, devoted beings – only then there is a possibility for you all to

GROW. **SAT SANGHA** – is the key to your transformation – it is said that company matters – with whom you live matters – whom you are friends with – matters, whom you follow – matters – because at the end of the day – it is the 'vibrations' that you receive is what is going to make you or break you.

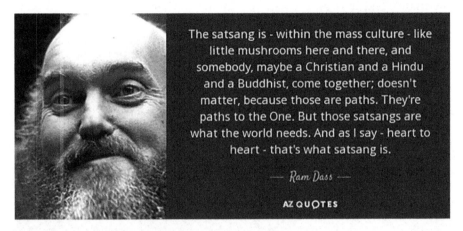

The satsang is - within the mass culture - like little mushrooms here and there, and somebody, maybe a Christian and a Hindu and a Buddhist, come together; doesn't matter, because those are paths. They're paths to the One. But those satsangs are what the world needs. And as I say - heart to heart - that's what satsang is.

— *Ram Dass* —

AZ QUOTES

Mohan asked, "For **SAT-SANGHA** (communion), how to identify real men of values, men of heart?"

The answer is simple – for that, first you have to get REAL! And to get REAL – you have to first JUMP WITHIN – look within and change the focus from OUTSIDE to INSIDE – only then can you find real gems in your life – only then you can listen to the 'music of your life' that others can't – only then can you change your life – it all begins from YOU – YOU have to let change happen – YOU cannot change yourself – the old cannot change itself – it has to give way to the OTHER – and so it is only when YOU SURRENDER to your lord – your master that the change within you is initiated – this is how it happens, this is the way of its happening – the larger question that you all should ask yourself is – 'Are you ready to surrender?'

If you are – then let me tell you from the bottom of my heart – nobody can stop you from being what you are – nobody can block you – the whole essence is in living your life in total surrender – that is what Arjuna did – that is what Ananda did, that is what Sariputa did – that is what

Peter did – that is what John the baptist did – and that is what you can also do…everything is available – and everything is possible – only if you are willing to take one step towards HIM – only if you are willing to take the backseat and let HIM drive your life.

It is only when you live your life in total surrender – that you can meditate. And it is only when you meditate that you can come to your own self-realization.

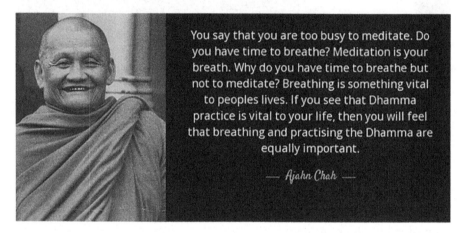

You say that you are too busy to meditate. Do you have time to breathe? Meditation is your breath. Why do you have time to breathe but not to meditate? Breathing is something vital to peoples lives. If you see that Dhamma practice is vital to your life, then you will feel that breathing and practising the Dhamma are equally important.

— *Ajahn Chah* —

The need of the hour is to meditate.

Meditate.
Jai Shri Ganesha. Jai Guru.

Question 26

How truthful
is Astrology?

A strology is within you. Truth is within you. God is within you.

God is Love and Love is REAL.

If you can realize your SELF - you can realize Astrology.

All the planets, all the stars, all of the universe is WITHIN you.

The Ancient Vedic Scriptures specifically mention - AHAM BRAMHASMI - meaning I AM THE UNIVERSE - in simple words - the WHOLE UNIVERSE IS WITHIN ME. Brahma is the UNIVERSE and the enlightened sages state, "I am the UNIVERSE (BRAHMA)."

अहं ब्रह्मास्मि

Aham Brahmāsmi

I am Brahma, I am the Divine.

Brihadaranyaka Upanishad 1.4.10 of the Yajur Veda

thelotusinthepond.com

Vedanta

Einstein addresses the UNIVERSE as WHOLE.

> A human being is a part of the whole called by us universe, a part limited in time and space. He experiences himself, his thoughts and feelings as something separated from the rest, a kind of optical delusion of his consciousness. This delusion is a kind of prison for us, restricting us to our personal desires and to affection for a few persons nearest to us. Our task must be to free ourselves from this prison by widening our circle of compassion to embrace all living creatures and the whole of nature in its beauty.
>
> **ALBERT EINSTEIN**

This WHOLE is within you, within me, within every human being.

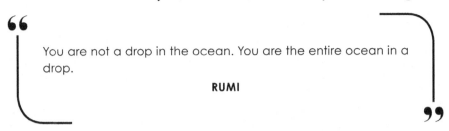

> You are not a drop in the ocean. You are the entire ocean in a drop.
>
> **RUMI**

The ONLY DIFFERENCE between a common man and the Yogi - is that the Yogi has REALIZED THE SELF - HE is a self-realized man - while the common man is still to realize HIS self - still to turn inwards - still to become ALIVE in the true sense.

The moment you self-realize the WHOLE within you - all the stars, all the planets, all the energies of this Universe (whole) start revealing the many deep mysteries of this human life. The SOURCE of ASTROLOGY is WITHIN and not Without.

Many times, people come and someone is a divorced woman, someone is a divorced man - someone is an abandoned old mother or old father - and then out of frustration, depression they all ask one question, "Is there any purpose for our existence?"

Today, through this answer, I want to tell them all - there is ALWAYS a PURPOSE for every HUMAN BEING who is yet living and ALIVE.

> Each person comes into this world with a specific destiny – he has something to fulfil, some message has to be delivered, some work has to be completed. You are not here accidentally – you are here meaningfully. There is a purpose behind you. The whole intends to do something through you.
>
> **OSHO**

NOBODY IS USELESS - NOBODY - and let this penetrate into your being as much as possible. NOBODY IS USELESS IN THIS HUMAN WORLD - everybody in HIS or HER own small way is CONTRIBUTING to somebody's life - be it human life, animal life - but some contribution is happening through each one of us - NOBODY IS USELESS - NOBODY.

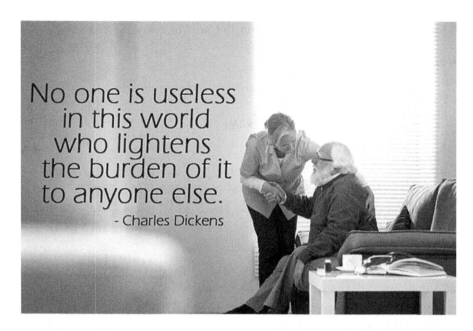

No one is useless
in this world
who lightens
the burden of it
to anyone else.
- Charles Dickens

The Master always says - that even though this world is filled with more of SAND - within this SAND - there are also few particles of SUGAR - you cannot deny everybody - you have to be selective and select these beautiful souls -- the SUGAR particles - the REAL ONES - the God-Lover Souls !

There was one such God Lover - a poor man - and he was a cobbler. He lived on the streets. And every day he would pray - his prayer would sound like this - "GOD - give me a chance and I will be so happy to serve you. I will cook food for you, my wife is not a great cook - but I am. I will also give you a good bath - I know you have been so ancient - I can understand how it feels when there is water to take bath - I can understand how it feels when there is a lot of dust on the body because I have been spending my whole life on the streets...I know how it all feels...but you don't worry - I will serve you in every way I can - I love you God...I love you..."

And this was his daily prayer - every day, this poor cobbler would pray with so much of love that GOD secretly would come in the form of a bird and listen to his prayer. And God would rejoice in that poor man's love - and the cobbler was also always found to be happy. He had no cars, no properties, no power, no status - but HAPPINESS stayed in his heart - in his life and life was sailing smoothly. A man who LOVES GOD is always found to be happy!

But GOD always loves to TEST his loved ones.

> God tests those HE loves the most, just look at HIS messengers.
> **BUDDHA**

Jesus was tested. Prophet was. Buddha, Mahavira, Arjuna - the messengers were tested very deeply! This poor man wasn't aware that one test was coming his way...

A very precious diamond was stolen from the King's treasure and the search was on. The officials were scanning every street and the residents of the streets! Our poor cobbler was also scanned - screened - and they found one beautiful diamond in his bag. The cobbler was not shocked, nor was he surprised - he just looked up and said, "God - so you are up to something. No problem, I am ready for whatever is to come. I trust you - I have always trusted you."

The officials arrested the cobbler and took him to the court. The King asked, "How you dared to steal the diamond from my treasure?"

The cobbler said, "His highness, I am an old man - I can barely walk, how can I come all the way and trespass all your security and steal a diamond? And even if I would have had, why would I stay in your kingdom?"

The King was a wise man. But the diamond was found in the old man's bag. There was absolutely no chance to let him go. He had to be punished.

With a heavy heart, the King decided to declare the punishment. But something strange happened - the young princess came and she whispered something in the King's ear. The King could not believe his ears. He declared, "The cobbler is no more to be punished - he can go back to his home."

The old man, our cobbler smiled. He bowed before the King and left his palace. On his way - a very old man met him and said, "You scoundrel - how can you LOVE me so much!" - and then HE smiled and disappeared.

The TEST was passed. The cobbler fell down, tears flowing through his eyes, he had no words - GOD had finally appeared - GOD had to finally come in his search - GOD finally had tested him and GOD finally had also passed him. WHAT MORE WAS TO BE EXPECTED - the cobbler went back to his home. But he was no more the same - everything around him was the same - but he was no more the same. Miracles started happening through his hands - he became one of the greatest healers the world had ever known! Wherever he would go - the sick would heal - the miseries would evaporate - one day the KING fell sick and the cobbler was invited to the Palace - the cobbler went, with his touch - the King healed - but the King won't let him go - the King thanked him and asked, "You never asked - why you were not imprisoned?"

The cobbler said, "The day I left your Palace - that day itself I truly became FREE - God appeared before me and then LIFE was no more a CAGE - a prison - the MIND was no more - so where was the question of asking anything? The road was clear and I kept walking..."

The King said, "But I will tell you the reason."

The King looked into the cobbler's eyes and said, "The Diamond miraculously came back into my treasure - while your bag still had the same diamond."

The cobbler smiled and said, "And today I am giving you the diamond that is still in my bag - as a gift. Keep it with yourself - this meeting and you falling sick was just an excuse - the real purpose was this - and now let me go."

The King's eyes became wet - he wondered who the REAL KING is - this man or him?

The old cobbler started walking towards the gate of the Palace - the King with a heavy heart returned to his Palace. But till his last breath, he kept the diamond with him - whenever anybody would ask about his fondness towards the diamond - he would say, "The 'real diamond' went away - leaving this 'false' diamond with me."

People would not understand - because the diamond was real - and they never understand their whole life. Because they had never seen the real diamond - the cobbler.

> The most precious jewels are NOT made of stone BUT of FLESH.
> **ROBERT LUDLUM**

"In my whole life, I have had all the real diamonds that this world had to offer - but NO diamond could be as precious as the old cobbler of my kingdom - he was the only precious diamond I had in my life." - The king had these words inscribed on his Grave - nobody knew where the cobbler went, but he certainly lived in the heart of the KING - and the people of his kingdom.

An illiterate cobbler can become a Saint - that is the power of FAITH - that is the strength of LOVE - that is the beauty of PATIENCE. The transformation inspired the KING - the people - the whole kingdom - this is how it happens - one candle can lighten the other - the need is to lighten one candle - and then the joy spreads - the love spreads - then those who have been walking away from GOD - turn back to HIM - to the SOURCE.

> The time you spend alone with God will transform your character and increase your devotion. Then your integrity and godly behaviour in an unbelieving world will make others long to know the Lord.
> **CHARLES F STANLEY**

The SOURCE is WITHIN you - always remember this. And I say this specifically to all my followers and readers - The SOURCE IS WITHIN YOU - what stands BETWEEN YOU and the SOURCE is your MIND.

Somebody INSULTS you and the MIND quickly TARGETS the insult-er who is on the outside. The ARROW OF YOUR MIND starts targeting the man who has insulted you - and YOU MISS - you simply MISS - you get carried away - you move away from the SOURCE that is WITHIN you - and the more the DISTANCE grows between you and the SOURCE WITHIN YOU - you become a lost man - a lost woman - then you don't know what to do!

Understand the fact - that the ARROW of the MIND has to turn inwards - whenever anybody INSULTS you - and this is very significant for you all to understand. The MIND should be turned inwards and the first QUESTION that you all should ask yourself is - "Why I feel INSULTED?"

If somebody calls you a FOOL - you feel insulted - because you have been considering yourself as a very WISE MAN! Had you not been considering yourself a WISE MAN - and somebody would have called you a FOOL - you would have stepped up and HUGGED that man or woman! Then you would have said, "Right - very right that is how I feel" - then where is the question of being insulted?

If somebody calls you a THIEF - you will feel insulted only if you have been considering yourself as a great MORALIST - when in reality you have been a thief! So, now the man or woman has put the finger exactly on the point where it PAINS - because there IS indeed something that is NOT RIGHT within you! Had you been a truly SAINTLY man or woman - no matter even if the whole world calls you a THIEF - you would have never felt insulted or offended.

I always say - and it is very significant - that if you have a million dollars in your bank account and if somebody looks at you and says, "You beggar" - then you will simply laugh - you would have a good laugh!

But YOU will FEEL INSULTED only if you REALLY HAVE ABSOLUTELY NO PENNY IN YOUR BANK ACCOUNT - then you will feel insulted! So then who is the CULPRIT?

YOU.

So in such a situation - only TWO things can happen - EITHER YOU JUMP ON THE PERSON WHO IS INSULTING YOU - OR - YOU TURN INWARD and go back to the SOURCE and SELF REALIZE where exactly you are missing - what exactly is wrong within you.

Jesus addresses this process in one word - REPENT - which means go back, go inside yourself - to the SOURCE.

Buddha addresses this process in one word - PRATYAHAR (self-evaluation by turning inwards)

Mahavira addresses this process in one word - PRATIKRAMAN (going back to the SOURCE - within)

Words differ from religion to religion - although the essence in simple words is - TURNING INWARDS.

But people are shallow. They are looking outside for ANSWERS - when the ANSWER is within!

But who wants to listen? Common man or common woman has just one question - When will I get this and when will I get that! Beyond this - they cannot go - they have made a terrible prisoner of themselves - a prisoner of the MIND!

"To know that you are a Prisoner of your Mind is the dawn of Wisdom."
- Sri Nisargadatta Maharaj

During the ancient times - a sage would spend eight hours in meditation, then he would share the many beautiful aspects of this human life and spiritual experiences with those who would come with love and devotion - and then some time that was left - he would guide a few by looking within and reading the planetary placements - such was the life of a real Sage, a Yogi - a life that was blessed with more spiritualism - because one needs to understand and I specifically tell this to all my followers and readers - that LIFE should be filled with HIS love - that LIFE should be devoted to HIS feet - then astrology comes on its own - but people go the other way round - they keep reading books and books and books and in the process they become 'parrots' - but I am encouraging you all to become 'Eagles' - EAGLES who dare to LOOK WITHIN - who dare to question themselves.

Meditation is not for cowards. Meditation is for the ones who are COURAGEOUS.

Because when you sit down and close your eyes to MEDITATE, it is the very beginning stage of your spiritual journey - you come across a HELL OF A THOUGHTS ALL SWARMING OVER YOU LIKE THOSE NOISY BEES! NOW only if you are COURAGEOUS - you can SUSTAIN - you can CONTINUE - you can IGNORE all that noise and all those thoughts and FOCUS on your BREATHING by reciting the name of the HOLY LORD.

So to meditate - tremendous COURAGE is required and along with COURAGE - lasting PATIENCE and FAITH.

"Meditation is just a courage to be silent and alone. Slowly slowly, you start feeling a new quality to yourself, a new aliveness, a new beauty, a new intelligence - which is NOT borrowed from anybody, which is growing within you. It has roots in your existence." - Osho

It is good that you have come up with the question that doubts whether there is TRUTH in astrology. But this is the question of the MIND - the MIND is targeting the ARROW towards that which you think is OUTSIDE you! When in reality it is inside you - so IF YOU CAN

FIND TRUTH WITHIN YOURSELF - only then can you find TRUTH in astrology!

And this is very significant - and I say to you all - WHATEVER IS WITHIN YOU - YOU WILL 'SEE' or 'PERCEIVE' on the OUTSIDE. IF you can EXPERIENCE TRUTH WITHIN - you will experience TRUTH in astrology - it is all RELATIVE - what comes through you is what decides the future course of your life.

But in general, PEOPLE are not willing to turn inwards - they want READYMADE information - READYMADE INFORMATION is 'Knowledge'.

Information that evolves through your SELF - your MEDITATION is 'WISDOM'.

People are busy gathering INFORMATION - which is readily available.

By reading books and watching videos of astrology - you are becoming educated. But one should remember that an educated person is not always an intelligent person. You become knowledgeable - Gyani - not a Yogi.

"It is very rare that a man can come from the university and yet be intelligent, still remain intelligent. Very few have been able to escape the University, avoid the university and yet save their intelligence - very rarely. It is such a great mechanism to destroy you. The moment you become educated, you have become unintelligent. The educated person behave very unintelligently. Go to the primitive people who have NEVER been educated and you find a pure intelligence functioning."

- Osho

Many times it has happened. CEOs, MDs, and Directors - they all have tried to approach me - but I have given my time to only a few, very few.

In fact, the other day - somehow a man reached me - and he said, "My name is Chandan. And I don't know anything about God or astrology - I am a very poor man and I have called you to find a solution for my only daughter - please help."

I helped him. I also would always respond to his calls - until his problem was solved. Not a single penny was charged - but he was happy and so was I.

Mohan always wonders on why I am so open to those who comparatively are poor - while I take a hell of a time to respond to others.

I said to him, "It is simple. Very simple. The so-called educated and intellectual men and women will go round and round and round - they will NOT understand my language and I cannot stand their stupidity. But the poor man, the uneducated man - he has a lot of LOVE in his heart - he can JUMP - he can FOLLOW - simply because he LIVES more by his HEART and less by his HEAD. But these intellectual educated people - they will go on raising DOUBTS, and DOUBTS and the smell of their INTELLECTUALISM simply makes me go away from them than otherwise."

The poor can JUMP. When I say poor - it has nothing to do with your bank balance - you may have 1 million dollars in your bank account and yet if you may have REALIZED your 'poverty' - within, then you are POOR. You may have realized that whole life was spent running behind money, power, sex and yet at the end - there is nothing that can be forever - that can open the doors to eternal happiness. A man who has SELF-REALIZED this - is POOR and Jesus, therefore, says that only the 'POOR can find his way towards GOD.'

> Blessed are the poor in spirit, for theirs is the kingdom of heaven. Blessed are those who mourn, for they will be comforted. Blessed are the meek, for they will inherit the earth.
>
> **MATTHEWS 5:3-5 (BIBLE VERSE)**

"By talking and talking - externally you may be gaining something, but WITHIN you are certainly losing contact with *Yourself*. You are getting closer to people while you are becoming further removed from yourself. And the more adept you become at this game, the harder it will be for you to go into silence." - Osho

Understand the deeper meaning of the word 'POOR' - this poverty is the poverty WITHIN you - where you have been spending your whole life in TALKING and TALKING and TALKING and while you may have gained many material gains - you have gone too far from your SELF. This distance has made you RICH from the outside - but utterly POOR from the inside.

And once you self-realize this - you start realizing how POOR you have become from the inside. From the outside - there are many cars, and many bungalows and all the pleasures that one wishes for - but within - you have LOST THE CONTACT WITH YOUR 'SELF'. And the moment you realize this POVERTY - Jesus says such a self-realized man will be blessed and can find a place in the KINGDOM OF GOD.

"BLESSED ARE THE POOR IN *SPIRIT*, FOR THEIRS IS THE KINGDOM OF HEAVEN."

How beautiful are these words of Jesus. When Jesus is saying - BLESSED ARE THE POOR - HE is NOT referring to your possessions - HE is simply stating POOR IN SPIRIT - how deep are these words, how deeply moving are these words!

EDUCATED man, EDUCATED woman - they are very HIGH in spirit - if you let them in - they will never ask you the relevant question and they will never understand your answer. Because they are so much TRAPPED in their INTELLECTUALISM - their EGO - their IGNORANCE - their STATUS that they will be a pure waste of time.

When you ask about TRUTH in ASTROLOGY - let me tell you and to all who have been following me - NOT A SINGLE FRAGMENT OF TRUTH WILL BE REALIZED BY THOSE WHO ARE JUST GETTING THEMSELVES EDUCATED WITH THE SCIENCE OF ASTROLOGY.

TRUTH is hard, it always is.

Once it happened, a young woman was trying to open a lid of a tin box. She could not open and so she went to find a 'book' that would help her to open the lid of the box. When she returned, she was surprised to see that the lid of the box was opened - she asked the cook, "Did you open it?"

The cook said, "Yes, I opened it."

The woman was surprised - for half an hour she was trying to open but failed - and how come this man opened it. She asked, "HOW?"

The cook smiled and said, "When you don't know how to read - you have no other choice than to use your Intelligence."

Something that happens WITHOUT any BOOK - WITHOUT any help - but happens spontaneously - comes from WITHIN you - and that *is* INTELLIGENCE.

And I am, therefore, for INTELLIGENCE and NOT INTELLECTUALISM.

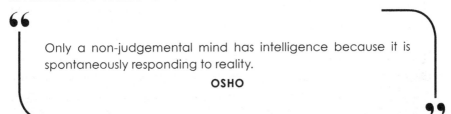

> Only a non-judgemental mind has intelligence because it is spontaneously responding to reality.
>
> **OSHO**

Mohan once asked, "How to identify an intelligent man or woman?"

I replied, "An intelligent man or woman is one who has the CAPACITY TO BE REBORN!"

Mohan said, "Please explain further..."

I said, "Look at this woman..."

There was a woman who had a relationship breakup - Mohan knew about her.

I said, "If this woman can DIE to her PAST - only then can she be REBORN - then she can find joy again, then she can blossom like a flower - then she will be a dance, a poem, a beautiful painting…"

Your intelligence is purely based on whether you can live your life by BEING HERE NOW.

The Body is always Here now, the Mind is never here now; and that is the whole conflict.

PAST IS PAST - it is GONE. FUTURE IS NOT YET. NOW is the moment - if you can BE HERE NOW - you are living with intelligence. The whole purpose of meditation is to bring you all to this stage - the stage - TO BE HERE NOW.

> 66
>
> Yoga is the science to be in the here and now.
> **OSHO**
> 99

THE PRESENT IS THE ONLY TIME YOU HAVE. Always remember this - always.

Educated people are too much into their HEAD. This HEAD then makes them miserable. This HEAD brings TOO MUCH OF INTELLECTUALISM leading them to nowhere.

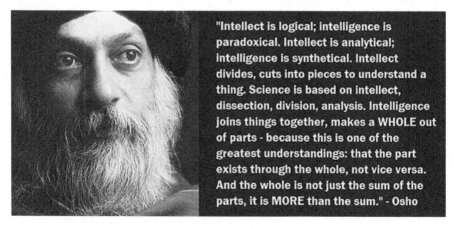

"Intellect is logical; intelligence is paradoxical. Intellect is analytical; intelligence is synthetical. Intellect divides, cuts into pieces to understand a thing. Science is based on intellect, dissection, division, analysis. Intelligence joins things together, makes a WHOLE out of parts - because this is one of the greatest understandings: that the part exists through the whole, not vice versa. And the whole is not just the sum of the parts, it is MORE than the sum." - Osho

In contrast - the illiterate is intelligent - but if you ask me about the EDUCATED CLASS - then as long as they continue to FOLLOW THEIR MIND - they remain blocks of INTELLECTUALISM - and this intellectualism goes on BLOCKING their REAL GROWTH - the GROWTH WITHIN.

A man, a woman - simple, followers of HEART, prayerful - such a man, such a woman can understand my language - can understand my sharing - can understand my answer - then I can let them have some of my time, it is worth it.

But an intellectual man, an intellectual woman - they are a PAIN IN THE NECK. They will go on ANALYZING - they forget the fact that ANALYZING can make you a good scientist - you may collect INFORMATION - but you will NEVER be able to realize or RELATE to the TRUTH.

Jesus is joyous when someone LOVES HIM. Buddha is in bliss when someone LOVES HIM. KRISHNA can only be realized when you LOVE HIM - Arjuna LOVED HIM IN TOTALITY - HE was able to relate to KRISHNA.

An INTELLECTUAL MAN CANNOT LOVE. HE will says, "I think I love" - he is still thinking - even when it is the question of love - he is *still* thinking.

Once it happened - Immanuel Kant, one of the greatest systematizers- a great intellectual - was proposed by a girl. The girl fell in love with him - but this man would not propose - so finally she had to.

She said, "I love you. I want to marry you."

Immanuel said, "I will think over."

Now the question is How can you THINK - when the matter is ABOUT LOVE! Either you say 'YES' or 'NO' - what is to THINK about it?

But intellectuals like Immanuel cannot understand this - they are TOO MUCH into their HEAD.

You THINK when it is a BUSINESS PROPOSAL - but this was a LOVE PROPOSAL. And the girl loved him deeply.

But Immanuel must be like MERCURY - he noted what she had said. Then the following days and weeks and months - he would go to the libraries and try to learn more about love, about marriage, about relationships...and time flew by...and finally his 'calculations' and his 'analysis' made him realize that 'MARRIAGE' is beneficial in many ways! And so then he rushed to that girl's home.

He knocked at her door - her father opened the door - Looking at Immanuel, he said, "She is already married and a mother of two - you came a little late."

And this is what happens with every intellectual man - the answer he gets is, "You came a little late!"

The HEAD would never let you JUMP - the HEART can. Intellectualism is of your HEAD - Intelligence is of your HEART - one who follows his or her heart - experiences LOVE - experiences GOD - experiences the TRUTH.

The question that you all should ask yourself is - What are you? A follower of your HEAD or your HEART?

The intellectuals will answer cleverly - the mind is very clever and cunning - they will answer, "We balance both" - and then they remain at the mediocre level. The intelligent have the answer ready - "HEART"! Such an intelligent man or woman can attain the beyond - the unseen - the peak - the state of Buddha.

Only a man who follows his heart can become a Buddha. Such a man is intelligent.

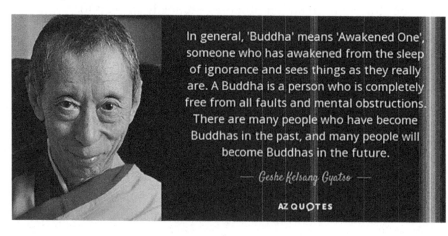

In general, 'Buddha' means 'Awakened One', someone who has awakened from the sleep of ignorance and sees things as they really are. A Buddha is a person who is completely free from all faults and mental obstructions. There are many people who have become Buddhas in the past, and many people will become Buddhas in the future.

— *Geshe Kelsang Gyatso* —

AZ QUOTES

INTELLIGENT MAN CAN LOVE. HE simply says, "I LOVE YOU." - There is absolutely NO THINKING and IT IS ONLY WHEN THERE IS ABSOLUTELY NO THINKING - that LOVE can happen - LOVE can be experienced - LOVE can be felt - that your HEART MOVES - and when the HEART moves - the whole world of yours starts moving and then you are no more the same - everything around you is the same BUT you are NO MORE THE SAME - then there is a song to it - a dance, a beautiful poem!

Life is lived when you DON'T just BREATHW - but when you LOVE!

LOVE is the SOUL's LIGHT. If there is NO LOVE within you - if you cannot feel LOVE - then you will never feel GOD's presence - because GOD IS LOVE and LOVE IS REAL.

And if you CANNOT FEEL GOD, if you CANNOT realize GOD - then how will you realize ASTROLOGY - then HOW CAN TRUTH BE FOUND IN ASTROLOGY?

Intellectual people are always TRYING TO FIND THE TRUTH on the outside - their SEARCH will never end.

Intelligent people never seek TRUTH outside - they simply start turning inwards - they simply start losing their MIND - because it is only when the MIND is LOST that you can FIND THE TRUTH - you can FIND YOURSELF.

I am in YOU and I am YOU. No one can understand this until he has lost his mind.

RUMI

It has always happened - the pundits, the intellectuals, the so-called educated men and women have always surrounded the divine masters - and have created many scriptures on them - but the truth is they have never ever realized their true essence - they kept on asking many questions - raising many intellectual questions - thoughts - ideas - and that's all they could reach to - they made a lot of noise - but that was all they could do - noise and just noise. Knowledge is noisy - they tried to gather knowledge - but KNOWLEDGE is information that can be used - it is NOT the ultimate TRUTH - the intellectuals remained away from the TRUTH - they remained trapped in the WEB of KNOWLEDGE.

Knowledge can help you to establish great organizations - logic can help you to run these organizations very efficiently - but that is all. Beyond this - knowledge becomes impotent to help you any further - you remain a beautiful-looking PLASTIC rose - everything looks perfect in your life - but that perfection is the DEATH OF ALL THAT IS CREATIVE - ALL THAT IS REAL.

Always remember - NEVER RUN BEHIND PERFECTION - if the world would have been PERFECT, it would have been DEAD by now. The world is growing because it is IMPERFECT. NATURE rejoices in its imperfection - I am imperfect, the whole universe is imperfect and because it is imperfect, it is GROWING, had it been PERFECT it would have been DEAD by now!

Perfection is a myth.

> 66
>
> The sooner you stop chasing the idea of perfection and start focusing on 1% progress is when you'll finally have the mindset to permanently achieve your health goals.
>
> **MARK MACDONALD**
>
> 99

Only a mad man is behind perfection and in the process, makes others miserable. Only an intellectual man is behind perfection - the INTELLIGENT is always focused on BEING TOTAL.

TOTALITY is possible - PERFECTION is not.

> 66
>
> Perfection is a neurotic goal, totality is sane goal. Perfection is in the future, totality is here now. You can be TOTAL this moment. You can be TOTAL in anger, you can be TOTAL in sex, you can ne TOTAL in whatsoever you are doing - it needs no preparation, it needs no cultivation. By being TOTAL you will enter into existence, nirvana.
>
> **OSHO**
>
> 99

The very question of finding TRUTH - comes from men who are behind perfection. Such were those pundits, scholars who were always surrounding the Buddha - the Mahavira, the Prophet, the Christ - they TRIED to KNOW THE TRUTH - they forgot that TRUTH CANNOT BE KNOWN - TRUTH has to be REALIZED.

"When a Buddha exists in the world, or a Muhammed, or a Krishna, or a Christ, then pundits and scholars and learned people, intellectually clever and cunning people, gather together around them. They start working hard: "What does Jesus mean?" They start creating a theology, a creed, a dogma. They are very successful people because they are very logical people. They cannot give you GOD, they cannot give you TRUTH, but they give you great organizations." - Osho

These pundits and these scholars and these intellectual beings - they can STIMULATE your MIND - they can GIVE GOOD ENTERTAINMENT to your MIND - they can say EXACTLY that your MIND wants to hear - you will like them. WHATEVER YOUR MIND WANTS TO LISTEN - THEY ARE SAYING - then the question arises - HOW ARE YOU GOING TO CHANGE - if the OLD is being repeated - making you COMFORTABLE - making you feel warm in your COMFORT ZONE - then what change are you talking of - what transformation are you expecting?

As long as you keep nodding your HEADS with AGREEMENT and DISAGREEMENT - TRUTH CAN NEVER PENETRATE INTO YOUR BEING - because the very action of AGREEING AND DISAGREEING is of the MIND - it simply means that you are listening with your MIND - the penetration cannot happen - the MIND won't let the words of the master sink into your being - you remain trapped in the MIND's AGREEING and DISAGREEING - and then you start wondering - "WHY AM I NOT CHANGING?"

How will you - to CHANGE, to TRANSFORM - first you have to STOP AGREEING AND DISAGREEING - only then some possibility of those beautiful divine words sinking - penetrating into your being is possible - and then a moment comes when those words 'spark' a realization within your being - but all this is possible only when you learn to LISTEN without the MIND - without the AGREEING and DISAGREEING.

"Kabir says: Please don't agree and disagree with me. Just listen. Listen attentively, totally. Kabir says: Please don't be in a hurry to decide and conclude. I am not preaching anything here. I am simply saying something that has happened to me, that has grown in me, that I have experienced, I am simply singing my own song.

All agreement, disagreement, is foolish, stupid. When truth knocks at your door you will simply be suddenly silent, unmoving. And that is real agreement - which is not of the intellect, not of the mind. That is not from you; that is from such a depth in your being that you can almost say it is from God."

- Osho

You don't have to agree. And you don't have to disagree. Just LISTEN. Just let the words sink into your Heart. Then the heart will respond, then the heart will start vibrating - then those divine words of the master will start bringing the change that you have been longing for - then the miracle starts happening - this is the way of its happening - this is how it all happens - only IF you learn to LISTEN without AGREEING or DISAGREEING.

I become very alert when somebody says, 'I AGREE' - it is a signal that this man or woman is still caught up in the MIND. That this MAN or WOMAN is still listening by bringing the MIND in between - logic is still in play - intellectualism is still active - it is a signal for me to stay away from such a man - such a woman - they are still a mess - a total mess.

You are trying to find if ASTROLOGY IS TRUTHFUL - I would request you and to all who have been following me - to FIRST FIND OUT IF YOU ARE TRUTHFUL TO YOURSELF. IF YOU ALL

CAN FIND TRUTH WITHIN YOURSELF - only then CAN YOU ALL FIND TRUTH IN ASTROLOGY - only then you CAN REALIZE THE BEAUTY OF TRUTH, OF LOVE, OF GOD.

TRUTH IS INDEFINITE. And it can SHAKE YOUR WHOLE BEING - it is like a sleeping man suddenly waking up and coming FACE to FACE with the TRUTH.

FIRST, the fire has to be from WITHIN - only then can it BURN UP ALL THAT IS MATERIAL and BRING FORTH THE TRUTH that has NO END - NO LIMITS.

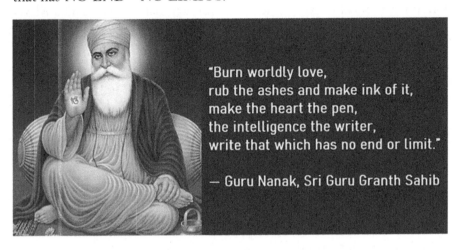

"Burn worldly love,
rub the ashes and make ink of it,
make the heart the pen,
the intelligence the writer,
write that which has no end or limit."

— Guru Nanak, Sri Guru Granth Sahib

The worldly love represents material love - material world. Guru Nanak is saying that first come out of this worldly love - these material attachments - and then you can experience that - which is BEYOND - which has NO END - which has NO LIMIT. Then whatever comes out of you is INTELLIGENCE - then whoever speaks out of you is your - HEART and once you get connected to your HEART then TRUTH is revealed - it is only when you go beyond the WORLD - the MIND is your WORLD - the WORLD is nothing but an extension of your MIND - once you BURN this WORLD, once you go beyond the MIND and merge within your HEART - then the TRUTH can be realized.

People have many fancy ideas about Astrology, about TRUTH, about ENLIGHTENMENT, about GOD - as if sitting in a cosy room - thinking a lot about TRUTH, about ASTROLOGY - about GOD - GOD can come to you, Astrology can come to you - as if by reading millions and millions of books on astrology you can become an astrologer - you can, but that is for those who want ENTERTAINMENT - for those who want to stimulate their MIND - but if by chance you ever come face to face with a man who has gone beyond ASTROLOGY - you will be in trouble - because this man is saying exactly that your MIND is NOT comfortable with - this man is simply NOT making you feel comfortable - you will condemn such a man - the human world has been doing it for AGES - they condemned the BUDDHA - they crucified JESUS - they ridiculed the MAHAVIRA - they forced the Prophet to go in exile - the common man cannot stand a MAN who HAS TRUTH - who has ABSOLUTE TRUTH.

Society likes KNOWLEDGEABLE MEN AND WOMEN. They LIKE the PUNDITS, the SCHOLARS - they are NOT a threat to the society because they say exactly THAT - which the SOCIETY wants to hear, so they are NOT a THREAT.

THREAT is the INDIVIDUAL - the man who has gone beyond the MIND - who has attained - who CANNOT speak anything BUT THE TRUTH - such a MAN is a THREAT to the society - the society fears such a man - the society goes all its way to ridicule - to insult - to condemn such a man. It had happened with JESUS, it had happened with the BUDDHA, it had happened with the PROPHET - it had happened with SAI BABA - every enlightened being - has been severely condemned by this so-called SOCIETY.

> 66 No society wants you to become wise, it is against the investment of all societies. If people become wise they cannot be exploited. If they are intelligent then they cannot be subjugated, they cannot be forced in a mechanical life, to live like robots. They will have the fragrance of rebellion around them. In fact, a wise man is like the fire, alive, aflame. He would like to rather die than to be enslaved.
>
> **OSHO** 99

People want to know the TRUTH - but they are simply unwilling, incapable of LISTENING to the TRUTH and yet they always keep asking:

"Is there TRUTH in Astrology?"

"Is there TRUTH in BUDDHA's words?"

"Was Jesus really a great messiah?"

You see - such questions they will ask - they will go on asking because this asking is of the MIND and the MIND IS CUNNING - the MIND IS ABSOLUTELY CUNNING.

> 66
>
> The mind is very clear and cunning; it distorts every great teaching. It jumps upon words; catches hold of the word and starts giving meanings to them which are NOT the real meanings.
>
> **OSHO**
>
> 99

One very significant point that you all should understand is - WHAT IS WITHIN YOU - IS WHAT THE ULTIMATE RESULT YOU ARE GOING TO GET.

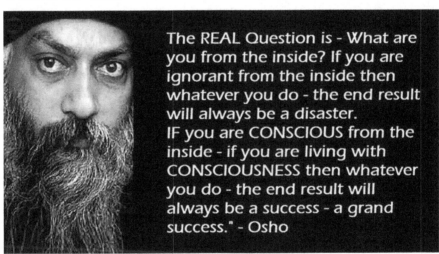

The REAL Question is - What are you from the inside? If you are ignorant from the inside then whatever you do - the end result will always be a disaster.
IF you are CONSCIOUS from the inside - if you are living with CONSCIOUSNESS then whatever you do - the end result will always be a success - a grand success." - Osho

If TRUTH is what you are following, if LOVE is what you are following, if GOD is what you are following then let me tell you and to all my followers, readers and fellow travellers - NO MATTER HOW DIFFICULT THE PHASE OF YOUR LIFE IS - in the END - you will have the LAST LAUGH - you will have the LAST DANCE.

If you CANNOT cleanse the DIRT, the DUST, the IGNORANCE that has accumulated within you - and I say it to all - then no matter how great a scholar you are - you will always remain short of peace, the absence of bliss is always going to be there - because you can PARROT the WHOLE SCRIPTURES of ASTROLOGY, you may repeat the WORDS OF BUDDHA - but that is all - you have NOT realized BUDDHA - because to REALIZE BUDDHA - first you have to TURN INWARD - first you have to WALK the TALK - first you have to let HIS words penetrate your being.

> " To understand Gautama Buddha, you don't have to be a Buddhist. By letting the words of Buddha absorbed by your intelligence - you can understand Buddha. The moment those words become yours - they blend with your breath, your blood, your existence - then you start transforming. Until then it has remained Gautama Buddha's, and there is twenty-five centuries distance. You can go on repeating Buddha's words - they are beautiful, but they will not help you attain what you are after.
>
> **OSHO** "

Buddha's words can help you to attain ONLY when you vibrate - when you FOLLOW HIS words - when you don't just become a PARROT - when you don't just imitate - when you WALK THE TALK - then you no more remain a parrot - then you transform into an EAGLE - then you can experience the essence of Buddha-hood - then you can feel the HIGHER REALMS OF CONSCIOUSNESS. Then TRUTH comes through you - AND SO ASTROLOGY IS REAL - IS TRUTHFUL - what MATTERS is HOW MUCH TRUTH YOU ARE FROM WITHIN - the more the depth of TRUTH is within you - the more the depth of TRUTH is in every KARMA - you do - then be it ASTROLOGY, or anything under the sky.

GOD EXISTS. TRUTH EXISTS. LOVE EXISTS.

The question that each one of you should ask yourself is - WHETHER YOU CAN BE TRUTHFUL. WHETHER YOU CAN BE GODLY.

> " God is a person; godliness is a quality. You cannot become God, but you can be godly.
>
> **OSHO** "

TRUTH is in every aspect of human life - and astrology is just one small aspect of life - it is like a drop in the ocean. This ocean is the ocean of spiritualism - of which astrology is just a tiny part. And so I always say and have been saying my whole life - that ASTROLOGY SHOULD NOT BLOCK YOU - you MUST NOT GET TRAPPED IN THE four WALLS OF ASTROLOGY - my whole effort - my whole presence and my answers to the questions put are SIMPLY to help you all understand that ASTROLOGY is just a TINY - a very TINY PART of the WHOLE. Einstein has very beautifully coined this word - WHOLE - for the UNIVERSE - BRAHMA!

But common souls - cannot understand my language - they CANNOT relate - and then they do one thing they are good at - and that is to CONDEMN - to RIDICULE - to BAN me - that is all they can do - because TRUTH is very HARD and even though they say they want to know the TRUTH - they really CANNOT face the TRUTH. They really CANNOT digest the TRUTH.

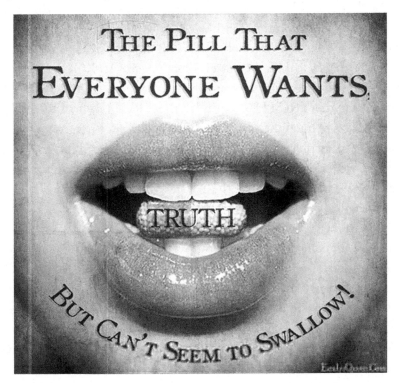

A young woman asked about her husband. And her husband was such a JACK - I could see that this man is having a secret affair with the OTHER WOMAN! Now would you want me to tell her this - she would have collapsed there itself.

This OTHER WOMAN is always DANGEROUS - and those married women who have been through such situations - know exactly what I mean.

A PROSTITUTE is better than the OTHER WOMAN. TRUTH is hard.

A PROSTITUTE at least is NOT BREAKING the MARRIAGE - the HOUSE - she is atleast not FORCING DIVORCE on that innocent married woman - but...the OTHER WOMAN - she is dangerous - she is bound to break the house of a married woman and, therefore, I have absolutely NO HESITATION to state that a PROSTITUTE is far better than the OTHER WOMAN!

But TRUTH is hard - it is possible that I may be condemned - it is possible that I may be banned - but nevertheless a copy of this answer will always be found on my website.

So, always remember that TRUTH is something that almost NOBODY wants to HEAR but everybody wants to KNOW! And that is the greatest irony of this human world.

To FACE the TRUTH - to FIND the TRUTH - to DIGEST the TRUTH - first you all have to PREPARE yourself. First, you all have to get READY. People ask - "WHEN CAN I SEE KRISHNA?"

My answer is - "Only when you will be like ARJUNA. Only when you are absolutely READY - that the Master will appear - the Divine will manifest before you."

When the disciple is ready, the master appears!

The sun is about to set. I said, "Sunsets are so beautiful."

Mohan said, "But after the Sun sets - darkness spreads all over..."

I said, "That is why sunset is so beautiful - because it is only when DARKNESS spreads all over your life that you REALIZE the significance of SUNRISE!"

We can appreciate the miracle of a sunrise if we have waited in the darkness.

Sunrise comes - you just have to be Patient, you just have to be Faithful.

Come, come you all and meditate. In the depth of your meditation, you will start finding the truth - you will start evolving to the next level - the level of consciousness.

Only a man of awareness can REALIZE the TRUTH, can FACE the TRUTH and can learn to LIVE with the TRUTH.

So before you dive into the TRUTH - first prepare yourself and the most effective way to prepare yourself is through deep meditation.

Meditate. In the beginning, many thoughts will attack you as soon as you close your eyes - let them attack - this attack is also an illusion - you should NOT entertain any of these thoughts.

> **❝**
>
> The ocean doesn't complain about the dance of ten million waves; so don't be concerned with the rise and fall of thoughts.
>
> **PAPAJI**
>
> **❞**

It is *time* to transform yourself into an OCEAN! Be like an ocean - no matter how many thought waves come - the OCEAN never complains - never gets disturbed - be like an ocean.

Disturbance is always there - outside it exists. Inside also it exists. But it is your job to ensure that FIRST you BRING PEACE WITHIN YOU - because it only when PEACE dwells WITHIN YOU that you will FIND PEACE EVERYWHERE. It is only when TRUTH is WITHIN YOU that you will be able to IDENTIFY TRUTHFUL MEN and WOMEN in your life. The whole FOCUS needs to be WITHIN.

> **❝**
>
> If there is peace in your mind you will find peace with evrybody. If your mind is agitated you will find agitation everywhere. So first find peace within and you will see this inner peace reflected everywhere else. YOU ARE THIS PEACE.
>
> **PAPAJI**
>
> **❞**

Once PEACE comes to your whole being - once you FIND YOUR PEACE WITHIN - only then can you walk your way towards ENLIGHTENMENT - the ultimate TRUTH - CONSCIOUSNESS!

Somebody asked – "How to identify an enlightened state?"

The answer is simple - and it is found in the divine words of Papaji, the disciple of Bhagavan Ramana Maharshi:

"If you see the illusion you are enlightened, but if you think that you are enlightened you are in the illusion!" - Papaji

One needs to overcome the illusions (Rahu) - and to do so - one needs to Meditate.

Always remember and I say it specifically for my close followers and readers - that there is absolutely NO process, NO technique to become SILENT. PROCESSES and TECHNIQUES - are the ways of the MIND and meditation happens only when there is NO MIND. NO THOUGHTS.

And so to stay SILENT - you simply have to be in the company of conscious beings - meditative beings - devoted beings - loving beings - in one word - SATSANG.

Always remember that there should be NO ATTEMPT to silence any thoughts - you just have to keep flowing like a RIVER - focusing on your breathing while you concentrate on the name of the Holy Lord.

If you feel ANGRY - if you keep getting any NEGATIVE thoughts - if you keep getting any TEMPTATIONS - then just find out - where it came from by turning inwards - by going back to the SOURCE - by coming back 'Home'.

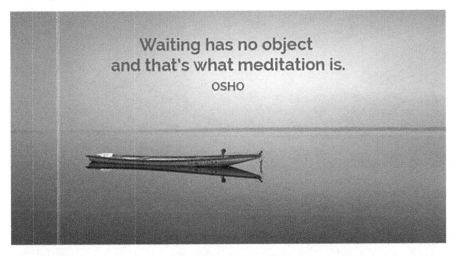

Waiting has no object
and that's what meditation is.
OSHO

If you meditate with some agenda - nothing will ever fructify - nothing will ever manifest. But if you meditate with LOVE - with DEVOTION - with FAITH - then one day, the 'bud' within you will start blossoming into a beautiful flower...

And once you blossom into a beautiful flower - then there is a dance, then there is a song to it - then life is no more a misery but a beautiful garden of bliss!

Everything is possible - the greatest failure can transform into the greatest success - darkness can be evaded by the light of consciousness - the setbacks can get you back to the top - today's low can become the stepping stone towards tomorrow's High - everything is possible - the real question is - **Are you Ready to Turn inwards and meditate?**

Meditate. Look within because Astrology is within you - if you cannot look within - if you cannot turn inwards - you will remain a 'parrot' - and parrots are good as long as they can answer from the 'book' - but one has to understand that there are certain questions that cannot be answered by referring to any book - but can be answered ONLY by turning inwards.

And the moment you start turning inwards - you remain no more a 'parrot' - you start transforming into an EAGLE - and then the 'sky' (consciousness) is available - then the real freedom comes - and you are 'READY' to *fly*...

Meditate - and find your freedom.

Jai Shri Ganesha. Jai Guru.

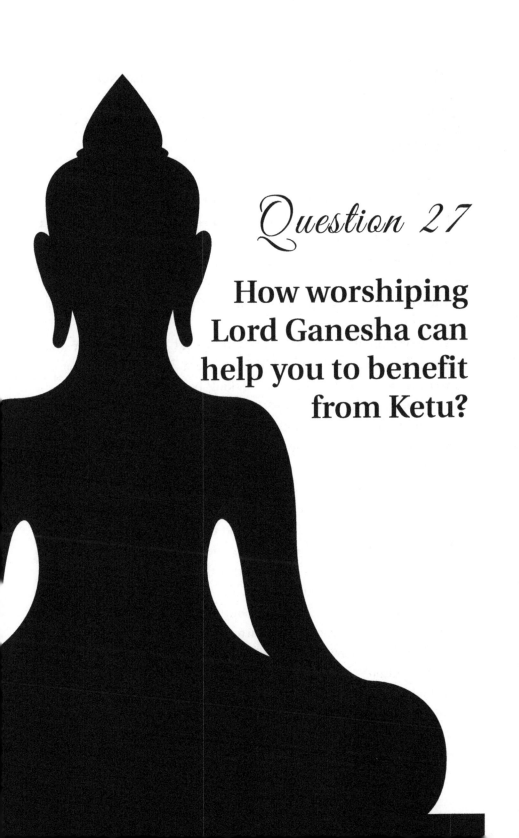

Question 27

How worshiping Lord Ganesha can help you to benefit from Ketu?

Lord Ganesha is the only God that has NO HUMAN HEAD.

Lord Ketu is the only entity in the whole gamut of astrology that has NO HUMAN HEAD.

The divine message that they share with us is to – TURN IN.

But the majority is always concerned with TURNING ON. (RAHU)

It is not a fact that Lord Ganesha's human head was cut by Shiva. It is just a symbolic representation – a divine message that human beings should think less and feel more. That human beings should start moving beyond mind.

Thinking helps to solve problems/puzzles that are created by thinking – by the mind.

Whatever problems are created by the mind – you can solve them by using the same mind – the thinking pattern. Mind is mathematics – so you can solve mathematics by thinking because it is created by the Mind. The trees that you count – 1 2 3 – this is the mathematics of your mind – the trees have nothing to do with it. It is a creation of your mind – whatever is the creation of the mind can be solved by the mind – by thinking.

BUT – what is NOT of the mind – but of the HEART or of the NATURE – of the COSMOS - cannot be solved by the MIND – then you are trapped – then you all cannot find the answer – that is how the so called intellectuals then start struggling – they become impotent in solving the case – because they miss to realize that the problem is existential.

Love is also an existential problem. You cannot solve love problems by thinking – you may go on thinking and thinking and thinking but you will come back to where you had started – you will find yourself trapped in a circle that just never ends and still you go on thinking…with no absolute solution!

Thinking won't help in such situations. Only when you stop thinking – only when there is NO HEAD – NO MIND – that you can FEEL and it is only when you FEEL that you can find the way – the solution – the answer to your problem.

There are many such existential problems – DEATH. BIRTH. LOVE. These all are existential problems – they are beyond mind and when you try to solve them by using your Mind – you fail, you fail miserably because you miss to understand that these existential problems cannot be solved by thinking – but only when you stop thinking and start feeling – thinking won't let you 'vibrate' with the existence – it is only when you start feeling that you can vibrate and it is only when you vibrate that you start coming close to the source of the problem.

When there is TOO MUCH OF THINKING (HEAD) – you are simply missing to identify the source of the problem.

When there is absolutely NO THINKING, NO MIND – TRUTH appears before you – you find the source of the problem and when the source is found – the solution comes on its own!

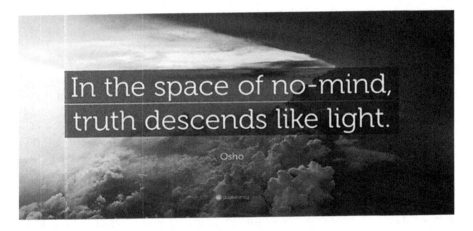

In the space of no-mind, truth descends like light.

Osho

Meditation is the state of NO MIND. When there is absolutely NO THINKING – meditation happens. When there are 'thoughts' – it is a distraction and when there are NO THOUGHTS – it is Meditation.

Lord Ganesha is Meditation.

Lord Ketu is Meditation.

The idol of Lord Ganesha simply reflects HIS state of Meditation. There is absolutely NO HEAD, NO MIND – Ganesha is deeply engrossed WITHIN – what a beautiful representation is this – one of the greatest wonders with such a great message – that IF YOU REALLY

WANT TO EXPERIENCE JOY, HAPPINESS, PEACE then – look at me, says Ganesha – I have NO HEAD – NO MIND – I am deeply engrossed within by TURNING INWARDS.

Mohan asked, "Then how come the Elephant face?"

The HEAD or FACE of Elephant is just a representation of HIS deep wisdom. Elephants are the wisest animals and so the ancient Seers and Sages – instilled the idol of Ganesha with an Elephant Face or Head – when in reality this deity has NO HEAD, NO MIND and that is what MAKES HIM one of the GREATEST LORDS – without taking the name of Lord Ganesha – NO SCRIPTURE begins – it only begins and completes when one says:

|| **"Shri Ganeshaya Namaha"** ||

One of the most striking similarities between Ketu and Ganesha – is the quality of BEING DETACHED!

"How?" asked Mohan.

I asked him, "What do you do after worshiping the idol of Lord Ganesha for 10 days during Ganesha festival?"

"I immerse the idol in a clean flowing water – river or sea," said Mohan.

So you understand. And I appeal to all my close followers, fellow travellers and readers – understand the fact that the action of immersing the idol in itself is a message – that you should live with DETACHMENT! For 10 days you worship HIS idol – but in the end – what is he asking you to do? To NOT remain ATTACHED but to detach yourself and immerse (LET GO) HIS idol by dropping it in the flowing water!

Understand this and this is very significant – the whole message of the VISARJAN process (immersing the Ganesha idol) is to help you realize the fact that LIFE SHOULD BE LIVED WITH DETACHMENT.

And that is EXACTLY the divine message of Lord KETU – DETACHMENT!

Real success in life comes only through DETACHMENT – one who self-realizes this truth goes a long way...

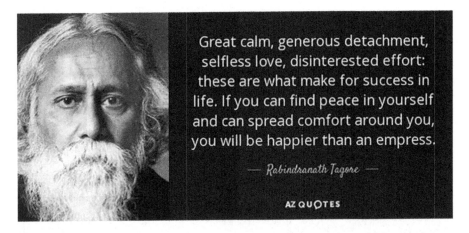

Great calm, generous detachment, selfless love, disinterested effort: these are what make for success in life. If you can find peace in yourself and can spread comfort around you, you will be happier than an empress.

— *Rabindranath Tagore* —

AZ QUOTES

India is the only country and Hinduism is the only religion – a unique religion where people make the mud idol and then the same people immerse the mud idol! And it is a very deep message from the Hindu civilization that – NOTHING is permanent and nothing can be permanent, even your image of God!

To throw away the idol of Ganesha – to immerse the idol of Ganesha – great courage is required – and this is deep, very deep. You have put everything that you had in your Father – to nurture Him, to comfort Him – for many days you have loved Him, worshiped Him and now you have to LET HIM GO – how difficult it is going to be…how much courage is required to let him go…and you don't know next year, if you would be there again to bring him back! But it has to be done – the message of Ganesha is simple – 'LOVE ME – but Let that LOVE be detached!'

Detachment is being lovable – but without being possessive.

Detachment means not that you should not own bungalows and cars and beautiful things in life – YOU CAN HAVE ALL OF THEM – BUT you should not be attached to those things. Even if you have 10 bungalows and a dozen cars – still you SHOULD NOT GET ATTACHED to them. But unfortunately that is what happens! The things in your life possess you – you think you possess them but you become so attached to them that they start possessing you and then you are trapped – you are deeply trapped!

> Detachment is NOT that you should own nothing. But nothing should own you.
>
> **ALI IBN TALIB**

Look at the beautiful lotus flower – it is rooted in water – but it is always found – above the water!

The real Yogi is like a lotus flower – HE is very much with us but not attached. His whole being is LOVE – if you come, he will offer you as much love as you can receive – and if you leave, he will not be disturbed – because HIS love is not dependent on the outside factor – he is no more falling in love – he has become LOVE – whoever comes to HIM – will be touched and blessed by the fragrance of his detached love.

"Love is always an attachment to you; the deeper the attachment the more you think - it is love! But the MASTER's love is utterly detached. He loves, yet he is NOT bound by it. He loves, but he is NOT binding on you. You know a love which creates excitement. The master's love is utterly peaceful; there is no excitement. It is nothing to do with romance." - Osho

The Master is a contented man. He has absolutely NO expectations. HE asks for NOTHING. So then, it becomes difficult to understand HIM – especially those who are always HUNGRY! Buddha calls those people HUNGRY who always want more and more and more – this MORE is RAHU. And NO MORE is KETU!

Lord Ganesha wants nothing – HAS no expectations – HE is in his peace and so, whenever anybody is suffering because of RAHU – I ask him or her to visit Lord Ganesha temple, to worship HIM, to read His Shlokas – His Stotras.

It is NOT that Ganesha and KETU are the same. Whenever I mention in my answers – and I have been mentioning many times – that when I say Ketu is Sri Ganesha – I mean when you worship GANESHA – the QUALITIES of KETU will start enhancing within your being. Then you will understand KETU – then you will RESONATE with HIS energy – then you will start TURNING INWARD!

And this is significant – this is very significant for you ALL to understand that the more you WORSHIP GANESHA – the more you would NURTURE the KETU QUALITIES within YOU and that will be a great blow to RAHU! That will be a great danger to RAHU – because NOW you are becoming intelligent – now you are TURNING

INWARD – now you are becoming WISE – now you are NO MORE interested on the outside – now you are slowly, steadily getting ROOTED WITHIN YOURSELF – and that is indeed a great transformation – a great transformation in the making.

Once you are rooted in your own center,
nothing from outside can move you.

OSHO

The more you go deep within your being – the more you meditate by focusing on your breath – breathe in – breathe out – between these two actions the whole story of your life is scripted. AND the more your meditation improves, the more you – yourself will be able to READ the SCRIPT of your life – then NO astrologer will be required and no Pundit – but then these men will be in trouble because then how will their business run! And that is exactly what this SOCIETY wants – the SOCIETY NEVER wants you to become WISE because then you will become INDEPENDENT – then you cannot be exploited – then the

SOCIETY will be in trouble – whereas the SOCIETY always wants you to be in TROUBLE so that the 'meter' of money continues – uninterrupted!

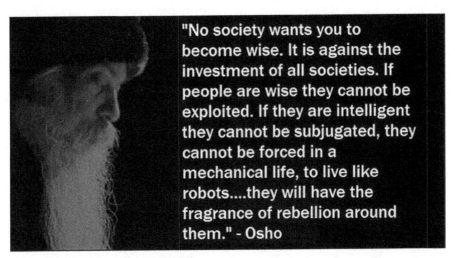

"No society wants you to become wise. It is against the investment of all societies. If people are wise they cannot be exploited. If they are intelligent they cannot be subjugated, they cannot be forced in a mechanical life, to live like robots....they will have the fragrance of rebellion around them." - Osho

A wise man is an 'Individual' – he is not behind personalities – he has thrown away the 'mask' of personality and lives his life by being himself. A wise man is ALIVE – is AFIRE – he is COURAGEOUS – he would rather die than to be enslaved!

Lord Ganesha represents the wisdom of such a wise man. It is through LORD GANESHA – that you realize the beauty of KETU.

By and by – whatever DEITY you worship – certain QUALITIES of the planet or the entity such as KETU develop within you!

When you worship:

Lord GANESHA: KETU qualities develop within you.

Lord DATTATREYA: JUPITER qualities develop within you.

Lord VISHNU: JUPITER qualities develop within you.

Lord KRISHNA: JUPITER and MERCURY qualities develop within you.

Lord SHIVA: SUN MOON KETU qualities develop within you.

Lord HANUMAN – MARS QUALITIES

Lord MHASOBA (a well-known deity of Maharashtra) – MARS QUALITIES

GODDESS LAKSHMI – VENUS and MERCURY

GODDESS DURGA – MARS and VENUS

RAHU qualities are developed when you worship TANTRIK GODS – or GODS that rule the UNDERWORLD – meaning the PATAL LOK. Generally, the reptile Snake Gods represent the qualities of RAHU. Some Tantrik Goddess' or Goddess' of Tantra also represent RAHU qualities.

So every DIETY is in a way – a BRIDGE between YOU and the concerned PLANET energy.

If you ask me – then to me, the GREATEST BRIDGE is the MASTER – the GURU! Through the benevolent master – you experience GOD. And Sant Kabir beautifully mentions the significance of the GURU through his divine words and those words should be inscribed in GOLD:

"If here before me stand both - my Guru (master) and Govind (the almighty), I would first prostrate before my Guru. Because - it is HE who revealed to me - the Govind." - Saint Kabir

Beautiful. Kabir goes deep into our heart – one of the greatest saints that the world has ever known! I humbly prostrate before His Holiness – Sant Kabir.

All the divine saints would not have become saints – had it not been the grace of Lord Ganesha and the matured state of KETU within them!

WITHOUT KETU – there is absolutely no enlightenment. KETU, therefore, is one of the greatest 'tools' of the benevolent GURU – because KETU is DETACHMENT, and unless you start becoming

DETACHED, there is absolutely no way for you to PROGRESS in the true sense!

You have asked a very beautiful question – and it has many dimensions to it. The last dimension is of Mercury!

One has to understand that Mercury is your INTELLECT.

But Intellect is a very poor substitute for Intelligence!

When you come in contact with Lord Ganesha – when you start worshiping HIM with a pure heart, unwavering faith and devotion – the INTELLECT within you starts TUNING with your HEART and when INTELLECT tunes with your HEART – INTELLIGENCE is born – Intelligence, therefore, is of the HEART and NOT of the HEAD.

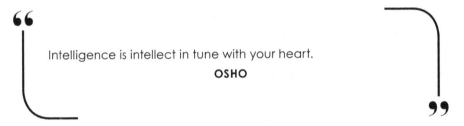

> **"**
> Intelligence is intellect in tune with your heart.
> **OSHO**
> **"**

Intellect is of the MIND. Every day, I receive all kinds of emails, hundreds of emails from 'intellectual' men and women – and all they do is that they write long emails asking about this house and that house and that yog and this yog. But one in a million comes and asks ONLY that which can help him realize the real thing! And because he or she knows what is the REAL thing – that they can ask some real good questions – the rest are yet to realize what is the REAL THING and so the questions they ask are also not real – just a lot of noise, and nothing else!

Mercury, therefore, is disliked by the master – Jupiter! Because the master is all for the heart – and mercury is all in the HEAD! Through the HEAD you can travel from A to Z – but beyond Z the doors close – there is no further going, you are trapped – you are utterly trapped in your intellectualism.

This intellectualism is TRANSFORMED into intelligence only when you worship Lord Ganesha – the more your SEVA (service) towards

HIM grows – the more the 'PLASTIC ROSE' starts transforming into the 'REAL ROSE'!

And REAL ROSE is beautiful – yes, it has many imperfections and yet it is BEAUTIFUL because now it has a certain FRAGRANCE to it, a certain LIFE to it!

REAL MEN, REAL WOMEN – I like them, in fact, I love them. But let me tell you – they are in minority – in fact, one in a million. In this KALI YUG, men and women also disguise themselves as REAL – when they are just FAKING it – so you have to be really cautious before opening the doors of your heart.

Such fake men and women – come up with the idea of non-attachment – but that is again an escape route – they are AFRAID that if they get into a relationship, they might get attached and then the pain.

Non-attachment is NOT detachment.

Non-attachment is a makeup for those fake men and fake women who are afraid of getting attached and so they keep running away from any relationships.

Detachment – a detached man or woman is NOT AFRAID of getting attached. The 'Inner Engineering' is so strongly developed through meditation that nobody can move him or disturb him – such a man is a man of awareness, he lives, laughs with you but he is absolutely detached – if you take him to your Palace – he will come, if you ask him to stay beneath a tree – he will stay – for him PALACE or TREE doesn't make a difference – he may sleep on the Royal Bed and he is also happy to sleep on the hard ground – for him there is NO attachment – he can come anytime and he can also leave anytime – he is not bound to anybody – he remains detached but with abundance of LOVE in HIS heart.

There is a very deep connection between detachment and intelligence! An intellectual man can never live a detached life. He may live a non-attached life – but for him living a detached life is next to impossible!

Such an intellectual man goes on living his life by believing that – SHE is MY WIFE. SHE is MY DAUGHTER. THAT is MY Bungalow. THAT is MY CAR. THAT IS MY DESK. THAT IS MY COMPANY. THAT IS MY…MY and MY and MY and this MY never gets him out of the CAGE. He himself prepares a nice CAGE around him and then starts feeling suffocated and then comes and asks, "Why is my life so miserable?"

Now what to tell him? And first of all, is he going to ever understand a single word that I may share with him?

People are running all over the world in search of the Master – in search of a Guide – the question is – even by luck you found one – how is it going to help you – if YOU are yet NOT READY to understand his words, his language?

Therefore, I say – read, read some of my books and then come to me – then there is a possibility that you may relate to what I am saying to you – you may understand what I am trying to tell you. I already have ENOUGH – so by buying my books you are not going to make me rich. But by reading my books you can certainly become rich – WITHIN.

And a man who is becoming RICH from WITHIN is a man of worth. It is worth helping such a man – because the THIRST in him is now for that – which is beyond – the divine – the unseen…

> 66
>
> Blessed are they which do hunger and thirst after righteousness: for they shall be filled.
>
> **MATTHEW 5:6 BIBLE VERSE**
>
> 99

The real blessing is when you start turning inward. Lord Ganesha is the most significant deity whose message for all HIS devotees is to turn inwards. Through HIS appearance – the message is loud and clear – HE is saying – "Look I have NO head, No mind – I am deeply engrossed within…and so why can't you do so?"

Through the ritual of immersing HIS idol on the tenth day of Ganesha festival – the Sages are simply conveying the message that DO NOT GET ATTACHED TO EVEN THE IDOL GOD – TIME comes and YOU HAVE TO LET GO – YOU HAVE TO IMMERSE by becoming DETACHED!

> **❝** The dispersion of Lord Ganesha Idol is a very deep transformative process, because to throw a God needs courage, to throw a God needs DETACHMENT - to throw a God you were worshipping for 10 long days! You were falling at the feet of the God - crying, dancing, singing and NOW you yourself go and throw the idol into the sea. So it was just a device to make you realize that NOTHING is PERMANENT and you should learn to live a detached life.
>
> **OSHO** **❞**

KETU's message is also the same. Live a detached life. You are married – then do not become POSSESSIVE. The moment you become possessive – love ceases to exist! Love feels suffocated when there is NO FREEDOM! Why you become POSSESSIVE? Because of your fear of losing! When I say – you – it is for all readers and followers. You fear of losing and so you want to possess. In this madness, you go on missing love – the more you become possessive, the more you are moving away from love – then your wife starts feeling suffocated – the children, the mother, the father – everybody feels suffocated when somebody tries to POSSESS them – love ends and what remains is POSSESSION – what is the point in living such a life?

"Why be possessive? The possessiveness shows simply one thing – that you cannot trust existence. Non-possessiveness is basically trust in existence. There is no need to possess, because the whole is already ours." - Osho

When you LOVE – you simply LOVE. When you love – let there be no doubt – let there be no fear of losing – REMEMBER that is the message of KETU – that is what DETACHMENT is – you love – you simply love!

An innocent man goes on loving – people may cheat him, he may be cheated by his lover – he may be cheated by his wife – but his INNOCENCE remains. Those who cheated him – those lovers and partners who left him must be utterly 'POOR' – but he remains RICH and his RICHNESS is in his INNOCENCE – he may go on experiencing cheaters but HIS innocence always remains and it is this INNOCENCE that eventually moves him to the HIGHER ALTITUDES – then one day, the benevolent master comes and says, "You idiot – do you still want to remain in this mud – or now you want to come with me?"

The heart of an innocent man or woman is like butter. Then the man starts crying then he goes in deep meditations – then he starts self-realizing that what an idiot he has been his whole life – running behind fake gold, fake beauties, fake world – then a great transformation starts happening – then the qualities of KETU start developing – then he starts TURNING INWARD...then he starts realizing the many treasures of the higher altitudes – then there is no looking back – the sky (consciousness) is clear and he is ready to fly!

It happens, it always happens that a man who is transforming is CRITICIZED by those 'plastic' men and women who don't know themselves!

Once it happened – a young man and he was changing for good. He was taking efforts to rise above the Mind. He was meditating. He was coming closer to the realms of consciousness...but the society won't let him GROW so easily! You see – that is how this fake society is – then some so-called intellectuals and moralists started saying, "Look...look at him...all his life he was such a womanizer and was such a drunkard and look, now how he is acting out as a virtuous man – as a prayerful man..."

You see – those who have been 'acting out' their whole life by wearing 'masks' – will only find the other also as 'acting out' – whatever is within you is what you will see on the outside!

They all were making fun of him – talking about his shady past – they forgot the fact that every SAINT has a PAST and every SINNER has a FUTURE!

Whenever the young man would walk to the temple – they would gossip between themselves, "Look, look how he is being saintly – taking Lord's name..."

But they were unaware that Kabir was walking around. And Saint Kabir heard them gossiping – he looked at them and said, "He has got up from his SLEEP – but what about you all?"

And this is a very significant question that EACH ONE OF YOU SHOULD ASK YOURSELF BEFORE YOU POINT YOUR FINGER ON ANYBODY WHO IS TRYING TO TRANSFORM – to CHANGE HIMSELF FOR GOOD.

At least, he has got up from HIS 'SLEEP' – it doesn't matter what he had been doing while he was SLEEPING – what matters is that HE HAS GOT UP FROM HIS SLEEP – he is no more ASLEEP.

But those who are gossiping – those who are JUDGING him – are still living a plastic life – they themselves are fast asleep – how can they realize the beauty of a person who has AWAKENED from his sleep?

A person who is awakened – has self-realized the futility of SEX, of MONEY, of WEALTH, of POWER, of STATUS – he had enough of it – and because he had it – he has come to the point of awakening where he has realized that all of this – is NOT THE ANSWER.

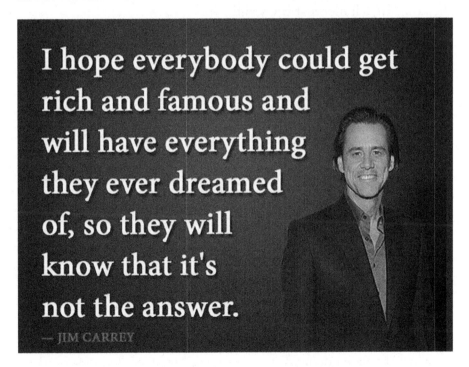

This realization has to be EARNED through your own experiences and awareness.

That is why it is necessary that one goes through the experiences of sex, experiences of power, experiences of status building, experiences of love, experiences of relationships – all these stages enrich him and help him to come to the SELF-REALIZATION that – it's NOT the ANSWER.

Monks and priests, celibates and nuns – who suppress their sexuality – their greed – their lust – their attractions to power, status and money – simply end up in disastrous situations!

Three priests were travelling – and they had to get their tickets at the airport. One was a young priest – the other two were elder men. They told the young priest to go and get the tickets from the ticket counter. The priest goes – stands in a queue. After a while, his turn comes to collect the tickets but he is totally taken aback, his hands start shaking, he goes weak on his knees because the lady sitting at the ticket counter is extremely sexy – her whole attire is so attractive that he can't get his eyes off her – she says, "Sir, tell me what you want?"

And the priest quickly responds – a slip of tongue – "YOU!"

Then knowing that he has committed a SIN – he runs back to the elderly priests!

So you see – what happens when you go on suppressing your sexual needs? Suppression is NOT the answer. You have to EXPERIENCE sex – only then can you realize that it is ENOUGH. Only then can you realize that it cannot last for longer – someday, the body is going to give up – someday, the bed is no more going to shake – because by then you would have started shaking...

Sex makes man a fool. But unless he becomes a fool – he cannot realize the beauty of being wise! Unless you experience darkness – you cannot appreciate the sunlight – the sunrise!

In the West – sex has become a boring thing – too much of it has been done and experienced – now they don't find it interesting. You see – when you have it beyond limit – it goes on making your life hell.

SEX is your bondage. It keeps you unconscious. It does not allow you to see what you are doing. You are possessed by it. SEX possesses you – and you remain ignorant – this ignorance then goes on making your life hell – more hell and more and more hell.

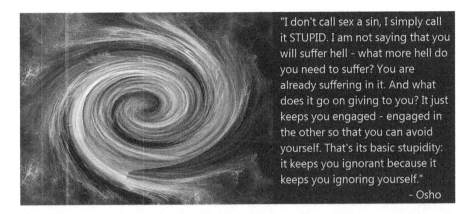

"I don't call sex a sin, I simply call it STUPID. I am not saying that you will suffer hell - what more hell do you need to suffer? You are already suffering in it. And what does it go on giving to you? It just keeps you engaged - engaged in the other so that you can avoid yourself. That's its basic stupidity: it keeps you ignorant because it keeps you ignoring yourself."

- Osho

But one should go through THIS HELL – THIS PLEASURE OF SEX – only then can you WAKE UP – that too if that much awareness is there – that much consciousness is there – that much blessings are there – in store for you!

People come and ask, "Is there a place called – hell?"

The master laughs – a loud belly laugh and says, "Are you crazy? You are living in HELL and asking if there is a place called Hell?"

IGNORANCE is your HELL. The more one gets driven by SEX, by MONEY, by POWER, by FAME, by WEALTH, by STATUS – he gets deeply into the clutches of IGNORANCE (RAHU).

And KETU is the KEY that gets you all out of this HELL (IGNORANCE). WHY KETU?

KETU is the source, the energy that helps you to TURN IN. Whole life you have been engaged in TURNING ON – the whole essence of your life has been to TURN ON – now KETU is helping you to TURN IN – Lord Ganesha is showing through HIS appearance – that I AM TURNED IN – I AM MEDITATION – you can also do it – you can also make something out of your human life that you can carry forward after you DIE – after this human body is DEAD.

The question is – how many are willing to listen? How many are willing to TURN INWARD? How many are willing to RISE ABOVE SEX? – Only a man who can rise above SEX can experience the beyond – to rise above sex – first, he has to go through the experiences of sex – and so you will find many men who were married – had children – but later rose to greatest heights of spiritualism – because they SELF-REALIZED the futility of SEX by EXPERIENCING IT – they realized that there is something much beautiful – much lasting – much higher than SEX – their EVOLUTION to the HIGHER ALTITUDES has been through their journey from SEX to SUPER CONSCIOUSNESS!

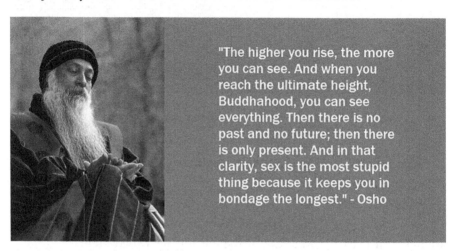

"The higher you rise, the more you can see. And when you reach the ultimate height, Buddhahood, you can see everything. Then there is no past and no future; then there is only present. And in that clarity, sex is the most stupid thing because it keeps you in bondage the longest." - Osho

RAHU is highly sexual. Ketu is highly asexual. Ketu is disinterested in SEX – he had it ENOUGH in the PAST – now he is interested to TURN INWARD – to look within – to meditate!

The very appearance of Lord Ganesha is of meditation – there is NO MIND, NO HEAD – but there is immense TRUST – immense FAITH in oneself – deeply engrossed WITHIN...

TRUST is very important. In fact, LOVE is impossible without TRUST. Relationships break – when TRUST starts evaporating – first TRUST evaporates – then LOVE evaporates – the basis is always TRUST.

TRUST can get you everywhere – but first TRUST has to be there.

Once a young man came and said, "People worship Buddha – but Buddha is not alive..."

The master smiled and said, "No Master Ever Dies For Those Who Can Trust." Your Trust matters! But the reality of this human world is – people cannot trust those who are living – so how can they trust those who are dead! Your TRUST can change your perception towards life. Then even if the master is dead – you can connect. Then even if the master has dropped his physical body – you can connect. The key is – TRUST. When you trust Buddha – then no matter even if there is distance of centuries between you and HIM – still you can connect. Distance doesn't matter – when TRUST happens – time and space don't matter – you stay 'connected'…

"TRUST is the miracle. You can be in closeness with Mohammed or Jesus or Buddha right now if **trust** is there. But it is difficult! It is difficult because you don't know how? You cannot trust a living person, *how can you trust a dead*? If **trust happens** then you are close to Buddha right now. And for persons **who have faith**, BUDDHA is ALIVE - **very much ALIVE.**"
- Osho

You can appreciate the qualities of Lord Ketu only when you self-realize the significance of Lord Ganesha! It is all connected – linked-in!

MOON dislikes KETU – the MIND is always against KETU – because it is the power and strength of Sri KETU that destroys the MIND – and it is only when there is NO MIND – that meditation can happen – that the TRUTH can be revealed.

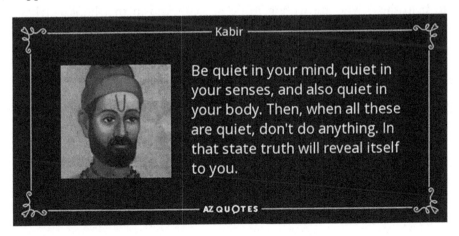

Kabir

Be quiet in your mind, quiet in your senses, and also quiet in your body. Then, when all these are quiet, don't do anything. In that state truth will reveal itself to you.

AZ QUOTES

It is only when the MIND is QUIET that the SOUL can speak! The SELF can be realized.

But how to Quieten the MIND? Yesterday, my family doctor asked me the same question – How to Quieten the MIND? And the answer is simple and it has been given to the whole mankind – again and again and again through many divine men and women – the answer is in one word – NAAM.

And Sant Kabir reveals the answer in the most beautiful way…

> **Says Kabeer,
> he alone is poor
> who does not have
> the Naam,
> the Name of the Lord,
> in his heart. ||4||8||**
>
> - Sri Guru Granth Sahib Ji I Ang -1159

A whole book of over 300 pages 'NO MIND' is what I have written just to help those who are willing to be helped! And in that book – I have again and again mentioned that unless you move beyond MIND – there is no coming to the TRUTH – and the way to move beyond MIND is through CHANTING THE NAME OF THE LORD – there is absolutely no other miraculous key to your transformation than the chanting the Lord's holy name!

But who wants to listen? Shallow people and their shallowness is so much that they will run behind everything – do everything – churn out thousands of rupees to a magician – to a tantrik – but will never listen to the most simple and most effective means that the benevolent masters have so compassionately shared with mankind – chanting the Lord's holy name!

> " To chant the holy name and dance in ecstasy is so easy and sublime that one can achieve all the benefits of spiritual life simply by following this process.
>
> **SRIMAD BHAGAVATAM** "

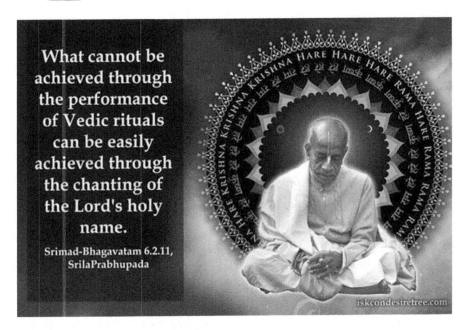

What cannot be achieved through the performance of Vedic rituals can be easily achieved through the chanting of the Lord's holy name.

Srimad-Bhagavatam 6.2.11, SrilaPrabhupada

iskcondesiretree.com

People want everything 'ready-made' – but one must understand that HAPPINESS is NOT ready-made – it comes only through your OWN actions.

The joy of meeting the TRUTH – the GURU – the MASTER is beyond the expression of words. Language is really poor – but Sant Kabir reveals it in the most beautiful way.....

> " When you meet the true Guru, He will awaken your heart; HE will tell you the secret of love and detachment, and then you will know indeed that HE transcends this universe.
>
> **KABIR** "

457

There is absolutely no better way than to realize the depth and beauty of the GURU through the 'eyes' of KETU! Ketu has absolutely NO HEAD – no intellectualism – HE is like Peter, the fisherman who starts following Jesus without thinking – without bringing any doubts, any intellectualism in between! Jesus says, "Follow ME – I will make you the fisher of men." And Peter is like our KETU – a man of heart with NO HEAD – he simply 'jumps' into the unknown – he is so much moved by the presence of Jesus – HIS aura, HIS bliss – HIS Peace – that even though he is meeting Jesus for the very first time in his life – still without giving any second thought, he starts following Jesus and then the rest is history!

Arjuna is like our KETU – Krishna tells him, "SHOOT – shoot your arrow on that old man…"

That old man is Arjuna's great grandfather – BHISHMA. Whole life he has loved that old man and that old man has loved him immensely – and now the master is telling him to shoot and kill that old man…

How difficult it would have been for a common man – for a man who is ATTACHED – for a man who is yet sleeping – but ARJUNA is an awakened man – without wasting a second – he shoots and the old man is dead. BHISHMA is dead – at the point itself the victory is guaranteed – not because BHISHMA was dead – but BECAUSE ARJUNA PROVED HIS ABILITY TO LISTEN TO THE WORDS OF THE MASTER – WITHOUT BRINGING THE MIND IN BETWEEN – without BRINGING the so called intellectualism in between – HE just followed Krishna's words and the rest is history.

That is KETU – listening to the WORDS of the MASTER and letting those WORDS penetrate into your being – and then a day comes when those words – those golden words start transforming you inside out – that is the day of your life – that is the REAL TURNING POINT!

But who wants to LISTEN? People have many fantasies of having a turning point and those are so shallow – so material that the less said the better.

Sant Kabir says – that when you LISTEN to the words of the master – DO NOT AGREE and DO NOT DISAGREE – just LISTEN because when you get into AGREEING AND DISAGREEING – you bring the MIND in between and the MIND is a monkey – it won't let the words of the master penetrate into your being – because it is very much aware that if those words get into your being – its existence will be in danger – and so the MIND obstructs you – you remain with the master – but no change – no transformation is seen within you – because you have never LISTENED in reality – you have just been lost in the madness of agreeing and disagreeing.

"Kabir says: Please don't agree and disagree with me. Just listen. Listen attentively, totally. Kabir says: Please don't be in a hurry to decide and conclude. I am not preaching anything here. I am simply saying something that has happened to me, that has grown in me, that I have experienced, I am simply singing my own song.

All agreement, disagreement, is foolish, stupid. When truth knocks at your door you will simply be suddenly silent, unmoving. And that is real agreement - which is not of the intellect, not of the mind. That is not from you; that is from such a depth in your being that you can almost say it is from God."

- Osho

Many times it has happened – that those who were CLOSE have never realized and those who have been at far distances – have realized! It is, therefore, not necessary to be with the Master – it is necessary to LISTEN and ACT by following the words of the Master.

Judas always remained close to Jesus. Like a shadow he would be with Jesus – but it is Judas who sold Jesus to the Romans for a few silver coins! Being CLOSE is useless if you CANNOT RELATE to the MASTER's words – HIS message – HIS LOVE!

And when Judas came to know that the Romans have nailed – crucified Jesus – he could not control himself – he started crying – a few moments of IGNORANCE had made JUDAS a man of betrayal! Unable to control himself – he HANGS himself – commits suicide!

Being close is not important – resonating with the words of the master without bringing your intellectualism in between is important – and that comes when you start turning inwards – the way of KETU is turning inwards because it is only when you start turning inwards that you can RELATE with Jesus – then you will no more remain a Judas – you will become JOHN who loved JESUS – the love between John and Jesus is beyond the power of words – the disciple moving towards the master – the master moving towards the disciple – ONENESS - how to express such a pure love – language is really poor.

Only a man who is turning inward – who is chanting the name of the Lord can realize – can identify with the awakened – the enlightened being. He can 'see' such an enlightened being – he can find the whole universe in HIM.

> A drop, melting into the sea, everyone can see. But the sea, absorbed in a drop, only a rare one can see.
>
> **SAINT KABIR**

Lord Ganesha is the bridge that helps you to gain the strength of Lord Ketu and it is through Lord Ketu that you can transform the Intellectualism (Mercury) into intelligence – and so you have come up with a real good question – it is all inter-connected, it is all linked.

When intelligence comes – you stop seeking God in temples – you stop doing all the unwanted rituals and ceremonies and all those poojas and havans.

Then you realize that GOD is not on the outside – HE is not in the TEMPLE – TEMPLES are built just to ENCOURAGE the common man towards RIGHTEOUSNESS – towards having more FAITH in GOD – it is a MOTIVATIONAL SPOT but it is certainly NOT GOD's HOME!

God's home is in your heart. It is in every human being's heart. God dwells within and not without.

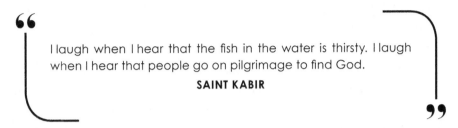

I laugh when I hear that the fish in the water is thirsty. I laugh when I hear that people go on pilgrimage to find God.

SAINT KABIR

If you are going on pilgrimage to meet GOD – to experience GOD then you have got the wrong address – the right address goes through your heart – the dwelling of GOD is within you.

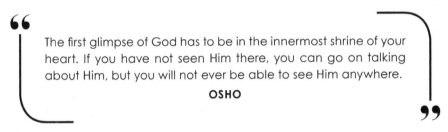

The first glimpse of God has to be in the innermost shrine of your heart. If you have not seen Him there, you can go on talking about Him, but you will not ever be able to see Him anywhere.

OSHO

KETU and LORD Ganesha simply are encouraging you to LOOK WITHIN and SELF-REALIZE the GOD that is within you – and let me tell you and to all my readers and followers that there is absolutely NOTHING as GREAT than to experience the state of your own self-realization.

Ketu is meditation. Ganesha is meditation and the whole essence of meditation is to bring you to the PRESENT MOMENT. The whole essence is to help you realize that GOD is NOT in the heaven. GOD is in the PRESENT moment – when you are able to BE HERE NOW – you have Entered the Temple – the joy – the bliss – the peace – the dance has begun...

Then life is no more the same – everything around you is the same but you are no more the same – then there is a song to it, a poem, a dance – and it all comes when you turn inward – when you become more and more DETACHED!

Ketu is detachment. Ganesha is detachment. Their message is simple –
DETACH YOURSELF. And if you miss to listen to their message –
then you miss, you simply miss this life – and this is how you all go
on missing – you remain on the surface – flaunting your intellectualism
(mercury) – and in this futile process, you miss – you simply miss to self-
realize that 'intellectualism' is a very poor substitute to INTELLIGENCE.

Be Intelligent and NOT intellectual.

And the way towards intelligence goes through your HEART and
NOT the HEAD. Get out of your HEAD and get into your HEART –
that is the message of KETU, that is the whole essence of Lord Ganesha!

Meditate.
Jai Shri Ganesha. Jai Guru.

Question 28

If Jupiter is the guru of Ketu then who is the guru of Rahu?

 **B**eautiful question.

Ketu exalts in the sign of Sagittarius - the sign of Guru (Jupiter).

Rahu exalts in the sign of Gemini - the sign of Budh (Mercury).

On one side is RIGHTEOUSNESS - Jupiter! Jupiter is the master of Ketu.

On the other side is INTELLECTUALISM - Mercury! Mercury is the master of Rahu.

AND - Jupiter - Mercury are enemies of each other. Simply because their energies are in total contrast! Rahu Ketu are also in contrast to each other - Rahu is Intellect (knowledge). Ketu is Intelligence (wisdom).

Intellect is of the Mind (Moon, Mercury). Intelligence is of the Soul (Sun, Jupiter).

> The more consciousness you have, the more eergy flows upwards.
> Intelligence moves upwards, intellect moves downwards.
>
> **OSHO**

Once it happened - there were two disciples, **Sohan** and **Mohan.**

Mohan was a very simple man. The master would fondly address him as 'Bhola'. He was an illiterate man - never had been to school, never had been to any town - he was a farmer. One day, he found the master walking through his farmland - and something moved WITHIN him - the Glow of the master, His Bliss, His Joy, His Peace - there was something about this man - he could feel the 'presence' and then he simply dropped everything - left everything behind and started following the master. The master said, "What are you doing? Go back home."

But Mohan said, "You are my home - after so many years I have found my home - and you are saying to go back home - you are my home…and I cannot go back."

The master smiled. He was accepted.

Mohan became an ardent lover of the master. Along with Sohan, Mohan continued to follow the master.

After many years, one day Mohan and Sohan said to the master, "We need to be initiated. ***When will you initiate us?***

The master said, "I will initiate you both, but before that happens - I want you to do something…"

Sohan said, "I am ready."

Mohan said, "Master - You just tell me what I have to do, and I am certain that I will be through it with your Grace."

The master gave one bird to each disciple - and said, "Go to an absolutely lonely place - where there are no people and then kill the bird. And once you have killed, come back."

Sohan took the bird - went out in search of a lonely place, found one place - looked around to ensure that nobody was around and then with a sharp knife killed the bird. He came back to the master and said, "I am done. I have followed your instructions accurately."

The master said, **"Wait - let Mohan come back too. He is still to come back."**

But Mohan did not return. Days passed, weeks passed - months - and yet Mohan did not return. And the master waited. The master can always wait…

And one day - on a very hot afternoon, Mohan returned - he came, bowed before the master - and the master was deeply engrossed in meditation. Looking at Mohan, the master smiled and said, "Where have you been? And why it took so long for you to come back?"

Mohan rushed towards the feet of the master - and holding the feet of the master in his hands - he started crying…

Master said, "What happened?"

Mohan said, "I am sorry - I cannot follow your instruction - I could not kill the bird."

"Why?" asked the master - His eyes twinkling with light.

Mohan said, "I took the bird everywhere - to the mountains, to the deep valleys - to the most lonely places - and yet I could not find any of these places to be lonely - whenever I would try to kill the bird - I could feel that there is GOD - who is WATCHING! I tried to close my eyes and yet I could not kill because I could feel the presence of GOD - I drugged the bird - made it unconscious and yet I could not kill because I could feel GOD present in that bird - I am sorry - I cannot do this - if this is the CONDITION for initiation then I am willing to Let Go - but I cannot do this - because I could feel God present all around me - within me - outside me and so there was absolutely NO LONELY place that I could find - I also experienced the presence of GOD in that bird - its innocence, its chirping, I am sorry - but I cannot do this and I tried for months and weeks but I could not. It is okay if you don't initiate me - but I cannot do this."

The master got up - rushed towards Mohan and gave him a tight hug.

The master said to Mohan, "You are the chosen one - my son - you are the one. It was a test and you have passed..."

Then he called Sohan and said, "**You get out - get lost - and *never come back.*** You are stupid. You will never understand what I teach - you will never understand the essence that I share - you please get lost."

Sohan is **Rahu** - he goes by the INTELLECT. He could not go to the depth of the matter - he could not relate to the essence of the master's teachings - he simply followed the HEAD - went out and KILLED the BIRD.

Mohan is **Ketu** - he has tremendous sensitivity - because there is absolutely no head - no intellect and because there is no head, no intellect - there is abundance of HEART energy - and it is HIS HEART that won't let him kill the bird - he went all around the world - but he could not kill the bird - the heart won't let - the CONSCIOUSNESS won't let him - he had truly matured to be initiated. His CONSCIOUSNESS made him realize that GOD is present everywhere - within and without - and that was what the Guru, the master wanted to test - and Mohan had passed the test - the master had finally taken HIM under HIS Wings!

Jupiter loves Ketu. Mercury loves Rahu. And the whole story is divided into two parts - the whole world of human beings is divided into two parts - HEART & HEAD.

The DEVTAS (YOGI) dwell in the HEART.

The ASURAS (BHOGI) dwell in the HEAD.

And for millions and millions of years, friction has always been happening between these TWO SIDES - and it is going to happen forever - because they are TWO contrast energies - two polarities - that can never get along with each other!

Hitler will not understand Buddha's love. In this material world - in every house, in every family, at every place - there is someone who is a Hitler, a Judas, and there is someone who is a Buddha, a Mahavira!

Every BIRTH CHART is either inclining towards RAHU or towards KETU!

Every BIRTH CHART is either a HITLER, a JUDAS or a BUDDHA, a MAHAVIRA!

And the whole gamut of your life results is based on - which side your birth chart is on. And that is the real secret - that is the reason why the ancient seers and sages have given immense importance to RAHU and KETU over all other planets - because FIRST, it has to be decided if you CAN KILL THE BIRD or YOU CANNOT!

If you CANNOT - then the CONSCIOUSNESS is PRESENT. If you CANNOT - then the higher love is present. If you CANNOT - then the HEART is over the HEAD - and such a man - such a woman is welcomed in the KINGDOM OF GOD - in the KINGDOM of JUPITER.

If you CAN - then IGNORANCE is at its peak. If you CAN - then the lower love is all that is present. If you CAN - then the HEAD is over the HEART - and such a man - such a woman is not welcome - because they simply CANNOT understand the language of the HEART - the language of LOVE - and GOD is LOVE and LOVE is real.

Mercury presides over RAHU - and that is why - LORD VISHNU should be worshiped if you are going through RAHU difficulties. After all, it was Sri VISHNU who beheaded the Asura RAHU!

Jupiter presides over KETU - and that is why - LORD GANESHA should be worshiped if you are unable to relate to the message of Sri Ketu - the message of turning inwards! Lord Shiva should be worshiped to realize the immense significance of living your life selflessly and by being more and more DETACHED.

Marriages fail when the energies are in contrast - one is RAHU-ish while the other is - KETU-ish.

But strange things happen - one day, a young man and his name was Gopal, came and said, "I have fallen in love with a woman, and I cannot help - I want to marry her."

The master said, "Come tomorrow - it is very late."

He came the next day. The master went into deep meditation and then said to Gopal, "This marriage will not work - you are getting yourself in a deep mess."

But ATTRACTION brings IGNORANCE - the man was attracted - he married the woman. And then began the many miseries of his life - then he could not sleep with peace - then he could find his joy no more, then he became a plastic rose - the fragrance was lost.

The master remembered the young Gopal - a very lively man, an honest man, a man of heart - his innocence, his compassion and what a beautiful person he was! But with one wrong move - the same Gopal had turned into a miserable man - a man who was no more willing to live - a man who once was full of life - was now thinking of giving up life!

Life can change 360 degrees towards the deepest valleys - if you fall for your TEMPTATIONS - if you fall for ATTRACTIONS - if you fall by following your MIND!

And the same life can change 360 degrees towards the highest peak - if you rise above your TEMPTATIONS - if you remain indifferent towards ATTRACTIONS - if you RISE ABOVE your Mind!

RAHU traps you.

Suffocation happens when you get into the tight clutches of RAHU (IGNORANCE).

KETU relieves you.

A man moving towards KETU - becomes more and more detached. He becomes a Buddha - you CANNOT distract him. You CANNOT attract him.

RAHU exalts not just in Gemini (Mercury) - but also is empowered when He is in the Nakshatra of Mercury.

RAHU is empowered in **Ashlesha (Cancer), Jyestha (Scorpio), Revati (Pisces).**

Whenever RAHU is in **Ashlesha/ Jyestha/ Revati** - he is empowered to give more intense results - if he is placed well - he may benefit, if he is not placed well - he may do what he likes the most - cause more harm!

Ketu exalts not just in Sagittarius (Jupiter) - but also is empowered when he is in the Nakshatra of Jupiter.

KETU is empowered in **Punarvasu (Cancer), Vishaka (Scorpio), Purvabhadrapada (Pisces).**

Depending on which side the birth chart is inclined - an empowered KETU will manifest the results. If the chart is on the KETU side - then whenever KETU is in **Punarvasu (Cancer), Vishaka (Scorpio), Purvabhadrapada (Pisces)** - you will benefit. But if the chart is RAHU-ish - then the same empowered KETU appears as a hurdle - because you are 'pressing' channel 1 for happiness when the real button on your remote is not channel 1 but channel 9!

So you see, astrology can be interesting simply because it is so relating - so ALIVE.

People run behind MATCH-MAKING - they MATCH everything - MOON SIGN, SUN SIGN, LAGNA/ASCENDANT - GUNAS - everything is matched - but they miss - they simply miss to see if the Man and Woman who are planning to marry - fall in the same category of KETU or RAHU!

A RAHU-ish man and a RAHU-ish woman can stay together - the 'marriage' generally works - because both belong to the same world - the world of RAHU.

But if you are KETU-ish and you are marrying a RAHU-ish woman - then you in for trouble - deep trouble!.

Young Gopal was suffering in his marriage because he was a KETU-ish man, and he had fallen for a woman who was RAHU-ish. He was not willing to listen - the master said to him twice - alerted him - but he went ahead and got married - and now he is suffering - he is miserable - now he comes to the master - the master says, "It is not late - it is never late - even if you WAKE up at the very last moment of your life - it is ENOUGH to bring a positive change. But now, if you want to come out of this marriage - you will need COURAGE. Courage to FACE all the consequences whatsoever."

RAHU obstructs the COURAGE within you. I have seen many men who suffer in marriage but they cannot get out of it - because they lack the courage - they FEAR - they are so much trapped in the clutches of RAHU that they appear totally impotent in making any move towards FREEDOM - real FREEDOM.

Rahu is FEAR. Ketu is COURAGE.

What stops you from coming out of a MARRIAGE that is FULL OF MISERIES and HUMILIATION - is YOUR FEAR. (RAHU).

And what CAN help you to come out of a MARRIAGE that is FULL OF MISERIES and HUMILIATION - is YOUR **COURAGE. (KETU).**

KETU, therefore, EXALTS in the MOST **COURAGEOUS** SIGN - the SIGN of **SAGITTARIUS.** It is the SIGN OF A WARRIOR - you better watch - you better be careful when you are dealing with a SAGITTARIUS - for HE or SHE has the COURAGE to FIGHT BACK and FIND FREEDOM!

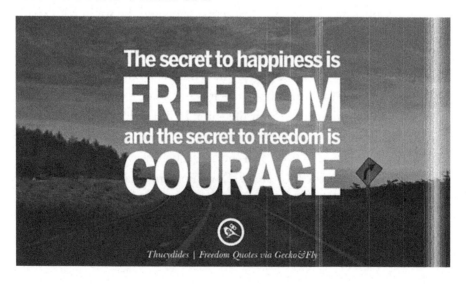

Courage is an affair with the unknown! You don't know what is going to happen - what matters to you is the PURPOSE - and if your PURPOSE is to get out of a FAILING MARRIAGE or a FAILING JOB - then the KEY is KETU - **COURAGE!**

Life is simple. Astrology is also simple. Because GOD is simple! And TRUTH is simply found in simplicity. Beauty is simply found in simplicity.

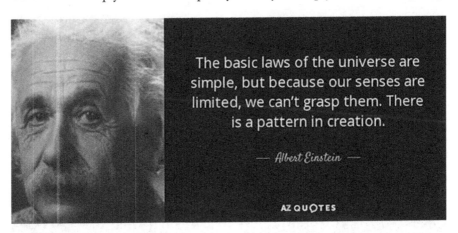

The basic laws of the universe are simple, but because our senses are limited, we can't grasp them. There is a pattern in creation.

— *Albert Einstein* —

AZ QUOTES

A simple man, a simple woman - and they are beautiful - they can understand the language of the heart - and Astrology is indeed the language of the heart!

"Without thinking of the letters, *listen* to the language of the heart."
- Rumi

But who wants to listen? The man of Head (Intellectual) goes round and round and round and yet finds himself exactly at the point where he had started!

The HEAD cannot find the answer - the HEART can!

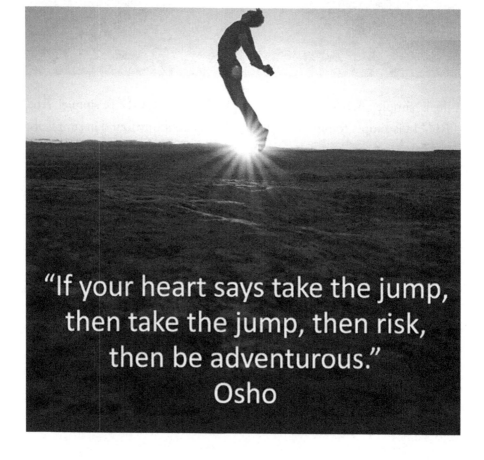

"If your heart says take the jump, then take the jump, then risk, then be adventurous."
Osho

Your HEART is natural - it is a BORN GIFT! But your MIND is NOT NATURAL - it is given to you by the SOCIETY - you are NOT born with the MIND - but you are born with the HEART! And the HEART has it all - the HEART is the most beautiful GIFT - every HEART is beautiful - but what makes it impure and ugly is the MIND!

And that is the whole message - that is the whole message of the master - that is the whole message of **Sri KETU** - get out of your HEAD and get inside your HEART. THINK LESS and FEEL MORE.

But the majority is caught up in thinking TOO MUCH, and then they come and ask, *"Why is my life so miserable?"*

The fault is not with LIFE - the fault is with YOURSELF.

LIFE is like a beautiful flowing river - if you can flow with it - if you can SWIM through it - then you can ENJOY the Journey - the whole effort of the divine masters is simply to HELP YOU ALL to ENJOY the journey by TURNING INWARDS - MEDITATING and making **yourself more and more aware** by introducing the higher realms of CONSCIOUSNESS to your awareness.

The key to growth is the introduction of higher dimensions of consciousness into our awareness.

OSHO

GROWTH comes NOT by a fat bank balance but by bringing a great transformation WITHIN you - by raising the level of CONSCIOUSNESS within you. Once you become AWARE - once the LIGHT OF CONSCIOUSNESS becomes aflame - then it BURNS all the IGNORANCE within you!

And so come, come you all and spend some quality time with yourself - spend some time in meditation - if you have too many people at home - find a secluded place outside your home - but seclusion is required.

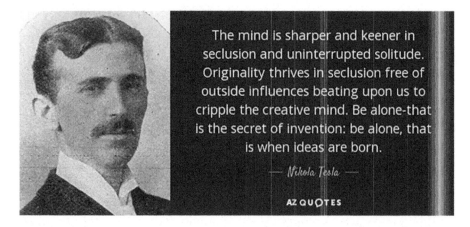

The mind is sharper and keener in seclusion and uninterrupted solitude. Originality thrives in seclusion free of outside influences beating upon us to cripple the creative mind. Be alone-that is the secret of invention: be alone, that is when ideas are born.

— *Nikola Tesla* —

AZ QUOTES

In seclusion - you will be able to quieten the chattering mind. Seclusion is necessary for meditation.

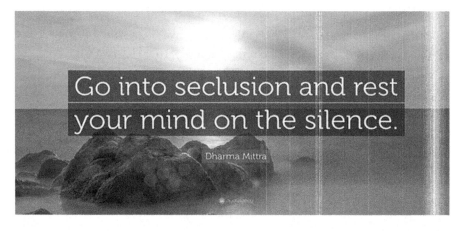

Go into seclusion and rest your mind on the silence.

Dharma Mittra

KETU loves seclusion. KETU is home in a secluded place - that is why KETU feels HOME in the **12th House** - the house of seclusion - the natural house of Jupiter - the master!

KETU is beautiful - simply beautiful - only if you can RESONATE with its energy - only if your 'Antenna' is placed in the right direction! And the direction of the master - of the Guru is simple - Turn Inwards and master yourself. The 'CONTROL' that you are seeking on the OUTSIDE is not possible - many have tried and many have failed miserably - because the CONTROL that you seek is possible WITHIN and not on the outside.

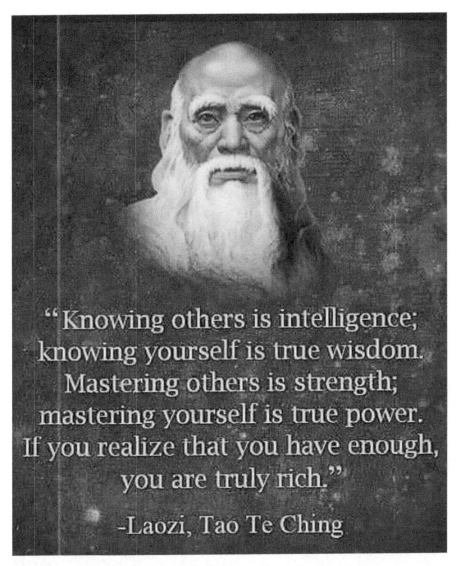

" Knowing others is intelligence; knowing yourself is true wisdom. Mastering others is strength; mastering yourself is true power. If you realize that you have enough, you are truly rich."

-Laozi, Tao Te Ching

A man of KETU is a man who is content with what he has. He is a man of awareness - he lives moment to moment - because he is perfectly aware that LIFE IS NOW - life is neither in the PAST nor in the FUTURE - Life is NOW and his whole effort - his whole direction is simply to - BE HERE NOW.

Meditation happens only when you are HERE - when you are able to STILL your MIND in the PRESENT MOMENT - only then

Meditation happens - only then the bud starts blossoming into a beautiful flower...

So, the whole focus should be to - **BE HERE NOW.**

The blessings of the benevolent compassionate Guru and the support of Sri Ketu enable you to BE HERE NOW.

A certain depth to your meditations and to your spiritual journey comes when you become compassionate towards others - when you help those who are in need.

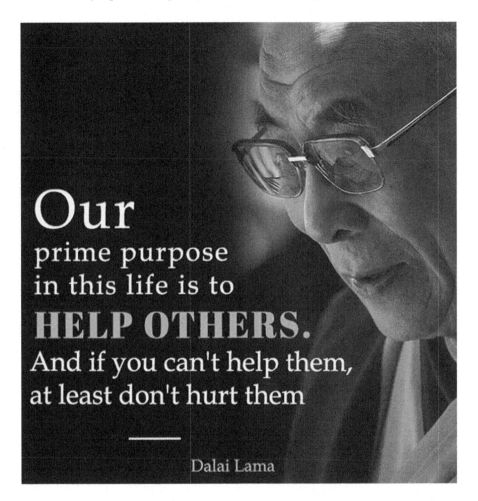

Our
prime purpose
in this life is to
HELP OTHERS.
And if you can't help them,
at least don't hurt them

Dalai Lama

Meditation is the KEY, but the KEY works only when you are helpful to others, when you are compassionate toward others - it is all interlinked!

And once you find BALANCE - once your ACTIONS fall in place - then Meditation starts blossoming - then the 'dance' begins - then the 'song' is heard - then life starts changing - **then everything around you will be the same** - *but you will be no more the same* - then there will be a song to it - then life will start transforming into a garden of bliss...

The 'key' (Meditation) is with you all - it has been with you all from the very beginning of time - many births have passed by - this birth is also 'passing' by - the sooner you all become 'aware', the better it is going to be. Always remember - your moment goes on shaping, and the shape that it eventually takes becomes your future! So the MOMENT is of great significance - we remember life by remembering the moments of our life and not the days. Focus on the MOMENT - a man of awareness lives totally in the 'moment' - present moment.

Awareness means to be in the moment - a man of awareness is always found to be in the moment - be a man of awareness - let awareness become the torch of your life, and then you all will find your answers.

Meditate.
Jai Shri Ganesha. Jai Guru.

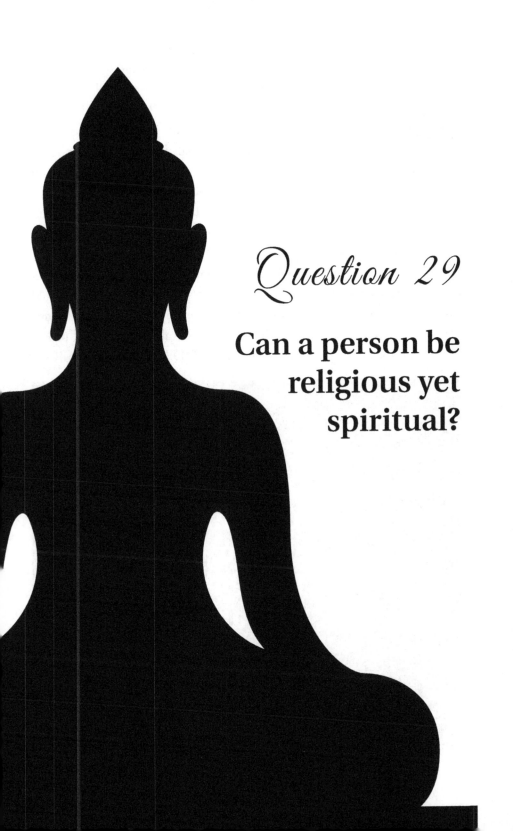

Question 29

Can a person be religious yet spiritual?

Religion traps you. Spiritualism liberates you. Religion is full of rules and laws. Spiritualism is full of freedom and LOVE! A person can either be RELIGIOUS or SPIRITUAL - a spiritual person is not religious and a religious person is not spiritual. KABIR was a spiritual being - Jesus was a spiritual being - Buddha was a spiritual being. Religion was formed later on their NAME - they never established any religion - they simply shared the TRUTH - that can help people progress in their life - all the great saints, masters and human beings - in the whole history of mankind - were purely SPIRITUAL by heart and not religious.

Whenever anybody would come to seek Sai Baba's blessings - Baba often used to answer with a hidden message! If the person was Hindu - Baba would say "Allah Malik - Allah bless you." AND if the person is a Muslim - Baba would say "Krishna bless you." - This was specifically done so that people understand that all religions are ONE - and GOD HAS NO RELIGION!

There is only one caste, the caste of humanity. There is only one religion, the religion of love. There is only one language, the language of the heart.

- Sai Baba

Mahatama Gandhi always used to say that GOD HAS NO RELIGION. Mahatma Gandhi was a spiritual person and not a religious person.

Religion need not be dropped - religion simply has to become a WAY OF LIFE that ACCOMMODATES & VALUES HUMANITY ABOVE ALL - then RELIGION CAN BECOME A BRIDGE THAT CAN HELP YOU TO REACH GOD. But that is NOT WHAT HAPPENS IN REALITY! RELIGION instead of becoming a BRIDGE - becomes the greatest BLOCKAGE to your REAL GROWTH - your SPIRITUAL GROWTH!

Once it happened - a great Saint and his name was Saint Eknath - he had carried the water of Holy Ganges all the way from Varanasi to his hometown - Paithan (Maharashtra). And during those days - long journeys were very tiresome and would happen only once in a life. And so Saint Eknath was about to reach his home with the bottle filled with the holy water of Ganges - when he came across a thirsty crow!

And guess what - Saint Eknath quickly stepped ahead and gave the holy ganges water to a CROW! Now imagine - who can do such a beautiful random act of kindness? ONLY A SPIRITUAL MAN - only a Saint! A religious man would have found it very difficult to offer such a holy water of Ganges to a crow! He would have simply walked away - letting the crow die of thirst! But someone as beautiful as Saint Eknath offered the holy water to a crow - saved his life and the then whatever water was left - he returned with it - back home!

FEELINGS. COMPASSION. And more over throwing all your knowledge is possible only for a SPIRITUAL PERSON - because only such a person can UNDERSTAND LOVE, can UNDERSTAND FEELINGS.

> Understanding means throwing away your knowledge.
> **THICH NHAT HANH**

Saint Eknath understood the sensitivity of the situation - the thirsty crow was dying - and so Saint Eknath DID NOT BRING KNOWLEDGE IN BETWEEN - any RULES OF RELIGIONS in between - HE SIMPLY OFFERED the holy water to the crow and saved his life! And the crow flew away happily - in his own way blessing the pious man who saved his life!

There is only ONE RELIGION that can HELP YOU and I share it with all my followers and readers - only ONE RELIGION that can HELP YOU ALL to embark on your SPIRITUAL JOURNEY and that RELIGION is called the RELIGION OF HEART.

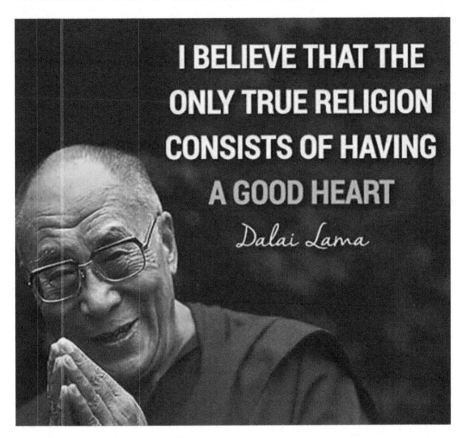

A spiritual person can be religious only if the RELIGION IS THE RELIGION OF HEART!

And beyond HEART - if you can start living your life with consciousness - then as the master says - life itself will be the religion!

> If you can bring consciousness, your awareness, your intelligence to the act, if you can be spontaneous, then there is **no need** for any other religion, life itself will be the religion.
>
> **OSHO**

Consciousness is the ultimate fragrance of GOD! The moment you come to the state of consciousness - whole life becomes a religion - a beautiful religion that can forgive, that can LOVE, that can UNDERSTAND and that can RELATE to the higher dimensions of humanity.

Meditate.
Jai Shri Ganesha. Jai Guru.

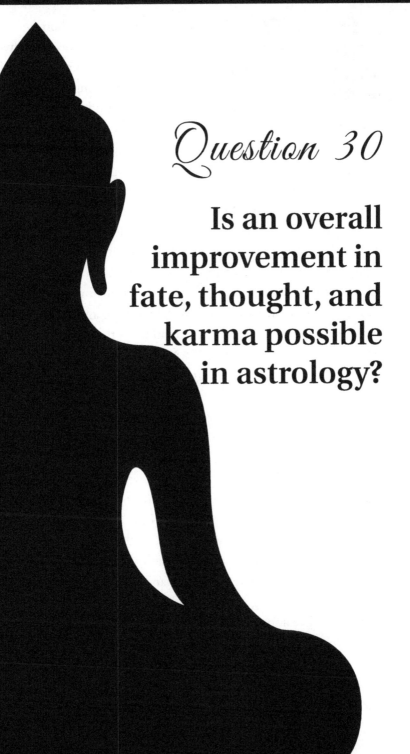

Question 30

Is an overall improvement in fate, thought, and karma possible in astrology?

Beautiful question – one in a million.

It is said that wherever the **Mahavira** would stay, people around HIM, towns around HIM, villages around HIM – would start changing for good! Places that were miles and miles around him would become full of LIFE! Barren lands would transform into fertile lands, barren wombs were blessed with babies, poor men would never have had to sleep without having food. Mahavira would simply stand or sit beneath a tree, for hours and days, but for miles, life would start throbbing with a new rhythm. It is said that trees would bloom out of season; trees would start growing faster than ever; dead trees would start producing new fresh leaves…

Just the presence of the master is enough to bring a certain change, a certain transformation within you – and when you start transforming – the quality of your KARMA also starts transforming – up-scaling to higher altitudes – then you start realizing the many virtues of this human life – the many qualities of this human life – then you CAN forgive, then you CAN Let Go – then you CAN Meditate.

Mahavira moved from village to village – the master never stays at one place!

So one day, Mahavira arrived in a town and decided to stay for a while, for a few months. A small campus was setup, Mahavira and his hundreds of disciples stayed in that campus. People of the town – would come to seek HIS blessings and the whole town was happy, was rejoicing – it was a dream come true for them – Mahavira staying in their town – was the greatest blessing that they could ever think of!

But not everybody was of this view. In that town lived a master thief – and he was such a master thief that nobody – not even the King and his men were able to catch him red-handed. He would always sneak out safely. He had a young son and when he came to know that Mahavira has arrived – he became tensed – he said to his son – "You – *Listen carefully, you are free to do everything, but don't go close to that man Mahavira. I am a master thief, but I also avoid him, because that man is dangerous. Something magical surrounds him, and once you are caught in it there is no way out. So remember, go everywhere else, but avoid the campus where Mahavira is staying.*"

His son agreed. But he always would wonder that his father never feared anybody – not even the King! How come he fears the Mahavira... that he says – Do not go close to Mahavira!

The boy was young – temptation was natural, so one day secretly he went close to the campus – stood outside the main wall of the campus and he could listen to a few words of the Mahavira... Mahavira was in the campus – and he was sharing – speaking to his disciples...

Mahavira was saying – "*In **paradise**, the angels and the female angels are **tremendously beautiful**, but just one thing is wrong: their feet point in the opposite direction. The angels go one way, but their feet go in the opposite direction.*"

Just one sentence – only one sentence of Mahavira – was what the young boy was able to listen to and he quickly went back to his home. He thought that Mahavira was telling just a fictitious story – and that's all!

The next day – something strange happened. The young boy and father (the master thief) were caught by the King's men. But the father was not revealing any information. The police beat him but he would not open his mouth. The King said – focus on the young boy – he will open up – he must be aware of the many loots that his father has done till date – do everything that you can to get information from the young boy.

And so the young boy was taken to a beautiful palace, he was given intoxicating drugs, so he slept for hours, completely unconscious. He was taken to the most beautiful room in the palace, and **all the beautiful girls** were *serving him,* **bringing food, drinks**. As he came back to consciousness, he thought, "My God, I am dead. I am in paradise. This is the paradise that fellow **Mahavira** was describing, and the girls are really beautiful. Everything is great."

But then he looked **at their feet,** and immediately he understood that there was some conspiracy — **"This is not paradise, because their feet are just like our feet."**

Only ONE SENTENCE of the MAHAVIRA was heard by the young boy – only one sentence, Mahavira had said: "*In **paradise**, the angels and the female angels are **tremendously beautiful**, but just one thing is wrong: their feet point in the opposite direction. The angels go one way, but their feet go in the opposite direction.*"

The young boy again looked at the feet of those beautiful girls – they were not pointing in the opposite direction – they were very much like a normal woman – a normal human being…the young boy quickly realized that this is NOT a paradise and these young beautiful girls are not angels – he would not fall prey to the King's strategy – they would ask him to confess and he would simply smile.

Those beautiful women would try to make him believe that he has died and entered the paradise and now he should tell everything about his life – all the secrets and do all the confessions – because now he is in paradise!

But the young boy would just smile – he would not say anything but smile – They asked him, "Why you smile?"

The boy said, "Because I am AWARE. I have heard the words of the Mahavira. I have heard him saying that angels in paradise have feet pointing towards the opposite direction. And so I know that you all are fooling me. I am not dead and I am not in paradise because in paradise the angels' feet point to the opposite direction whereas yours are just like a normal human being's. *Your feet have given me the clue that this is the palace of the king. And this is a strategy. Tell your king to try to fool somebody else.* **I am a disciple of Mahavira.**"

They all were taken aback – they said, "When did you become a disciple of Mahavira?"

And the boy said, "*Just passing by I heard one sentence, and that one sentence has saved me today.*"

Finally, the King had to let him go – **the young boy and his father were released.**

And as soon as they were released – the young boy looked at his father and said, "You said – never go to the Mahavira, not even close to his campus – but it is HIS words that saved me and you. Else, by now we would have been hanged to death. I am not going to listen to you anymore – right now I am going to MAHAVIRA – and you cannot STOP me."

The father's eyes were filled with tears – he had no words – he let his son go to Mahavira.

And the young boy came, he entered the campus – rushed towards the feet of the Master – and Mahavira was smiling – the boy dropped at His feet and said, "You have SAVED my life. Now I don't want to go away from you – now I want to spend my whole life at your feet – with your grace I will be able to come out – now I don't want to go back to the world of crime and loot – now please take me under your wings – please accept me – even if I become the dust of your feet still it will be the GREATEST blessing that I could ever have – O master, please ACCEPT me…"

And Mahavira accepted him. The young boy – once a thief – went on to become one of the greatest disciples of Mahavira that the world has ever known!

Just the **omnipresence** of the divine master can move the mightiest mountains!

Out of curiosity – the young boy went near HIS campus and by accident – he listened to **just a few words of Mahavira** – and those few words led the young boy to such a great transformation…**how to express such a fascinating transformation** – how to…!!

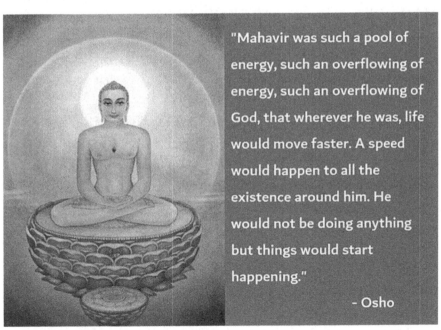

"Mahavir was such a pool of energy, such an overflowing of energy, such an overflowing of God, that wherever he was, life would move faster. A speed would happen to all the existence around him. He would not be doing anything but things would start happening."

- Osho

I fondly remember the Mahavira – one of the greatest masters of India – **I love Mahavira as much as I love the Buddha!** I humbly prostrate before His Holiness – *the Mahavira!*

It is said that many Yogis attain self-realization – enlightenment on a FULL MOON DAY – Poornima – when the Moon is FULL.

But it was only MAHAVIRA who attained on a day when there was NO MOON – AMAVASYA and that makes him a MAHAVIRA – because HE did something that was unusual – he did something that only a MAHAVIRA can do – and so the name Mahavira!

Mahavira and **Gautama Buddha** were **contemporaries – however** the influence of Buddha and His teachings was so much that the westerners often considered Mahavira and Buddha as ONE! It was later when they started with their research that they realized that Mahavira is not Buddha and Buddha is not Mahavira – they both are separate individuals and they also have a totally different approach.

Mahavira was like a Warrior. If you read about Mahavira – if you can relate to His teachings and His way of life – you will realize that MAHAVIRA goes to the EXTREME. All of the Jain monk's way of life is to the EXTREME.

Buddha is softer than Mahavira. Buddha brings BALANCE. HIS approach is a BALANCED approach – HE believes that with balance – you can attain more than with EXTREME!

When you are in the middle of TWO EXTREMES – the two extremes become two wings of a bird and then you can FLY to the farthest shores of this planet – Buddha emphasizes on maintaining BALANCE – Mahavira emphasizes on going to the Extremes!

The PATHS are different – the APPROACH is different – but people at large found Buddha more appealing because going to EXTREME is always difficult – than living with a BALANCED approach!

There was much talk about an incident when both crossed each other's path – they were present at the same place with their disciples – but they never met each other!

Many pundits and scholars tried to find an answer – **Why they never met when they were at the same place – same village?**

Because they wanted to save their disciples from confusion – when approach is different – it is always better not to meet!

Buddha and Mahavira never met – though they remained at the helm of Indian spiritualism – driving hundreds and thousands to their teachings and wonderful sharing!

You have asked a beautiful question and you must be wondering why I am sharing with you – and through you – with all my followers, fellow travellers and readers with the many transforming enlightening stories of the masters – I am doing it because I would want you all to REALIZE that – **IMPROVEMENT in fate, thought, and karma is POSSIBLE – but it is POSSIBLE not through ASTROLOGY but through the DIVINE intervention of the benevolent compassionate master!**

You all – and I say it to all my close followers that you all can TRANSFORM – can IMPROVE – can become GODLY – only when you STOP SUFFOCATING YOURSELF in the FOUR WALLS OF ASTROLOGY that you yourself have built around you – that is your IGNORANCE and my whole effort is to help you come out of this IGNORANCE.

ASTROLOGY has become GREATER than GOD, the pond has become GREATER than the SEA – and this is the greatest irony of this human world – that the REAL is forgotten while you remain STUCK on the path of ASTROLOGY!

ASTROLOGY is just a tool – but people have made the TOOL as their GOD – while the GOD who holds this tool in HIS hand is forgotten – completely forgotten!

And that is what Buddha had been doing His whole life – trying to help people – REMEMBER the forgotten language, the language of the HEART.

When Buddha was about to leave his body – when he was ready to die – on his last day, he said to all his disciples, "Today – I am going to depart. This body has become too old and I will be leaving soon. If there is anything that you want to ask – then ask Now – because once I am gone – I cannot answer your question."

The disciples were moved – it came as a shock – they were unaware that the master would take such a decision in such a casual way! Now they all started crying – they could not control themselves – some of them fell on the ground – some of them fainted – some of them burst out with tears – the whole monastery went into a state that is difficult to express…Buddha was watching and looking at them – HE said, "Time is running out. Don't waste time! Don't be in such a hurry to cry, you can do it later on. Right now – **do you want to ask anything?**"

The disciples were so much moved by this abrupt decision of the master that they had absolutely no strength to think or ask any question – they all said, "No question comes to the mind – we have no question to ask."

Buddha said, "Then it is fine – now go and do your work and let me do mine."

Buddha then goes to the tree – sits beneath it and then starts moving towards DEATH.

Buddha had mentioned about four steps of Death. HE entered the first step, then the second – was coming closer to the EXIT point – DEATH when suddenly a man came running from a nearby village and said, "I have heard that Buddha is going to die – BUT I have something to ASK – I have a question to ASK…"

The disciple said to him, "You are TOO late – the master is already on the way towards DEATH – now we cannot help."

DEATH is just a JOURNEY for Buddha. It is NOT that DEATH was coming HIS way – it was HE who was CONSCIOUSLY moving towards DEATH! The master can always move out of the body as and when he wants – it is just a matter of his own WILL and he can leave the body with ease!

The man insisted. He said, "PLEASE, please let me ask my question to Buddha – else I will always remain in my misery – please… I plead to you all, please help me…please do something – I want to meet the Buddha…"

The disciples said, "Are you mad? Where were you all these days when the master was staying in your village – where were you then? And now when the master is about to die – you have come!"

The man said, "Now this is not the time to give explanations – I knew that Buddha was moving around my town – but then I was busy with my customers, my children, my wife and I went on postponing thinking that at some point I will meet Buddha but now he is dying and I really don't want to miss this moment – this moment is all that I have got – please let me go and meet him…"

Buddha must have realized what was happening – he came back. And he said, "Don't stop him. I was still in the second stage – and I don't want to be remembered as someone who was still ALIVE – while a man with a question had to go away without an answer. Let him have his answer."

And Buddha takes the last question of his life – answers it and then moves back to DEATH – to the last two steps – and then the NIRVANA!

This is a unique way of DYING – a very conscious way – so much so that I am short of words.

There is a very strong similarity between MEDITATION and DEATH. In both situations – in both states – you are moving away from the BODY – the MIND.

The only difference is that when in MEDITATION – you are moving away from the BODY – from the MIND – consciously.

But when DEATH is coming – you hesitate because then it is not a conscious choice to move out of the body – out of the mind!

For Buddha – DEATH is similar to MEDITATION. He moves out of the body with choice just as we – while meditating – move out of the body with choice!

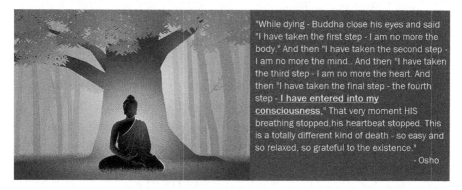

"While dying - Buddha close his eyes and said "I have taken the first step - I am no more the body." And then "I have taken the second step - I am no more the mind.. And then "I have taken the third step - I am no more the heart. And then "I have taken the final step - the fourth step - I have entered into my consciousness." That very moment HIS breathing stopped,his heartbeat stopped. This is a totally different kind of death - so easy and so relaxed, so grateful to the existence."

- Osho

To be with the master is to be with God! With the blessings of the master – all your bad qualities start moving out of your being and all your good qualities start blossoming into your being! The whole story of mankind and if you may say so – Astrology – is about QUALITIES (GUNA)! And it is with your own determination, FAITH, LOVE towards the benevolent master that you can TRANSFORM your life into a garden of bliss – the question is – "Are you willing to? Are you ready?"

There was a man, he must be like me. He was Ready – and so he set out on his journey towards the Himalayas…

And he travelled through many villages and towns – until he came across a small village situated at the foothills of the Himalayan Mountains. In that village – he met the master – HIS bliss, HIS peace, HIS grace – how to express it – the young man was moved – deeply moved – he decided to stay near the master.

But the master hardly paid any attention towards him. There were many villagers who would come to seek HIS blessings – he would talk with everybody – but he would never look at the young man. But the young man remained. And he remained for many days and months – in his own way, he would continue to serve the master – but the master would never talk with him, never let him come closer.

After two years – for the very first time – and it was a sudden moment – the young man was cleaning the ground – when the master just looked at him – for the first time – for the very first time – JUST A GLANCE of HIS and the young man's heart moved – something happened within his being – his eyes became wet – tears started flowing – those were the tears of joy – how beautiful was that glance of the master – so much love, so much compassion – that it was enough for the young man to spend another two years…

And then after four years – on a beautiful morning – the young man was seated looking at the villagers who were asking questions to the master – and the master was so compassionately answering – sharing – His love – His light – that the young man was deeply engrossed in observing it all – when the master looked at him and he was sitting far away – but the master looked at him and SMILED!

And what a beautiful smile was that – it was a message that 'I know what you have been doing all these four years. I am totally aware of YOU – your whole being….' – that one smile was enough for the young

496

man to move closer to HIS self – that one smile was enough to motivate him on his path towards the beyond. And he continued to serve and meditate – his meditation became more and more deeper – and then after two more years – a strange thing happened....

It was a dark night – a no-moon day and he was preparing to sit for meditation – when suddenly the benevolent master appeared before him – and for the first time – touched his forehead – just a soft touch and then looking at him – the master said, "You can NOW leave – you are READY to spread the message – the message of love."

The young man started crying – those were the tears of joy – six years had passed – and only three times the master had interacted – only three times that too for a moment!

After the first two years – the first time – the Master had showered his glance on him.

After four years – the second time – the Master had smiled at him.

After six years – the third and the last time when he had seen the master – the Master had touched him – just a soft touch on his forehead!

Even after 40 years – the young man who was now no more young but had become a very old man – when his disciples asked him, "Was that all that you could share with us about your master?"

He said to them, "That was all and so if HE had said that 'You are ready' – then I must have been ready and so then listening to his words – I left his place – we never met in person – but not a single moment of my life was ever spent without HIS holy name – without experiencing HIS presence at every stage of my life!."

Only two QUALITIES are required – FAITH and PATIENCE!

A student cannot wait for six years – a disciple can, a devotee can!

A student cannot surrender himself in totality – a disciple, a devotee can!

A student comes with an agenda – he wants to KNOW and then use that KNOWLEDGE to his benefit – a disciple has NO AGENDA – the only reason he is with the master is because HE LOVES the MASTER – and LOVE has NO AGENDA!

One has to understand the difference between a student and a disciple. Often people come – they become disciples but in reality they remain as a student – that is the reason why only a few disciples can transcend while the other disciples remain on the surface – because unless there is ABSOLUTELY NO AGENDA – and unless there is ABSOLUTE LOVE – FAITH – PATIENCE – the REAL – the TRUTH – the GOD cannot be experienced – cannot be realized.

Sai Baba – His whole life emphasized on two QUALITIES – FAITH and PATIENCE. SHRADDHA aur SABBURI – one who has it is the most fortunate man – a man who can then EVOLVE to the next level – the higher altitudes of CONSCIOUSNESS!

I want something from you..Can you give it to me? It requires big heart to give...Weak people can't give..I want faith and Patience (Shraddha or Saburi) from you.. When you give me these two then you have to walk on path of this..Now ask yourself that are you strong enough to give me : Sai Baba

To reach Delhi – the capital – there are many ways. You can go from city to city until you reach Delhi. Or else you can simply focus on 'flying' your way straight to Delhi Airport!

Through ASTROLOGY – when you try to correct yourself – transform yourself – upgrade yourself – you are moving from city to city – it is going to be a very difficult 'journey' – instead of reaching Delhi you may simply reach somewhere else – you may also get lost and that is exactly what is happening – by getting ENTANGLED in ASTROLOGY and the many ways of ASTROLOGY – people get STUCK – people get TRAPPED – in this POOJA and that POOJA – in that RITUAL and this RITUAL – in this HAVAN and that HAVAN – and in the whole process – the man, the woman is trapped and interestingly they become so much enslaved to such things that it becomes a habit and all habits are bad because all habits – good or bad – make you mechanical – you do it because it has become a habit – you never do it with awareness – with consciousness!

498

Through the MASTER – nothing is required. ABSOLUTELY NOTHING – no SPENDING of thousands on RITUALS – on POOJAS – on anything. WHAT IS REQUIRED IS YOUR PATIENCE AND YOUR FAITH. WHAT IS REQUIRED IS YOUR LOVE. WHAT IS REQUIRED is YOUR UNWAVERING DEDICATION AND PERSISTENCE towards STANDING FIRMLY no matter how many storms come – but NOT moving away – even an inch from the benevolent master. That is all required – it costs nothing – not a single penny and yet what it can bring forth in your life – and I say to all my followers and readers – what it can bring forth in your life is beyond the power of expression – is beyond your imagination!

But people are shallow. The majority is shallow – so not everybody can understand this. People try all kinds of rituals and poojas. Some have even gone to the extent of using black magic ways – when they come to me – I tell them all – to watch the Airtel Advertisement. They ask me, "What has that to do with our miseries?"

I tell them – "Just watch."

Then one of them realized why I had insisted on watching that advertisement – the advertisement has a very beautiful message – it says:

"Sab kuch try karo aur phir sahi chuno."
(Try everything and then choose the right.)

And that is exactly what I have been telling my whole life – TRY EVERYTHING – and when you come to your SENSES (that too if you are a blessed soul) then and only then you will come to seek that which is REAL – only then will you be able to come out of ASTROLOGY and get into SPIRITUALITY – because ASTROLOGY is just a drop of the OCEAN called SPIRITUALITY!

But people are at large lost in the drop – they are lost in the dancer and they forgot the DANCE!

The master is saying – Forget the DANCER and become the DANCE.

Forget the dancer, the center of the ego; become the dance. That is the meditation.

Osho

'I' should fade away – the 'dancer' should move out – and only the 'dance' should remain!

And when your whole life becomes a 'Dance' – when your whole life becomes a 'meditation' – then all the good qualities that you seek – start blossoming. If God can bring life to million buds and transform them into beautiful flowers – why cannot it happen with you? Why it cannot happen with every person who wants to become the 'dance' – who wants to rise above the mind – who wants to experience the joy – the bliss – the peace within!

It is possible. Everything is possible – only if you choose the path of love and devotion. I say it again and again – that no matter you all – at what stage you are in your life – in what difficulties you are going through – if you are living your life with love and devotion – if you are bringing COMPASSION to your being – then no matter what – no matter how difficult the DASHA or period of your life is – YOU ARE GOING TO COME OUT OF IT – and there is absolutely no second thought to this.

One has to focus on his or her eating habits. People are afraid of RAHU – people are afraid when RAHU MAHADASHA begins – but they don't want to CHANGE THEIR EATING HABITS!

They want to continue eating spicy food, oily food, street food, non-veg food – and then they come and ask, "Please help me with a remedy on RAHU."

Now that is a joke – and how am I supposed to answer that which is a joke!

RAHU is in GARLIC. Rahu is in ONION. Rahu is in CHILIES. And you all are eating it freely – you are encouraging the CARNAL ENERGIES (sexual, anger, negativity) by eating garlic onion food and then you wonder – Why do I get so angry on small things? Why do I react so much?

Remember – WHAT YOU EAT is WHAT IMPACTS YOUR BODY – YOUR MIND.

One day, Bhagavan Ramana Maharshi shared the secret of Garlic. He said, "When Rahu's head was cut – a few drops of his blood and saliva fell on the earth. And that gave birth to a plant called GARLIC. And because he had drank a few drops of 'Immortal Nectar (Amrut)' – the plant of Garlic may be good as a medicine but is also extremely disastrous for meditation – for a man who is set on spiritual journey!"

I prostrate before His Holiness – the divine master whom I love and admire the most – **Bhagavan Ramana Maharshi.**

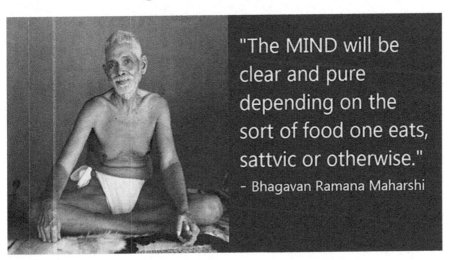

"The MIND will be clear and pure depending on the sort of food one eats, sattvic or otherwise."
- Bhagavan Ramana Maharshi

Many things are there – from the FOOD you intake – to the THOUGHTS that you entertain – to the ACTIONS (Karma) that you execute – and when I say 'YOU' – it depends on which 'YOU' you follow – whether it is your MIND that you follow or it is your CONSCIOUSNESS (Self) that you follow! Based on what YOU – is followed – the RESULTS manifest! Then either you keep 'falling' or you continue 'Rising' – this falling and rising is totally based on the QUALITIES within you…

To overcome the negative qualities – the TAMAS GUNA – you have to start meditating – you have to start focusing on having a sattvic diet food – you have to focus WITHIN – you have to turn inwards!

You have to become the DANCE – only in dance – the moment comes when you are no more – and Godliness exists! When the 'mind' – the ego has taken the backseat and the 'SELF' has taken control of your life. The Bhagavan says, "SELF is the GURU!"

This SELF is your consciousness – when you start living with consciousness – you can become a dance – you can transform into a beautiful person – you can attain all that you had wished for – the key – is your consciousness!

"THE KEY TO GROWTH IS THE INTRODUCTION OF HIGHER DIMENSIONS OF CONSCIOUSNESS INTO OUR AWARENESS."

~ LAO TZU

So come – come you all and focus on your meditation. Nothing is as transforming – as the art of meditation! When you drop all those thoughts about YOGAS, PLANETS, STARS and you start turning inwards – then you start self-realizing the whole essence of this human life – then all stars, all planets and all zodiacs and the 'beyond' will be available to you – the whole universe will be available to you – the way – the answer – the solution – the GOD that you seek – the LOVE – the happiness that you seek – it is all WITHIN and so you should meditate – no matter how long the 'journey' is — the **'Dance'** *should begin...*

"The greatest miracle in the world is that you should DANCE and disappear in the DANCE - then let the DANCE do whatever it can do. That you should LOVE and disappear in the LOVE - then let the LOVE do whatever it can do. You cannot claim that you are doing it - you already have disappeared."
- Osho

Disappear in your DANCE (Meditation) – disappear in your LOVE (God) – and then *life will never be the same* – then *there will be a song to it – a dance –* a beautiful enlightening dance!

Jai Shri Ganesha. Jai Guru.

AFTERWORD

The energy of KETU helps in fructifying the MANTRA. EVERY MANTRA is POWERFUL. Every MANTRA helps you to move beyond MIND. Every MANTRA helps you to turn inwards and meditate. The real question is how deeply, faithfully, devotedly you recite the Mantra provided to you by your Master. The greater the devotion, love – the greater is the showering of HIS Grace upon you and then there is no looking back, the sky (consciousness) is clear and you are ready to 'fly'.

Death is necessary for you to get enlightened with the TRUTH! This Death that I am referring to is the Death of the MIND – because it is the MIND that goes on creating many miseries and as long as you continue to follow your MIND – you will continue to face many miseries in your life.

Rule your MIND else the MIND will rule over you and then you will be in a mess, says the Buddha.

Jesus says to Nicodemus – "To experience the ultimate TRUTH, to experience GOD – you have to be REBORN."

To be Reborn, one has to die first! When Jesus indirectly refers to DEATH – it is the DEATH of all that you have been carrying all along within your MIND. It is, in short, the DEATH of the MIND and not of your physical body.

KETU has the capability and the potential to bring DEATH to the MIND – so that you move on to the state of NO MIND!

But how it happens? How can it happen? What is the way by which we can make it happen?

And the answer is – Meditating by chanting MANTRA. MANTRA consists of certain letters that create a specific sound vibration within your being. And the more you recite with love and faith, the more these positive sound vibrations heal you inside out. And it is only when you can heal yourself that you can heal others. It is the energy of KETU that helps you recite and fructify the **MANTRA. This MANTRA then** acts as a MEDICINE for removing all the illusions of the MIND and slowly helps you to move beyond MIND. CHANTING OF MANTRA is, therefore, the most effective KEY in this KALI YUG to overcome the monkey MIND and find the many answers that you seek, the peace, the bliss, the joy and the eternal happiness that you seek.

MANTRA is the most effective medium, tool - a beautiful bridge that can help you and everybody to walk beyond MIND and experience the bliss within!

Every Mantra is a powerful Mantra - *only* if you recite it with **DEEP FAITH and LOVE.**

The Bhagavan beautifully explains the immense importance and significance of MANTRA - which in simple words is a SPECIFIC POSITIVE DEVOTED **THOUGHT.**

"Meditation is sticking to one thought. That single thought keeps away other thoughts; distraction of mind is a sign of its weakness. By constant meditation it gains strength; that is to say, its weakness of fugitive thought gives place to the enduring background free from thoughts."
- Bhagavan Ramana Maharshi

The MIND is a TRAFFIC OF THOUGHTS. And to break this TRAFFIC JAM - and find a way beyond - only one VEHICLE can HELP - that is your MANTRA - ONE THOUGHT - the THOUGHT of the Holy LORD can keep away all the other thoughts - the real question is - **HOW DEEPLY YOU CAN CONCENTRATE *ON THIS ONE THOUGHT*** - THE THOUGHT OF KRISHNA - the THOUGHT of the HOLY LORD.

MANTRA is basically the 'MEDICINE' to FINISH the MONKEY MIND and merge it with the HEART - and once the HEART starts vibrating - once the KNOCK on your HEART goes deeper and deeper - then one fine day - the DOORS open up and you are 'in' for the most wonderful experiences of your spiritual journey - but it all STARTS from the MEDICINE that is called the - MANTRA!

And with deep respect and love - I salute and prostrate before all the divine masters who have spent their whole lives in sharing the immense SIGNIFICANCE of MANTRA - NAME OF THE HOLY LORD - one of them that I closely can relate to is **His Holiness Bramha Chaitanya Gondavalekar Maharaj** - the divine holy master who not only did many miracles but also shared the fact that - RECITING MANTRA in itself is one of the greatest steps towards living a life of miracles!

A beautiful picture of **His Holiness Bramhachaitanya Gondawalekar Maharaj.** Today, if you all visit HIS Samadhi at HIS birthplace - Gondawale, near Satara, you will be surprised to see that every devotee who comes - is engrossed in chanting the Mantra of 'Shri Ram Jai Ram Jai Jai Ram'.

|| Shri Ram Jai Ram Jai Jai Ram||

The MIND can be controlled when you continue to focus on chanting the Holy name of the Lord with utmost devotion and unwavering faith and love.

> 66 In this universe there is no such sin that can sustain before the NAME OF THE LORD. In today's AGE, without giving a form to the ultimate TRUTH, we cannot realize the SELF. Lord's name gives the TRUTH – its form. Therefore always meditate on the Lord's holy name.
> **SRI BRAMHACHAITANYA GONDAVALEKAR MAHARAJ** 99

Wherever you go, always remain engrossed deeply in the name of the Lord. Even if you take the name of the Lord out of compulsion, it is OKAY. If you take the name of the Lord with pure devotion, it is GOOD. And if you take the name of the Lord by maintaining a **positive attitude** than it is BEST for your self-growth says His Holiness Gondavalekar Maharaj!

I remember that when I had visited **His Holiness Bramhachaitanya Gondawalekar Maharaj Samadhi Mandir** - there were many devotees with their Japa Mala and chanting silently - and amongst them was a very poor man - he must be very poor - but in his hand also - was a very very long Japa Mala - and he was doing his bit - by focusing on chanting the Lord's holy name! And I said to myself - **what a great revolution the Master has brought** - just through HIS AVATAR - HE has and HE still **is motivating and inspiring so many of them - especially the weakest section of the society to *chant the holy mantra* and experience the beautiful transformation within!**

I Salute to HIS great work - may HIS grace be on all of us.

The second name that instantly comes to me is that of His Holiness **Srila Prabhupada! The Modern Age Messiah who spent his whole life in making people realize the immense significance of CHANTING the holy MANTRA.**

This chanting of the Hare Krishna mantra is enacted from the spiritual platform and thus this sound vibration surpasses all lower strata of consciouness - namely sensual, mental and intellectual.

— A. C. Bhaktivedanta Swami Prabhupada —

Today - the world is a better place to live only because a major portion of the majority has been guided and made to realize the immense significance of chanting the MANTRA - and His Holiness **Srila Prabhupada** contributed immense efforts to make this happen. I humbly prostrate before His Holiness **Srila Prabhupada.**

||Hare Krishna Hare Krishna - Krishna Krishna Hare Hare||

"You should chant *"Hare Krishna"* every day and read books and in this way you will make advancements in Krishna Consciousness. We have to understand that I am *not* this body, but part and parcel of the supreme Lord Sri Krishna"

- His Holiness Srila Prabhupada

Now let us see how the chanting of Mantra helps one to OVERCOME the most difficult situations of life.

One has to understand the fact - everything operates at the SOOKSHMA (**Subtle**) level. But the results are derived at the physical level.

Every human being's SOOKSHMA (**Subtle**) body goes on taking birth in physical form. The root is in the SUBTLE state - the SOOKSHMA state.

"The subtle body is the casual body; it is the body that takes on the new physical body. You see many light bulbs around here: the electricity is one, that energy is one, but it is manifesting through different bulbs. The bulbs have different bodies, but their soul is one. Similarly, the consciousness manifesting through us is ONE, but in the manifestation of this consciousness, two vehicles are applied. One is the subtle vehicle, the subtle body (Sookshma body); the other is the gross vehicle, the gross physical body." - Osho

The SUBTLE (SOOKSHMA) BODY is of great SIGNIFICANCE. MANTRA impacts and nurtures the SUBTLE BODY - the more you recite, the more the SUBTLE BODY gets nurtured - and it is only when the SUBTLE BODY is empowered that you operate efficiently and consciously at the PHYSICAL BODY LEVEL!

Understand the fact - that even if death comes - still only the physical body is going to die - the subtle body remains - the soul is still NOT liberated - it dwells in the SUBTLE BODY (SOOKSMA BODY).

When you focus on chanting the Krishna Mantra or any positive Mantra - the level of your consciousness EXPANDS - making the subtle body more active - it is through the subtle body that you can then do many wonders - many miracles - the SUBTLE BODY is at the very root of your existence - of human existence.

People fall SICK - when the SUBTLE BODY is disturbed - your THOUGHTS are CONSTANTLY impacting the SUBTLE BODY - understand this - every time you THINK NEGATIVE FOR OTHERS - for YOURSELF - you are lowering the quality of your subtle body - you are paving a path for more miseries.

Yesterday Mohan came and said, "My friend is losing badly on his VITAMINS - he is young and still doctor says - he has very low vitamins. Now he is suggested for regular injections of vitamins."

Injections can supply vitamins and you will feel good. But the larger question is WHY such things happen? There are cases where the man is taking all nutritious diet and yet he loses vitamins - why such things happen?

BECAUSE OF YOUR NEGATIVE THINKING. BECAUSE OF YOUR TAMAS GUNA. BECAUSE OF YOUR AGGRESSIVE ATTITUDE. All that is negative - all that creates a LOT OF NOISE within your MIND - SUCKS THE VITAL VITAMINS OUT OF YOUR BODY - and then you wonder - what is wrong with me?

There is nothing wrong with you - what is wrong is your WAY OF LIVING that you are not willing to change - and that actually affects the subtle body - paving a guaranteed path for many miseries for your physical body.

This physical body will leave someday. Someday I will die - but my subtle body remains. Someday you will die but your subtle body remains. Then it waits for the NEXT BIRTH - that BIRTH - nobody knows whether it is of human or of a reptile or of a bird or of an animal. That is NOT in your hand but what is in your hand is RECITING THE MANTRA and EMPOWERING your SUBTLE BODY - which can thereby help you to overcome the miseries caused by your own past karma which is signified by SHANI and RAHU.

RAHU SHANI also represent the EVIL ENERGIES - that first ATTACK your SUBTLE BODY. These EVIL ENERGIES can be in the form of BLACK MAGIC, SPIRITS, and GHOSTS. When you focus on chanting 'Hare Krishna' - the Subtle Body gets strength to defend itself - chanting is the most powerful 'tonic' that can help you sustain the many UNSEEN attacks from the astral world.

> **66**
>
> One can be free from all sinful reactions after reaching a place of pilgrimage, but one can have the same benefit at home or at any place simply by chanting the holy name of the Lord.
>
> **SRILA PRABHUPADA (ISKCON)**
>
> **99**

SHANI - PAST KARMIC DUES and Responsibilities in this life

RAHU - DESIRES to be fulfilled in this life

Now this CONJUNCTION of SHANI RAHU is one of the UNHOLY conjunctions - and I have been stating this all along.

Why?

SHANI - KARMA. KARMIC DUES. Responsibility - is impacted by DESIRES (RAHU). RAHU brings so much of TEMPTATIONS – yes, that is the word - TEMPTATIONS that the otherwise sincere, obedient, honest woman starts CROSSING the boundaries of TRADITIONS, MORALITY, VALUES and then it becomes messy - very messy!

It is a placement where TOO MUCH DESIRE, OBSESSION - force the otherwise very moral, very honest SATURN to SLIP - to FALL from the GRACE!

If there is absolutely no positive aspect or support to this aspect, then life indeed becomes a circle of miseries that goes on and on and on...

Until one fine day - the question that you have asked - comes and then there is some possibility of change - some sign of slipping out of this vicious circle of miseries!

Reciting the KRISHNA MANTRA somehow BLOCKS the dominating RAHU - and lets SHANI takeover. Then the person starts feeling better - then there is a song to it - then life can change for good - then transformation is possible.

RAHU may bring TEMPTATIONS to you - it may bring forth a beautiful sexy woman - and then if there is absolutely no chanting happening in your life - then the same sexy woman becomes RAHU and ensures that your life becomes miserable.

This RAHU may bring TEMPTATIONS to you - it may bring the GREEDINESS to have more and more and more money - and then you go on like an out of control horse - and then someday CRASH so badly that you start thinking if there is a way to 'stand up' again!

But a man, a woman who CHANTS the KRISHNA MANTRA or any positive MANTRA - can CONTROL THE MONKEY MIND - he can STOP the MIND from falling for a woman who has absolutely NO values, NO ethics, NO principles - but only a sensual sexy body. Such a man can help himself by taming the MIND - and preventing it from being a victim of GREED, LUST.

You understand - that is the beauty - the whole beauty of MANTRA!

But who wants to listen? People are more interested in manipulating things - they will go to magicians and ask them to do this and to do that. Now the greatest joke is that neither the man who commands knows what is good for him and neither the magician is bothered to understand what is good for the man. He is only concerned with money - for him that is GOOD enough!

You think that by manipulating - you can benefit. But you don't know if this 'benefit' that you see is going to be a boon or a CURSE!

"It is very difficult to know exactly what good should come out of a particular situation. To attempt to manipulate circumstances so that *your idea of good* can come about is to <u>let the ego play God</u>-and that, as you know, can and does backfire."

- Neem Karoli Baba

I have been telling my whole life - DO NOT TRY TO MANIPULATE the HAPPENINGS of your LIFE. DO NOT try to INTERFERE with the flow of your life. But PEOPLE - the majority is ruled by the MIND and the MIND cannot wait - the MIND has absolutely no patience - the MIND has absolutely NO FAITH - the MIND is mechanical - and SAI BABA, therefore, has been always emphasizing on practicing FAITH AND PATIENCE - SHRADDHA AUR SABURI - because the Master is perfectly aware that the MIND is never willing to be patient - the MIND is mechanical. So, man is mechanically efficient but with NO AWARENESS. And that is the greatest irony of humans.

But a YOGI has gone beyond MIND - HE can relate to the voice of the higher realms of consciousness - HE can communicate with GOD - because HE has self-realized that GOD is not on the outside - **God is within.**

"The 'Guest' is within you, but you have to turn in. You are too focused on the outside and on the futile. You are leaning on your scriptures: reading, reading and thinking that by knowing more and more of the scriptures you will become enlightened. You will only become burdened with knowledge and knowledge is noisy. Truth is to be found only in silence - when you are deeply meditating - turning inward. Look into your own body - HE is there. Your body is the temple, HE has already chosen it; He abides there. Turn in." - Osho

Turn in. Just two words - and you all have to remember these two words. Sammasti. The last word of Buddha was Sammasti - which means 'REMEMBER'.

Just **Remember to turn inward - and go back to your source - again and again - whenever you feel lost - whenever you feel low - REMEMBER - to TURN IN.**

The reciting of MANTRA helps you to TURN IN. It is NOT that only through the MANTRA that you can TURN IN - but through the MANTRA you all can TURN IN much easily and much quickly than otherwise! So, Srila Prabhupada emphasizes on the significance of reciting the MANTRA. Sai Baba, Meher Baba, Gondavalekar Maharaj, Sant Dyaneshwar Maharaj,Tukaram Maharaj, Neem Karoli Baba - the DIVINE MASTERS have always emphasized on the significance of CHANTING MANTRA. When you CHANT MANTRA - CHANT CONSCIOUSLY - do not make it a habit because all habits are robotic in nature - there is absolutely no consciousness to the actions that become a HABIT!

When you chant - chant with awareness - by FOCUSING on every word and by remembering the HOLY LORD whose name you chant. Let there be love, let there be devotion, let there be a dance - and whenever you chant - let there be a sense that the chanting is also happening THROUGH HIM - THROUGH HIS GRACE and you are just a medium - the DOER is the LORD - the compassionate benevolent master.

It is a long journey - and people have many fancy ideas about chanting - as if they start chanting today and miracles start happening the next day! Even a child takes NINE MONTHS to take birth - PATIENCE is the key, FAITH is the source. SHRADDHA AUR SABURI.

Whatever you do - do it with FAITH (SHRADDHA) and PATIENCE (SABURI).

I always like those things that take time - because the one that takes time is bound to be far more beautiful, stronger and more reliable than something that is happening faster!

There was a young man. His name was Rahim. And Rahim was one of the most faithful men of the town. But somehow he felt restless - something was missing from his life - everything was there - all the pleasures and riches were at his command but something was missing... and it was missing badly - very badly.

What was it? And Rahim realized that it was the absence of the master. So, Rahim decided to go in search of the master. He must be like our Mohan - he just wasn't ready to stay any longer in his palace - one dark night, he slipped out in the jungles - never ever to be seen again.

The journey was difficult because Rahim had always been pampered with all the pleasures that a man can think of! But Rahim continued, his feet started bleeding - there were many thorns on the way - but a man who is fired up with a higher purpose never stops, his journey continues...

After many days - Rahim reached a village where a great Sufi Saint lived. But the Sufi was a very strange man - he would never talk - never met anybody - he remained in his own bliss - even if you had to talk to him - you had to stay a few feet away from him - else he might just pick up a stone and throw at you - it is a different story that if you got hurt - the very next moment by his miracle - you may also get healed! But this old man was something - and the whole village loved him - worshiped him - but nobody would dare to go near him - else they knew - the stone was always ready...

Rahim reached and the villagers warned him - they said, "There is a Sufi saint in our village - but he is a very strange man - for us - he is our GOD - but we again warn you - HE is a very strange man."

Rahim had lost all his body weight - had become fragile - but still he decided to meet the Sufi Saint. Rahim went and the Sufi shouted back, "You idiot - Why have you come? - Go back - go back to your palace."

Rahim said, "I have come not to disturb you - but just give me some message - give me some direction - that is all I need - that is all that I pray for - at your feet - I can find the answer - show me the way - show me the answer."

The Sufi said, "Take the name of Allah - day and night take HIS name - and now never come back again - leave now."

Rahim never came back again...but whenever his disciples would ask, "Who is your master?" His eyes would fill with tears...he would start crying, and then he would go back to his abode. Forty years went by - but still the fond memory of the master (the Sufi Saint) remained within his heart - just one message the master had given - just one -"Take the name of Allah - the name of the lord - chant his name."

And Rahim from that moment - never ever missed to chant the name of the Lord - he moved from that village - there was nothing that he could carry with him - there was no photo of the master, no piece of the master that he could keep with himself -NOTHING - absolutely NOTHING was given to him except one message - CHANT THE NAME OF ALLAH (HOLY LORD)! And that one message was EVERYTHING - EVERYTHING for RAHIM - He took it so deeply into his whole being - that for the next forty years - he would simply MEDITATE on the LORD's holy name - by chanting HIS holy name!

In these forty years - Rahim became a master of many miracles - many disciples followed him. One day, a close disciple said, "Rahim Baba - there is one function happening in a nearby village - the whole village and nearby villagers are coming to that function - they all say that it is a function held in the remembrance of a great Sufi Saint - HE passed away last year."

Rahim quickly realized who the Sufi Saint was. He started crying - like a child he burst out in tears - never had the disciples seen such a cry - they all were moved - they said, "Why are you crying...?"

Rahim said, "The Sufi Saint that you mentioned was my GURU - my MASTER - after 40 years - we had come so close to his village and now comes this news...let us go - I cannot wait here - let us go..."

And Rahim and his followers rushed towards the same village where Rahim had met his master - the same tree, the same lingering fragrance... the same people...but the MASTER was no more - instead there was a small shrine built in HIS remembrance, near the same tree where he used to meditate.

Rahim rushed towards the Shrine - now there was nobody to say, "I will throw this stone if you come close - now there was nobody to shower love - those eyes - how deep were those eyes - how much love was in those eyes - Rahim fell down at the entrance of the Shrine...he was about to get up and enter when a very old villager stepped ahead and said, "Rahim Baba...wait..."

Rahim looked at the villager - his followers also were puzzled - who is this villager and why is he asking to wait?

The old villager brought a beautiful garland made of red roses - handing it to Rahim - he said, "Bade Baba (the Great Master) had said to me - that one day my Rahim will come - and when he comes - you provide him with a rose garland...here it is."

The whole village went into silence. Rahim could not control himself - he hugged the old villager - how much the master loved me - even after forty years - he remembered him - he was certain that he would come back - Rahim's tears could not stop - the followers could not control themselves - the whole gathering was moved - deeply moved.

When you REMEMBER and FOLLOW the word of the MASTER - the MASTER also REMEMBERS YOU and DIRECTS you every moment of your LIFE - NO MATTER where you are.

Rahim followed the WORD OF THE MASTER - and the WORD was **"Chant the holy name of your LORD"** - Rahim never missed to chant - a time came in his life - when there was no need of chanting - he himself had become the chant! There was no need to meditate - he himself had become the meditation! He himself had become the dance! And that is how life should be - a dance, a poem, a beautiful painting! And this is possible only - and ONLY when you CHANT the name of the LORD with love, with devotion - with TOTAL SURRENDER.

> What we hear about the Lord, we should hear with a spirit to serve the Lord. When we chant His name, we should chant so that He is pleased to hear us chanting. That is the beauty of life – the real Art of Living.
>
> **RADHANATH SWAMI (ISKCON)**

No PUJAS - NO HAVANS - NO RITUALS can be of as much help as the CHANTING OF MANTRA - the name of the LORD!

How much does it take to chant? And the answer is ZERO RUPEES or ZERO DOLLARS.

If you need a Japa Mala - then only then - you may have to spend a few rupees to buy - that too not more than 100 Rupees or 10 Dollars.

In 10 Dollars - you can attain Enlightenment - you can improve the QUALITY of your life - you can OVERCOME the many difficulties of your life - you can bravely FACE the many miseries of your life and turn them around - you can transform your WEAKNESS into your STRENGTH - and you say, "WHAT MIRACLE CAN HAPPEN WITH CHANTING?"

If this is NOT THE MIRACLE then what is the MIRACLE? But people are shallow - they don't want to do ANYTHING on their own - they just want to spend money and get something quickly - they miss to REALIZE that GOD IS NOT READY-MADE - HAPPINESS IS NOT READY-MADE.

> Happiness is not something 'ready-made' – it comes from your own actions.
>
> **DALAI LAMA**

Unless you ACT - **unless you start turning inwards** - unless you start **meditating** - unless you all start **chanting** - there is absolutely NO CHANCE for REAL GROWTH. It is only through MEDITATION - it is only through CHANTING - it is only through LOVE and DEVOTION that you can turn in - you can evolve to the higher realms of Consciousness.

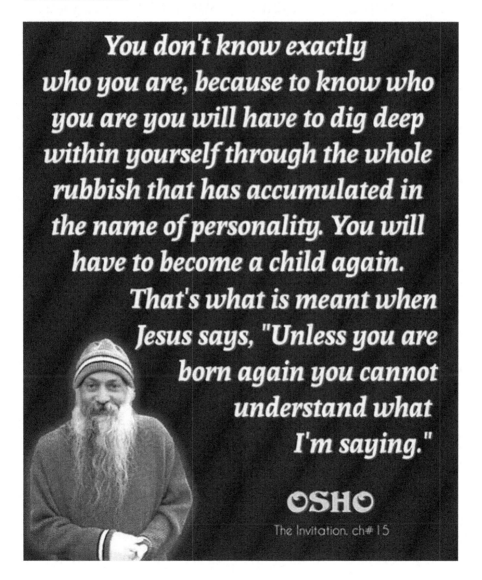

You don't know exactly who you are, because to know who you are you will have to dig deep within yourself through the whole rubbish that has accumulated in the name of personality. You will have to become a child again.
That's what is meant when Jesus says, "Unless you are born again you cannot understand what I'm saying."

OSHO

The Invitation. ch# 15

To be reborn - first you have to die. This death is of all your notions, and EGOs and learning - until you become an absolute ZERO - there is no possibility for you to experience the divine - the beyond. That is why whenever - I meet a man or a woman - who has lost everything - who has fallen to the absolute low - I say to them that this is the opportunity - this is the GOLDEN CHANCE - if you cannot EVOLVE through the PASSAGE OF THIS FIRE OF SUFFERING - then you have missed - you have simply missed!

The fires of suffering become the light of consciousness.
ECKART TOLLE

Suffering is a 'Blessing in Disguise' - it brings out the best in you - it helps you to evolve to the next level - the higher consciousness.

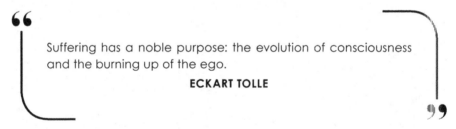

Suffering has a noble purpose: the evolution of consciousness and the burning up of the ego.
ECKART TOLLE

Suffering is of the MIND - always remember this - this is significant in many ways.

If the MIND has some guidance - some direction, then this MIND starts turning inwards - it makes you more meditative - you start looking within - you start turning inwards and the more you do it - the more you start self-realizing the many aspects of your life that otherwise you would have never known!

Suffering is the start of a great Beginning! The Ending is the Beginning and the *beginning* is the first step, and the first step is the only step.

> The end is the beginning of all things. Suppressed and hidden, awaiting to be released through the rhythm of pain and pleasure.
>
> **JIDDU KRISHNAMURTI**

Life is ever changing. Everything changes except change! Change is constant. Always remember - NOTHING LASTS FOREVER. So when you are going through GOOD TIMES - don't let the EGO penetrate into your HEAD and when you are going through the low phase of life - do not let the feeling of depression and frustration and humiliation slip into your being. The Earth is never still - it is rotating - moving - revolving - bringing many experiences to its tenants - happy, sad, crying, laughing - there are many colours to human life - the colours keep changing - times keep changing - people keep changing - what remains STILL is your SELF - the CONSCIOUSNESS!

> Remain still, with the conviction that the SELF shines as everything yet nothing, within, without, and everywhere.
>
> **BHAGAVAN RAMANA MAHARSHI**

You can remain STILL - only when you STILL the MIND.

Chanting the holy MANTRA helps you to STILL the MIND. CHANTING with love and devotion by focusing on your breathing - slowly helps you to STILL the MIND - it is a long process - but every human being is fortunate - who has begun on this wonderful journey - I must say - that to begin with this journey is the GREATEST BLESSING one could ever have in his or her life!

The nature of the MIND is being restless. A man or a woman who follows the MIND is always found to be restless - but a man who is meditating - chanting with devotion - slowly starts getting control of the

MIND - such a man - such a woman is truly the most fortunate person - they may have NOTHING but they are blessed with EVERYTHING!

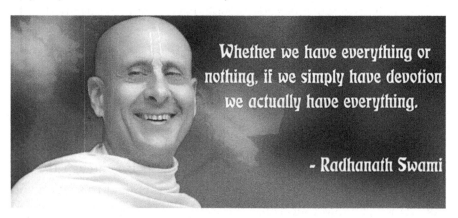

Whether we have everything or nothing, if we simply have devotion we actually have everything.

- Radhanath Swami

A great FAKIR once had said, "I am not a beggar - but you all certainly are."

And he is absolutely true. Because the YOGI is never seen standing in a QUEUE of DESIRES AND WANTS AND DEMANDS - but people are seen. So then the question arises – "WHO IS POOR IN REALITY?" - the NAKED FAKIR - the NAKED YOGI or those who are standing with precious jewellery - gold and diamonds and pearls and all those attractive expensive robes around them?

The QUESTION REMAINS. And it remains for all of you and you have to answer it - your answer determines the course of your future.

WHO IS THE REAL KING? One who has realized his SELF or one who is living in PALACES?

The great FAKIR says, "You fools - your whole life you have been chasing the FAKE GOLD - time is still there - before it gets too late."

And he would say to everybody - the question is - who wants to listen?

One who wants to listen **will find the REAL GOLD** - HE will come back to the SOURCE - HE will come back HOME.

Many come - they all want to experience GOD - experience KRISHNA - but nobody is willing to be ARJUNA! It is only when you become ARJUNA that you can experience KRISHNA. It is only when you are READY to SURRENDER YOURSELF in TOTALITY - that you can experience KRISHNA. It is only when you CAN KEEP YOUR

INTELLECT ASIDE - your MIND aside - your AGREEING and DISAGREEING aside that you can let the words of the MASTER penetrate into your being - and then those words will bring a light unto you - then the transformation begins - then the flowering begins - the question is - Are you willing to rest your whole life - your whole being at the feet of the Master?

CHANTING fructifies - CHANTING flowers - CHANTING manifests into a MIRACLE only when you don't just CHANT - but CHANT by surrendering yourself in totality - at the feet of the Master.

Let there be more love, more affection, more dedication to your Chanting and then there will be a song to it - then no matter how much NOISE is on the outside - within you are always at peace, in bliss and in the ever flowing joy - and that is the state of Nityananda (Eternal Joy)!

Meditate on the Lord's name. Chanting must happen from **within** - not without. The name of the Lord should penetrate into your HEART - the HEART is the place where GOD dwells - the whole journey of human evolution begins from MIND - but it has to end in the HEART!

"The heart is the hub of all sacred places. Go there and roam." - says the divine master Bhagavan Nityananda - whole life he spent in helping millions and millions find the right direction.

"One must seek the shortest way and the fastest means to get back home - to turn the spark within into a blaze, to be merged in and to identify with that greater fire which ignited the spark."
-Bhagavan Nityananda

A beautiful real meditative picture of the Bhagavan. I humbly prostrate before the divine master **Bhagavan Nityananda Swami of Ganeshpuri.**

The shortest way and the fastest means to get back home - to get back to the Source is the **way of Chanting - but that chanting has to be real, from within.**

So come you all and chant - meditate on the name of the Lord. Every morning - 1 hour - every night - 1 hour before sleeping - if you cannot find two hours for meditation - then the whole life of many million hours goes down the drain. Your 2 hours of meditation can change - can overcome many difficulties of your life - can help you to evolve into a matured person - always remember, MATURITY is NOT based on AGE - MATURITY is based on how long you have been on the JOURNEY WITHIN.

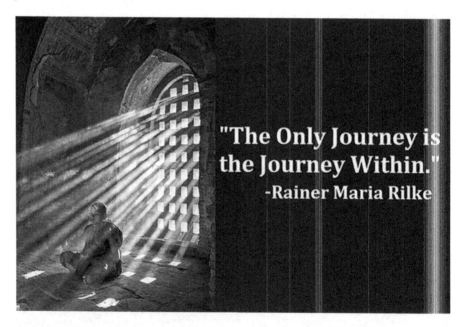

"The Only Journey is the Journey Within."
-Rainer Maria Rilke

When you chant, when you meditate - do it without any expectations - because expectations don't let you flow freely - you are not 100% available to the WHOLE - the chanting then cannot flower - the meditation then cannot blossom.

Blossoming happens when there are absolutely NO expectations - you do it just because you love to - and when there is love - there is a certain fragrance and there is a certain music - then the 'Knock' can be heard - then the 'doors' can open...

Love should be the way - and Love has no agenda, absolutely no agenda and, therefore, Love is beautiful - love can transform - it is love that leads you to Miracles - the answer never completes without Love - life never completes without love - our whole existence never completes without love.

"This is love:
The flowering of
love is meditation."

—Jiddu Krishnamurti

Everything comes to a full circle - only when there is LOVE. Let there be Love to all that you do - and then get ready to experience the greatest Miracles of your life.

Meditate.
Jai Shri Ganesha. Jai Guru.

Love & Light
Addittya Tamhankar
July 20, 2020
Pune, India

Get 'Ready'

The colour *Black* reflects the nature of CLINGING – being possessive, being attached.

The colour *White* reflects the nature of LETTING GO – being detached.

The story of human life is caught up between **Black & White**.

The story of human life is caught up between **Rahu & Ketu**.

The ancient seers therefore have held these two opposite energies (Rahu & Ketu) as the most mighty ones, so much so that they can completely change the very course of your destiny!

And it is true because your whole life's journey – is based on the intensity of your desires (Rahu), quality of your desires & your ultimate liberation is based on your state of desirelessness (Ketu)!

Birth happens because of desires. Liberation from the cycle of birth and rebirth happens when there are no desires – you reach the stage of desirelessness – the state of a Yogi!

(Rahu) Bhogi to (Ketu) Yogi – that is how the 'journey' of this human life has to progress, not everybody is able to become a Yogi – those who have – are the blessed souls, are the chosen ones!

It is God who chooses men and not the men who chooses God. It is the Master who chooses the disciple and not the disciple who chooses the Master!

Jesus choose all his 12 disciples (Apostles). Krishna choose Arjuna. Buddha choose Ananda. It is always the Master who chooses the disciple.

527

Ketu's nature is to **Let Go**. And Meditation *is* a **Let Go.**

It is only when you are able to LET GO – meditation starts flowering within you and then you are no more the same, everything around you is the same but you are no more the same – *then there is a music, a song, a dance, a bliss!*

LET GO, LOOK WITHIN & LET THE JOURNEY WITHIN BEGIN – that is the message of Ketu…those who can follow the message of Ketu – **can heal themselves,** those who cannot will continue to suffer.

KETU's whole focus is WITHIN. KETU is Meditation. Only a man who has KETU in prominent placement in the birth chart - can understand the language - the language of the heart, the language of Silence. **And only such a man can understand the essence of this book!** My blessing to such men and women – who are taking the efforts to turn inwards and experience the silence – within.

One should become silent and allow that Silence to communicate.

Once a young man asked the master "What are you?" And the master said "I am the **'Silence'** between your two words. Now don't ask me the same question again - until you learn the language of 'Silence' -"

Remember – the language of the Master - is the language of **Silence.**

Real communication happens in silence - when you are **'Ready'** to relate with the blissful 'Silence' - the benevolent compassionate Master will appear…

Focus on getting **'Ready'**.

Meditate every day.

The Useful Purpose of Life

"The only useful purpose of the present birth is to turn within and realize the Self."
- Bhagavan Ramana Maharashi

We all are born out of desires (RAHU) – but our real journey, our real life begins only when we start moving away from desires and come to the state of desirelessness – the moment we reach the state of desirelessness – we are 'home'.

The whole purpose of this book is to help you all realize the true purpose of this human life. Always remember – it doesn't matter when you start, what matters is that you start – and once you start never look back, and never stop until you are back 'home'.

Walk in the river, but don't allow the water to touch your feet. Be in the world, but don't be of the world. Be in the world, but don't allow the world to be in you. When you come home, you come home – and the whole world disappears. And what remains is Silence.

Silence is the language of God. It is only when you come to the state of 'silence' that you can connect with God. Let there be silence within.

Blessings to all my readers and followers.

And now I rest at the feet of my master. 🙏

Love & Light

Addittya Tamhankar
Pune, India
August 1ˢᵗ, 2020

|| Gurudev Datta ||

Read Other Insightful Books:
Written By Addittya Tamhankar

➤ Gift of Consciousness ◄

➤ Beauty of Acceptance - Tathata ◄

➤ No Mind - The Journey Beyond ◄

➤ How to Overcome Rahu ◄

Available on
Amazon, Flipkart,
Barnes & Noble and WFP Store

Made in United States
North Haven, CT
30 March 2022

17702171R00311